THE ENCYCLOPEDIA OF PRACTICAL PHOTOGRAPHY

THE ENCYCLOPEDIA OF PRACTICAL PHOTOGRAPHY

MICHAEL FREEMAN
Contributor : Richard Platt

NEW
BURLINGTON
BOOKS

A QUARTO BOOK

Published by New Burlington Books
6 Blundell Street
London N7 9BH

British Library Cataloguing in Publication Data:
    Freeman, Michael, 1945.
        Encyclopedia of practical
        photography
        1. Photography
        I. Title
        770'.28   TR146

        ISBN 1 85348 020 7

This book was designed and produced by
Quarto Publishing plc
The Old Brewery, 6 Blundell Street
London N7 9BH

Senior editor Patricia Webster
Project editor John Farndon
Editors Jane Laing Emma Foa
Designer Alex Arthur
Assistant designers Fraser Newman Eva Ratanakul
Illustrators Ray Brown Fraser Newman
Steve Gardner
Studio photography Rose Jones
Picture researcher Anne-Marie Ehrlich
Indexer Diana LeCore
Also thanks to Sabina Goodchild Michelle Newton
Peter Bowen Paul Owens Stewart Larking

Art director Nigel Osborne
Editorial director Jim Miles

Quarto would like to extend special thanks to
Keith Bernstein; Neyla Freeman; Sumana Ray;
Peter Weaver; Mike Shailes, Photopia
International; Charles Smith, Samcine Ltd; Steve
Dunning, Nikon Uk Ltd; Derek Morgan, Bell &
Howell; Nobby Clark and Keith Johnson, Keith
Johnson Photographic; Alfa Romeo Ltd; Atlas
Photography Ltd; Carl Henry Photography Ltd;
Durst Ltd; Kodak Ltd; Lens Photography Ltd;
Nikon Ltd; Pat Wallace, Polaroid Ltd.

Typeset by Leaper & Gard Ltd, Bristol
Colour origination by
Hong Kong Graphic Arts Limited, Hong Kong
Printed and bound by
Leefung-Asco Printers Limited, Hong Kong

CONTENTS

INTRODUCTION

In recent years, photography has undergone a technological
revolution, and this has had a dramatic effect on the way it is practised
— and even on the type of people taking pictures and on their
motivations and standards. Integrated circuitry, miniaturization,
programming, computer-aided lens design and advances in
film structure and chemistry may sound at first to be several stages removed
from the way in which a photographer chooses an image, but
they are all, in fact, in a direct line with the practice of taking pictures
— the true art of photography.

Most of the limits on what can be photographed are set by
the insensitivity of the process — that is, how much exposure the film needs,
how much light the lens can transmit, how accurately metering
systems can measure the image, and so on. The result is not just a matter of
being able to take photographs in less and less light, or in more
complex arrangements of lighting, important though both of these are.
There are considerably more subtle effects. For instance, the
combination of faster film and lens design that allows wider apertures has
made it possible to use longer lenses hand-held at useful
movement-stopping shutter speeds. This in turn has made candid
photography possible from a distance — and so easier for the
majority of people who lack the enthusiasm for and practice in
photographing from close to, and yet want to achieve
candid results.

The organization of this encyclopedia of photography is deliberately different from that of traditional encyclopedias. It has been felt that, as this is a practical rather than theoretical subject, it is easier to follow and absorb if structured rather than presented as an alphabetical list of entries. Moreover, as the practice of taking photographs involves much more than just the mastery of the camera, film and other technical matters, photographic subjects are treated separately. Current technology is both advanced and complex, and to be understood thoroughly and in detail it needs a concentrated treatment, at a distance from the variety of uses to which it can be put. At the same time, there is a danger of assigning too much importance to it in the making of a photograph. Consequently, this encyclopedia is divided into two distinct parts: the first deals with the means available to photographers, the second treats the subject matter from a practical, realistic perspective.

It is perhaps worth bearing in mind that this is a field which encompasses a wide range of approaches, from scientific record to artistic expression. The variety is such that all these different types of photography seem to have in common is the basic equipment, materials and processes—the basic, photographic technology covered in the first part of this encyclopedia. Not only do the techniques and methods differ among photographers, but often their standards and ideas bear little resemblance. Manipulation and stage management may be anathema to some photojournalists, while the ethos of subject-before-technique may seem lacking in craft to those studio photographers who are used to a high degree of control. A balanced view is only possible if we are prepared to accept the validity of every use of the camera, whether humble or elaborate, objective or opinionated.

PART ONE: EQUIPMENT, MATERIALS AND PROCESSES

For most of the history of photography, technical improvements have been relatively slow — certainly slow enough for there to be, at any one time, sets of standard working procedures. At the beginning, there was a certain amount of individuality in, say, the preparation of chemical formulae, but the general trend has been towards standardization. In colour film developing, for instance, just two processes now dominate, one for negatives and one for transparencies, both developed by the largest of the film manufacturers.

This trend has been a fairly obvious and expected one, but in an activity that combines both technology and art, it is arguable that standardization of equipment and materials encourages conservatism — a belief that there are appropriate and inappropriate ways of taking photographs. So, for example, certain assumptions tend to develop and harden — that certain focal length of lens should be used for portraiture, or that there is standard equipment for one type of photography, or even that back-lit subjects should be exposed at just one stop more than the meter reading.

These traditional assumptions are easy enough to fall into but dangerous because they give too much importance to equipment and materials. It is, moreover, especially dangerous in view of current trends in camera and film technology. There are changes in the air right now on a scale that surpasses anything seen before in photography. The rapid improvement in film quality and sensitivity is probably only a taste of things to come. Already, the first of a new generation of 'smart' through-the-lens metering systems are in the market, analysing the tonal distribution in a photograph and making pre-programmed decisions accordingly. This kind of decision-making process can, and undoubtedly will, be much more complex and sophisticated. An even greater technological leap is likely to be in the area of electronic, digital imagery. At the point where a photographic image can be recorded or processed as a very large number of dots (pixels, as they are usually known), every kind of alteration to the image is possible, from contrast control to colour balancing to exotic combinations of different pictures.

This technology may not be with us yet, but certainly will be in the forseeable future, and when it arrives, in stages, the traditions of photography are likely to take some hard knocks. When contrast control becomes a matter of selecting a programming mode electronically, techniques such as fill-in flash, the Zone System, and spot metering will cease to be needed as practical solutions (though fill-in flash may survive for its visual effect). With the prospect of accelerated change in equipment, materials and processes, it has become even more important to see them in proportion — as means to an end rather than as the source of images.

The purpose of all technological innovation is two-fold: to make specific types of photography easier to perform, and to improve the image quality. Assessing cameras, lenses, accessories, film and processes on these basic criteria makes it easier to put them into perspective. However radically they may change in the future, they will still stand or fall on how much they facilitate shooting and improve image quality. Of the two, the first is probably the most obvious and most equipment and materials are classified functionally. The operational design of modern single-lens reflexes — the most successful of all types of camera — is basically ergonomic; it has proved so successful because they are easy and comfortable to use. Modular designs of camera, which exist for all formats, facilitate shooting in a different way, by offering interchangeability of parts and so great versatility in the types of photography for which they can be used. For specific photographic tasks there is a large selection of

The quality of a photographic image depends on a number of variables, each of which can be deliberately enhanced or played down by the photographer, either in the negative or in the print. For this picture, a good tonal range, with dark shadows and brilliant highlights, is crucial.

BRIGHTEST HIGHLIGHT

HIGHLIGHT DETAIL

equipment and materials, including perspective-control lenses for architectural photography, different kinds of remote triggering systems for wildlife photography, and high-speed film designed for adjustable processing to make shooting easier in dim and uncertain lighting conditions.

All the equipment, materials and processes described in the first half of this encyclopedia, however, have some effect on the image quality as well. Image quality in a photograph is determined by a number of variables, some of which are inter-related. They are:

1 Tone
2 Tonal separation
3 Tonal range
4 Maximum density
5 Brilliance of highlights
6 Sharpness
7 Grain texture
8 Apparent depth
9 Physical texture
10 Permanence

and additionally, for colour photographs:

11 Colour accuracy
12 Colour saturation

The first five of these qualities all concern tone — the density of the image — and all are linked. The overall tone is usually determined most by the exposure at the time of shooting, although it is influenced by other factors and can be altered substantially by other means. The decisions involved in how dark or light the general impression of the image should be may not necessarily be simple, and a realistic interpretation is only one of several. Within the image is a mixture of different tones, and tonal separation concerns how distinguishable these are, one from another. Lens and film are influential in this and filters, particularly with black-and-white film, can offer an immediate control. The range of these tones — from light to dark within one picture — determines the contrast of the image, otherwise known as its tonal range. In addition to the range of tones in the subject, hard lighting increases contrast, while soft, diffuse lighting lessens it, and in the studio there is ample opportunity for controlling this with appropriate lighting equipment. Emulsions, from film to paper, also vary in their tonal range, and are further affected by the way in which they are processed. Finally, the limits of this tonal range — the density of the deepest black and the brilliance of the purest white — are affected not only by subject, lighting and exposure, but by such material qualities as the density of silver in the film, the surface finish of a print (a glossy surface reflects less light and so shows darker blacks), and the inclusion of chemical whiteners in paper. Even viewing conditions can affect the tonal range — a glossy print will only show maximum whites and blacks if viewed and lit from the right angle. And slides, of course, give a tonal range well beyond any print.

The sharpness of edges and detail has long been a prime quality sought by photographers, and while there are occasions for softening the image, these are much less common than the traditional ideal of crisp, highly resolved detail, with plenty of visual information in the picture. The quality of the lens and the accuracy of focus are obviously important (in enlargement and copying as well as in original shooting), but other factors can also affect sharpness. For instance, the camera design influences how steadily it can held. Emulsions also differ in their ability to record detail, and the graininess is an overlying texture. Nevertheless, although resolution in grain size can be measured, other, unmeasurable qualities in the picture contribute to the visual impression of sharpness and sharpness remains essentially a subjective quality.

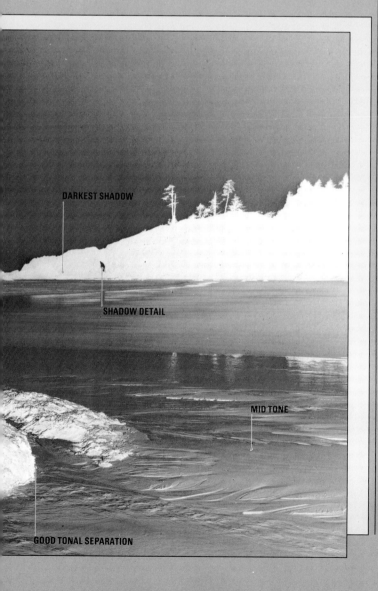

DARKEST SHADOW

SHADOW DETAIL

MID TONE

GOOD TONAL SEPARATION

35MM SLRs

Without doubt, the camera type that is today most commonly used by serious photographers is the 35mm single lens reflex, or SLR. The reasons are not difficult to find. 35mm film provides an ideal compromise between picture quality on the one hand, and convenience and economy on the other. Held in the hand and loaded with fast film, a 35mm SLR can catch fast-breaking news stories. Yet locked on a tripod and using slow, fine grain colour film, the same camera can produce images capable of great enlargement.

SLRs have an edge over other 35mm cameras because their reflex viewfinders show the photographer exactly what will appear on film, regardless of the lens in use or the subject distance. Until a few milliseconds before the film is exposed, the image formed by the camera's lens is projected onto a bright matt screen, so that every aspect of the picture, and every subtle change in lighting or composition can be instantly seen and evaluated.

Success breeds success, and as the SLR has become more popular, so more energy and effort has gone into finding ways of making it more useful and versatile still. Now, there is a 35mm SLR to cater for every level of experience and interest. The most fully automated models offer the benefits of reflex viewing and produce good results even in the hands of someone without any photographic knowledge. Yet for the professional or serious amateur, advanced 35mm SLRs form part of elaborate systems of equipment, some of it highly specialized. Every permutation of lens and accessory is available, so that the creative possibilities of the medium are not limited by the equipment.

At the heart of the camera is the reflex viewing system. This so dominates the design of the camera that, in broad terms, virtually all 35mm SLRs are outwardly very similar in appearance. The core of the camera houses the reflex mirror: this rests diagonally for viewing, and flips up during exposure, as explained opposite. In front of the mirror is an interchangeable lens; behind the mirror, the film, protected by a wafer-thin shutter. Above the mirror is a matt screen on which the image can be seen and focused, and above this is a glass prism which enables the photographer to see the screen and compose the picture with the camera held at eye level.

Also fitted into this 'core' zone of the camera is the exposure metering system which measures the light passing through the camera's lens. Aperture and focusing mechanisms, though, are housed in the lenses, rather than in the camera body.

Opening the back of the camera reveals the shutter, with a chamber on the left for the 35mm cassette, and one on the right containing a take-up spool. The film is wound onto this frame-by-frame after exposure using a

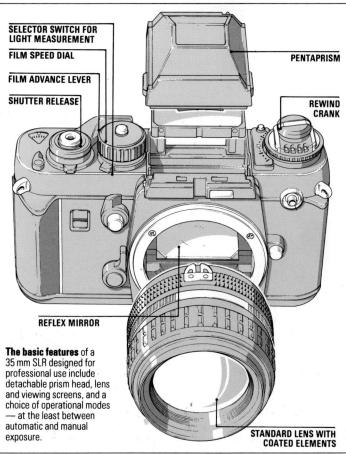

SELECTOR SWITCH FOR
LIGHT MEASUREMENT

FILM SPEED DIAL

FILM ADVANCE LEVER

SHUTTER RELEASE

PENTAPRISM

REWIND
CRANK

REFLEX MIRROR

The basic features of a 35mm SLR designed for professional use include detachable prism head, lens and viewing screens, and a choice of operational modes — at the least between automatic and manual exposure.

STANDARD LENS WITH
COATED ELEMENTS

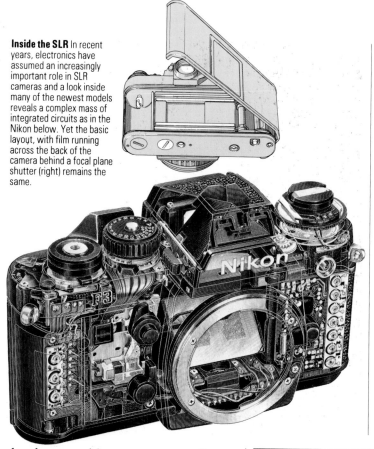

Inside the SLR In recent years, electronics have assumed an increasingly important role in SLR cameras and a look inside many of the newest models reveals a complex mass of integrated circuits as in the Nikon below. Yet the basic layout, with film running across the back of the camera behind a focal plane shutter (right) remains the same.

These inexpensive SLRs will see comparatively gentle use: their owners may expose fewer rolls of film throughout the life of the camera than a prolific professional photographer might use in the course of a day. Consequently, these cameras are of light construction and will not stand up to long periods of intense photography. This does not mean that they should not be taken seriously. Indeed, many budget SLRs share the same lens mounting flange as complex and expensive system cameras. So they provide the inpecunious photographer with a foothold in a system that is comprehensive enough to accommodate the photographer's abilities and aspirations as these grow and broaden.

Mid-range SLRs
More expensive cameras offer more options and facilities. By paying more, the photographer gets a camera which is more versatile, and which allows greater scope for manual control over picture making — or one which perhaps offers a greater range of automatic functions, as the box on page 12-13 explains.

Mid-range SLRs are generally equipped to take a broader range of non-optical accessories than their entry-level counterparts — so, for example, the camera back may be detachable, to be replaced by a data back. The

thumb-operated lever or — optionally — a motor that screws onto the base. The back of the camera carries a spring-loaded pressure plate to keep the film flat.

Over and above this shared constructional concept, 35 mm SLRs differ from each other in three broad areas: first, in the extent to which the camera is constructed in demountable modules — the more modular the camera, the more versatile it is likely to be; second, in the degree of automation, and the number of different operating models; and third, in the quality of construction.

Budget SLRs
The cheapest of SLRs are intended to be used as snapshot cameras. Thus they are designed as integrated units, with fixed viewfinders, focusing screens and backs. They have simple-to-use exposure systems which require the user to set either the aperture or shutter speed. The camera then sets the other control according to the prevailing lighting conditions, and the speed of the film in use. Some cameras of this type have 'programmed exposure'; that is to say that the camera sets both shutter speed and aperture without the photographer's intervention. Most cameras of this type give the photographer minimal manual control over the exposure setting.

If there is a danger of over- or under-exposure, or if the shutter speed set is so slow as to introduce the risk of camera-shake, a warning signal appears in the viewfinder.

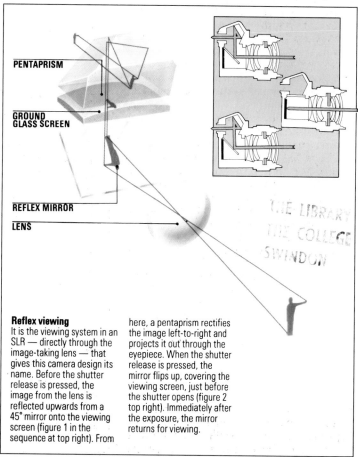

Reflex viewing
It is the viewing system in an SLR — directly through the image-taking lens — that gives this camera design its name. Before the shutter release is pressed, the image from the lens is reflected upwards from a 45° mirror onto the viewing screen (figure 1 in the sequence at top right). From here, a pentaprism rectifies the image left-to-right and projects it out through the eyepiece. When the shutter release is pressed, the mirror flips up, covering the viewing screen, just before the shutter opens (figure 2 top right). Immediately after the exposure, the mirror returns for viewing.

focusing screen may also be removable, enabling the photographer to fit a screen designed for a special purpose. Additionally the camera is likely to be built more substantially — a reflection of the greater wear-and-tear that it will receive in the hands of an enthusiast.

System cameras

The most sophisticated 35 mm SLRs are those that take the principles of modular construction to its logical conclusion. These cameras generally have interchangeable viewfinders, backs and focusing screens, and provide the photographer with a broader range of accessories and ancilliary equipment than other cheaper cameras from the same manufacturer's range.

System cameras are very robustly built; they have to be, to withstand constant heavy use over a period of years. The standard of construction is reflected in the camera's weight and size: these are quite large, heavy cameras.

Perhaps surprisingly though, 35mm system SLRs may not be as electronically sophisticated as less expensive models. The traditional market for system cameras is the working professional photographer, who is more interested in reliability than in how many exposure modes the camera has. Consequently system cameras are often conservative in design, and rarely take advantage of state-of-the-art developments in optics, engineering and electronics.

Applications and limitations

The applications to which the 35 mm SLR lends itself are tremendously diverse, and any listing would necessarily be incomplete. It is perhaps simplest to look at the strong points of this type of camera, and examine the application in which these virtues are most relevant.

■ PORTABILITY This is important in all photo-applications which oblige the photographer to carry large amounts of equipment — or modest amounts of equipment in difficult conditions. Thus, for example, the 35 mm SLR is the ideal tool for travel photographers and mountaineers.

■ EASE OF USE When fitted with a motordrive, the 35 mm SLR can expose film very rapidly, and requires virtually no preparation before exposure — the photographer can point, focus and shoot. In any fast-changing situation, such as news photography, this is vitally important, and the 35 mm SLR is now the pressman's standard kit.

■ LENS AVAILABILITY The range of lenses that can be fitted to a 35 mm SLR is greater than for any other type of camera. At one

MODES AND METERS

Modern cameras use sophisticated integrated circuits to meter the light reflected from the subject, and to set exposure. Analogue inputs, such as film speed and light passing through the lens, are converted into digital form, and used to control all camera functions, principally shutter speed and aperture.

Initially, camera manufacturers made only limited use of the digital output from the camera's central processing unit, but advances in engineering and electronics have made multi-mode control over the camera a practical reality.

These are the principal operating systems that are currently in use — though many cameras offer the photographer a choice of several modes.

Manual In manual mode, the camera measures the light reflected from the subject, and indicates in the viewfinder whether the shutter speed and aperture selected by the photographer will yield correct exposure. The camera is thus totally under the control of the photographer, who is free to follow its recommendations — or to disregard them.

Aperture priority automatic (or aperture preferred automatic) In this mode, the photographer sets the camera's aperture, and the shutter is automatically set to a speed that will give the correct exposure. This mode is most useful in conditions where control over depth of field is important — landscape or close-up photography, for example.

Shutter priority automatic (or shutter preferred automatic) Conversely, in this mode the photographer sets the shutter speed and the camera chooses the aperture. This mode is most useful when photographing subjects that must appear 'frozen' on film — action and sports photography, for example.

Programmed automatic This is a 'point and shoot' mode in which the photographer completely relinquishes control to the camera. In progressively brighter light, the camera picks smaller and smaller apertures, and faster and faster shutter speeds. 'Sub-modes' include *shutter-preferred programs*, which choose faster shutter speeds before closing down the aperture; and *aperture-preferred programs*, which as the name suggests, pick

smaller apertures in preference to faster speeds. A few of the most recently introduced cameras sense the focal length of the lens in use, and will program faster shutter speeds when a telephoto lens is fitted. This helps prevent camera shake, which is more likely to cause problems with telephotos.

Flash mode The exact function of the camera when set to this mode varies from model to model. In the most simple example, the camera will operate at the flash synchronization speed as long as there is a dedicated flashgun in the accessory shoe, and fully recycled; while the flash is recycling, the camera meters and responds to ambient light as if no flash was fitted.

Other modes Some cameras may switch between one mode and another to provide optimum results even when the photographer makes an erroneous setting — perhaps by failing to set the lens to its minimum aperture (this is a prerequisite in certain programmed modes). To increase the mode count, some camera manufacturers dub this 'crossover mode'.

One camera has a mode that sets the shutter to the ideal speed for

TYPES OF SLR

The electronic revolution in camera design has resulted in a basic polarization between heavily and moderately automated models. Cameras aimed at professionals tend to feature several modes, of which one is called 'manual' — although in practice this means doing little more than matching the controls to the TTL meter measurement.

Full automation, in which most of the control decisions are removed from the photographer, is aimed at the amateur market. The models shown here represent the range.

photographing TV screens and video monitors, but this and other gimmick modes are of debatable advantage in everyday photography.

METERING

Most 35mm SLRs meter the brightness of the light reaching just a portion of the frame, and ignore the remainder. This is known as *selective area metering*, and prevents the camera from being misled by, for

SELECTIVE AREA METERING

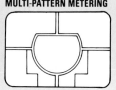

SPOT-METERING

MULTI-PATTERN METERING

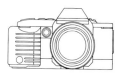

example, a bright sky. The pattern of exposure metering, though, is very variable: some cameras meter just a small area of the frame, others sample a much broader area.

Spot-metering is an extreme form of selective area metering. A small circle in the middle of the camera's focusing screen marks the area of the meter's sensitivity. The photographer places the spot over the area to be metered. This system, however, needs to be used with intelligence to produce consistent results — spot metering is not for the hasty photographer. A variation of spot metering permits the photographer to take several spot readings and average these out to determine the exposure.

One option that has been recently introduced is *multi-pattern metering*. This system makes use of several light-sensitive cells that individually meter the four corners of the frame, and the central area. The camera then compares the readings from each cell with a stored computer algorithm to determine the best exposure. This system copes better with unusual lighting then does selective area metering.

1 NEEDLE

2 NEEDLE POINTER ON SCALE

3 DIGITAL LED NUMBERS

1000 5.6 M

4 DIGITAL LCD NUMBERS

P5oo   F:6

5 LCD SCALE

2.8

Viewfinder metering displays

1 Centered needle
2 Needle on scale
3 Digital LED numerals
4 Digital LCD numerals
5 LCD scale

There is now a considerable range of different display systems for conveying essential information in a 35mm SLR, and this has some influence on the choice of camera. The amount of information given varies, and while a full display can be valuable, it can also be complex and distracting. A basic difference is between analog and digital displays — as with wristwatches, there tend to be sharp distinctions in individual preference.

Focusing screens

There is even greater variety of focusing screens. The standard screen fitted to most cameras at the time of purchase is a matte/Fresnel screen with a split-image microprism rangefinder in the centre (1). This is ideal for general purpose use. A plain matte screen (2) gives a clear view for long-focus shots. An etched grid over a plain screen is useful for alignment, as in architectural photography (3). A plain screen (4) without ground glass is for aerial image-focusing, useful in photomicrography. The scale is used for measurements of specimens.

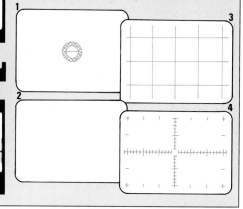

Canon T70 This multiple program model features 8 modes of operation, is very heavily automated, and its manufacturers make a strong design feature of 'computer-age' display.

Minolta 7000 An example of the trend towards total electronic control of all camera functions is the Minolta 7000. In particular, it features an autofocus system that is integrated into the body, so reducing the cost, size and weight of lenses.

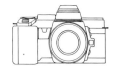

Olympus OM-4 Also a highly automated camera, the OM-4 is designed for near-foolproof operation in unskilled hands, but provides a highly sophisticated metering system for more experienced photographers.

Canon AE-1 Program One of the pioneering 'multi-mode' cameras, the AE-1 is a high quality camera offering both shutter priority and fully programmed automatic exposure plus full manual metering.

Rollei SLR 3003 Distinct from other 35mm SLRs, this new Rollei model is modular in the sense of medium-format cameras, featuring interchangeable film backs and snap-on rapid recharging power packs.

Nikon F3AF One of the most advanced professional cameras, this is basically the top-of-the-line F3 with an image-displacement sensing prism. Micro motors in a small range of lenses use this information to focus the lens automatically.

extreme, fisheye lenses have a field of view exceeding 180°, so they can take in the whole of a room in a single picture. At the other, a 2000 mm telephoto mirror lens can pick out distant detail that is virtually invisible to the unaided eye. This range of lenses gives the 35 mm SLR a special value in pictorial applications where interesting pictures must be conjured from dull subjects; and in those fields where a subject is unapproachable or presents special difficulties, such as wildlife photography.

■ SPECIALIST APPLICATIONS Whenever a camera must be linked to some other piece of apparatus — such as a microscope or endoscope — the 35 mm SLR is usually the camera chosen on account of its easy-to-use viewing system, and through-the-lens meter.

Despite its versatility, there are some areas of photography where the SLR does not excel. The principal limitations on the general application of the 35 mm SLR are the size of the film format, lack of fully interchangeable magazine backs, and slow flash synchronization. Of these, the first is the biggest handicap.

Many pictures taken by professional

photographers are greatly enlarged in reproduction. To fill the page of a quality newspaper, a 35 mm frame must be enlarged some 16 times, and this tests film quality to the limit. Fine-grain 35 mm transparencies have been enlarged to poster-hoarding size, but in general, larger format images are better suited to great enlargement.

None of the system cameras from the major manufacturers currently accept film magazine backs that can be exchanged in mid-roll. To change from one film type to another, photographers must rewind the 35 mm film into its cassette, and load another roll. Although the expense of doing this is insignificant for the professional photographer, the inconvenience can be considerable. Most roll-film SLRs offer interchangeable backs as a standard facility, so in circumstances where time is short and frequent film changes are needed, 35 mm SLRs are used less often than roll-film cameras.

Many roll-film cameras are fitted with leaf shutters that operate with flash at all speeds — whereas few 35 mm SLRs synchronize with flash at speeds faster than 1/125. This again means that 35 mm SLRs are passed over when flash synchronization speed is critical — as it is when combining flash and daylight (see pages 78-79).

ROLL-FILM SLRs

Roll-film cameras are in many ways a compromise between size and simplicity. The film they use produces pictures around four times larger than a 35 mm frame, yet the cameras are not as cumbersome and unwieldy as those that use sheet-film.

The most convenient and easy to use of all roll-film cameras is the SLR. Like its smaller 35 mm cousin, this type of camera has a diagonal mirror that relays the image from the lens up into the viewfinder until an instant before the shutter opens.

However, few roll-film SLRs outwardly resemble 35 mm SLRs. The body of the larger species of camera is much more box-shaped, without the broad 'wings' on either side of the lens and mirror box.

There are other differences, too. On the whole, roll-film SLRs are more modular in construction than 35 mm SLRs, with lens, focusing screen, viewfinder, and film magazine all removable. The camera body is just a frame, onto which the other working components of the camera clip. The body itself contains the reflex viewing mechanisms, a shutter, and often some other electronic and mechanical components.

Shutter types

Whereas all 35 mm cameras have focal-plane shutters positioned just in front of the film, not all roll-film cameras are arranged like this.

Many instead have leaf shutters within the camera's lens. This approach has significant advantages, the most important of which is flash synchronization; leaf shutters will operate with flash at all speeds, whereas focal plane shutters usually synchronize only at speeds slower than 1/60. Additionally, should the leaf shutter in one lens break down, the photographer can continue to take pictures with another lens. If the focal-plane shutter in the camera body fails, a new body is needed.

Focal-plane shutters are not without their advantages, either. The top speed of a focal-plane shutter is usually 1/1000 or 1/2000, compared to the 1/500 of a leaf shutter. And because the photographer does not buy a new shutter with each lens, these are often cheaper.

Viewfinders and screens

The standard viewfinder fitted to a roll-film SLR is usually a folding hood. This is just a construction of metal plates which, when erected, cast a shadow across the focusing screen, making the image easier to see. Folded down, the hood takes up little space, and protects the focusing screen from damage. In the top of the folding hood is a magnifier which enables the photographer to see an enlarged view of the centre of the focusing

Composing in a square format

Although a square is neither traditionally nor aesthetically a normal frame within which to compose an image, the early development of rollfilm cameras has made it a feature of medium-format photography. Most professional photographers are accustomed to using the square frame loosely, shooting to crop in later to the shape of the magazine or layout that will be using the picture. Otherwise, there are a number of ways of designing an image to fit well into this very formal, symmetrical border, as the examples above show.

Compositions that work better than most in a square are:
1 Formal, regular designs
2 Designs that are organized around the centre
3 Patterns and other formless areas where texture matters more than shape. The centred, geometrical interior above and the textural pattern of leaves in the forest shot are both examples of natural square composition.

Image-size The traditional advantage of rollfilm is that it gives nearly four times the picture area of 35 mm but cameras can still be hand-held. The picture below is actual size.

FILM AND FORMATS

Traditional roll-film cameras take 12 square pictures each 6 cm wide, on a roll of paper-backed 120 film. With unbacked 220 film, this is doubled to 24 frames. However, many cameras now offer formats larger or smaller than this standard size.

6 × 7 cm cameras take ten frames this size on 120 film, and 6 × 4.5 cm cameras, 15 frames. Since pictures made by these cameras are rectangular, more of the film area is used when making rectangular prints than if the starting point was a square negative or transparency. However, rectangular film presents certain difficulties in composition, because turning the camera to change from landscape to portrait format moves the folding focusing hood from the top of the camera to the side. Turning the camera also inverts the image in the viewfinder.

There are two solutions to this. Certain 6 × 7 cm format cameras have revolving backs, so that only the back moves, not the whole camera. A more common, and equally practical answer is to fit an eye-level prism.

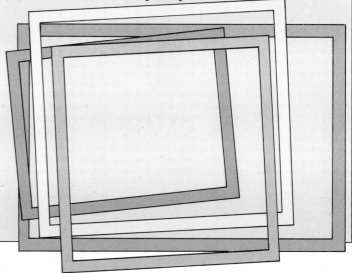

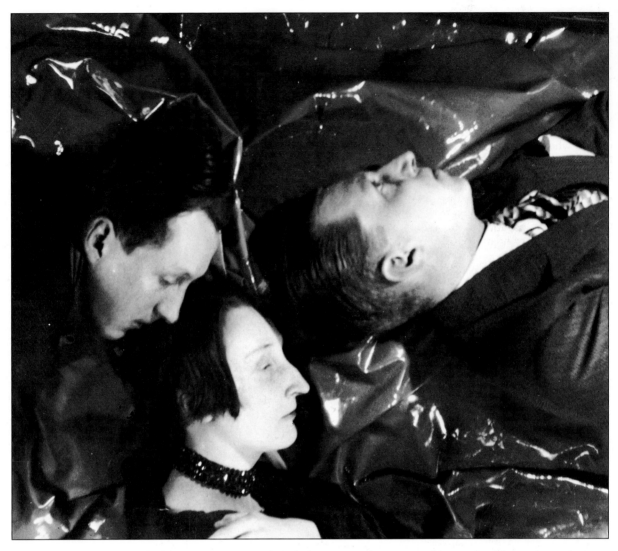

Studio portraiture is one of the fields in which roll-film cameras excel, as this picture of the Sitwell family by Cecil Beaton illustrates. The speed of operation (moving from one exposure to the next) is by no means as slow as with a large-format camera, yet the negative size allows relatively grain-free enlargements with most print-sizes.

screen — and sometimes the whole image.

Folding hoods do not exclude all ambient light, and when compactness is not a primary consideration, many photographers prefer to use rigid hoods. These are absolutely light-tight, and generally have a magnifier that adjusts to suit each individual's eyesight. However, like folding hoods, these rigid ones suffer from a major disadvantage — they present an image of the focusing screen that is laterally reversed, so that subjects moving from left to right in front of the camera appear to move in the opposite direction on the focusing screen. Prism viewfinders provide a right-way-round image that eliminates this problem.

The prism viewfinder most familiar from 35 mm SLRs turns the image of the focusing screen through 90°, so that the camera can be held up at eye-level. However, supporting the camera at eye-level can be tiring, and a slightly different prism, which turns the optical axis through just 45°, can make the camera more comfortable to hold. Both types

of prism add considerable weight to the basic camera body.

Cameras that are supplied without an integral meter can be fitted with metering prisms, which meter the light falling on the focusing screen. These may be coupled to the camera's controls to a greater or lesser degree: some simply indicate the required exposure and leave the photographer to set the shutter speed and aperture, while others effectively give the camera fully automated exposure metering. The newer roll-film SLRs, though, generally have metering systems installed in the camera body, and do not need separate metering prisms to provide auto-exposure.

Compared to a 35 mm SLR, the standard focusing screen on a roll-film model is simple. Often the screen will be just plain matt, with crosshairs in the middle. Focusing aids are less important with this larger format, because the screen is larger and therefore easier to see. However, interchangeable screens optionally include split-image rangefinders and/or microprisms.

Film magazines

On most roll-film SLRs, the back of the camera, which holds the film and its transport mechanism, is removable. To take it off the camera, the photographer inserts a metal sheath which protects the film inside the magazine, and then pushes a catch to one side to release the magazine. Putting on a new magazine simply means reversing the procedure. Interlocks fix the magazine to the camera when the sheath is removed so that film cannot be fogged, and prevent the shutter from firing when the sheath is in place.

Magazines can be loaded with film either when fitted to the camera, or when removed, so the busy photographer can employ an assistant to reload magazines when film runs out.

Removable magazines have a further advantage. The standard roll-film magazine can be replaced by an instant-film magazine, so that the photographer can make instant checks on lighting, colour and exposure. Other magazines may change the film format — perhaps from 6×7 to 6×4.5 cm on 120 roll-film — or the film stock, allowing the use of long rolls of 70 mm film, or cassettes of 35 mm film.

Lenses for roll-film SLRs

Each different format of roll-film uses a different focal length as standard: 75 mm for 6×4.5, 80 mm for 6×6, and 90 mm for 6×7 cm

Roll-film SLRs in use

These cameras fill a gap between 35 mm and sheet-film models. Though not as quick and easy to use as 35 mm, they are nevertheless small enough to hand-hold, yet produce usefully large pictures. Consequently, they are often used by professional wedding and social photographers.

In the studio, they are very much more convenient than sheet-film cameras, and therefore find favour for portrait and fashion work where the photographer must catch a fleeting gesture, or a flowing garment.

One of the pioneer manufacturers of medium-format SLR cameras is Hasselblad. This is very much a system, designed in a modular way, that allows quite different configurations. There is a choice between bodies that incorporate a focal plane shutter and those that do not (relying on leaf shutters in each lens). A distinctive feature is a selection of interchangeable film magazines, permitting not only rapid change between different types of film during one shoot, but also different formats.

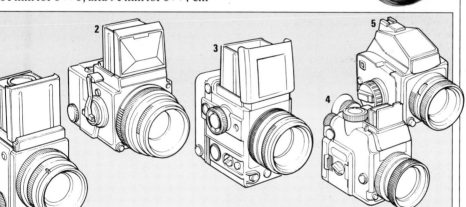

Other roll-film designs include the following makes, illustrated at left:
1 Mamiya RZ67
2 Mamiya 643
3 Rolleiflex 6007
4 Rolleiflex 2000F
5 Bronica

pictures. Wide-angle lenses tend to have comparatively modest specification, providing — even in the extreme — angles of view that correspond to 20 or 30 mm lenses on 35 mm cameras.

Telephoto lenses give limited magnification, too: the longest focal lengths usually available for roll-film cameras magnify the subject no more than a 250 or 300 mm lens on a 35 mm SLR.

Most systems additionally have a fisheye lens, a macro lens, and possibly a perspective control lens (see pages 36-37). Systems fitted with focal plane shutters often also have a portrait lens with its own integral leaf shutter, for faster flash synchronization.

Other roll-film cameras
Although roll-film cameras are dominated by the SLR type, not all roll-film cameras fall into this category. Twin-lens reflex cameras (TLRs) were once very popular, though less so today. TLRs as the name suggests, have two lenses stacked one above the other. The lower lens serves only for picture-making, while the upper one of the pair relays the image via a fixed mirror to the focusing screen. Both lenses slide back and forth on a single panel for focusing, so when the image on the screen at the top of the camera is sharp, so too will be the image on the film.

TLRs are generally cheaper and quieter than SLRs, but they suffer from parallax error (see page 23) which can cause problems at short subject distances. Usually TLRs have fixed lenses — though one make can be fitted with pairs of lenses ranging in focal length from 55 mm to 250 mm.

Rangefinder roll-film cameras have become increasingly popular over a period when use of TLRs has declined. These models resemble overblown 35 mm rangefinder cameras, and are very light and compact compared to roll-film reflex cameras. To make them even smaller the lens often extends from the camera body on a bellows, and folds away when not in use. Lenses are not interchangeable, though different models of camera are available, each with lenses of different focal length.

SHEET-FILM CAMERAS

The image of the photographer standing behind a large and unwieldy camera, a black cloth covering his head, may today seem archaic and irrelevant, but it is not. These cumbersome cameras are still in use, and indeed, for colour images used in poster advertising, such sheet-film cameras are essential.

Though modern technology has made these cameras lighter and somewhat easier to use, the changes are partly cosmetic, and a photographer from a century ago would probably feel quite at home with one of today's sheet-film cameras. The converse is also true — some portrait photographers in particular still use cameras the design of which has not changed in 50 years.

Professional 5 × 4in monorail camera

Basic principles

The sheet-film camera is the most basic form of apparatus. It is composed of two flat panels: the front one supports the lens, shutter and aperture; and the back one holds a ground glass screen for focusing. To take a picture, the screen is pushed aside, and a film holder takes its place.

The two panels — called the lens or front 'standard', and film or rear 'standard' — are joined by a leather cloth bellows that excludes light. The whole apparatus is supported on a rail, or a third panel.

To take a picture, the photographer fixes the camera to a tripod, and locks open the shutter and aperture inside the camera's lens so that the lens projects a dim image onto the ground-glass at the back of the camera. By excluding light, using the prominent black cloth, the photographer can see the image, and move the two standards closer together or further apart until the image is sharp.

At this point, the shutter is closed, and the aperture stopped down to the chosen setting. The photographer now loads a sheet of film into the film-holder (a flat, shallow box), and pushes this into the back standard of the camera. After pulling out the light-tight sheath which protects the film, the camera is ready for operation. Pressing the shutter release exposes the film.

Pictures can only be taken one at a time, of course, because the film is in the form of cut sheets, instead of a long roll. However, there

CAMERA MOVEMENTS
On a 35mm camera, the lens is locked in position relative to the film, and can move only along its own axis — closer to, and farther from the film for focusing. Sheet-film cameras are not restricted in this way, and both the lens standard and film standard move in several other directions. In addition to the fore-and-aft movement found on smaller formats, the standards can shift left and right, and up and down while remaining parallel. Each standard can tilt forwards and backwards along a horizontal axis, and swing to the left and right around a vertical axis.

These camera movements, as they are called, are used to control the appearance of the image on film. Shifting either the front or back of the camera changes the field of view, because this action moves the film plane to a different part of the large circular image formed by the lens, as shown at right.

This technique finds practical application when photographing a building. Tilting the camera upwards to include the whole of the structure causes the parallel sides to converge on film, so photographers always aim to keep the camera back vertical. However, with the lens in the normal position, the top of the building is cropped out of the picture. The solution is to shift the lens — and with it, the circular image that falls on the film — upwards. This brings the top of the building into view at the bottom of the sheet of film. (Camera lenses always form inverted images.)

Swings and tilts perform different functions. Front swings and tilts — angling of the lens standard — alter the distribution of sharpness within the image. When both standards are parallel, as they are on a 35mm camera, the plane of sharpest focus lies parallel to the film. However, tilting

or swinging the lens re-orientates the plane of sharp focus. For example, when photographing a carpet on the floor, a photographer wishes to keep the whole floor in focus. This is made possible by tilting the lens forward so that the plane of sharpest focus is horizontal, rather than parallel to the film. The whole carpet will thus be sharp, even at full aperture. Note, though, that the vertical walls of the room will drift rapidly out of focus as they rise upwards from floor level.

Back swings and tilts change the shape of the subject. This is because swinging or tilting the film plane is equivalent to turning the whole camera. A photographer may want to change the apparent shape of a still-life set, for example, to emphasize some object in the foreground. This could be done by tilting the rear standard of the camera backwards at the top.

Image quality

One of the principal, and least complicated, virtues of large film size is the exceptional quality that is possible in terms of resolution, rendering of smooth tones, and the gradation of tones. This subtropical landscape view (right) is reproduced here at the actual size of the film; without enlargement, the grain of the film is much smaller than the dot size of the printing on this page. The emulsion — ISO 64 Ektachrome — is essentially the same as that used for 35mm and 120 film, yet the same image is recorded over a much larger area of film.

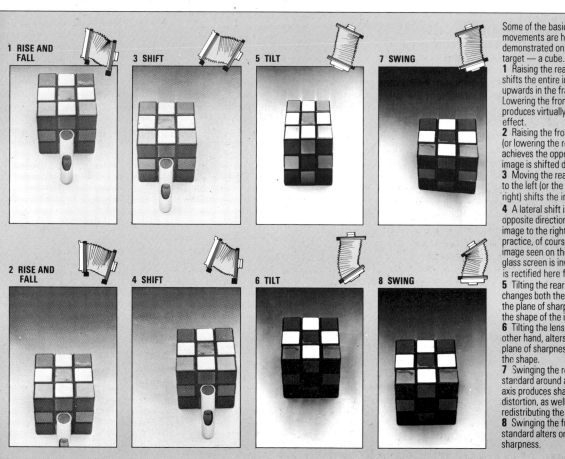

Some of the basic camera movements are here demonstrated on a standard target — a cube.
1 Raising the rear standard shifts the entire image upwards in the frame. Lowering the front standard produces virtually the same effect.
2 Raising the front standard (or lowering the rear) achieves the opposite — the image is shifted downwards.
3 Moving the rear standard to the left (or the front to the right) shifts the image left.
4 A lateral shift in the opposite direction shifts the image to the right. In practice, of course, the image seen on the ground-glass screen is inverted; it is rectified here for clarity.
5 Tilting the rear standard changes both the angle of the plane of sharp focus *and* the shape of the image.
6 Tilting the lens, on the other hand, alters only the plane of sharpness and not the shape.
7 Swinging the rear standard around a vertical axis produces shape distortion, as well as redistributing the sharpness.
8 Swinging the front standard alters only sharpness.

1 RISE AND FALL

3 SHIFT

5 TILT

7 SWING

2 RISE AND FALL

4 SHIFT

6 TILT

8 SWING

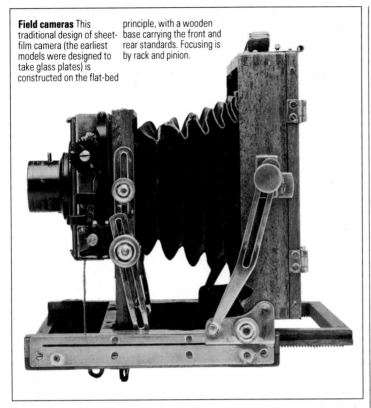

Field cameras This traditional design of sheet-film camera (the earliest models were designed to take glass plates) is constructed on the flat-bed principle, with a wooden base carrying the front and rear standards. Focusing is by rack and pinion.

Monorail and technical cameras The two most commonly used current designs of view camera are the monorail (below left and right inset) and the technical camera. The monorail is a highly versatile instrument, but not especially robust, and is used principally in studios. The technical camera is in many respects a more strongly engineered version of the field camera.

are several compensations: first, the large pictures produce superb quality images. Second, by tilting, shifting and swinging the front and rear standards relative to each other, the photographer can change the camera's field of view, the apparent shape of the subject, and the distribution of sharpness within the picture (see box on page 19).

The third advantage is less tangible, because it relates more to human nature than to technique. Portrait subjects respond differently to these large-format cameras than to smaller equipment. So the photographer captures an image that is quite different in mood and quality — though it may have the same content as a picture taken using a 35 mm camera.

Sizes and types of camera

The two commonest sizes of sheet-film are 5 × 4 in, and 10 × 8 in (12.5 × 10 cm and 25 × 20 cm respectively). However, there is a profusion of other less commonly used sizes, such as $4\frac{3}{4} \times 6\frac{1}{2}$ in or 12 × 15 in. The larger the film, the larger is the camera in which it is exposed, and only cameras taking the smallest size — 5 × 4 in — can really be hand-held.

Broadly speaking, there are two types of sheet-film camera: the monorail, and the field camera. *Monorail cameras*, as their name suggests, have standards mounted on a single metal rail. The two standards are very manoeuvrable, offering the largest possible range of camera movements, so this type of camera is very versatile. However, it is also time-consuming to set up, and ungainly to use, so monorail cameras are most often used in the studio. Outdoors, they are used only when extreme movements are required.

Field cameras, on the other hand, are designed for use out of the studio. They are much more rugged than monorail cameras, and easier to use in difficult conditions — in high wind, for example. They do not have such extreme movements as monorail cameras, though, so they are not as versatile. A few field cameras are fitted with range-finders similar to those on 35 mm cameras. This enables the photographer to focus the camera without resorting to the ground-glass screen. The rangefinder usually operates only with a limited range of lenses, though.

Lenses for sheet-film cameras

The lens standards of sheet-film cameras have removable centre panels, into which the lens screws. Generally the panels are cheap, so each lens is left fitted into its own panel, which can then be quickly locked onto the camera.

Choice of focal length is more limited than for either 35 mm or roll-film cameras, particularly at the long focal length end. However, since a portion of the large film sheets can be enlarged with little loss of quality, this rarely presents problems.

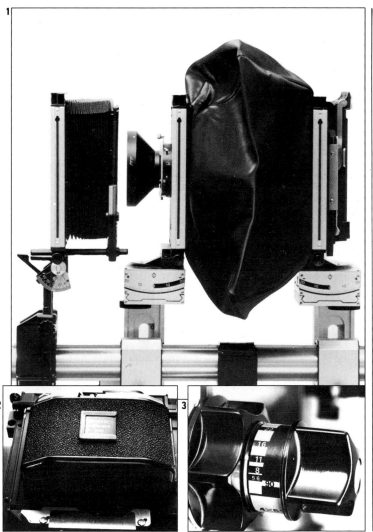

The most suitable lens for any given application depends not only on the angle of view that the photographer wants, but also on the film format in use, and on the degree of lens coverage required, as explained on page 29. A standard lens for a 5 × 4 in camera, for example, would have a focal length of 150 mm or 210 mm. These lenses give fields of view equivalent to focal lengths of 40 mm and 55 mm lenses on 35 mm cameras. A typical wide-angle lens for 5 × 4 in has a focal length of 90 mm (equivalent to 24 mm on a 35 mm SLR) though lenses as short as 65 mm (17 mm) are available. In the telephoto range, a focal length of 360 mm is typical — equivalent to 95 mm on a 35 mm SLR. Coverage for lenses of different focal lengths is on page 39.

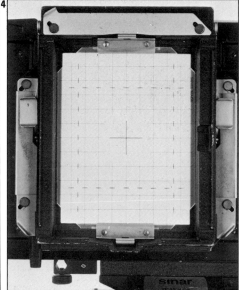

1 Bellows lens shade To avoid flare, a shade can be made from one of the standard bellows with one standard.

2 Roll-film back Several makes of roll-film back are available. These fit into the rear standard in place of the ground glass screen and spring-back roll—film is more economical than sheets.

3 Depth of field scale As view cameras do not normally have focusing mounts for their lenses, any depth of field scale must be incorporated into the focusing knob or rack. The version shown here is for a Sinar P.

4 Viewing screen the viewing screen in modern view cameras is located in a spring-back — at rest it lies in the film plane, but is opened and moved back to accept the film holders.

35MM NON-REFLEX

Non-reflex 35mm cameras appeal to photographers at opposite ends of the skill spectrum. In autofocus-snapshot form, these cameras provide unskilled photographers with a simple and reliable way of taking sharp, colourful pictures. At the other end of the scale is the precision rangefinder camera — a sophisticated picture-making machine beloved of photojournalists, which is barely recognizable as a member of the same family.

Snapshot cameras

The enormous majority of today's 35mm non-reflex cameras are totally automatic snapshot cameras. As far as possible, all functions of these cameras take place without the photographer's intervention — apart from the pressing of the shutter release, of course.

To operate an autofocus 35mm camera, the photographer simply inserts a 35mm cassette, draws the tongue of the film across the back of the camera, and tucks the end into the take-up spool. On closing the back of the camera, film is advanced to the first frame, and picture-taking can begin after the film-speed has been set on a dial. (On the most recent cameras even the setting of film speed is automatic.)

Taking pictures just means pointing the camera and pressing the shutter release. The camera then measures the light reflected from the subject and sets the aperture and shutter speed; and using a sophisticated electronic rangefinding device, judges how far away the subject is before setting the optimum focus. In low light, a visual or (exceptionally) spoken warning advises the photographer to use the flashgun.

The camera's few manual controls include the film-speed setting dial, a switch to supply power to the flash unit, and sometimes a preset-focus switch for the autofocus mechanism. The preset-focus control allows the photographer to point the camera at the principal subject to set the correct focus, then turn the camera and recompose the picture with a subject off-centre before pressing the shutter release. Cameras lacking such a control focus on subjects in the very centre of the viewfinder, and produce unsharp pictures of, for example, off-centre figures in the foreground of a spreading landscape.

The most suitable applications for autofocus snapshot cameras are broadly similar to those for cartridge-loading cameras. However, since autofocus cameras use fully controlled exposure, 35mm film, and lenses that are adjusted to match the subject distance, these cameras are capable of very much better results than their cartridge-loading counterparts: negatives on slow colour film can be blown up to 60 or 80 cm across without serious loss of quality. An addi-

tional advantage is that users have a vast range of films to choose from — there is a greater variety of film made in 35 mm than in any other format.

Not all non-reflex snapshot cameras have autofocus facility. A few of the cheapest or most miniature models have scale or symbol focusing (see page 40) and either weather-symbol exposure control or simple auto-exposure mechanisms. These budget cameras otherwise have specifications that closely resemble those of cartridge-loading cameras.

Rangefinder cameras

In marked contrast to the profusion of autofocus models, rangefinder cameras are now few and far between. The most well-known is the Leica — an expensive, high-quality system camera that can be fitted with a large range of interchangeable lenses. Other models of this type are similar in concept to

The Leica The first-ever 35mm still camera, the Leica remains the standard non-reflex 35mm camera the professional. Despite the inherent disadvantage of a rectangular viewing and focusing system when compared with modern SLRs, a regular programme of design improvements keeps the Leica the choice of many photojournalists.

the Leica, but may have fixed lenses and are generally less sophisticated.

None of these cameras are designed with the novice in mind. Most camera functions are set manually, though there may be an automatic exposure system. However, the most obvious difference between rangefinder and autofocus cameras is in the viewfinder. This is still separate from the camera's main lens, but on rangefinder cameras the viewfinder is mechanically coupled to the camera's focusing mechanism, as explained on page 42. The mechanics of the coupling causes subjects that are out of focus to appear as double images in the central area of the viewfinder. Turning the focusing ring merges the two images into one, showing sharp focus.

Changing lenses affects the viewfinder image, too. Bright rectangles in the viewfinder indicate the field of view of the lens in use, and changing from one lens to another changes the size of the rectangles.

Rangefinder cameras are particularly

Leica M6 As is customary from this manufacturer, external design changes are few. The main feature of the M6 is a new selective light metering system.

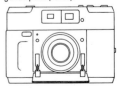

Contax T35 At 270gm (9½oz), the Contax T35 is a high-performance pocket camera with aperture-priority auto metering and good optics (Zeiss).

popular among photojournalists, many of whom feel that the direct-vision viewfinder puts less of a barrier between subject and photographer than does the ground-glass screen of a reflex camera. This, they suggest, enables them to take pictures that show the subject in a more sympathetic light, rather than as a pattern on a piece of film.

There are some practical advantages, too: the viewfinder shows more of the subject than will appear on film, so that the photographers can see a subject before it enters the frame. They can thus anticipate action and activity more readily than when using a 35 mm SLR (the viewfinder of which generally shows *less* of the subject than will appear on film).

Other advantages are that rangefinder cameras are very quiet in operation compared to SLRs, and are mechanically simpler and therefore more reliable in adverse conditions.

CARTRIDGE AND DISC CAMERAS

Cartridge and disc cameras are the direct descendants of the world's first cameras. Just like their ancestors — the 'mousetrap' cameras that Fox Talbot used — these modern cameras are essentially no more than boxes with lenses.

The passage of a century, though, has changed the box camera out of all recognition. Circular plastic wafers or strips of film have replaced salt-soaked writing paper as the image-forming medium; and hour-long exposures have been reduced to milliseconds.

Disc cameras

Disc cameras are aimed at the amateur photographer who knows little about the technology of photography — and does not wish to learn any more. These cameras are therefore extremely simple to load and operate, and produce acceptable results almost all the time.

This simplicity and ease of operation comes at a price: disc cameras are limited in scope, versatility and picture quality. Each frame of film measures less than a square centimetre — so the picture is recorded on an area just one eighth of the size of a 35 mm frame. Enlarging the negatives to bigger than postcard-size yields prints in which the grains — the particles of dye that make up the colour picture — are very prominent. Additionally, the pictures look fuzzy and unsharp when greatly enlarged.

Nevertheless these are perhaps small sacrifices to make to achieve totally foolproof and convenient photography. Disc cameras are tiny, and wafer-thin. The smallest leaves hardly a bulge in the pocket, and any of them can be whipped out in an instant and brought up to eye-level, ready for picture-taking. Many professional photographers find this carefree ease of use so attractive that they carry a disc camera constantly as an ever-ready visual notebook.

Parallax error Because the viewing window of a rangefinder camera is displaced slightly from the picture-taking lens, the image viewed differs from the image recorded. This difference is insignificant at distances of more than several metres, but close up it must be allowed for. Sophisticated rangefinder cameras like the Leica have parallax correction built into the viewing system.

Rangefinder focusing Because the image cannot be focused visually with a non-reflex camera many cameras of this type intended for the serious photographer have a rangefinding system. This is essentially a form of triangulation, in which the slightly different angles of view from two windows on the top panel of the camera are measured accurately and linked to the lens focusing system. The lens focus can be adjusted until the two halves of the image match.

Disc cameras Kodak disc film, shown here, is available in colour negative form, giving 15 frames per loading. The small image size and the unique film format allows a convenient, pocketable camera and discs are suitable for automated processing, but only small prints are satisfactory in quality.

Disc cameras in use

Disc film (which is available only in colour-negative form) comes in a thin plastic envelope that protects the disc within from light. A small window in the envelope opens to admit light when the film is inside the camera. Before and after loading, though, a tiny trap-door seals the window.

Loading could not be easier: the disc just drops into the camera, and only fits one way round, eliminating the possibility of incorrect loading. Closing the camera back and pushing a catch or lever opens the film window and activates a tiny motor to advance the film to the first frame. The same motor rotates the film disc about 24° between each of the 15 exposures.

Exposure measurement varies from model to model, but typically a photoelectric cell on the front of the camera measures the brightness of the subject, and adjusts both aperture and shutter speed to match the scene brightness. In dim conditions the camera switches to flash exposure — a flash unit is built in.

Most disc cameras are focused with a two-position switch — the viewfinder is just a simple window above the lens, and gives no indication of when the picture is sharp. With the focusing switch in the normal position, the camera will make sharp images of subjects at least 1.5 m from the camera. Moving the switch to 'close-up' swings a supplementary lens into place — and the camera then takes sharp pictures of subjects between 0.5 and 1.5in distant. Closing the camera's integral lens-cover resets the lens to suit distant subjects. (This action also turns off the camera's electronic circuits.)

Disc cameras work best with their intended subjects: family snapshots; pictures at parties or on the beach; portraits of friends; landscapes and travel pictures. Certain other subjects are less successful: in low light, for example, the flash on many disc cameras will fire automatically, and this can sometimes spoil the atmosphere of the scene. A few subjects, such as wildlife, are impractical to photograph with a disc camera — but this could be said of any non-interchangeable lens camera.

Cartridge-load cameras

Like the disc cameras that superseded them, cartridge-loading cameras are designed primarily for ease of use. Film is contained in a drop-in cartridge made of plastic. The cameras themselves are simple box-cameras, but are technologically more primitive than disc cameras.

A typical cartridge-loading camera has a fixed-focus lens that forms sharp pictures of subjects two metres away or more. The picture is framed using a simple 'reversed telescope' viewfinder that shows the subject approximately as it will appear on film. There

126-size cameras The Kodak Instamatic 77-X shown below accepts 126 cartridge film, available for colour prints, colour slides and black-and-white prints. A fixed lens gives sharp focus from 1.2metres (4ft) to infinity. Flash cubes give illumination for indoor photography.
There is one shutter speed, of 1/50 second, suitable for photography in bright or hazy sunlight and with flash.

110-size cameras The Kodak Ektra 200 and Ektralite 400 are both examples of simple amateur cameras that accept 110 cartridges. They both have a fixed-focus, one-aperture lens, and a choice of three shutter speeds. The Ektralite 400 has, in addition, a built-in electronic flash. The Ektra 200 uses an accessory flash.

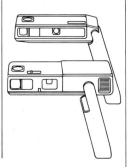

Disc cameras The Kodak Disc 4000 and 8000 cameras are a simple, pocketable system for the amateur market. Both have built-in electronic flash, automatic exposure and automatic film winding; in addition, the 8000 model has a rapid-sequence capability — of 3 frames per second if needed.

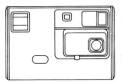

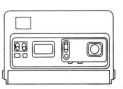

is no real exposure metering system; instead of exposure controls, the cheapest cameras are set to give optimum results in 'cloudy-bright' conditions. In duller or brighter weather, such cameras fall back on the easy-going nature of colour negative film, which can forgive all but gross exposure errors. Middle range cartridge-loading cameras sometimes have 'weather-symbol' exposure setting, and only the most expensive models are fitted with variable exposure and an electronic exposure measurement system.

Flash units sometimes form an integral part of these cameras, but more often there is a socket for expendable bulb flash arrays: either flashcubes (four bulbs) or flipflash panels (eight bulbs).

A few cartridge-loading cameras are highly sophisticated precision instruments, with single-lens reflex viewing and fitted with lenses as good as many of those found on 35 mm SLR cameras. However, the quality of pictures produced by these cameras is limited by the lack of a pressure plate in the film cartridge. This means that the film is not held flat at the back of the camera, and pictures are not reliably sharp across the frame.

Cartridge-loading cameras are made in two sizes. 110-size cartridges yield frames measuring about 13 × 17mm. The larger 126-size cartridges make square pictures that measure 28mm across. The cameras that accept each cartridge type are broadly similar in most respects, with the exception of size and shape. 126 cameras are larger and more boxy, whereas 110 cameras tend to be flat and elongated, as shown in the centre above.

Film choice for cartridge-loading cameras is broader than for disc cameras: black-and-white and colour transparency films are available in 110 and 126 cartridges, in addition to the more popular colour negative film.

Cameras designed for use exclusively with instant film are in two categories — those accepting integral print film, such as the SLR 680 (1 below), and those accepting peel-apart film, such as the Polaroid 600SE (2 below).

Instant transparencies
A recent development in instant photography has been the introduction of instant slide film. The Polaroid varieties, shown here, include a colour transparency film, continuous-tone black-and-white transparency film, and high-contrast black-and-white line film (positive and negative).

Instant backs for 35mm
Two specialty equipment manufacturers produce film holders for Polaroid 3¼ × 4¼inch pack film that fit Canon and Nikon cameras. In use, the Teckno model shown here (left) replaces the hinging back of the camera.

INSTANT-PICTURE CAMERAS

Instant-picture cameras very nearly eliminate the delay between pressing the shutter release, and seeing the photograph — nearly, but not completely, because the chemical reaction that makes the picture visible must still take place at a finite speed. Nevertheless, instant-picture cameras have tremendous appeal to amateur photographers, and, in their more esoteric incarnations, are of increasing importance in scientific and technical fields.

Amateur cameras

Instant-picture cameras are fairly rigidly divided into amateur and professional models, because the requirements of each group of users are very different. To the snapshooter, the instant-picture camera is as much a toy as a camera, something which is as likely to be used for the purposes of entertainment as for serious picture-making. Serious amateurs and hobbyists may own both a conventional camera and an instant-picture camera. But the aim of all non-professional users is to produce the maximum possible number of sharp, correctly exposed pictures per pack of film, and the cameras are constructed to make this as easy as possible. (Paradoxically, the aims of the professional are quite different — the 'bad' photographs may be as important as the 'good' ones.)

Instant-picture cameras are quite bulky, because the film itself must be the same size as the final pictures. Although a few ingenious solutions have been found to this problem, notably by Polaroid, instant cameras are still very much bigger than, say, 35mm snapshot cameras. This does not, however, seem to have handicapped their acceptance.

The more prestigious Polaroid cameras fold up to about the size of a large paperback book, making them very convenient to carry. Opened out, these cameras form a single-lens-reflex design, with all the attendant advantages.

Other instant-picture cameras have boxy shapes, direct-vision viewfinders, and bumps and bulges that conform to the corners of the mirrors and other optical components within the camera. The precise shape of the camera depends on the geometry of the image-forming process — Kodak film forms the image on the side facing away from the lens, whereas on Polaroid film, the image appears on the side of the film that faces towards the lens. To make a true image of the subject, rather than one that is reversed left-to-right, each kind of film demands a different optical system.

The principle of operation is the same, though, regardless of the camera. Film is loaded into the camera in a small, light-tight pack, containing ten sheets. This is pushed into the camera through a small door, and

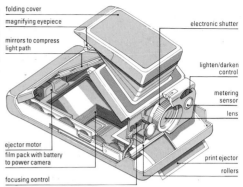

labels: folding cover, magnifying eyepiece, mirrors to compress light path, ejector motor, film pack with battery to power camera, focusing control, electronic shutter, lighten/darken control, metering sensor, lens, print ejector, rollers

Polaroid integral cameras
The SX-70 and its successor the SLR 680 both feature a design that is unconventional by the standards of most cameras. A hinged, folding construction and a system of mirrors make for a compact camera that can be folded flat when not in use. Batteries contained in each pack of print film (SX-70 for the original model, 600 Supercolor for the SLR 680) power a motor in the camera that operates the internal viewing mirror and ejects the film through the pod-squeezing rollers.

when the shutter release is pressed, a small motor ejects an opaque cover sheet. The camera is then ready to take pictures. The same motor ejects pictures after exposure, forcing them through a pair of rollers that burst and spread the pod of processing chemicals to make the image visible.

The ejected print looks like a piece of plastic — white on one side, black on the other. The picture gradually appears on the white side. (The principles of instant picture development are discussed fully on page 108.)

As with most snapshot cameras, picture-taking is as automatic as possible, but with one or two extra considerations. Instant prints are less forgiving of exposure errors than colour print film. Consequently, exposure measurement and the setting of controls must be much more accurate than with cameras that use conventional film. Additionally, users of instant cameras tend to be far more critical of colour and exposure problems, because they can instantly compare the print with the original subject.

On the other hand, instant pictures that are failures can be retaken straight away, so, at least in theory, users should never be disappointed. The features of instant cameras are obviously designed to make picture-taking as problem-free as possible.

To this end, all instant-picture cameras have 'electronic-eye' exposure control. They also have a manual 'lighten/darken' control that enables the user to adjust the tone of the prints manually. This control plays an essential role in cold and hot climates, where the developing process proceeds at different speeds, leading to prints that are too light or too dark respectively.

Focusing on the more expensive models is automatic, but the control is manual on simpler ones, and fixed on the very cheapest.

Integral instant print film
Integral print film such as this Polaroid 600 Supercolor has the advantages not only of speed (it self-develops completely within a few minutes), but of special image values. These derive from the combination of a mild diffuse haze overlaying the crisp, rich dye image, all protected by a tough polyester window.

Professional instant photography

Professional photographers use large amounts of instant film. The most commonplace use is for lighting and exposure tests — a studio photographer might use a whole pack of film while setting up just one picture.

In other areas of professional practice, instant film is invaluable, too. In scientific photography, instant film provides a ready reminder of the results of an experiment, or records the trace on a cathode-ray tube.

The cameras used for these applications, though, are only rarely the same as those used by amateurs, and in fact there are very few professional instant-picture cameras as such. Most instant film used by working photographers passes through instant film backs — adaptors that fit onto existing equipment, enabling just one camera to be used for either conventional or instant film.

Not only are the cameras different, but the film is, too. Professional instant film takes the form of two sheets. The first of these is light-sensitive, and it is onto this sheet that the image from the camera's lens falls. After exposure, rollers press this first sheet into contact with a second receiving sheet, and the image diffuses from one to the other. Processing chemicals from a burst pod fill the gap between the sheets.

After a short wait, the two sheets are peeled apart. The positive image is on the receiver sheet, and the other sheet is usually discarded (though it can be used as a conventional negative with certain types of instant black-and-white film).

SPECIAL CAMERAS

Most cameras are designed as general-purpose tools. However, there are sometimes special photographic problems that cannot be easily solved using any general-purpose camera. Coping with these special problems often means resorting to certain highly-specialized types of camera.

Panoramic cameras

Even the widest of wide-angle lenses is limited in its field of view by the aspect-ratio of the film in the camera. 35 mm frames measure 36 × 24 mm, so they have an aspect-ratio of 1.5:1. Panoramic cameras have much greater aspect-ratios, usually 2:1 or more.

The simplest type of panoramic camera has an ultra-wide-angle lens, and a film plane that is fixed relative to the film. The film, though, is very much wider than it is high. This type of camera produces zero distortion — all lines that are in reality parallel appear parallel on film, as long as the camera is not tilted.

Other types of camera use rotating components to take in a broader view. The Widelux camera has a curving film plane, and a lens that rotates during exposure. This enables the camera to make pictures on 35 mm film with a field of view of 140°, and an aspect-ratio of 2.4:1. However, parallel lines appear to bow outwards on the resulting pictures.

The cameras that take in the broadest fields of view of all actually rotate bodily on top of their tripods. As the camera turns, film is cranked continuously past a slit at the back of the camera, exposing a picture of a full 360° field. This camera therefore produces a continuous strip of film, from which the photographer is free to select as much or as little as needed. The Alpa Roto, which uses 120 roll-film, is of this type, and like the Widelux causes parallel lines to apparently bulge towards the camera.

Linhof Technorama This special roll-film camera produces panoramic images with an aspect-ratio of 3:1, using an extended body and a lens originally designed for larger film — a 90mm Super Anglon.

The panoramic image The special appeal of panoramic photographs derives from their wide horizontal coverage, eliminating the distraction of foreground and sky. Used for vistas that benefit from a side-to-side scanning, they give the impression of a grand view.

Amphibious cameras
Although amphibious cameras like the Nikonos are intended principally for underwater photography, they can also be used simply in wet-conditions. For the Nikonos, the 35mm and 80mm lenses work as well in the air as in water, and are useful for water sports photography.

Underwater cameras

Regular cameras obviously will not function underwater unless specially protected. Though housings are available for water-proofing 35 mm and roll-film cameras, a few special models are amphibious — they can be used above or below water.

Most of these cameras are snapshot models, but one, the Nikonos, is a true 35 mm system camera. Though lenses and film must be changed on the surface, the camera will otherwise function normally at depths down to 70 m. Four lenses are available: two of these, which have focal lengths of 90 mm and 35 mm, will function in air and in water; the other two, the 28 and 15 mm lenses, work only underwater. Lenses are also available from other manufacturers.

Stereographic cameras

The sensation of depth that we perceive in our surroundings springs from the fact that our two eyes each see a slightly different view of the world. Early photographers were not slow to realize that this same sensation of depth could be recreated by presenting each of the viewer's eyes with a slightly different aspect of the same subject.

To make the two pictures simultaneously requires a camera with twin optical systems. This means either two lenses, shutters and apertures, or a single assembly with beam-splitting prisms to provide the required separation of a few centimetres.

Many twin-lens stereo cameras were produced, but the only surviving stereo camera uses not two, but four lenses. This Nimslo camera makes four separate images on 35 mm colour negative film, using four lenses in a row. The sensation of depth is created by printing in sequence wire-thin strips from the four negatives onto special prismatic photographic paper. The embossed plastic prisms on the surface of the paper ensure that the viewer's left eye is presented only with images from the left-hand pair of lenses, and the right eye with images from the right-hand lenses.

Aerial cameras

Aerial photography frequently involves the photographer leaning from a light aircraft in a 70 mph slipstream, so it puts unusual demands on both camera and operator. Special aerial cameras are simplified to make operation easier, and are reinforced to withstand the rigours of life aloft. Focus is fixed on infinity, since most photographs are of the ground or of distant aircraft.

Not all aerial cameras are hand-held. Those used for mapping or survey work are mounted below the aircraft, and operated from a remote console in the cockpit.

Electronic imaging
Still video camera technology is as yet only at the experimental stage, but the prototype Canon video camera (right) was used with some success at the Los Angeles Olympics in 1984 for instant news pictures.

Electronic cameras

Just as videotape stores moving images, so magnetic tape or discs can store still images. This principle is utilized in electronic cameras, which operate in broadly the same way as the one-piece video 'cam-corders'. Video still cameras are very much smaller than moving-picture cam-corders, though, and resemble oversize 35 mm SLRs. They record images on small magnetic discs — so-called video-floppies.

Currently, electronic imaging is in its infancy, and video still images are of very much lower quality than those of even 110-size film. This is because conventional film can record a staggering amount of information. Digitized and recorded on a floppy disc, the data from one 35 mm transparency would occupy as much magnetic storage space as half of the text from this book. State-of-the-art video imaging is far behind this, but the situation is changing rapidly.

LENSES

The lens is the heart of the camera — the component that turns the three-dimensional world outside the camera into a two-dimensional image on film inside. The quality of the lens determines, to a considerable extent, the quality of the photograph. With a good-quality lens, even the simplest, most inexpensive cameras are capable of creating technically good pictures. The converse is not true — fitting a poor lens to a good camera will invariably lead to inferior results.

The lenses used with most cameras today are very complex works of engineering, designed by computer and manufactured with extreme precision. They form images, though, in the same manner as the simple magnifying glass that gathers the light of the sun to burn a hole in a piece of paper.

Lenses and image formation

Lenses work because light travels more slowly in glass than in air. A beam of light striking a block of glass at an oblique angle is slewed round as it enters the glass. This is because the edge of the beam that enters the glass first is slowed down significantly sooner than the far edge of the beam.

This bending of light on entering a different transparent medium is called refraction. Different substances refract light by different amounts and the amount of refraction — the bending power of the substance — is called the refractive index. The refractive index of glass is between 1.5 and 2.

To understand how a lens works, think of parallel beams of light passing through a prism. The prism bends the light round at an angle. The degree of bending depends on the roof angle of the prism — the closer to parallel the sides of the prism are, the less bending there is. A lens is like a series of prisms stacked up. The prisms in the centre of the lens have parallel sides, and closer to the edge of the lens, the prisms have steeper and steeper angles. Light passing through near the centre of the lens is only bent a little; further from the centre, light is bent more and more. So parallel light beams passing through the lens all converge on the same point, called the *focus* of the lens.

For a simple lens, such as a magnifying glass, the distance from the middle of the lens to the focus is called the focal length. When using a magnifying lens to burn holes in paper, the lens is held at its focal length from the paper to get the maximum burning effect — the parallel rays of light from the sun then all converge to form the hot spot, which is actually a small picture of the sun on the paper.

Though simple magnifying lenses can form images, they are not very efficient and would be useless on cameras. Simple lenses have many faults, known as *abberations*, and the aim of the lens designer is to minimize these abberations and create the best lens possible.

The process of optimizing the lens is very long and difficult, but by way of example, consider just one lens fault, chromatic abberation. Because glass bends different colours by different amounts, the colours of the sun that the magnifying glass projects will not all be brought to the same focus. Instead, the sharpest image of red light will be formed farther from the lens than the image of blue light. Invisible infrared radiation will come to a focus even farther away from the lens, which is why the glass burns best when the sun is a little bit out of focus.

These coloured images are unsuitable for photography, for reasons that are clear to anyone who has ever used a cheap pair of binoculars: everything in the field of view is surrounded by coloured fringes. This is because the field-glasses have uncorrected chromatic abberation.

Lens designers minimize the problem by combining two lenses made from two different kinds of glass, each with a different refractive index.

Chromatic abberation, however, is not the only problem that lens designers face. There are many more types of aberration, including aspheric aberration, created by the very slight difference in the focusing of light passing through the centre of the lens and light passing through the edges. Correcting, or at least minimizing, them all means using many more than two glass elements in the lens. Modern lenses often have seven or eight elements, and zoom lenses even more.

Correction of abberations is not the end of the story. Lenses must not only form good, sharp images, but they must fulfil other criteria as well. The lens must not be too big or too heavy; it must have a fairly wide maximum aperture, so that picture-taking is possible in dim light; and the lens must not be too costly to manufacture. An optically perfect lens that is big, expensive and slow is of only theoretical, not practical interest.

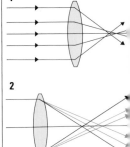

Spherical aberration It is cheaper to produce a lens with a spherical curved surface than one in which the curvature changes. The cost of this is spherical aberration (below **1**) where the edges of the lens focus the light waves at a different point from the centre of the lens, causing unsharpness.

1

2

Chromatic aberration The different wavelengths that comprise white light travel at different speeds through the lens, and pass through a lens at slightly different angles and come to focus in slightly different places; this is called chromatic aberration.
Blue-violet light is focused slightly closer to the lens than green light, which in turn is focused closer than red light. As the focus is spread in this way, there is some loss of definition.

Covering power A lens projects a circular image. The image quality is highest at the centre, deteriorating towards the edges. The point at which the image falls below an acceptable standard marks the circle of good definition, and this represents the covering power of the lens. In photography, the film format must fit within the circle (left). On a camera, the covering power is increased slightly by stopping down the aperture.

Diffraction The edge of an opaque surface, such as the aperture blades, scatters light waves slightly. If the aperture stop is closed down to its smallest size, this scattering, called diffraction, is increased (stopping down, which tends to correct most lens faults, actually worsens this one). In practice, most lenses perform at their best when stopped down about three aperture stops from their maximum — called optimum aperture.

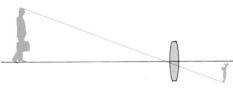

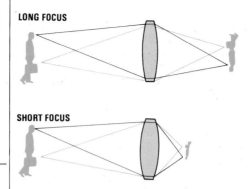

LONG FOCUS

SHORT FOCUS

Focal length and image size By altering the design of the lens to change the focal length, the size of the image at the focal plane can be altered. Reducing the focal length makes the image smaller (below); increasing it makes the image larger. With a smaller image, there is a greater angle of view.

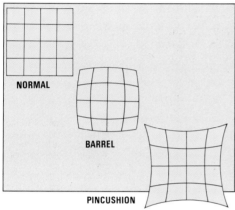

NORMAL

BARREL

PINCUSHION

Distortion The aperture stop of the lens prevents oblique light waves from passing through the centre of the lens, and, as the lens surfaces at the edges are not parallel, the image-forming light is bent. This does not affect sharpness, but does distort the image shape. If the shape is compressed, it is called barrel distortion; if stretched, pincushion distortion. Symmetrical lenses (that is, with complementary elements at the front and back) cancel out this distortion.

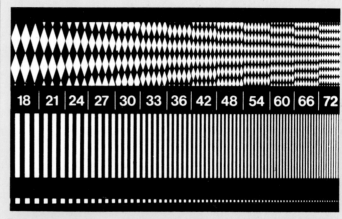

| 18 | 21 | 24 | 27 | 30 | 33 | 36 | 42 | 48 | 54 | 60 | 66 | 72 |

Testing lens resolution The standard method is to find the smallest pair of lines (in pairs per millimetre) in a photograph that remains distinct. The test target shown is designed to be photographed on finegrain film at 40 times the focal length of the lens — with a 50mm lens, the target should be 2000mm from the camera (below right). To avoid confusing the results with the structure of the film, use a very fine grain emulsion. Examine the negative on a light box with a loupe. The point at which the lines in the target begin to merge with each other is the limit of resolution. The number above them gives the line pairs per millimetre.

Covering power

All lenses form circular images, with the sharpest part of the image in the middle. Towards the edges of the circle, the image gets dimmer and more blurred.

The size of the usefully sharp part of the image is the covering power of the lens and must be great enough to give a good picture right across the frame of the film in use. For example, 35 mm film measures 24 × 36 mm, and the frame diagonal is 43 mm. So lenses for 35 mm cameras must form sharp images at least 43 mm in diameter. For a roll-film camera, the circle must be more than 90 mm across. So a lens for a 35 mm camera cannot be used on a roll-film camera, because the lens would just form a circular image in the middle of the frame.

Some lenses have covering power that far exceeds the area of the film. The extra coverage is needed so that the lens can be moved around relative to the film, as detailed on pages 18 and 39. Perspective control lenses for 35 mm cameras are of this type, as are most lenses for sheet-film cameras.

Focal length and magnification

For a simple lens, focal length is the distance from the film that the lens must be held to form a sharp image of distant objects like the sun. However, for complex camera lenses, this definition is not of much practical use, because the lens barrel holds the glass elements in the right place in relation to the film.

In day to day photography the significance of focal length is that it controls how much the image of the subject is magnified. Take as a starting point the standard lens of a 35 mm camera. This lens has a focal length of 50 mm. Lenses with longer focal lengths such as 100 mm or 200 mm will form magnified images on film, but show a more restricted field of view. Lenses with shorter focal lengths, such as 35 mm, take in a broader field of view, but render all subjects within the picture a smaller size than a 50 mm lens does. Short focal length lenses are called wide-angle lenses. Lenses with focal lengths longer than standard lenses are usually called telephoto lenses; like a telescope, they magnify the subject.

FOCAL LENGTH

Standard lenses

The focal length of a camera's standard lens depends on the size of the film. The larger the film, the longer is the focal length of the lens. In general, standard lenses for each film format are roughly equal to the film's diagonal.

A common definition of the standard lens is that it shows the subject roughly as the human eye does. While this may be true for pictures enlarged to average sizes, and viewed from normal distances, defining 'standard' in this way overlooks a fundamental characteristic of human eyesight: we see a very broad view of our surroundings, and are aware of things through a field of view about 120 degrees wide. A 'standard' lens for a 35mm SLR, though, has a diagonal field of view of just 50 degrees — rather like looking down a cardboard tube.

The standard lens is a photographic workhorse. It is usually very well corrected, and therefore produces sharp, clear images; it is compact and light; it has a large maximum aperture — generally larger than other focal lengths; a standard lens focuses quite close without accessories; and because many are made, standard lenses are the cheapest lenses in a manufacturer's range.

Because of its jack-of-all-trades status, a standard lens is used in all sorts of photographic applications, often more by default than because of any specific virtues of the lens. However, for full-length portraits the standard lens is probably ideal because it allows the photographer to stay close enough to the subject to communicate easily, yet not so close as to be intimidating. For still life, the standard lens is a good choice, too: it introduces less distortions of shape and perspective than do telephoto and wide-angle lenses.

Some photographers deride the standard lens because it seems to give neither the selective view of a telephoto nor the all-encompassing view of a wide-angle. But a standard lens often gives high quality at relatively low cost — and many variations can be achieved simply by moving closer to and further away from the subject.

Standard lenses for 35mm cameras have focal lengths of 50mm, and usually have apertures of f1.8 or f1.4. Faster lenses are available, but these are usually heavy and expensive, and more suited to their intended application — pictures in low light — than to general photography.

For other formats, there is often a choice of focal lengths as standard. For example, many 6 × 6cm roll-film cameras are available with either an 80mm or a 100mm lens as standard (the film measures 84mm across the diagonal). And on 5 × 4in sheet-film cameras, photographers may use 150mm, 180mm or 210mm lenses as standard; for 10 × 8in, 240mm or 300mm may be standard.

Focal length and format
The effect of a particular focal length lens on the coverage varies not only on the size of the film format but the shape. The standard 80mm lens for the 6 × 6cm format (picture above) has much the same angle of view as the standard 50mm for the 35mm format (left), but the square format means that it actually takes in a little more of the scene.

Standard lens Over the years, the 50mm lens has become established as the standard for the 35mm format, primarily because it gives relatively normal-looking perspective with typical subjects. 50mm is also the length of the diagonal of the 35mm film format.

15mm FISH-EYE

24mm WIDE-ANGLE

35mm MODERATE WIDE-ANGLE

50mm NORMAL

180mm MODERATE LONG-FOCUS

400mm EXTREME LONG-FOCUS

600mm EXTREME LONG-FOCUS

800mm EXTREME LONG-FOCUS

1200mm EXTREME LONG-FOCUS

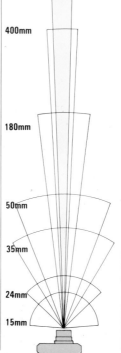

The range of focal lengths
This sequence of nine photographs taken from the same position demonstrates the range of focal lengths available from most system SLR 35mm camera manufacturers (excluding fish-eye lenses). The range of magnification from the 15mm shot to that taken with a 1200mm telephoto is 80 times.

GRADIENT-INDEX LENSES
Traditional lens design uses two main variables to control the light path — the type of glass (which determines the refractive index) and the shape of each glass element. By combining several elements of different shapes and composition, a wide range of optical effects is possible. Although computer-aided design has been able to produce considerable improvements in recent years, the limitations of size, weight and difficulty of manufacture are severe, particularly for multi-element zoom lenses. One line of research that has already made progress in fibre optics is into gradient index (GRIN). In this, the actual refractive index of the glass (its light-bending power) is varied continuously. In theory, this could do away with the need to shape a glass lens — the variable refractive index would do the same work. In practice, this development should make possible improved performance, fewer elements, and lighter, smaller lenses.

LENS COATING
Flare created by internal reflection within the lens is reduced to a minimum nowadays by coating lens surfaces with several layers (a multi-coating) of material such as silicon dioxide. Each layer is a precise thickness that corresponds to a particular wavelength of light — plus half that wavelength. Light reflected from the lens surface is either reflected from the inner surface of the coating or travels harmlessly back out of the lens. Because the surface is a precise thickness, the peaks in the waves of light reflected from the inner surface of the coating meet the troughs in light of similar wavelength entering the lens for the first time, cancelling each other.

800mm
400mm
180mm
50mm
35mm
24mm
15mm

Angle of view
The proportion of the subject included in the frame — that is, the angle of view — depends on the focal length of the lens and the film format. The diagram on the left shows the range of different angles of view encompassed by the commonly available focal lengths for 35mm format. At one extreme, there is the 16mm fish-eye, which takes in almost 180° of the scene — though with considerable circular distortion. At the other extreme is the 800mm telephoto, taking in a mere 3°. The standard 50mm lens falls in between, taking in about 40°. Although there seems to be a dramatic difference in the appearance of perspective in pictures taken on lenses of different focal length, there is, in fact, none at all; the only difference is in angle of view. Indeed, the long-focus, narrow angle view can be cut, quite literally, out of a photograph taken on a wide-angle lens.

Wide-angle for involvement

Used close to a deep subject, a wide-angle lens has a useful ability to draw the viewer into the scene, if used as above. Here, the subject distances are layered, from close foreground at the edges of the frame to the background near the centre. Both the depth of field of the 20mm lens used — (infinity to less than one metre (three feet) at f8) — and its 84° (side to side) angle of view help create an involving effect.

35mm — an alternative for standard

The newest of the wide-angle focal lengths for 35mm SLR cameras is 35mm. This is used by a number of photographers as a standard lens.

Wide-angle lenses

Wide-angle lenses — those with focal lengths less than the film diagonal — have obvious value in applications where the standard lens just cannot fit everything into the frame. Interiors, for example, are difficult to photograph without a wide-angle lens as are exterior views of buildings when obstructions prevent the photographer from moving back. When photographing groups of people, a photographer using a wide-angle lens need not move back so far, so instructions can be spoken, not shouted.

The wide-angle lens has other characteristics that are not as obvious as its broad field of view. Because the lens forms a smaller image of the subject, the photographer can move closer. Taking a pace towards a subject two metres away halves the subject distance — but has an insignificant effect on the distance between the camera and a far-off hill. The background of the picture therefore appears farther away if a wide-angle lens is used, when the photograph is compared to images made with a standard lens. Thus a wide-angle lens seems to expand perspective and stretch out space.

Wide-angle lenses have greater depth of field, too, so that they are a good choice when everything in the picture must be recorded sharply, from close-up through to infinity.

For 35mm cameras, the wide-angle range starts at 35mm, but many photographers regard this moderate wide-angle as a standard lens. It introduces virtually no distortion, yet has a field of view that is usefully broad. In a crowd, a 35mm lens is ideal for candid people pictures — whereas a standard lens permits only tightly-cropped faces.

Progressively shorter focal lengths take in broader fields of view. 28mm lenses on 35mm cameras are the ideal choice for the photographer who has just a single wide-angle lens. A 28mm lens has a field of view broad enough to give good interior pictures and scenics, with such little distortion that it usually goes unnoticed. By tilting the camera, though, the photographer can exploit the distortion and use the characteristics of the lens to create startling images.

24mm wide-angle lenses are the other common focal length for 35mm SLRs. They have a very broad field of view, but must be used with greater care than 28mm lenses. Circular objects at the corners of the frame become smeared out to ovals and, unless the camera is held absolutely horizontal, parallel vertical lines in the scene converge violently towards the top or bottom of the picture.

Lenses with shorter focal lengths than this are usually regarded as ultra-wide-angle and tend to be expensive. Their characteristics are similar to regular wide-angles, but more pronounced. For 35mm cameras, ultra-wide-angle lenses have focal lengths between 21mm and 13mm.

Colombia

Wide-angle for graphic effect

Wide-angle lenses produce a whole range of distinctive perspective effects, depending on the focal length and also the particular optical configuration. While panoramic coverage is the most obvious use of very short focal lengths, such as the 16mm lens used above, these perspective distortions can be deliberately exploited for graphic effect. Here, the lens is a full frame fisheye, and the barrel distortion is left uncorrected. The result is that straight lines away from the centre of the picture bow outwards in curves. The effect here, in a downward looking view from a tall building, is to produce a series of curves that help impose a unity on the image.

Fisheye lenses

Ordinary lenses produce rectilinear images — this means that straight lines in the subject look straight on film. At increasingly wide angles of view, though, it becomes more and more difficult to keep straight lines straight, and on the cheaper wide-angle lenses, lines close to the frame edges may appear to bow out slightly.

Fisheye lenses are extreme wide-angle lenses in which no attempt has been made to prevent straight lines from bowing out. By sacrificing the rectilinear requirement, the lens designer is able to make a lens that has a very much broader field of view. Some fisheye lenses take in a full 180 degrees or even 220 degrees. With these lenses, the photographer must take extra care that the legs of the tripod do not appear in the picture! Extreme fisheye lenses tend to be very expensive and have a limited range of applications, so they are generally hired for specific shots rather than bought outright.

There are two types of fisheye lens. Circular image fisheye lenses form a round image in the middle of the frame. These lenses are generally more useful for scientific applications, such as photography of the sky to estimate cloud cover. For pictorial photography, full frame fisheyes are of greater value, since they fill the frame with the picture, making presentation simpler than it is with a circular picture.

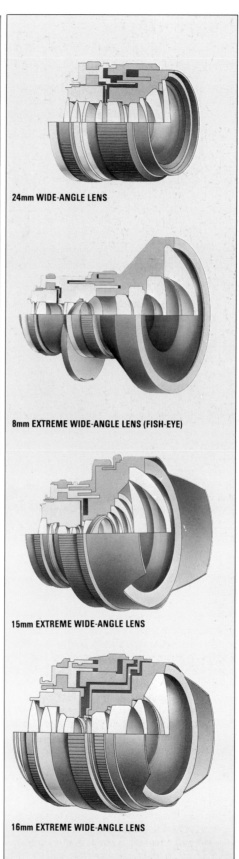

24mm WIDE-ANGLE LENS

8mm EXTREME WIDE-ANGLE LENS (FISH-EYE)

15mm EXTREME WIDE-ANGLE LENS

16mm EXTREME WIDE-ANGLE LENS

WIDE-ANGLE LENSES

24mm (On a 35mm camera), a 24mm lens has a 84° picture angle across the diagonal and 90° from side to side. Its wide-angle effect is pronounced but not extreme, and the 24mm is probably the most popular of distinctly wide-angle lenses. Major camera manufacturers offer this focal length in two or more designs — with a modest maximum aperture of around f2.8 or with more light gathering power of around f2 or even f1.4.

8mm fisheye
A fisheye lens has a domed front surface and gives a circular picture covering a very wide field of view — 180° in the case of this 8mm f2.8 design. Certain models such as this are constructed so that the back focus is longer than the focal length. Consequently the instant return mirror on a standard 35mm SLR does not have to be locked. Filters are built in to a rotating turret.

15mm One of the shortest focal lengths for a 35mm camera to give a corrected image, this is an ultra-wide-angle lens designed for the extreme coverage requirements of photography in confined spaces. Its angle of view across the diagonal of the picture is 110° (100° across the longer edge of a 35mm picture frame). The oddly shaped integral lens hood is designed for maximum shading effect, and a selection of filters is built into a turret at the back of the barrel.

16mm full frame fisheye
Although virtually the same focal length as the corrected 15mm lens above, this fisheye design covers 170° across the diagonal and 137° across the longer side. Unlike other fisheye lenses, which are designed for scientific and industrial applications, this projects its image over the entire film frame and is intended for pictorial use. As with other extreme wide-angle lenses, a selection of filters is built in to a rotating turret. The photograph at the top left of this page was taken on this lens.

Telephoto lenses

Telephoto lenses form magnified images of the subject, or permit the photographer to fill the frame with the subject from a more distant viewpoint. For head-and-shoulders portraits, short telephotos avoid the photographer having to move uncomfortably close to the subject and create pictures that have more pleasing proportions.

Because telephotos fill the frame from a greater distance, background detail seems to advance towards the camera, and objects that are in reality quite far apart look crushed together. Telegraph poles in a row seem more tightly packed than they really are, when seen through a long telephoto lens. These lenses appear to compress perspective — just as wide-angle lenses appear to do the opposite.

For 35 mm cameras, telephoto lenses have focal lengths of between 85 and 2000 mm, and as might be expected, the characteristics of each lens become more pronounced with increasing focal length. The more popular focal lengths fall between 85 mm and 200 mm — longer lenses are bulky and expensive.

The shortest focal lengths — 85 mm and 105 mm — are most useful for portraiture, as they provide suitably moderate magnification of the subject. The longer of the two, though, is a favourite among photojournalists because of its light weight, small size and ease of use. It is not as conspicuous a lens as its longer cousins, an important point in a tension-packed trouble spot.

135 mm, 180 mm and 200 mm lenses are all easy to hand-hold, but produce useful subject magnification. They are commonly used in sports photography, particularly indoors, where their comparatively wide maxi-mum apertures are valuable.

Longer focal lengths are more difficult to use. They generally have quite small maxi-mum apertures, and need substantial support to prevent camera-shake. These lenses are essential working tools for sports and wildlife photographers and in many other applications.

Teleconverters multiply the focal length of the lens to which they are attached. They fit between the camera body and the prime lens, and generally double the focal length of the lens, or increase it by 1.4 times. However, a teleconverter reduces the marked aperture of the lens by an amount to the converter's power, so that combining a 200 mm f4 lens with a 2x converter yields a 400 mm f8.

The combination of lens and converter always produces lower quality pictures than would a longer focal length used on its own, but then a converter is very much lighter in weight than a second, longer lens, and much cheaper, too.

Mirror lenses

Lenses longer than 200 mm are cumbersome and heavy, but by folding the optical path using mirrors, it is possible to make a much more compact telephoto lens — just as roof-prism binoculars are very much smaller than the conventional straight-through design.

Mirror lenses have a number of drawbacks, though, that take the edge off the considerable savings in weight and size. They have fixed apertures, so exposure can be controlled only with the shutter speed and with neutral density filters; they rarely give such good results as ordinary refracting lenses, and pictures have less depth of field; and they form circular shaped images of out-of-focus points, which some people find unattractive.

Zoom lenses

Zoom lenses have variable focal lengths; turning or sliding a ring on the lens barrel makes the subject larger or smaller in the viewfinder. One zoom lens can therefore take the place of several fixed focal length lenses.

A zoom lens allows the photographer to crop the picture very precisely, framing the subject perfectly. This is especially important when taking colour transparencies, because there is no opportunity for cropping the picture in the darkroom.

For 35 mm SLR cameras, the zoom lens is now extremely popular — three zoom lenses are sold for each lens of a fixed focal length. The most successful lens designs are those which offer focal lengths in the range from 50 mm up to about 210 mm. Typical lenses run from 80-200 mm or 75-150 mm. These lenses are small and light and provide comparatively good image quality at a low cost.

Wide-angle zooms are less common and generally produce poorer quality pictures. A

Technically speaking a zoom lens offers a continuously variable focal length within a certain range. Practically, this gives the photographer the opportunity to alter the framing of a shot without having to move, as the pair of pictures below illustrates. This is useful not only when there are physical restrictions on moving closer or further, but also simply in terms of speed — movement of the zoom control makes it possible to shoot substantially different compositions in seconds.

Zoom lenses are optically complex, incorporating at least several separate glass elements that must be moved in co-ordinated groups. 14 elements in 11 groups, for example, is not unusual for a high ratio zoom lens. The zoom ratio (or range) is the key consideration in choosing lenses, particularly if more than one is to be carried. To make up a full range of focal lengths the following lenses go well together:
28-45mm
43-86mm
80-200mm
200-600mm (for specialized use)
Some manufacturers make lenses with a very wide zoom range approaching the ideal of a 'unilens'.

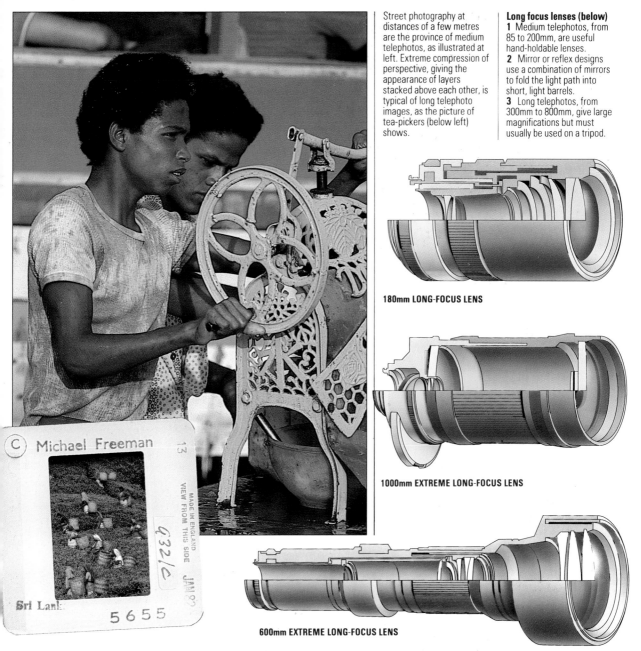

Street photography at distances of a few metres are the province of medium telephotos, as illustrated at left. Extreme compression of perspective, giving the appearance of layers stacked above each other, is typical of long telephoto images, as the picture of tea-pickers (below left) shows.

Long focus lenses (below)
1 Medium telephotos, from 85 to 200mm, are useful hand-holdable lenses.
2 Mirror or reflex designs use a combination of mirrors to fold the light path into short, light barrels.
3 Long telephotos, from 300mm to 800mm, give large magnifications but must usually be used on a tripod.

180mm LONG-FOCUS LENS

1000mm EXTREME LONG-FOCUS LENS

600mm EXTREME LONG-FOCUS LENS

typical focal length range would be 25-50 mm, though various other lenses are available, some of them varying between ultrawide and wide-angle.

Professional photographers are on the whole less likely to use zoom lenses than are amateurs. This is because a professional cannot trade quality for convenience and no zoom lens yet offers as good quality as a top fixed focal length lens. There are other reasons, too: zoom lenses have smaller maximum apertures than fixed focal length lenses, and though lighter than the two or three lenses that it replaces, a zoom lens is heavier and more bulky than any one of those lenses, and so is harder to handle.

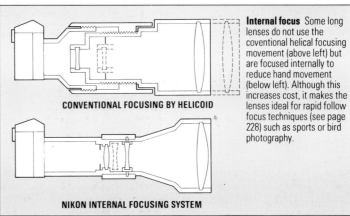

CONVENTIONAL FOCUSING BY HELICOID

NIKON INTERNAL FOCUSING SYSTEM

Internal focus Some long lenses do not use the coventional helical focusing movement (above left) but are focused internally to reduce hand movement (below left). Although this increases cost, it makes the lenses ideal for rapid follow focus techniques (see page 228) such as sports or bird photography.

Special lenses

Many photographic applications make special demands on the photographer and equipment, and special lenses have evolved in response. Some of these special lenses, such as the *shift lens*, enable the camera to be used for tasks that would otherwise force the use of a larger format. Other lenses, such as the *night lens*, make photography practical in apparently impossible conditions.

■ NIGHT LENSES are ultra-fast standard lenses. They have apertures of f1.2, or exceptionally, f1. They are several times heavier and more expensive than ordinary standard lenses and are formulated to give optimum performance at full aperture — rather than closed down by two stops like ordinary lenses. Though these lenses make picture-taking possible at very low light levels, image quality at moderate apertures rarely matches that from an ordinary lens.

Shift lens
Perspective correction lenses for rigid body cameras feature a movement to slide the optics off-axis — typically by 10mm for a 35mm camera. This enables, for instance, buildings to be photographed without converging verticals; the camera back remains vertical, and the optics shift upwards, as for the example at right.

■ SHIFT LENSES — often called perspective control lenses — mimic the functions of a sheet-film camera. The lens moves up, down and sideways relative to the film, to change the area of the subject that appears in the picture, as explained on pages 18-19. A few shift lenses also tilt, for control of sharpness distribution. Shift lenses are invariably wide-angle lenses.

Shift lens for architecture
A shift lens is often used to avoid the convergence of parallel vertical lines in buildings. In a situation such as above, for a fairly close view from ground level the camera would have to be tilted upwards to include the top of the building, and the result would be convergence. A shift lens, however, has sufficient coverage to be moved upwards and include the entire building with the camera aimed horizontally.

Night lens
Night lenses such as the Noct-Nikkor 58mm used for the candle-lit shot at right incorporate several design features for shooting at night and in other low-light conditions: large maximum aperture (f1.2 in this case); aspherical front surface to allow full-aperture shooting without chromatic aberration; matt black internal finish and multi-coating of elements to reduce flare and ghosting.

Insect close-ups Macro lenses can be focused down to a magnification of × ½ without attachments, and are computed to give their best optical performance at these close distances. Nature photography is one of the principal subject areas. More examples appear on pages 290-295.

Macro lenses vary in focal length from standard (that is, about 50mm for a 35mm camera) to medium telephoto (100mm and 200mm are not uncommon). Good optical quality is easier to maintain with a standard focal length, but the advantage of a longer focal length is that the working distance is greater; this can be convenient for insect photography on location, making it less likely to scare away the subject.

■ MACRO LENSES are specially made for photographing small subjects. Optically, these lenses are corrected so that they give good results even when the size of the image on film is the same size as the subject itself. Mechanically, a macro lens has a specially long focusing range, so that the lens can focus continuously from infinity down to eight inches or so. By comparison, regular lenses need accessories to focus this close and give poorer results in close-up than do macro lenses.

■ MEDICAL LENSES are similar to macro lenses but have a built-in ringflash (see pages 76, 79) for illumination of specimens and for photography during operations.

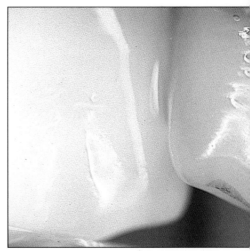

Lens flare and shading
Shooting towards the sun is likely to produce flare effects from the internal surfaces and apertures of the lens, as shown below. The difference that a hood makes (left) is usually striking.

LENS HOODS

Non-image-forming light striking the front of the camera lens always has a degrading effect on the image. At best, the effect is a pale haze that reduces contrast and weakens colour. At worst, flare spots — coloured images of the camera's iris diaphragm — will spread across the frame.

A lens hood or shade can prevent this problem, or at least reduce it. A few lenses have hoods built-in, notably ultra-wide-angles and some telephotos. For most lenses, though, the hood screws into the front of the lens.

A hood should only be used with the lens for which it is designed; too shallow a hood gives inadequate protection and too deep a hood may cut the corners off the picture. The best hoods are actually concertina-like bellows, that can be racked out to match exactly the coverage of the lens in use.

Lens hoods are available in several designs, of varying efficiency: integral sliding hoods on telephoto lenses (**1**), detachable round hoods (**2,3**), detachable rectangular hoods with bayonet fittings (**4**), collapsible rubber hoods (**5**), adjustable professional bellows shades (**6**).

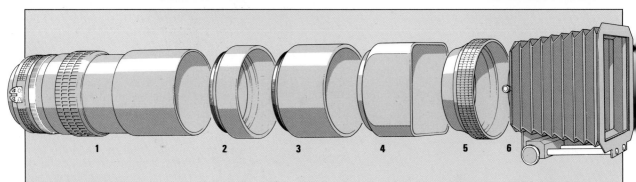

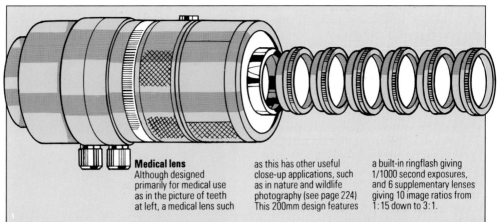

Medical lens
Although designed primarily for medical use as in the picture of teeth at left, a medical lens such as this has other useful close-up applications, such as in nature and wildlife photography (see page 224) This 200mm design features a built-in ringflash giving 1/1000 second exposures, and 6 supplementary lenses giving 10 image ratios from 1:15 down to 3:1.

4 × 5in

4¾ × 6½in

6½ × 8½in

8 × 10in

Circles of Coverage
In these four examples of the most popular view camera formats, the minimum and normal circles of coverage are shown. When a telephoto lens is being chosen, camera movements are less likely to be needed, and a lens with the minimum circle of coverage will normally suffice. For standard and wide-angle lenses, however, the circle of coverage should be larger.
Another point to remember is that between maximum and minimum aperture, there is normally a difference in coverage of about five to ten per cent.

CHOOSING A VIEW CAMERA LENS
As lenses for view cameras are invariably bought separately from the camera, there is considerable choice — confusingly so for many first-time purchasers. A lens for one format can, for example, be used on a smaller-format view camera. Apart from the choice of maximum aperture and focal length — a standard focal length for any format is equivalent to the diagonal measurement of the film frame — a major consideration is the covering power of the lens. At the very least, the lens must be capable of covering a circle slightly larger than the film format. If, however, use is to be made of the camera movements described on page 18, the covering power of the lens must be considerably greater — by about a quarter or one-third. In addition, as image quality from most lenses decreases towards the edges, there is an advantage in using only the central part of a lens.

Hand shading
This is one of the most effective means of shading a lens from flare, particularly if the camera is fixed on a tripod. Stand slightly in front, and watch the shadow of your hand. When it just clears the lens surface, it is just out of the picture frame.

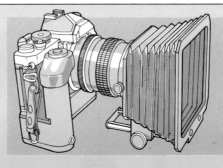

Precise masking
The special advantage of a professional bellows lens hood is not only that it is rectangular and relatively deep, but that its extension can be altered to suit the focal length of the lens. The picture can be masked right up to its edges.

FOCUSING

All but the simplest cameras incorporate a focusing mechanism — a means of controlling which parts of the picture appear sharp, and which parts blurred and indistinct. Together with the shutter and aperture, focusing is one of the camera's three fundamental controls.

At first sight, focusing appears to be straightforward, simply a matter of making sure that the subject is sharp. However, focusing is not always just a mechanical procedure, as anyone who has an autofocus camera that has got it wrong will know. Often, focusing involves complex decisions about the relative importance of different parts of the image; or about which areas to render sharply, and which to conceal in an indistinct haze. Even the most sophisticated autofocus mechanism cannot make such deductions, so cameras that delegate the task of focusing to a microchip sometimes focus on totally irrelevant trivia. Manual focusing puts the decisions in the hands of the photographer.

As the pages that follow show, the basics of focusing are easy to understand. The decisions about where to focus, though, are more subtle, and demand an aesthetic input and appreciation on the part of the photographer. These are things that cannot be taught, only learned by experience.

Focusing fundamentals

All lenses form three-dimensional images in space: sharp images of distant objects are formed close to the lens; and sharp images of nearby objects are formed farther back behind the lens. However, film is a flat plane, not a volume in space, so the lens projects onto the film an absolutely sharp image of objects just one distance from the camera. On film, these objects are described as being 'in focus' — they are sharp and clearly delineated, with textures well defined. Objects closer to the camera and farther away appear less well defined — they are 'out of focus', as if seen through a misted window.

Since film is a flat plane behind the lens, the parts of the subject that are in focus form a flat plane in front of the lens. This plane is called 'the plane of sharp focus', and is usually at right angles to the axis of the lens.

The act of focusing is the process of changing the position of the plane of sharp focus, moving it nearer to the camera to take close-up pictures; and farther away, for distant views. This movement is accomplished by moving the lens in and out — away from the film for close-ups, and closer to the film for scenic views. The separation between lens and film is mathematically related to the distance between lens and subject. With an understanding of the relationship, it is possible to move lens and film a measured distance apart to bring a specific part of the subject into focus.

Focus and depth
Essentially, focusing determines the sharpness of different areas of the image. As such, it cannot be treated independently of the depth of field, which, in turn, depends largely on the aperture. In the three photographs above, the row of mailboxes were focused at just over 2m (7ft) with a standard lens; the aperture, however, was varied from full (f3.5) at left, to a middle setting (f8) in the centre picture, to minimum (f22) at right. In effect, the view is selective at full aperture, concentrating attention on the middle of the row, but comprehensive at minimum aperture (all the mailboxes appear sharp), even though only one focus setting was used.
In the smaller set of three images at right, the effects of selective focusing at full aperture are shown.

The basic viewing screen
in most cameras comprises a sheet of glass ground matt on the underside, sandwiched with a Fresnel lens. This behaves as a simple condenser lens and distributes the bright image evenly over the screen. It does so by means of a series of stepped convex rings, each one a section of a convex lens surface (below).

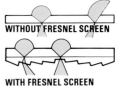

WITHOUT FRESNEL SCREEN

WITH FRESNEL SCREEN

Viewing aids and screens
For critical focusing, magnifying attachments can be particularly useful with the small 35mm format (whether projected or printed, a 35mm frame of film always has to be enlarged, and this sometimes reveals focusing errors). The two models at right give magnified views of this central portion of the screen. Eyepiece correction lenses are also useful for weak eyesight.

No photographer wants to carry a tape measure and a pocket calculator everywhere, and anyway, the lens position must be set with great accuracy — to within a fraction of a millimetre. So, on inexpensive cameras which have adjustable lenses, the lens moves in and out in a threaded barrel. This allows for very precise setting of the lens-film separation, and has the additional advantage that a large angular rotation of the barrel produces a small forward or backward motion of the lens. Thus the barrel can be marked with widely spaced indexes to indicate the correct position of the lens for a range of subject distances. This focusing scale runs from infinite distances (marked with the infinity symbol ∞) through to distances a metre or two from the camera. The markings are most widely spaced at close distances, but progressively more tightly packed for objects increasingly far away.

Using such a camera means guessing the subject distance. This is fine for far-off subjects, where focusing does not need to be so precise. But guesswork is less than adequate for close-ups, where the lens needs to be positioned with greater precision. So most cameras have some sort of focusing aid.

Large sheet-film cameras have a very direct and straightforward means of checking sharp focus. At the rear of the camera is a sheet of matt glass, on which the lens throws an image of the subject. The photographer

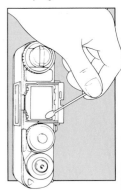

Most system SLR cameras offer a choice of viewing screen types (right), and if the prism head is detachable, these can be fitted and removed by the photographer according to the job.

can then move the lens in and out while watching the image change in sharpness on the screen. When the picture is sharp, the screen is moved out of the way, and its place is taken by a sheet of film. The camera is constructed in such a way that film is positioned in precisely the same place as the surface of the matt glass. So what was sharp on the glass will also be sharp on the film.

Reflex focusing

The direct focusing procedure used with a sheet-film camera is very positive and accurate, but suffers from two major drawbacks: it is very slow and cumbersome, and totally unsuited to even slow-moving subjects such as people walking; and the image on the screen is inverted and reversed left-to-right.

Reflex cameras get around these problems by using a mirror, which projects the image from the lens upwards onto a viewing screen positioned the same distance from the lens as the film is. The reflection by the mirror turns the image upside down, so that subjects appear the right way up on the screen. The addition of a prism above the screen eliminates the left-to-right reversal, making viewing even easier.

Twin-lens-reflex cameras (TLRs) have two identical lenses, one above the other. The lower lens forms the image on film, the upper one on the glass viewing screen. The lenses are linked rigidly together, and move in and out on the same panel for focusing. This ensures that the images on film and focusing screen are focused on the same point.

TLR focusing is not a perfect answer to focusing problems, though, largely because the two lenses are separated by several centimetres. This means that the viewing lens does not see precisely what will appear on film, so framing is not always accurate. This 'parallax error' is rarely a problem with distant subjects, but is very serious at short distances. The problem is partly solved by marking the

Elements of a focusing screen

There is a variety of screen designs for SLRs, but there are three standard elements, each particularly suitable for focusing on certain kinds of subject. The screens supplied with most cameras feature all three: split prism finder which shows displacement of an out-of-focus subject, microprism grid, which 'scrambles' unfocused images, and plain screen for detailed, but slower focusing.

GROUND-GLASS SCREEN BACKED BY FRESNEL SCREEN

CENTRAL SPLIT PRISM WITH ANGLED DIVISION

MICRO-PRISM GRID

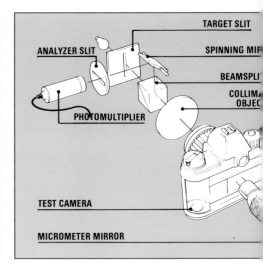

TARGET SLIT

ANALYZER SLIT

SPINNING MIR

BEAMSPLI

COLLIM
OBJEC

PHOTOMULTIPLIER

TEST CAMERA

MICROMETER MIRROR

viewing screen to show the different fields of view at short and long subject distances, or by fitting a sliding mask under the screen. The mask moves progressively downwards as the photographer focuses closer, indicating how much will appear in the picture. These measures alleviate parallax error but they do not eliminate it. The two lenses still see slightly different views of the subject.

Single lens reflex cameras (SLRs) eliminate even this problem by using one lens for both viewing and taking the picture. The mirror that reflects the image upwards to the viewing screen is hinged, and springs upwards out of the light path an instant before the shutter opens. After exposure, the mirror drops down again, so that the viewfinder image disappears for a split second.

SLR focusing is particularly valuable when taking close-up pictures, because there is no problem of parallax error, even when the subject is just a centimetre from the lens. And because the optics of the focusing mechanism are the same regardless of the lens in use, the system works equally well with telephoto and wide-angle lenses.

Rangefinder focusing

Reflex cameras are difficult to use in dim lighting conditions, and the swinging reflex mirror adds to the bulk of the camera, and the noise it makes. When silence is essential, in dim light and in certain other conditions, many photographers prefer to use rangefinder cameras.

These work on quite a different principle to reflex cameras. They have a viewfinder that is quite separate from the camera's lens, and that shows a slightly reduced image of the subject — rather like looking through the wrong end of a low-power telescope. The viewfinder image is sharp and clear over its entire area, because it does not contain the matt-glass screen of the reflex camera.

To focus, the photographer looks at the centre of the viewfinder, where there are two coloured spots. One of these spots is just a tint that overlays the middle of the viewfinder proper. The other spot of colour is actually a second image of the subject, formed by a small mirror or prism a few centimetres from the main viewfinder window. Mechanical linkages turn the mirror or prism as the lens is focused, thereby changing the area of the subject that appears in the second of the two coloured patches. When the image in each of the coloured patches is identical, the two images appear to fuse into one, and the picture is sharply focused.

Rangefinder focusing is equally precise with all focal lengths of lens, but since telephoto lenses require more precision in focusing than wide-angle and standard lenses, 35 mm rangefinder cameras function properly only with 135 mm lenses or shorter focal lengths. The other side of the coin is that focusing of wide-angle lenses is more accurate on a rangefinder camera than on an SLR.

Since the viewfinder of a rangefinder camera does not see through the taking lens, the same amount of the subject is visible regardless of the lens in use. To indicate the camera's field of view with different lenses, there are bright frame lines visible in the viewfinder. Changing from lenses brings a different frame into the viewfinder.

To compensate for parallax error, the bright frame lines also move down within the window, though simpler rangefinder cameras often lack this feature, and indicate parallax error by a couple of marks at the top.

Autofocus cameras

Automatic focusing is a comparatively recent innovation, but on snapshot cameras it is already the rule, and a few SLRs have autofocus built-in or available as an option. There are basically four different means of focusing a camera automatically.

Passive systems bear a close resemblance to rangefinder focusing systems, except that two

Focusing with long lenses

Selective focus with long telephotos can help picture design. In the photograph below, it is the softness of the background that helps make the figure of the woman stand out. In the photograph of the heron, selective focus blurs foreground leaves to the point where they do not obscure the image. The zebras are defined more sharply by the golden wash of unfocused foreground.

Calibrating the focus

Focusing accuracy is factory-tested with an electronic autocollimator (left). The match in focus between the image in the viewfinder and true film-plane focus is measured by the image reflected from the micrometer-adjusted mirror, via a collimator, converted to give an oscilloscope trace.

Optical auto-focus

The sophisticated Nikon system compatible with its F3 cameras measures distance optically in a special prism head. A TTL system like this can be used with a wide range of lenses.

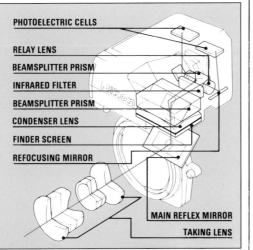

PHOTOELECTRIC CELLS
RELAY LENS
BEAMSPLITTER PRISM
INFRARED FILTER
BEAMSPLITTER PRISM
CONDENSER LENS
FINDER SCREEN
REFOCUSING MIRROR
MAIN REFLEX MIRROR
TAKING LENS

photoelectric cells (actually grids of light-sensitive elements) replace the photographer's eye as the detectors of sharp focus. An image from each of the two rangefinder windows is projected onto the photocells, which produce two slightly different signals when the subject is out of focus. When the image on each cell is the same — corresponding to the merging of the two coloured rangefinder patches — the signals are identical, and the camera knows that the point of sharp focus has been reached.

Passive systems work well in bright light and with heavily patterned or contrasty subjects, but are fooled by dim light and featureless subjects. On the positive side, these cameras can take pictures of reflective subjects, and through windows — situations that often fool other autofocus cameras.

Infrared triangulation systems function by projecting a spot of infrared radiation. As the lens focuses from near to far, the spot crosses the field of view. A narrow-angle infrared receptor pointing forwards detects when the projected spot of infrared strikes the subject, then immediately locks the lens, and releases the shutter. This system is again similar to a rangefinder camera, but instead of light coming into the camera by reflection off the rotating mirror, infrared radiation travels out of the camera on a similar optical system linked to the focusing action.

Infrared triangulation is the most effective autofocus system for everyday snapshots: it works with most subjects, and can operate even in the dark. However, this system will not work with reflective surfaces such as still pools of water. These reflect the IR beam, and the camera focuses on infinity.

Flash reflection systems are fitted to a few autofocus cameras. These rely on the fact that nearby subjects reflect more electronic flashlight to the camera than distant subjects. The camera releases a flash of light or infrared radiation just before the exposure, and measures the light reflected back. Electronic circuits then estimate the approximate subject distance, and set the lens accordingly. The advantages are: it is a simple and reliable mechanism, and cheap to manufacture. The drawbacks are: it does not work well with very dark or light subjects; its accuracy is limited.

Some instant cameras measure distance using sound, rather as bats' high-pitched squeaks enable them to navigate in the dark. The camera emits an ultrasonic 'chirp', and measures the time taken for the echo to return. Since the speed of sound is relatively constant in air, the delay is proportional to the subject distance. Again, a motor moves the lens to the best focus.

These 'sonar' systems are effective in the dark and with non-patterned subjects, but are misled by windows — the camera focuses on the glass.

SHUTTER

The earliest cameras had no shutters; they did not need them, because the light-sensitive materials of the day were very slow, and exposures lasted several minutes, even in bright sunshine. Photographers often covered the lens with their caps — even today, people still talk of 'uncapping' the shutter.

As photographic materials improved, so exposures got shorter — eventually to less than a second. Taking these 'instantaneous' pictures without a shutter proved difficult, because it was impossible to uncover, then re-cover the lens quickly enough.

Modern films are many times faster than those of even 20 or so years ago, and the speed of shutters has kept pace with the speed of films. The fastest of shutters in common use exposes film for just 1/4000 second, and can arrest the movement even of falling water, or the wings of a tiny bird. Nevertheless, the basic concept of the shutter remains very much the same as it did a century ago.

Shutter principles

The purpose of a shutter is to protect the film from light until the chosen moment, then to open for a precisely measured time before closing once more. In a sense, then, a shutter is like a fast-acting and completely opaque roller blind, opening and closing to briefly admit light to a room. (This metaphor is actually rather close to reality, because many shutters physically resemble roller blinds.)

All shutters — apart from those on the most rudimentary of cameras — have a range of speeds, usually in a doubling sequence that runs from one full second to 1/2 second, then 1/4, and so on, usually as far as 1/1000. The sequence is not an exact doubling sequence — 1/1000 should be 1/1056 — but the errors are negligible. Many modern cameras have speeds beyond this range — some as fast as 1/4000, and as slow as 8 seconds.

This doubling sequence of shutter speeds is important, because it matches the doubling and halving sequence of apertures, and simplifies exposure calculations. Changing from one speed to the next fastest exactly halves the time during which light can reach the film.

The time for which the shutter is open is controlled either mechanically, using clockwork mechanisms, or electro-mechanically. Electro-mechanical shutters, usually called electronic shutters, operate on battery power, and time the exposure using a quartz clock mechanism. Such shutters are capable of very precise speeds, but are generally totally reliant on batteries, so the camera is useless when the cells run out of power.

Speeds are marked as reciprocals on the control that is used for changing the shutter

Shutter speed and movement
At shutter speeds slower than needed to produce a sharp, frozen image of a moving subject, the visual effect can vary considerably — and not always predictably. The four pictures above, of a liquid pouring into a cocktail glass show how different shutter speeds can create subtly different effects. In the picture top left, shot at 1/250 second, nearly all movement is frozen, and individual bubbles can be seen clearly. Slower shutter speeds show blurring to varying degrees.

speed; 1/2 is marked just as 2. Full seconds often appear in a different colour.

Besides this series of numbers, shutter speed dials may carry other symbols. The letter B appears on many dials and stands for 'bulb'. This setting holds the shutter fully open for as long as the shutter release is depressed, and is a hangover from the days when expendable flashbulbs were common. The photographers would set the camera to B, press the shutter release, detonate the bulb by closing a switch and then release the shutter button again.

Today, the shutter mechanism itself closes the circuit that fires an electronic flashgun, but the shutter may not synchronize with flash at all speeds. Often the fastest speed usable with flash is marked with a lightning bolt or the letter X, or the fastest flash synchronization speed is engraved in a different colour. This speed is usually mechanically controlled, even on electronic shutters. So if the camera's batteries fail, the X speed is often the only one usable.

A few cameras have a letter T alongside the B. At this setting the shutter is locked open as soon as the shutter release is pressed. Pressing it again, or moving the shutter speed dial to a different speed, closes the shutter.

Leaf shutters
The ideal shutter is totally opaque when closed, and opens instantly to become totally transparent over its entire area. All the shutters used for everyday photography, though, rely for their effect on some sort of moving blades or blinds. Since solid matter cannot be accelerated from rest instantaneously, all shutters are a compromise of one sort or another.

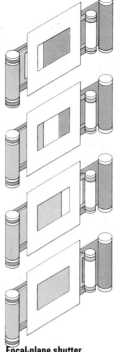

Focal-plane shutter Essential in SLR cameras because the reflex viewing system requires an open lens right up to the moment of taking the picture, focal-plane shutters operate on the principle of roller blinds. There is a pair of these flexible, tensioned blinds, and both travel across the frame through which the film is exposed. At slow speeds the entire frame is exposed, but at high shutter speeds the two blinds are timed to unroll so that a thinner gap is revealed. Adjusting the gap alters the shutter 'speed'.

Having opened, the blades remain at rest briefly before snapping closed to terminate the exposure. Light therefore reaches the whole of the film area simultaneously while the shutter is open, so electronic flash can operate with these shutters at all speeds.

Leaf shutters are limited by the mass of the blades, which cannot accelerate instantly, nor come to rest instantly. Consequently, few shutters of this type offer the photographer speeds faster than 1/500. And because the centre of the lens is uncovered marginally sooner than the edges, the shutter may give a degree of overexposure at small apertures. In practice, the error rarely causes problems.

Leaf shutters are used in many roll-film cameras, and in virtually all sheet-film cameras. Simple leaf shutters expose the film in 35 mm compact cameras, and in smaller formats, such as 110 Instamatic cameras, the leaf shutter may play the extra role of aperture, opening to varying sizes as well as for varying times.

Focal-plane shutters
The other major category of shutter is housed not in the lens but in the camera, just in front of the film. One of these focal-plane shutters therefore operates with all the interchangeable lenses fitted to a camera — whereas individual leaf shutters must be fitted into each and every lens if the camera lacks a focal-plane shutter.

Focal-plane shutters resemble roller-blinds that cross the area in front of the film. These shutters, though, are composed of twin blinds, so that the shutter is like a window with a roller blind both at the top and the bottom. Prior to exposure, the lower blind is unwound, covering the

Leaf shutter Usually situated between the elements of a lens, a leaf shutter works on the principle of an iris — a number of interconnected curved blades operate to give an expanding then contracting aperture. The sequence above illustrates half of the action, and so half an exposure sequence.

Leaf shutters come closest to satisfying the requirements of the ideal shutter. They are also called lens shutters, or Compur shutters. A leaf shutter is usually built into the lens with which it is to be used and consists of a number of thin metal plates. When the shutter is closed, the metal leaves overlap, stopping light from passing through the lens. Pressing the shutter release causes the leaves to spring apart, allowing light to pass.

Shutter and aperture together The same level of exposure can be achieved with different combinations of shutter speed and aperture. In the first photograph (above left) the aperture is small (giving good depth of field) and the shutter speed slow. In the next picture (above right), the settings are reversed. The photograph at left is a compromise.

Shutter speed test
Make an approximate visual check of the shutter speed accuracy as follows:
Open the camera back and remove the lens. Hold the camera up to the light, watch the shutter opening, and start by operating the slow speeds (one second or more). Rapidly work from one speed to the next: the slowest speeds can be timed, the faster ones can be judged by seeing if they are half the duration of the previous speed. Above 1/125 second speeds cannot be judged visually. Perform this test with the mirror in operation and also with it locked up.

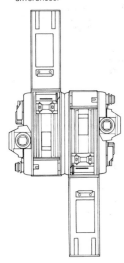

Comparative test A similar test of shutter speed accuracy involves taping two cameras base to base, as shown below. Perform the range test described above, pressing both shutter releases together. Look for differences.

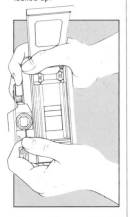

window. The upper blind is fully rolled up at the top of the window.

At slow shutter speeds, the exposure is made by releasing the top edge of the lower blind, which rapidly rolls up onto its roller at the bottom of the window. This uncovers the whole of the window for the prescribed time, and when it has elapsed, the upper blind is unrolled, covering the window from top to bottom.

After exposure, the overlapping edges of the two blinds are wound from the bottom of the window to the top, thereby unfurling the lower blind, and rolling up the top one, ready for another picture.

At faster shutter speeds, the action of the shutter is different. On pressing the shutter release, the lower blind starts to roll up, but as soon as a small part of the window is clear, the upper blind begins to unroll. The result is that the edges of the two blinds make a slit that travels across the film. The faster the shutter speed set, the narrower the slit. The time taken for the slit to cross the frame remains the same at all shutter speeds.

Although all parts of the film may therefore receive an effective exposure of, say, 1/500, the top of the film is exposed well before the bottom, and the whole of the film area is never exposed simultaneously. Electronic flash can therefore not be used when a focal-plane shutter is operating at the faster speeds — the brief flash of light illuminates just a narrow band of the film.

The blinds of a focal-plane shutter are not necessarily made from fabric, though many are. Some shutters are made from a complex arrangement of sliding metal plates, or from thin sheets of titanium foil. The lower the mass of the shutter, the better, because light shutters can travel faster. The faster the shutter travels, the faster its top speed will be, and the faster will be the speed at which the whole film area is exposed simultaneously. This speed is the fastest speed at which the camera can be used with flash — the flash-synchronization speed.

Most focal-plane shutters have top speeds of 1/1000 second, and flash synchronization speeds of between 1/60 and 1/90. A few have top speeds as high as 1/2000 or 1/4000, and flash-synch speeds of 1/125 or 1/250.

Stopping movement
The importance of fast shutter speed lies in the camera's ability to freeze the motion of speeding objects. However, the shutter is not the only factor that affects this ability.

The apparent sharpness of a moving subject on film depends on how far the *image* of the subject moved in the course of the exposure. Consider two examples — an aircraft a mile or so from the camera, and a sprinter a few yards away. The aircraft may be travelling at hundreds of miles per hour, yet it

takes, say, five seconds to cross the frame. During an exposure of 1/250, the image of the plane travels just 1/70 mm or so — an undetectable distance. The runner, moving at say 10 mph, crosses the frame in a second, and his image moves 1/7 mm during a similar exposure. When the photograph is enlarged ten times, the runner's image will have moved 7 mm across the print, and the picture will be visibly blurred.

So, besides speed, the other factors involved are: subject distance, focal length of lens, direction of movement, and even the degree of print enlargement. If subjects are far off, moving towards or away from the camera, photographed with wide-angle lenses, and with the resulting images enlarged little, then even slow shutter speeds will arrest motion. Conversely, nearby subjects crossing the field of view, photographed with telephoto lenses and then greatly enlarged may be badly blurred, even at the camera's fastest shutter speed.

Of course, absolutely sharp images do not always evoke subject motion. They can look static and dull, like a bronze sculpture depicting a figure in motion. At slow shutter speeds the camera blurs the image of moving subjects, and this can create a more convincing image of movement, as the picture to the right illustrates. Again, though, the same factors govern how blurred the subject appears on film.

Shutter speed and movement
Two alternative techniques for dealing with linear movement are shown here in the context of horse racing. In the larger picture at left, the camera has been panned with the horses to make the most of the shutter speed — the result is a blurred background of spectators at the finishing line. In the smaller photograph below, at Ascot, a more oblique viewpoint onto the rails makes panning unnecessary. Both photographs are by George Selwyn.

CAMERA-SHAKE
Besides arresting the images of moving subjects, fast shutter speeds also prevent movement of the camera from blurring the picture. Camera-shake causes especially bad problems when the camera is hand-held, but even mounted on a tripod, a camera can move significantly during exposure.

The slowest speed at which it is safe to hand-hold the camera is affected by the focal length of the lens in use. Telephoto lenses magnify the effects of camera-shake, while wide-angle lenses minimize them. A practical rule of thumb is that the slowest safe speed at which a lens can be hand-held is the reciprocal of the focal length. So standard lenses need speeds of 1/50 — effectively 1/60, and a 135 mm lens, 1/135 — for practical purposes 1/125. Heavy, bulky lenses need a faster speed.

Long telephotos have inevitable camera-shake problems, because of the size and weight of the lens and because of the mangified image (the effects of camera movement are similarly magnified). Use every support possible, such as the soft shoulder bag and wall in the long street photograph at left.

APERTURE

The camera's aperture is just that — a hole through which light passes on its journey from the subject to the film. What makes the camera's aperture unusual, though, is that it is adjustable, from a tiny hole — almost a pinprick — to the diameter of the lens itself.

Together with the shutter, the aperture controls how much light reaches the film. The aperture does more than this, though; it also affects how much of the picture is in focus. Small apertures let through little light, yet they enable the camera to render most of the subject sharply. Large apertures let through more light, but record only a shallow plane clearly. Choosing the right aperture is not, therefore, just a matter of getting the exposure right — it is necessary also to take into account the nature and depth of the subject and how the scene before the camera is to appear on film.

The iris diaphragm

The size of the aperture within the lens is controlled by the iris diaphragm. This is a series of crescent-shaped blades that makes a circular opening in the middle of the lens. Moving the blades enlarges or reduces the size of the central hole.

The aperture setting ring on the exterior of the lens controls the size of the hole made by the blades — turning the ring back and forth enlarges and reduces the size of the hole. On rangefinder cameras and certain other types, the aperture setting ring and the iris diaphragm are directly linked, and looking in the front of the lens, it is possible to see the aperture closing down as the ring is turned. However, on single lens reflex cameras, the linkage is more complicated, and until an instant before the exposure, the iris diaphragm remains fully open. Then, shortly before the shutter opens, the aperture closes down to the value preset by the photographer.

This rather complex arrangement is called a 'fully automatic diaphragm'. It is necessary because SLR cameras use a single lens for both viewing and focusing. Reducing the aperture of this lens prior to exposure makes the focusing screen darker, and the process of focusing less accurate. So it makes sense to keep the iris diaphragm wide open for focusing and composing the picture, closing it down just before the shutter opens.

Aperture calibrations

The aperture ring on the lens is calibrated with a series of numbers that at first glance seems curious and almost random, though progressively increasing. The series usually starts at 2, 1.8 or 1.4, and increases to 4, 5.6, 8, 11, 16, and perhaps further to 22, or even 32. The numbers, in fact, are far from

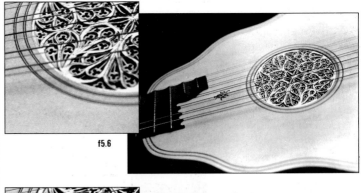

f5.6

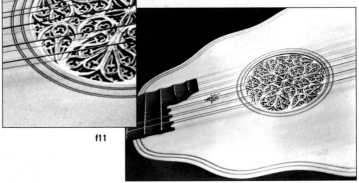

f11

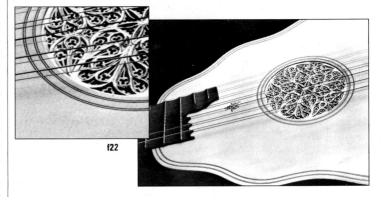

f22

random, as closer scrutiny reveals; the series doubles at every other value.

These numbers are called f-stops, or f-numbers and are a measure of the size of the lens aperture. Each number though, is not the diameter of the aperture, it is the number by which the focal length of the lens must be divided to yield the aperture diameter. So the numbers can be written as f/2, f/16 and so on — f being the photographer's abbreviation for focal length.

For example, when a 50mm lens is set to f/2, the diameter of the aperture is 50/2, or 25mm. When referred to in speech, the numbers become 'eff-two' and 'eff-sixteen' — the oblique line is ignored.

This may seem like a very complicated way of measuring the power of a lens to transmit light. However, it has certain advantages. Telephoto lenses form a magnified view of the subject, compared with wide-

Depth of field with aperture
These three progressively stopped down examples, each with the central portion magnified, demonstrate the practical effects of depth of field. Using a 100mm lens at a focused distance of 0.6m (2 feet), the depth of field at f5.6 (top) is from 60-64cm (23½-25in), less than the width of the strings. At f11, the field depth increases, covering 57-65cm (22½-25½in) — about the width of all the strings together. At the aperture setting on the lens of f22, most of the instrument appears sharp, the depth of field reaching from 53-71cm (21-28in).

Selecting views by varying aperture In the two photographs at left, a standard lens was focused on the distant trees. At f16, the minimum aperture, both foreground and background are equally sharp (top). At f1.2, however, the foreground is very much out of focus, and acts as a frame (bottom). With a long telephoto lens, the loss of foreground sharpness can isolate a subject. With a 600mm lens used at f16 (small picture in the pair below), the intervening grass almost obscures the image, in contrast to the main picture, taken at f4.

HYPERFOCAL DISTANCE When a lens is focused on infinity, depth of field ensures that subjects in the middle distance are still sharp. The depth of field on the far side of the plane of sharp focus, though, is wasted — for there is nothing beyond infinity.

This 'wasted' part of the zone of sharp focus can be put to good use by positioning the infinity symbol alongside the depth of field marking for the chosen aperture, instead of next to the focusing index. All the zone of sharp focus will then be on the near side of infinity — and more of the picture will be sharp.

When the infinity symbol is positioned like this next to the depth of field mark, the main focusing index will point to a setting known as the hyperfocal distance. This distance varies with the aperture — at small apertures, hyperfocal distance is closer to the camera than at large apertures.

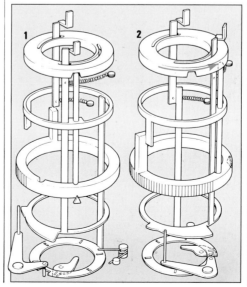

angle or standard lenses. So the light from a given area of the subject is spread over a larger area of film with a telephoto lens. This means there is less light for any given aperture diameter. The f-stop system gets around this problem because it is independent of focal length. An f-number is a ratio, not an actual measurement, so that an aperture of f8 on a 50mm lens admits exactly the same amount of light as an aperture of f8 on a 400mm lens.

This is important when changing lenses. A photographer who is switching from one lens to another can maintain the same f-number on both lenses. If the aperture was measured in millimetres, instead of as a numeric ratio, lenses of different focal lengths would need to be set differently.

Why then the curious progression of numbers? Again the choice is quite logical. Each setting of the aperture ring lets through twice as much light as the one before, so with the lens set at f4, the image on film is twice as bright as at f5.6, and half as bright as at f2.8. This doubling/halving sequence may be familiar — shutter speeds increase and decrease in a similar manner.

Note, though, that large f-numbers let through little light, and small f-numbers, such as f2, admit very much more light.

Shutter and aperture together

The matching progression of shutter speed and aperture makes setting of the two controls very easy and convenient. If the camera's meter indicates that a particular combination

Aperture stop mechanism A system of pins, levers and cams transmits the necessary information between camera body and lens, while allowing full-aperture viewing. In the Canon breech-lock system, an aperture signal lever is attached to a pre-set cam. When the lens is removed from the body (**1**), the cam activates a crank which in turn moves the diaphragm blades to their set position. On the camera, however, the normal position is with the blades fully open (**2**); they are activated only an instant before exposure.

of shutter speed and aperture will give correct exposure, then moving each control by an equal number of increments — but in opposite directions — will not affect the exposure. For example, when the meter indicates that settings of 1/60 at f8 will give correct exposure, then equal exposure will be given by settings of 1/30 at f11 or 1/125 at f5.6.

Because altering the shutter speed by one setting is exactly equivalent in exposure terms to changing to the next aperture, the term 'stop' is commonly used to refer to both controls. 'Give one stop less exposure' means 'change to the next fastest shutter speed, or the next smallest aperture'.

Different combinations of settings suit different picture-taking situations — stopping action, for example, would mean choosing a fast shutter speed such as 1/1000 at f2. Generally, though, choosing the best combination means making a compromise between shutter speed and aperture.

Lens speed

The widest aperture to which the lens can be set is a measure of its maximum light-gathering power — the 'speed' of the lens. This is an important consideration for photographers who take many pictures in restricted light. Most standard lenses for 35 mm cameras have maximum apertures of f1.8 or f1.4. A few have apertures of f1.2.

Telephoto lenses usually have smaller maximum apertures because with long focal lengths, the physical diameter of the lens must be greater for the same f-number. This makes fast telephoto lenses heavy to carry and expensive to manufacture.

Maximum aperture is limited ultimately by film flatness, because the wider the aperture to which a lens is set, the more precisely the film must be positioned at the back of the camera. With the lens set to f1.2, even a slight curl in the film will lead to uneven sharpness across the frame.

Depth of field

As explained on page 40, only one plane of the subject — the plane of sharp focus — is rendered absolutely pin-sharp on film. Subjects close to this plane but not actually in it are recorded less sharply, but they do not just snap suddenly out of focus. The transition from sharp to unsharp on either side of the plane of sharp focus is thus gradual and progressive.

In effect, subjects are in tolerably sharp focus not just in one plane, but over a range of distances — a zone of sharp focus. The depth of this zone is known as the depth of field.

Depth of field is directly proportional to aperture, and is least at wide apertures. Closing the lens down to smaller apertures increases depth of field, bringing more of the subject into focus.

When all of the subject must appear sharp, the lens must be stopped down to small apertures such as f11 or f16. However, great depth of field is not always desirable, and a photographer may deliberately choose a wide aperture to reduce the depth of field — perhaps to blur an unsightly background behind a portrait subject.

Aperture is not the only factor that influences depth of field. Focal length, subject distance and degree of print enlargement do too. Long focal length lenses have shallower depth of field, and wide-angle lenses more depth of field when compared with standard lenses. Similarly, depth of field increases in proportion to subject distance.

Enlargement is something that is frequently overlooked when considering depth of field, yet it is as important as focal length or aperture. Slight unsharpness that goes unnoticed on a contact sheet or on a transparency seen without a magnifier may render an image useless for great enlargements.

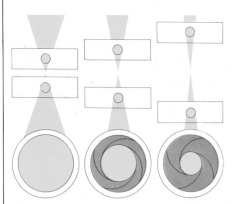

Depth of field depends on circles of confusion, the smallest circles in an image that the eye interprets as points (0.033 mm is a standard measurement). In the diagrams above, the circles of confusion are represented in the pairs of rectangular panels (the near and far limits of the depth of field). The steepness of the cones of light on either side of the point of focus depends on the lens aperture, and this determines the depth of field.

Estimating depth of field

On SLR cameras, the lens is set to full aperture until immediately before exposure, so the image on the focusing screen always shows depth of field as it is at the maximum aperture of the lens. This can give a false impression of what the picture will look like — particularly if the aperture set on the control ring is a small one, such as f22. A typical result of this is that a background that looks blurred in the viewfinder appears sharp on film, revealing all sorts of unwanted detail.

To enable the photographer to preview the depth of field, many SLR cameras have a manual stopdown control that closes the lens down to the preset working aperture. Pressing this control makes the focusing screen much

DEPTH CHECKS
1 Visually Depress the preview button on an SLR.
2 Lens scale
3 Depth of field table
4 Equation
a) Calculate the hyperfocal distance, H:
$$H = \frac{F^2}{f \times 0.033}$$
b) Near limit of field =
$$\frac{H \times u}{H + (u - F)}$$
c) Far limit of field =
$$\frac{H \times u}{(H - F)}$$
H = hyperfocal distance; F = focal length of lens; f = f stop; u = focused distance

There is often more than one way of using depth of field, as in the examples above, all shot with a 20 mm lens.

1 At full aperture of f3.5 the depth of field appears only moderate when the lens is focused on infinity.

2 Also at f3.5, but focused at 0.3 metres, the depth of field appears much shallower.

3 At f3.5, focusing at the hyperfocal distance (3.5 m) maximizes depth of field.

4 Full sharpness across the entire picture needs both focus on the hyperfocal distance (0.6 m) and a small aperture (f22).

darker, but gives a truer picture of how the final picture will look.

Additionally, cameras of all types have a depth of field scale. This is a series of markings on the lens barrel that indicates how much of the subject will be in focus. The markings are either numbered or coloured to correspond to similarly coloured engravings on the aperture ring.

Depth of field can be calculated, too, provided the photographer knows the focal length of the lens, the aperture, the subject distance and the degree of enlargement. The formulae are given in the box on the opposite page — in practice, scales on the lens and observation of the screen image are of greater value than calculations.

Sharpness and lens aperture

No lens gives its best performance at full aperture. This is because at the edges of the lens, the glass elements have to bend light more than at the centre, and the greater the bending, the more the faults in a lens — the abberations — are revealed. Stopping down the lens to a small aperture ensures that only the centre of the lens is used, so light needs to be bent very little to form the image and the performance of the lens improves.

There is a limit to the improvement gained by stopping down the lens. Usually the optimum aperture is two or three stops smaller than the maximum aperture. Stopping down to very small apertures may actually reduce sharpness.

EXPOSURE

Exposure is the product of the *intensity* of light that reaches the film, and the *time* this light falls upon the film. On this simple formula, fundamental to all photography, a very complicated structure of camera technology and individual creative decisions has been built, necessary in the eyes of some photographers, a distracting burden to others.

The intensity of light striking the film depends on the brightness of the scene in front of the camera, and on the size of the lens aperture. The brightness of the subject is controlled by its own arrangement of tones and colours, and by the intensity of the light source. It is, therefore, possible to break down the process of exposing film into this sequence:

1 Light of a certain intensity falls on a subject that may be light or dark, shiny or matt.
2 The product of this is reflected light, which passes through the camera's lens.
3 The aperture of the lens can be adjusted to allow more or less of this light through.
4 Inside the camera, the light has to travel a certain distance. The longer this is, as in close-up photography, the less intense the illumination at the film plane.
5 The sensitivity of the film, slow or fast, determines how much exposure it needs to record a particular image.
6 Finally, the shutter can be set to different periods of time, from a few thousandths of a second to several hours.

Essentially, exposure entails adjusting the amount of light that reaches the film so that the result, when processed, appears as the photographer wants it to. But this simple statement disguises a whole world of problems. While in a technical sense there are only two camera functions involved in actually making the exposure — the shutter speed and the size of the lens aperture — achieving a satisfactory image involves a complex mixture of sensitometry and personal taste.

Sensitometry is the study of the effect of light on light-sensitive materials. A certain amount of exposure of light will, when the film is developed, produce a given density in the silver or dye, and this can be calculated precisely. The characteristic curve graph is the standard sensitometric way of displaying this, and from this curve the results of particular camera settings can be worked out.

For any given film and picture situation, there is one particular exposure that will record the maximum amount of information. For a fairly typical outdoor scene, such as that on page 242, photographed on a medium-speed black-and-white film (ISO 125, for example) this exposure might be (1/125 second at f8). Less exposure than this would result in less information being recorded in the darker, shadow areas of the picture — a negative would be thinner and a transparency denser. More exposure would cause the highlights to 'block up', losing the detail in these brightest parts of the photograph — a negative would be dense with silver or dye, a transparency weaker.

This is an objective way of looking at exposure, making the most of any film's ability to carry tones and detail. However, maximum information is not the same as 'best' and the idea of correctness in exposure has grown to be something of a millstone for many people. A major concern for a large number of amateur photographers is achieving an acceptable exposure, a concern that may well distract attention that could be better spent on more interesting picture decisions. The response from camera manufacturers has been to apply more sophisticated technology to automatic metering than to any other area.

Contrast range and latitude

If the only kind of subjects that film had to record were of a single tone — a grey stone wall, for example — exposure decisions would be fairly simple. In fact, most scenes have a variety of tones, from light to dark, and this is called the *brightness range*. This range can be quoted as a ratio, such as 1:50, or more usefully for photographers as the number of stops of exposure difference.

Even those subjects that may look at first glance to have little difference between the darkest and brightest areas, such as a figure in diffuse lighting, may contain surprises when measured. The figure photographed on the following page actually has a brightness range of 1:80, or 6 stops. A sunlit landscape in clear weather with plenty of deep shade may have a range of 1:250, or 8 stops.

Two commonly used words in this respect are *shadow* and *highlight*. Precisely, they refer to the extremes of tone in a scene that contain useful or desirable detail and they set the limits of the brightness range.

Film emulsions vary in their ability to record all of a wide brightness range. The ability to record extremes of brightness is the film's *contrast range*. The contrast range of a slow black-and-white film, for example, is shorter than that of a fast emulsion; it is, in popular terms, 'more contrasty'. The contrast range of a transparency is shorter than that of a negative, and that of a negative longer than that of a print made from it. For practical purposes, the range of most negative films is about seven stops and that of most transparency films about five stops. Most instant films have shorter ranges — less than four stops for the most popular integral prints — and line films the least of all.

Now, if the contrast range of the emulsion is the same as the brightness range of the subject, one exposure setting will make the ranges match. Everything from the shadow detail to the highlight detail will be recorded.

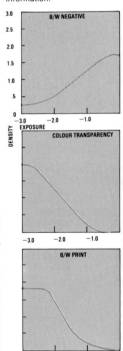

FILM RESPONSE
The graphs below are 'characteristic curves', which show the relationship between exposure and the density of the image — in other words, the response of film to light. The more light it receives, the denser the negative image (also consequently, the lighter the positive image in a slide or print), but emulsions react differently. The main slope of the characteristic curve represents the useful range of the film or paper; generally speaking, if this slope is steep, the film is contrasty and has little latitude. As the graphs demonstrate, a normal negative film has a gentler slope than transparency film or positive print, and so, as the example on the facing page shows, contains more information.

Film latitude vs. subject
When the range of brightness in a scene exceeds the contrast range of the film, as in (A), highlights or shadows suffer reproduction. If the brightness range is less than the film's contrast range there is some choice in exposure.

With no fill lighting to alleviate the shadows, this photograph of a cellar door opening out onto a sunlit courtyard has an extremely high contrast range — beyond the capacity of either the negative or print. However, what is obvious is that the negative carries much more information at the high and low ends of the tonal scale than does the print — even though this has been enlarged carefully. As this demonstrates, the latitude of a negative is usually greater than that of a positive, whether a print or film.

(A) SUBJECT BRIGHTNESS, RANGE OF 8 STOPS: CONTRASTY.

AVERAGE NEGATIVE: 7 STOPS

AVERAGE SLIDE: 5 STOPS

(B) SUBJECT BRIGHTNESS RANGE OF 4 STOPS: FLAT.

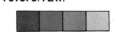

AVERAGE NEGATIVE: 7 STOPS

AVERAGE SLIDE: 5 STOPS

Understandably, this does not happen all the time. If the brightness range of the subject is less than the range of the film, then there is a choice of exposures that will deliver an acceptable, recognizable image. This spread is the *latitude* of the film. So, with a 'flat' subject, such as a block of weathered stone under a cloudy sky, a normal negative emulsion will have a reasonable amount of latitude. This can, at the least, allow for errors in making the exposure.

The other side of the coin, however, is when the subject has a long brightness range and the film has a short contrast range — that is, when both are 'contrasty'. Not only is there no latitude, but all of the tones in the scene *cannot* be recorded. In this common case, something has to give, and the decision can only realistically be made by the photographer, using judgement.

Compromise

In a situation where the film cannot cope with the range of tones in the scene, there are a number of things that can be done. Sometimes the lighting can be adjusted — in the studio a typical solution would be to add shadow fill with a reflector or another lamp, while outdoors fill-in flash might be used. An alternative might be a neutral gradated filter to make part of the image, such as the sky, seem less bright. It may also be feasible to alter the contrast range of the film, by reducing its development (see page 113).

However, these manipulations apart, the most common of all exposure problems is to decide on the setting when either highlight or shadow detail is bound to be lost. Then, the priorities of the image have to be followed. It is not enough to make an average exposure when the result can leave an area of sky washed out or when an essential part of the picture is deep in shadow. The subject itself, and the reasons for the photographer wanting to take the picture, come into play. Most experienced photographers in this type of situation quickly run through the visual consequences of different exposures in their minds, even if they make no conscious effort.

The exposure compromise is also affected by the film. With transparencies and with instant prints, the image is produced in one step, while negatives need a second stage — printing. Normally, washed-out highlights are more objectionable than over-dark shadows, so underexposure tends to be more favoured with transparencies and instant prints. With negatives, underexposure does not lead to washed-out highlights and there is always the chance of putting some tone back during enlargement.

Working methods

Most modern cameras have built-in exposure meters that measure the light reaching the

Readings in non-average conditions

This selection of pictures illustrates how the combination of varied lighting and differently toned subjects easily produces views that would be mishandled by an averaging meter.

1 The extreme contrast between the shiny mosaic pattern on the pyramid roof and the shadowed building behind is beyond the five stop range of a typical colour slide film. The double choice offered here (a two stop difference exposure), depends very much on what is considered important in the picture. Note that the placement of the key detail differs.

2 In this photograph, the most important consideration was that the large area of white should appear white in the photograph. Yet an averaging meter could easily be fooled into indicating too little exposure for a reading from the white and too much from darker areas. The correct exposure was given by adding two stops to a direct reading from the white.

3 Back-lighting offers a fairly wide choice of exposure. In this example, shot for a silhouette, details of the boatman were considered unimportant, but the colour was felt to be important. Consequently, the sky was the key element in the reading, and the exposure was set to only $\frac{1}{2}$ stop more than the average direct reading.

4 The mixture of subject tone and lighting in this picture stretches the capacity of colour transparency film a little too much, so the exposure was set for the reading off the adobe wall. This setting preserved detail on the cross but rendered the deep blue sky even darker than it appeared to the eye.

5 For this picture, the only consideration was that the rich colour of the sky should be retained, while the rest of the picture could be in silhouette. So the photograph was exposed for the sky.

● **KEY DETAIL**
○ **DARKEST SHADOW**
▽ **BRIGHTEST HIGHLIGHT**
□ **AVERAGE TONE**

film. However, measuring the light reflected from the subject is only one of three basic metering methods, each with its advantages and limitations.

■ DIRECT, OR REFLECTED LIGHT READING

In this, the brightness of a scene is measured directly. This naturally takes into account both the tones and textures of the subject, and the level of illumination. A basic direct-reading meter simply averages the different levels of brightness in the view that it takes in, and with most subjects the results are acceptable most of the time. If the meter is inside the camera, close to the film, it will also take care of such additional factors as light lost through filters or through lens extensions for closer focusing.

The main problem with direct readings is that the meter cannot discriminate between, say, a whitewashed wall and a black dress. It will, instead, give the reading that would record both as mid-grey. Direct readings work well for average subjects, but may be misleading for subjects with extreme tones.

■ INCIDENT READING

By measuring the light falling (incident) on the subject, any problems of tone in the subject can be ignored. This is done by fitting a translucent diffusing attachment over the meter's cell or the camera lens with TTL meters. The meter is then placed next to the subject, usually pointing towards the camera position. In situations where the lighting is consistent (and particularly where it can be controlled), incident readings are simple and have a high level of accuracy. They too, however, are less capable with very bright or very dark subjects, but in a different way — an incident meter will suggest slight overexposure of a bright object and underexposure of a dark one, the exact opposite of a direct-reading meter.

■ SUBSTITUTE READINGS

One reason for metering problems with the direct method is that the main subject may be surrounded by areas that are much lighter or darker, and so affect the reading — a bird flying against a light sky, for example. An alternative method is to take a direct reading of a substitute surface nearby. The most logical substitute would be a matt, mid-toned surface, and such 'grey cards' are available from suppliers such as Kodak. In fact, any surface, coloured or neutral, that reflects 18 per cent of the light will do — this level is the average. Some photographers use the palm of their hand, adjusting the setting slightly (Caucasian skin is in the order of one stop lighter than a mid-tone). Another method, particularly useful in dim light, is to read a pure white surface and then reduce the exposure shown by about $2\frac{1}{2}$ stops.

Of these three metering methods, each has some special advantage in certain situations, but personal preference also plays a large part. Experience, and constant practice at making readings, is the most valuable commodity in measuring exposure.

Just as there are three main methods of metering, so there are three types of reading:

■ AVERAGE

This is the most basic, in which the entire scene is measured over an angle of view similar to that of the camera's lens.

■ HIGH-LOW

Measuring the brightest and darkest parts of the scene shows the brightness range — an important reading if the scene appears to be contrasty or, indeed, if it seems flat and calls for some method of increasing the contrast. A spot meter, which usually has an acceptance angle of about 1°, is ideal for this more precise reading.

■ KEY

In extreme or unusual exposure conditions, it is often better to decide which is the important part of the scene to be recorded, and to measure just that. Again, spot meters are ideal for such detailed, key readings.

Individual choice

Exposure decisions clearly involve the photographer's own ideas, and while there are certain objective guidelines to 'correctness', personal taste is the final arbiter. Even scenes that have no excessive contrast and will record satisfactorily on any film with an average meter reading are open to interpretation. A landscape at dusk, for example, can be photographed so that the tones are average and most of the details can be seen; all it needs is sufficient exposure. However, it might be preferable to underexpose so as to convey the

Exposure values The exposure value, or EV, system, consists of combination numbers that are proportionate to the amount of light reaching the film. They combine, therefore, aperture and shutter speed, which are now always stepped by doubling and halving.

TTL metering Now by far the most common system of light measurement used in photography, through-the-lens metering has developed a variety of measuring patterns. A spot measurement is the most selective; an average reading is indiscriminate; centre-weighting pays little attention to the frame edges; multi-pattern metering calculates exposure under different conditions.

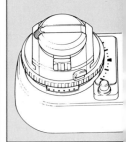

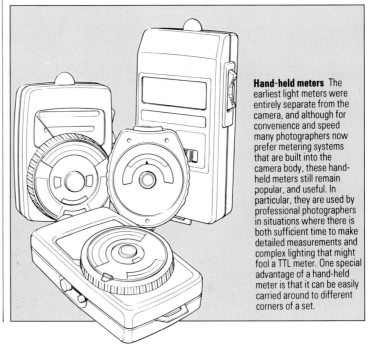

Hand-held meters The earliest light meters were entirely separate from the camera, and although for convenience and speed many photographers now prefer metering systems that are built into the camera body, these hand-held meters still remain popular, and useful. In particular, they are used by professional photographers in situations where there is both sufficient time to make detailed measurements and complex lighting that might fool a TTL meter. One special advantage of a hand-held meter is that it can be easily carried around to different corners of a set.

Shutter speeds (Sec.)

f-numbers	1	1/2	1/4	1/8	1/15	1/30	1/60	1/125	1/250	1/500	1/1000
1	0	1	2	3	4	5	6	7	8	9	10
1.4	1	2	3	4	5	6	7	8	9	10	11
2	2	3	4	5	6	7	8	9	10	11	12
2.8	3	4	5	6	7	8	9	10	11	12	13
4	4	5	6	7	8	9	10	11	12	13	14
5.6	5	6	7	8	9	10	11	12	13	14	15
8	6	7	8	9	10	11	12	13	14	15	16
11	7	8	9	10	11	12	13	14	15	16	17
16	8	9	10	11	12	13	14	15	16	17	18
22	9	10	11	12	13	14	15	16	17	18	19
32	10	11	12	13	14	15	16	17	18	19	20

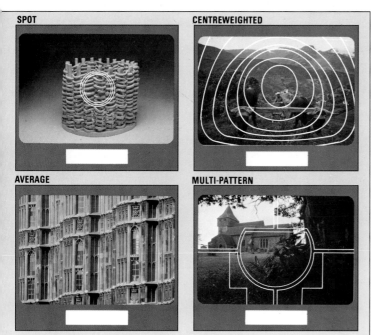

SPOT

CENTREWEIGHTED

AVERAGE

MULTI-PATTERN

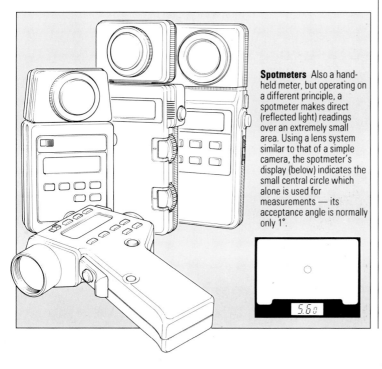

Spotmeters Also a hand-held meter, but operating on a different principle, a spotmeter makes direct (reflected light) readings over an extremely small area. Using a lens system similar to that of a simple camera, the spotmeter's display (below) indicates the small central circle which alone is used for measurements — its acceptance angle is normally only 1°.

darkness of the scene rather than the maximum information. In a transparency, less exposure will give more saturated colours and many photographers prefer to 'underexpose' slide film by half a stop or so. Overexposure in certain conditions will increase flare, give a pastel-like finish to colours, and create a less realistic, light-soaked appearance. These, and many others, are decisions about how the image should look, and can be made only by the photographer.

Automatic metering

Integrated circuitry, common on most modern cameras, allows the simple connection to be made between measuring the light and setting the exposure. As a result, automatic metering is now a standard feature and makes life easier in many ways for the amateur photographer. There are a number of possible choices in the system, and the word 'mode' is commonly used to describe them. The aperture can be set by the photographer and the shutter adjusts automatically (known as 'aperture priority'), or the photographer can set the shutter speed and the aperture changes automatically ('shutter priority'). Alternatively, the integrated circuits can be programmed to set both aperture and shutter speed, following certain rules such as keeping the shutter at a certain minimum speed to avoid camera-shake, unless light levels are low.

The manufacturer's problem in creating an automatic metering system is that of guessing how most of the camera users will take pictures. As most tend to place the main subject of interest in the middle of the frame, the basic TTL metering pattern in cameras is *centreweighted*. The patterns illustrated opposite reflect what different camera manufacturers have decided are typical pictures; variations such as spot patterns are ways of accommodating different situations. A newer method, multi-pattern metering, which involves sub-dividing the picture area and altering the meter priorities according to the distribution of tones, is a more sophisticated attempt to cover different types of image without bothering the photographer.

Basically, automatic metering is a statistical solution to exposure. The most successful produce acceptable exposures most of the time. They are only ever, though, a partial substitute for the photographer's own decisions. They have their place in freeing the camera user's attention, which can be useful in situations when there is little time to react, and for casual photographers. Their chief disadvantage however is that they can result in over-reliance. Just as pocket calculators do little to encourage basic mental arithmetic, so automatic metering can prevent camera users from becoming adept at judging light.

DIFFICULT EXPOSURE CONDITIONS

Most unusual, non-average exposure situations fall into one of the following categories (the numbers correspond to the photographs):

1 Light subject, dark setting The bird is the important detail, but appears so small in the frame that only a spotmeter reading would be useful, and this would normally be impractically slow to make. One solution is to take an incident reading in the same strength of sunlight, another is a substitute reading of an area of average tone also sunlit, outside the picture.

2 Dark subject, light setting A direct reading of neither the dark subject nor the white setting would be useful, and an average reading would be uncertain. The normal solution for a studio shot such as this is to take an incident reading, or a substitute reading directly off an 18% grey card.

3 High lighting contrast Here, the scene has a higher brightness range than a normal film could handle due to the lighting — sunlight verses shadow. As overexposed bright areas are usually unacceptable,

the normal solution is to silhouette the foreground figures by exposing for the background — with an SLR a 'spot' reading can be taken with the TTL meter.

4 Overall dark As envisaged, this landscape was to remain dark — an average exposure treatment would lose the drama. Consequently, the exposure was worked out on a rule of thumb basis — two stops less exposure than a TTL reading indicated. For later choice, a bracketed range of exposures was also made.

5 Overall light This telephoto shot of a white painted cathedral facade was intended to appear realistically white. Once again, the basis of the setting was a direct TTL reading, but the exposure given was one stop more than indicated.

6 High subject contrast White paint against a rich blue sky here gives a contrast range of about six stops — rather too much for colour transparency film. For an exposure that held detail in the paintwork and allowed the sky to appear darker, a spotmeter reading of the white was increased for the exposure by two stops.

The concept of a system camera is one of maximum versatility. The camera is designed in such a way that it can be adapted to suit the widest possible variety of applications. This is done by making the camera in a modular form; lens, viewfinder, focusing screen, film advance mechanism, and sometimes the film chamber itself are all removable.

35mm SLRs take the system camera concept to its logical conclusion, and the top cameras from the major manufacturers can be fitted with one of 50 or 60 lenses, and literally hundreds of accessories.

Close-up attachments

Most standard and wide-angle lenses for 35mm cameras focus on subjects no closer than about 18in (45cm) from the front of the lens. There are two good reasons for this. First, the optics of the lenses are computed to give best results for distant subjects, so optical quality falls off at short distances. The second reason is mechanical. Focusing on close subjects means moving the lens farther away from the film (see page 40). While the movement required to focus from infinity to 18in (45cm) is quite slight, focusing on closer subjects requires a much greater movement, and the mechanism to do this is complex and costly.

Macro lenses have a specially long focusing range, and are computed to give equally good results with distant or nearby subjects. However, to fill the frame with a small subject when using other lenses, you must fit a close-focusing accessory of some sort.

These fall into two categories: *mechanical accessories* simply move lens and film farther apart to form a bigger image; and *optical accessories* which change the focal length of the lens to which they are fitted.

Mechanical accessories have to hold the lens rigidly in position with its axis at a perfect right angle to the film surface, and form a light-tight seal between the lens and camera body.

The simplest way to achieve this is to fit a metal tube between lens and camera — an *extension tube*. Generally, extension tubes are supplied in sets of three different lengths, so that the user has a wide choice of different lens extensions — and therefore different subject distances. The tube lengths are designed to give a more or less continuous range of magnifications when used in combination with the normal focusing action of a 50mm lens. Most extension tubes maintain the automatic diaphragm coupling between camera and lens, but only the more expensive types allow you to use your camera's meter in the normal way.

Extension bellows support the lens in front of the camera body on a rail. A flexible tube of leather-cloth links the lens to the camera, keeping light out. The distance between lens and film is thus continuously adjustable over a range of distances, allowing the photographer to frame objects of various sizes. The exact focusing range depends on the length of the bellows, and the focal length of the lens fitted.

Although bellows extensions allow a continuously variable range of subject distances, they tend to be unwieldy and cumbersome to use in the field unless tripod-mounted. Additionally, most bellows lack mechanical couplings between camera body and lens, so metering and diaphragm stop-down must be carried out manually. This means that the use of bellows at fixed magnifications is generally slower than use of an automatic extension tube set.

A *reversing ring* can be used with both bellows and extension tubes. It is simply a metal ring with a filter thread on one side, and a male lens mount on the other. It enables you to mount a lens in reverse, and with certain lenses — particularly wide-angles — this produces better results at close subject distances.

All mechanical close-focusing accessories share one common drawback — the further

Reversing ring Most lenses are optically at their best when the subject at lens distance is greater than the lens-to-film distance. At magnifications greater than 1×, however, the film is further from the lens than is the subject. Reversing the lens by a special ring mount improves the image quality.

CLOSE-UP EQUIPMENT
The three basic attachments for close-up images are a bellows extension, a set of extension rings, and supplementary close-up lenses. A bellows extension is the most convenient for large magnifications. Extension rings are convenient for moderate magnifications and location use; supplementary lenses allow slight magnification.

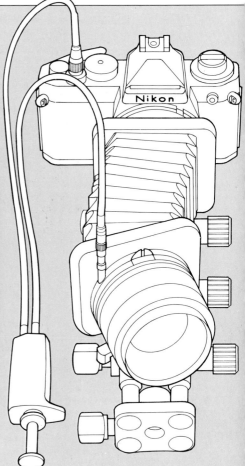

At approximately life-size reproduction (1:1), this small shell was photographed with a 55 mm macro lens extended by its own focal length — 55 mm. Extension rings were used, but a bellows would have been equally satisfactory.

the lens is from the film, the less light reaches it. With through-the-lens exposure metering (of flash or daylight) this does not matter, as the camera will automatically compensate. But when using non-TTL metering, exposure must be calculated, guessed or standardized by experiment. This can be tedious.

Optical accessories

The most well known of these is the close-up supplementary lens. This is generally a single-element meniscus lens, similar to a spectacle lens. It screws into the front of the main lens much as a filter does.

Close-up lenses reduce the focal length of the lens they are fitted to. For a fixed lens-to-film distance, magnification increases as focal length decreases, so fitting a close-up lens makes the subject appear bigger in the frame.

Like spectacles, close-up-lenses are supplied in a range of strengths, measured in *diopters*. The higher the diopter number, the greater is the power of the lens, and the closer it lets you focus.

Close-up lenses require no exposure compensation, so they are easy to use.

AUXILLARY LENSES

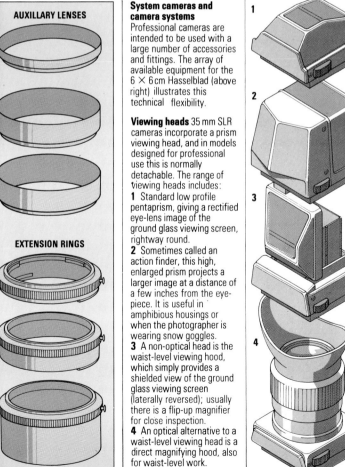

EXTENSION RINGS

System cameras and camera systems
Professional cameras are intended to be used with a large number of accessories and fittings. The array of available equipment for the 6 × 6cm Hasselblad (above right) illustrates this technical flexibility.

Viewing heads 35 mm SLR cameras incorporate a prism viewing head, and in models designed for professional use this is normally detachable. The range of viewing heads includes:
1 Standard low profile pentaprism, giving a rectified eye-lens image of the ground glass viewing screen, rightway round.
2 Sometimes called an action finder, this high, enlarged prism projects a larger image at a distance of a few inches from the eye-piece. It is useful in amphibious housings or when the photographer is wearing snow goggles.
3 A non-optical head is the waist-level viewing hood, which simply provides a shielded view of the ground glass viewing screen (laterally reversed); usually there is a flip-up magnifier for close inspection.
4 An optical alternative to a waist-level viewing hood is a direct magnifying hood, also for waist-level work.

Compared to mechanical close up accessories, they are cheap, but quality is rarely as good, and the main camera lens should be stopped well down.

Teleconverters can be used as close-up accessories, because they multiply the size of the subject in the frame (the magnification) — without increasing the minimum focusing distance of the lens.

Viewfinder accessories

35mm system cameras generally have a pentaprism fitted as standard, to permit eye-level viewing. On a few cameras the prism is removable, and can be replaced by one of a range of different viewing devices tailored to specific application.

Action or *speed finders* have a greatly enlarged viewfinder window that shows the whole focusing screen even when the photographer's eye is some distance from the camera. This can be a useful facility, especially when the camera is in a housing, or if the photographer must wear obstructive, protective headgear, such as a helmet or a visor.

Magnifying finders show an enlarged image of the focusing screen — or sometimes just the centre of the image.

Right-angle finders turn the axis of the viewfinder through 90° — so the photographer looks down into the camera, yet the lens points forwards. This is useful for low-level camera positions, and when the camera is fixed to a copying stand. Similar finders turn the viewing angle through 45°.

Non-removable prisms can be fitted with extra optical hardware that duplicates the functions of some of these accessory finders.

Roll-film system cameras usually offer a more restricted range of viewfinders and are supplied in their standard form with a simple folding focusing hood to exclude light. This houses a small magnifier for critical focusing.

Focusing screens can be interchanged on all system cameras, either by first taking off the prism, or by reaching into the camera body with the lens removed. Alternative screens may have a different arrangement of focusing aids. Some, for example, are completely covered in microprisms, and some are just plain matt plastic. Certain specialized screens make focusing easier with telephoto, wide-angle, or low-light lenses.

Motor drives

Almost all 35mm SLR cameras can be fitted with a bolt-on, motorized film-winding mechanism of some kind, and some even have a built-in motor drive. The benefits of instant film wind-on are not just the obvious ones of speed and convenience, though these are obviously important. Motor drives allow any photographer to concentrate fully on the subject, without the jarring interruption of winding film. This is particularly important for people who use their left eye for viewing, as manual film winding involves moving the camera away from the eye.

Most 35mm motor drives advance film at a rate of two frames per second or faster, though some camera manufacturers produce two different units. One, often called a

Motor drives in use When used in its continuous mode, the repetitive firing of a motor drive allows sequence of fast action to be captured in their entirety. From a sequence of several frames (12 were taken in the situation illustrated here) a few key shots can later be edited; it is unlikely that every frame will be needed.

motor winder, is slower, and generally has fewer facilities. The other winds film at a higher framing rate, may have motorized rewind, and sometimes incorporates a counter that stops the motor after a preset number of frames have been exposed.

Remote control

Pressing the shutter-release button of a motor-driven camera closes an electrical switch. This in turn opens the shutter. It is therefore quite simple to place the switch somewhere outside the camera body, perhaps at the end of a 9m (50ft) cable.

This, then, is the simplest of remote control mechanisms, and enables the photographer to take pictures while actually some distance from the camera. Remote control is often the only way to get a picture of dangerous subjects such as lions and other big cats; in hostile environments — nuclear reactors, for example; and with timid subjects like birds.

The disadvantage of an ordinary electric cable is that there must be a physical link between camera and photographer. Other

Motor drives Professional system cameras are designed so that motor-drive operation can be added. A true motor drive as opposed to an automatic winder not only drives the film transport and re-tensions the shutter, but allows continuous firing (between 4 and 6 frames per second is typical). Motor drive accessories, shown above, include a bulk film back (about 250 exposures) and an intervalometer for automatic operation.

remote-control devices do not require such a link. *Infrared releases* operate the shutter by means of a pulse of infrared radiation. The photographer holds a small handset — essentially a sophisticated flashgun with the reflector covered by a filter that is visually opaque, but transparent in the infrared part of the spectrum. Pressing a button on the handset sends a pulse of infrared to a receiver attached to the camera. This device closes the contacts to operate the shutter.

Infrared releases are limited to quite short distances — usually less than 100m (330ft) — and to line-of-sight operation. In other words, to operate the shutter, you must be able to see the camera. An additional drawback is that other photographers using similar handsets may inadvertently operate your camera — a major problem at news events heavily covered by the press.

Radio-releases do not suffer from any of these drawbacks. They can be operated on a narrow frequency band chosen by the photographer, and the camera can be a considerable distance away — even out of sight. However, radio releases are illegal in some countries, and in urban areas radio-frequency interference can trigger the camera at the wrong moment.

Automatic triggers
All the systems described above rely on the photographer observing the subject, and operating the shutter at the appropriate moment. However, in certain applications, it is more convenient if the subject itself triggers the camera. A typical example is in wildlife photography at night: catching an image of a flying owl is near-impossible in the usual way — how can you tell when the bird is in focus? With an automatic trigger, it is possible to prefocus the camera during the day, and then rely on a sensing device to detect when the bird is flying through the point of sharpest focus. At this instant, the shutter opens, and an electronic flash lights the scene.

The method of sensing is limited only by the photographer's imagination, ingenuity and budget. A few 'off the peg' devices are available, but more often, remote triggers are custom-built for specific applications. Here is a rundown of the principal detection methods:

● *Simple switches* can be operated by pressure pads or trip wires to catch images of, say, medium-sized and large creatures.

● *Passive infrared* systems detect body heat, and trigger the camera when a living creature approaches. In much the same way, visible light — say from a rocket exhaust — can be made to operate the camera.

● *Active infrared* systems trigger the shutter when the subject breaks one or more beams of infrared — some systems use visible light.

● *Sound triggers* take pictures when activated by noise — perhaps to catch an explosion.

Interchangeable backs
The standard back of a 35mm system camera generally carries nothing more complex than a pressure plate on the inside, and a film memo-holder on the outside. On most medium-format system cameras, though, the camera back is a modular film holder that can be removed and exchanged.

This means that the photographer is free to change from one film type to another in mid-roll. The basic back contains a load of 120 roll-film, but this may be replaced with a different back carrying long lengths of sprocketed 70mm film; instant film for test exposures; double-length 220 roll-film (for twice as many frames as 120 film); and in some instances, 35mm film, taking either regular 24mm × 36mm images, or perhaps panoramic pictures. Even for 120 film, there may be options of different formats — 6 × 4.5cm, 6 × 6cm or 6 × 7cm.

The design of almost all 35mm SLRs precludes the use of such a wide range of interchangeable film magazines. However, a few manufacturers now produce an instant-film back that can be adapted to fit most 35mm cameras. These backs produce pictures only the size of a contact print, but are often adequate for lighting and exposure tests.

Data backs can be fitted to many 35mm system cameras. They imprint alphanumeric characters on the film, usually by means of tiny LEDs mounted on the camera's pressure plate. Most data backs will imprint the time or date, or number each frame sequentially. More sophisticated models double as intervalometers, or imprint whole sentences on the frame-edge.

Camera housings
In hostile conditions, a complex system camera is very vulnerable to damage, particularly by water. To prevent this, 35mm and roll-film models can be fitted into waterproof housings. These protect the camera, while allowing free access to all the controls. The simplest type are just heavy-duty plastic bags that keep water out in storms, and underwater at snorkelling depths. For scuba dives, acrylic housings are necessary to withstand the increased pressure. And for very deep dives, only heavy, cast alloy housings are strong enough.

A *blimp* is a rather different kind of housing. Instead of keeping water out, it keeps sound in. This masks the noise of the shutter during performances of music or dance, and muffles camera sounds that might frighten away timid wildlife subjects.

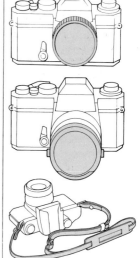

Basic protection Three of the most useful protection accessories are a lens cap, body cap (for when the lens has been removed), and neck strap.

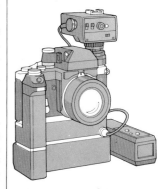

Light modulation For cable-free remote control, one of the most adaptable systems is a light modulation trigger. In this, an infrared pulse is emitted by a handset that the photographer aims at a receiver connected to the camera. Line of sight operation is possible up to 60 m (200 ft).

SUPPORTS

Today's fast films and high-speed lenses make hand-held photography possible with all but unwieldy sheet-film cameras. Yet camera supports such as tripods and camera stands are still widely used. The motive is not purely to avoid camera-shake, though this is a major consideration. On a tripod, a camera is fixed at one viewpoint, so the photographer can concentrate fully on the subject without worrying about what might intrude at the frame corners. Additionally, a hand-held camera generally covers the photographer's face during picture-taking. This can create a disconcerting barrier for human subjects. With the camera on a stand, the photographer is freer to move around and build up a rapport with the portrait sitter.

Undoubtedly, though, the biggest advantage of a camera stand is still the improved image quality it produces. Camera-shake does not always appear as a pronounced streaking of the image. Often it shows up simply as a very slight softening of fine detail. A good, heavy tripod prevents this, so that pictures look sharper and crisper than when the camera is hand-held — even at quite fast shutter speeds.

Tripods

The steadiness of a tripod is generally proportional to its weight. The heavier it is, the more resistance there is to vibration.

For this reason, the lightest portable tripods often provide little more support than the photographer's hands. Certain features, though, provide stability in even the lightest of tripods. Cross-bracing between the central column of the unit and the legs helps to keep the camera stable. And the most sturdy tripod is generally the one that has fewest leg sections. A tripod that fits into a pocket when folded, yet extends to over five feet is unlikely to be of any real value to the working photographer.

Other valuable features in tripods are the ability to spread the three legs wide apart to achieve a low camera position, and rapid adjustment of leg length, so that the tripod can be easily levelled on an uneven surface. Most tripods have an adjustable centre column for small changes in overall height; the rack-and-pinion movement which controls this on a few more expensive tripods is of real value only with very heavy cameras. Many centre columns are reversible — a valuable facility when taking low-level pictures, and for copying.

Tripod feet The surface actually in contact with the floor or ground also influences tripod stability:
1 Ball-jointed foot for surfaces that are not completely level.
2 Ribbed rubber foot.
3 Metal spikes for outdoor use.
4 Plain rubber stop for indoor use.

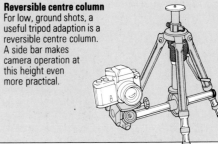

Medium and small tripods
There is considerable variety in tripod design, including such features as geared rising centre columns and horizontal arms (to avoid including the tripod legs in frame in vertical shots downward). Pocket tripods (right) are extremely portable, but need a raised, level surface for most shots. A monopod aids hand-held shooting.

Reversible centre column
For low, ground shots, a useful tripod adaption is a reversible centre column. A side bar makes camera operation at this height even more practical.

Studio support As portability is not a need in a studio, supports can be bulky and heavy for extra stability. A wheeled 'dolly' attached to tripod legs can be rolled around the floor and locked when necessary. The larger camera stand will carry the heaviest camera.

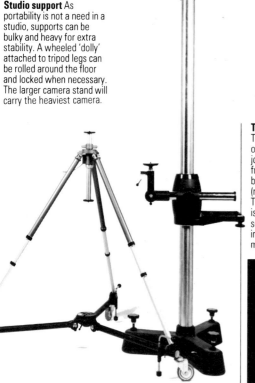

Tripod heads
The two most common types of tripod head are the ball-joint design (left and second from left in the picture below) and pan-and-tilt (right and second from right). The advantage of the former is rapid change, but the separate axis of movement in a pan-and-tilt head allows more precise adjustment.

Professional-standard tripods often form part of a large system of camera supports which includes studio stands, wheeled dollies, interchangeable feet, and lateral arms. As with a system camera, this versatility makes such tripods more expensive.

TRIPOD HEADS fit on top of the tripod, and carry a platform for the camera. The two principal types are pan-and-tilt heads, and ball-and-socket heads. They differ in the method of adjusting the camera's orientation.

Ball-and-socket heads have a single locking knob which, when slackened off, allows the camera to move in any direction. These heads facilitate large, rapid changes in orientation of the camera, but make fine adjustments rather difficult.

Pan-and-tilt heads usually have at least three separate controls, so that the camera can be moved on three individual axes. One knob controls fore-and-aft tilt; the second one, rotation of the camera atop the tripod; and the third, left-and-right tilt. Though slower to set up, pan-and-tilt heads allow the photographer to make fine adjustments to one axis — perhaps to level the horizon — without affecting other parameters, such as the height of the horizon within the frame.

Sophisticated tripod heads may have other devices fitted. A quick-release plate makes fitting and removal of the camera very easy; similarly, a levelling head permits rapid levelling of the camera without adjustment of the tripod legs or the pan-and-tilt head. A spirit-level allows the photographer to check that the tripod is properly set up and a panorama head is gradated in degrees, and often click-stops as well, to make light work of shooting panoramas by joining up normal frames.

Other stands and supports

In the studio, portability becomes irrelevant, and stability is the only consideration. Massive studio stands provide the ultimate support for the camera. Machined from cast alloy, and supported on a steel upright, these devices will hold even a heavy camera at ceiling level without any instability.

Copy-stands are specially adapted to the demands of photographic reproduction. They hold the camera with the lens axis pointing vertically downwards, so that the film is absolutely parallel with the base-board. Many have lights attached at either side of the camera.

Improvized camera supports hold photo-graphic apparatus steady in situations where the use of a tripod would be impractical. These include a variety of clamps for fixing to scaffolding poles or railings; ground spikes and plates for low-level pictures; tree-screws which can be inserted into a con-venient fence or other timber upright; and bean-bags which conform to the shape of the camera base, making a solid but por-table foundation for the camera in the field.

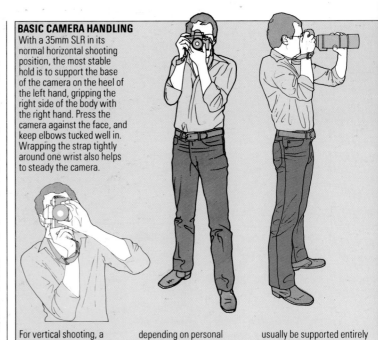

BASIC CAMERA HANDLING
With a 35mm SLR in its normal horizontal shooting position, the most stable hold is to support the base of the camera on the heel of the left hand, gripping the right side of the body with the right hand. Press the camera against the face, and keep elbows tucked well in. Wrapping the strap tightly around one wrist also helps to steady the camera.

For vertical shooting, a 35mm SLR can be supported either way, as shown above, depending on personal preference. With a motor-drive fitted, the camera can usually be supported entirely by a right-hand grip.

Auto stabilizer A specialized camera support for use from moving vehicles is a gyroscopically stabilized mount. Two small gyroscopes in the base rotate at up to 20,000 rpm, and compensate for the vibrations of a vehicle moving over rough ground. This is useful in wildlife photography, for example.

Pistol grips and their larger companions, rifle stocks, generally give a more ergonomic hold, and are useful with telephoto lenses.

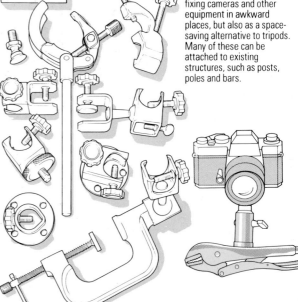

Clamps A variety of clamps, usually screw-locking, is useful not only for fixing cameras and other equipment in awkward places, but also as a space-saving alternative to tripods. Many of these can be attached to existing structures, such as posts, poles and bars.

Shooting in crowds

At popular events that attract crowds of other photographers, a satisfactory view may be difficult to find. A tall tripod (and camera box for the photographer to stand on) is one solution. A more mobile one is to remove the prism head and shoot with the camera held overhead, as shown above.

Extra steady support

Where conditions allow, and especially when using a telephoto lens — which is particularly prone to the effects of camera shake — make use of all available means of support. These include squatting, kneeling, using the camera bag as a rest, and nearby walls.

Camera-shake Movement of the camera during an exposure need not be gross in order to spoil the image. The most common effect is as below, in which the shaken picture seems just unsharp at normal viewing distances. An enlargement of the umbrella shaft shows the typical double image.

Maintenance and repair

Besides picture-taking accessories, a complete photographic outfit should contain a range of accessories for maintaining and repairing equipment. Like any equipment, cameras and lenses need a certain amount of attention if they are to continue functioning accurately. Heavy use, particularly on location, inevitably causes wear and tear, and certain moving parts, optical surfaces and integrated circuitry are sufficiently delicate to be affected by dirt, moisture, heat and cold. The basic maintenance programme consists of care in use, regular cleaning and regular checks of the major systems. In addition, damage may require field repair by the user, although this should always be approached with caution.

Care in use

Careful handling of photographic equipment under normal circumstances can avoid later problems of damage. Both front and rear lens surfaces, and the body aperture, can be protected with caps and clear glass filters. When carried, equipment should be packed carefully, as described on page 73. In use, moving controls like the cocking lever and the rewind lever, should be operated smoothly and without straining. In storage, tensioned parts, which include the shutter mechanism and the fully automatic diaphragm (FAD), should be left slack. Equipment should be regularly serviced by professionals. A well-used camera, for instance, should be serviced at least once a year.

Cleaning

Even the gentlest outdoor use can make equipment dirty and it is well worth cleaning equipment regularly. All the major interchangeable components, such as lens, prism head, battery drive and motor head, should be separated for cleaning, but only in surroundings that are free of dust. To avoid scratching and driving dirt further into the mechanism, a vigorous cleaning sequence is needed: air, brush and wipe. A hand-squeezed blower brush or a can of compressed air are the normal means of blowing fine particles away, but a miniature vacuum cleaner removes dust rather than circulates it. Compressed air should be used with caution close to focal plane shutter blinds, which are usually delicate. Brushes of different degrees of softness are needed for various surfaces: the most delicate is the mirror, followed by lens, prism and viewing screen, and these need a soft camel hairbrush. The body exterior is the toughest of all and can be cleaned with a toothbrush or typewriter cleaning brush. Once all abrasive particles have been removed, a cloth and dampened cotton buds can be used to wipe surfaces clean.

LENS CHECK
● Look for free play in the focusing ring, aperture ring and zoom ring. Shine a torch inside the lens to reveal bright reflection, loose parts etc.
● Check the state of the coating against the light by reflection.
● Look down through the lens onto a sheet of white paper, and check that colour is the same through the lens and by eye.
● With the lens on the camera, look through viewfinder and turn focus. Check for jerky, lateral movement of image.
● Open the back of the camera, and fire shutter at slow speed at different apertures.
● Check that all apertures work.
● Shoot clear sky or a white wall as metered and check results for evenness of tone.
● Shoot naked domestic lamp in dark; image should be sharp, without flare.
● Shoot test target on p29 for definition.
● Shoot any known parallel lines (a brick wall, for instance) and look for curving distortion.

REPAIR KIT
A photographer with considerable technical knowledge may find the selection of tools and tapes illustrated below useful for emergency repairs:

1 Tweezers.
2 Long-nosed pliers.
3 Angle-nosed tweezers.
4 Epoxy glue.
5 Needle files.
6 Pad and pen.
7 Camera tape.
8 Empty film cans for storing loose parts during repair.
9 Cross-head jeweller's screwdriver.
10 Spare batteries.
11 Jeweller's screwdriver.

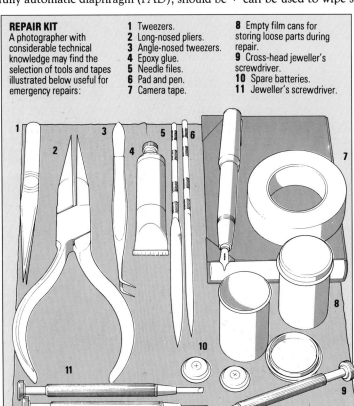

CLEANING AND MAINTENANCE
To avoid scratching surfaces with the dirt itself, follow this sequence:
● Blow or vacuum with air.
● Brush away remaining particles.
● Wipe.
Use soft materials on delicate surfaces, but for the exterior a toothbrush is fine. Clean battery contacts with an eraser.

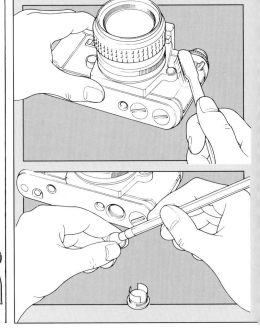

Precautions
If an attempt at repair is unavoidable, take these precautions: make notes of each stage of disassembly, including instant photographs if possible; compare the damaged camera with a similar model.

Maintenance checks

Regular checking of all the camera functions is an important precaution. Familiarity with the sound, feel and appearance of the mechanisms makes it easier to identify potential faults and can be an aid to repair. A good occasion is when the camera is empty.

There are, in most cameras, five major systems in the body — shutter, wind-on, mirror box, viewfinding and metering — and three in the lens — focusing, aperture diaphragm and aperture linkage (with most non-reflex cameras, the shutter mechanism is also in the lens). The slower speeds of the shutter can be checked visually by opening the camera back, holding the camera to the light and triggering the shutter from its slowest speed to its highest. Speeds of about half a second and longer can be timed, whilst progressively reducing the speed setting makes it possible to judge speeds even to about 1/125 second, as each should appear to be about one half the duration of the previous one. Faster speeds cannot be reliably assessed by eye.

The winding mechanism should feel and sound smooth (familiarity helps), and an additional check is to watch the movement of the film leader when a new cassette is installed. In use, the rewind lever on a 35 mm single lens reflex will move — although not necessarily each time the film is moved on. The mirror operation in a single lens reflex

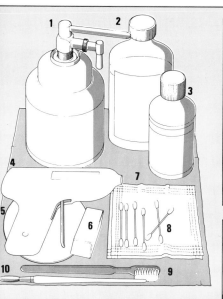

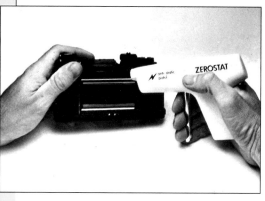

Cleaning kit
s basic set of equipment materials will cover all mal cleaning needs:
Compressed air.
Surgical spirit.
Lens cleaning fluid.
Anti-static gun.

5 Eraser for cleaning batteries and their contacts.
6 Lint-free cloth (such as a well washed handkerchief).
7 Cotton Buds.
8 Toothbrush.
9 Soft camel hair brush.

Cleaning inside
The interior of an SLR camera contains delicate surfaces, such as the instant return mirror and shutter blinds. Treat these with care. A thin plastic tube fitted to the nozzle of a compressed air can can be useful for directing short bursts of air accurately into confined spaces (below left). After cleaning, treat with an anti-static charge to prevent the re-attraction of dust (above left).

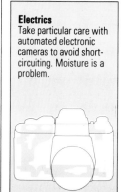

Electrics
Take particular care with automated electronic cameras to avoid short-circuiting. Moisture is a problem.

can be checked from the front with the lens removed, both during normal operation and by moving the mirror lock-up lever fitted to some models. Any significant problems in the viewfinder system will be immediately obvious, but the seating of the viewing screen should be checked by inspection. Any optical faults in the viewfinder which might affect accurate focusing can also be checked by opening the shutter and the camera back, fitting a lens and focusing an image on a piece of tracing paper held against the open shutter. This should compare with the focus as seen through the viewfinder. The best immediate check of the metering system is to compare it against the readings from at least one other meter. An even, mid-toned surface is the most suitable target.

Two likely lens focusing faults are a slack mechanism and lateral movements; both can

Cleaning the lens Clean first with air, then a brush, and finally by wiping in a circular movement gently with a soft cloth outwards from the centre. After cleaning, fit a clear glass filter.

occur through extended wear and tear. The first can be checked by holding the lens face down and watching to see if the focusing bow slips down under its own weight. Lateral movement can be seen through the viewfinder while shifting the focus; it does not affect the recorded image, but is distracting. The aperture diaphragm should be checked visually, with the lens both on and off the camera, for smooth operation and to make sure that it stops down to the full range of apertures.

EQUIPMENT HANDLING
Methods of storing, packing and carrying photographic equipment must take into account protection, bulk, weight and convenience. Location work, in particular, calls for safe means of transporting cameras and also for easy access. The actual cases and camera bags used depend very much on the type of photography and on the personal preference of the photographer.

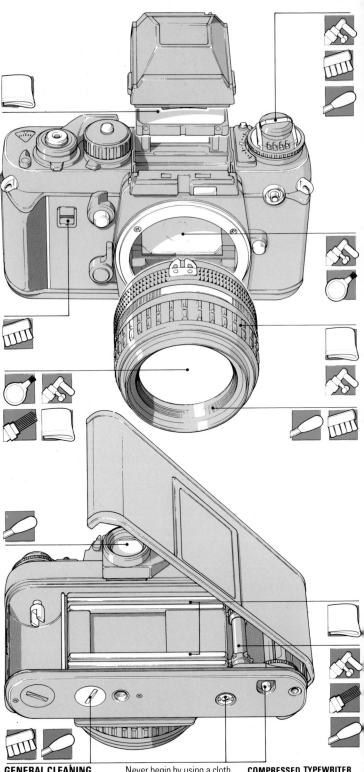

GENERAL CLEANING PROCEDURE Cleaning saves repair. Dirt can clog mechanisms, scratch film and glass and even wear down and loosen some moving parts, such as the lens focusing ring. Apart from full-scale cleaning after a trip, when the camera is obviously dirty, also clean regularly and as often as possible.

Never begin by using a cloth on delicate surfaces or you may simply wipe particles into the glass or plastic. Blow away loose particles with compressed air or your breath, then to brush away the remainder. Finally wipe with a clean cloth.

Use these cleaning diagrams to avoid missing essential parts. Always work on a clean surface.

COMPRESSED AIR **TYPEWRITER CLEANING BRU**

TOOTHBRUSH **LINT-FREE CLOT**

COTTON BUD **BLOWER BRUSH**

Dust and sand In a dusty environment leave equipment packed in sealed bags except for brief periods of shooting — wrap individual items in plastic bags sealed with rubber bands if possible. The most dangerous place of all is an ordinary sandy beach — it appears benign, but sand grains, made sticky with salt, adhere easily and work their way into the mechanism. Once sand is inside, do not continue to work moving controls, but strip the camera and clean it.

Heat and cold Modern cameras are unlikely to suffer actual damage at temperature extremes, except for the danger of condensation. But systems may malfunction due to battery failure and thickening of lubricants in cold, and the film may suffer due to heat-ageing or to breaking in cold. Check for cold weather malfunctioning by testing. Place in a freezer overnight and see if it works in the morning. Avoid condensation by keeping at a fairly constant temperature. Likely damage treatment will be for condensation, as for 'water damage' (below).

Water A light wetting from a rain shower generally does no harm — simply wipe down with a dry cloth. Immersion in fresh water is more serious. Remove the film in the dark and dry before rewinding. Open the camera, remove lens and other parts, and dry everything in sunlight, on a radiator or with a hairdryer. Have it professionally checked afterwards. Immersion in salt water is extremely serious. Immediately place the entire camera in a sealed container of fresh water and deliver to a repair shop.

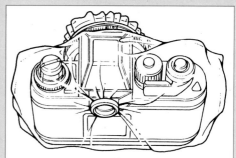

Instant dust-proofing
A simple answer to conditions in which dust, sand or water are flying about is to wrap the camera in a transparent plastic bag.

Use a tight rubber band to seal the bag's opening around the lens, trimming the surround with scissors.

Water damage (by wetting or condensation)

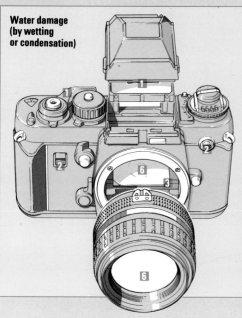

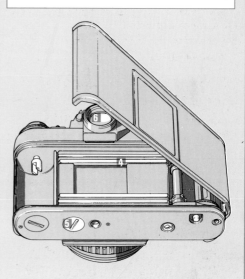

1 First points of entry after a wetting are the prism head, hinged back and controls on the top plate and baseplate. Opening the camera back will reveal to what extent water has entered.
2 The electronic circuitry and contacts are likely to short, which may make the camera immediately, but only temporarily, inoperable. Salt deposits from a salt water wetting can keep them shorted even after drying.
3 Many internal parts are liable to corrosion unless dried quickly.
4 If the film has softened from water entering the camera, parts of the emulsion may have stuck to the guide rails and film gate.
5 The battery may have shorted. Remove and dry.
6 Condensation due to extreme temperature changes is likely to occur first on the front lens surface. Beware of removing the lens if condensation is forming — it will then occur on the mirror and back lens element.

Dust and sand damage

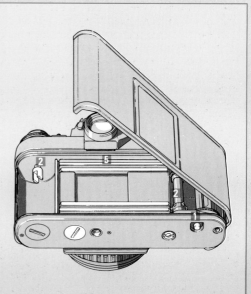

1 Entry points for particles include the gaps under moving controls such as the winding lever and rewind knob. Listen for grating sounds. Use compressed air and then a stiff brush.
2 Internal moving parts are at risk, particularly gears and linkages. Use a small vacuum cleaner or compressed air, but carefully.
3 The front lens surface is liable to abrasion. Protect with a clear glass filter. Clean with air or a blower brush. It will need regrinding if scratched.
4 Particles easily enter the aperture and focusing rings. Extend lens barrel by focusing to near limit, then use compressed air followed by a small stiff brush. Professional disassembly and cleaning is likely, as particles may become embedded in the lubricant.
5 The film emulsion is at risk of linear scratches if grit is lodged near the guide rails. Clean this area with particular care.

FAULT DIAGNOSIS AND TREATMENT

APPARENT PROBLEM	POSSIBLE CAUSES	CHECKING PROCEDURE
Winding mechanism jams	Part broken through impact Foreign body in gears End of film has been reached Film stuck in cassette damaged Battery failure if motorized	1 Inspect film counter, change film if ended. 2 If shutter failed to fire, see shutter problems below. 3 If motor-drive was fitted, remove and try manually, if not, attach motor-drive and try. 4 Remove film by rewinding; if this is jammed also, open camera in dark, pull out film and rewind into cassette by hand. Try winding with camera empty. 5 Check that rewind button in baseplate engages. 6 Turn sprocket wheel and take up spool by hand. 7 Rotate rewind lever. 8 Otherwise, have it repaired professionally.
Film does not wind on (but winding mechanism works)	Film leader not engaged No film Film torn inside camera	1 Gently rotate rewind lever to check for tension (this indicates film is tight). 2 If rewind lever loose, open camera in dark. 3 Feel for film. If torn, remove and place in light-tight tin for development; if still at start, switch on light and engage leader in take up spool. 4 Try fresh roll of film. 5 Otherwise, have camera repaired professionally.
Shutter stops working	Battery failure Shutter lock engaged Film transport lever not fully wound Circuit fault	1 Check the batteries, shutter lock and film transport lever. 2 Try without lens (diaphragm linkage may be jamming). 3 Try with instant return mirror locked up. 4 Gently ease blinds by hand (needs great care; perform only in an emergency). 5 Try mechanical back-up shutter, if camera is electronic. 6 Otherwise, have the camera repaired professionally.
Shutter speeds inaccurate	Normal for high speeds with age (mechanical shutter) Dirt, loss of lubricant (mechanical shutter) Grovit fault (electronic shutter)	1 Check if inaccuracy is across range or only at certain speeds. If latter, avoid these speeds. 2 Check if inaccuracy is by a consistent amount. If so, suspect speed setting or exposure compartment control. 3 If fault not due to operator error, have the camera repaired professionally.
Aperture diaphragm does not stop down automatically on exposure	FAD linkage malfunction	1 Check engagement of FAD linkage between lens and body. Use second camera and lens for comparison. 2 Try lens and body each with another body and lens respectively, to isolate fault. 3 If linkage is twisted out of shape, bend back carefully. 4 Otherwise, have the camera repaired professionally.
Focus is unsharp at infinity	Viewing screen unseated Normal with Flurite or rare earth glass (depends on temperature) Extension ring or close-up lens left fitted Loose lens element	1 Check the fitting of the viewing screen. 2 Inspect lens for physical damage, shake gently and listen for movement inside; also move focus and/or zoom control while looking inside for signs of jerky movements. 3 Have repaired professionally.
Focus is diagonally unsharp (ie sharpness not proportional to distance)	Normal if camera or lens has swing or tilt movements and these are in use Twisted mirror-box (from impact)	1 Remove lens and examine camera from directly in front. Check for misalignment of mirror-box. 2 Have repaired professionally.
Aperture diaphragm sticks	Bearings dirty Blades rusted or dirty Broken linkage	1 Remove lens and work aperture ring several times. 2 If this does not work, have it repaired professionally. (Never lubricate.)
Meter display does not work	Battery failure Circuit failure Failure of LED, fading of LCD with age, needle sticking	1 Switch on. 2 Check battery and replace if necessary. 3 Wind on one or two frames. 4 Dry camera if there is a likelihood of moisture inside. 5 If none of this works, have repaired professionally.
Meter inaccurate (wrong exposures)	Wrong film speed set Affected by exposure to strong light for a few minutes Out of calibration Unusual exposure conditions	1 Check film speed setting and exposure compensation dial. 2 Check against readings from another camera or meter, over a range of subject tones. If consistently inaccurate by a predictable amount, adjust film speed setting or exposure compensation dial accordingly. 3 If recalibration needed, have this done professionally.

Shoulder bag
This is the most generally useful way of carrying cameras and lenses. There is a wide variety of designs to suit personal taste. Important qualities are robustness, padding and not looking conspicuous.

Transporting equipment
(right) When taking camera equipment as baggage or sending as freight, a hard case is preferable to a soft bag. Foam-lined aluminium, fibre or compound cases are usual. Filters can be carried in special hard boxes in slotted racks.

INTERNATIONAL TRAVEL
On entry into a foreign country, any equipment more elaborate than one small camera and a couple of lenses may be liable to duty, although this is largely at the discretion of individual customs officers. There are rarely major problems but it is worth checking the regulations of the country

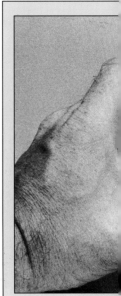

Lens cases
Individual bags for lenses are useful if the shoulder bag does not have individual compartments and when a lens is to be carried separately (below).

being visited. It may be necessary to complete a customs declaration and to show all the equipment upon exit. Professional photographers sometimes use the Carnet system, which can usually be arranged by a local Chamber of Commerce. This can save considerable time going through customs.

Carrying equipment

For certain types of photography, such as candid street photography and the stalking of wildlife, the photographer must be mobile and equipment be quickly to hand. So most photographers specializing in these areas work with a minimum of cameras and lenses — although the minimum varies from person to person. Some photographers carry just a camera on a neck strap and film in their pockets. Others take a shoulder bag with as much equipment as they can carry without great discomfort.

In every camera bag, the equipment should be well protected yet accessible. Protection is chiefly in the form of padding and waterproofing, and there is a fairly wide choice of materials available, both synthetic and natural. Modern synthetics such as Cordura are tough, waterproof and light in weight, although leather may be more durable. Internal padding, usually with foam, protects equipment against impact. Ease of access is largely a matter of design. Ideally, a standard shoulder bag should fit comfortably just below the hip, supported by a broad adjustable strap, and the opening should be immediately accessible. Separate compartments inside make the selection of lenses and other interchangeable parts easier.

Transporting equipment

When transporting cameras and lenses to locations, heavy-duty protection is usually more important than portability or rapid access — particularly if they will be handled by other people, such as in airports. Rigid cases are therefore better than soft bags. The strongest materials normally used for camera cases are metal and synthetic compounds like ABS. To keep weight down, aluminium is used in preference to steel, but is usually strengthened with a hammered finish or by moulded ribbing. The interior is usually divided into compartments, neatly fitting the specific items with dividers or by a specially cut block of closed-cell foam. Additional protection against moisture and dirt is possible by means of a gasket seal around the lid. With certain compound cases, complete waterproofing is possible.

Switching film in mid-roll
To change from a film of one speed or type to another in the middle of a roll, it may be necessary to unload a partly used film. Note the number of exposures, then rewind slowly and manually, until the release of tension indicates that the leader has come away from the take-up spool but has not been completely withdrawn into the cassette. Write the number of exposures taken on the cassette or the leader with a marker. To replace later, re-load, then wind on to the frame number noted *without allowing any light through the lens*. Ensure this by using the smallest aperture and fastest shutter speed, and a tightly secured lens cap. Without a lens cap, place the front of the lens flat against a dark surface at the bottom of a camera bag, in shade.

Long-term storage

With equipment in ordinary storage between sessions, dust and moisture are the main dangers so some form of concealed container is ideal, and a little silica gel dessicant helps to reduce moisture. Ordinary camera cases may be satisfactory but if the equipment must remain accessible, it is usually better to keep it in a cupboard. When equipment must be stored for a long period without use, it should have all tensioned parts, such as the shutter and wind-on, slackened and batteries removed. It can then be sealed in a kitchen cling-wrap, including a sachet of silica gel; a second wrapping of foil gives added protection.

Safe storage
When storing equipment for long periods at home or in a studio, loosen all tensioned parts, remove batteries and wrap with a dessicant in cling wrap and foil.

LIGHTING

What is loosely termed 'artifical lighting' covers a surprising range of forms, some made for photographic use and so suited to conventional films, others that are out of the photographer's control but often interesting in their effects. There are three principal sources of man-made light: incandescent, created by the slow burning of a filament such as tungsten; electronic flash, which is almost exclusively used for still photography; and vapour discharge, which includes fluorescent strip lighting, mercury and sodium lamps. Although the lighting quality, emission spectra and colour temperature of all these sources differ widely, all can, with some precautions and adjustments, be used for photography, in black-and-white and in colour.

Candle-light
One of the weakest and reddest sources of available light is a small naked flame. The colour temperature is below 2000 K and variable. Full correction to a visual white would require filtration in the order of three 82 C gels used with Type B tungsten-balanced film, but as candle-light is expected to have a reddish glow, it is usually acceptable to shoot with no filters at all.

After dark in houses, offices, streets and public buildings, there are several types of artificial lighting used — all tend to be difficult to take photographs by. These artificial lights are not only relatively weak and often give uneven illumination (a mixture of deep shadows and pools of light is typical); they also bathe subjects in light of a different colour. While the human eye adapts to these variations so quickly that they are barely noticed, film does not adapt so readily.

The chief restriction on photography by available artificial light is often the shutter speed. The light level in a typical modern office or department store is more than 100 times less than outdoors in ordinary sunlight — a difference of, say, seven stops. And, as a filter may be needed to balance the colour cast from some lamps, notably fluorescent ones, even less light will reach the film. Film makers provide charts giving typical shutter speeds and apertures for various available-light settings. They show that for useful shutter speeds — those that permit hand-held shots of people moving — a high-speed film and a fast lens help enormously.

Fluorescent and daylight mixed
When two different light sources are mixed, it is impossible to filter for both. Here, diffused daylight from the windows combines with overhead strip-lighting that appears distinctly green by comparison.

Fluorescent lighting
Fluorescent strip lamps are the most common kind of artificial lighting, and often give the most even illumination. However, though white to the eye, the light they throw appears green on colour film. Different coatings on the glass envelopes of these lamps give a variety of greenish casts, and it is difficult to predict the exact appearance on film. For most, a CC 30 Magenta filter, or any of the proprietary fluorescent correction filters, will give a reasonably neutral result on daylight-balanced film. For absolute accuracy, it is necessary to expose a test roll of film through different strengths of magenta filter and develop that before returning for a full photographic session. Alternatively, existing fluorescent lamps can be replaced with types made specially for photography, or can be covered with magenta stage-lighting gels.

With colour negative film, the colour can be balanced during printing, but slide film must be filtered at the time of shooting. Polachrome slide film uses an additive colour process and usually gives accurate results *without* filters.

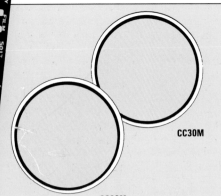

CC30M

CC20M

Testing colour balance

The most reliable way to overcome the uncertainty of exactly how green a particular set of fluorescent lamps will appear on film is to make a test beforehand. In this example, fluorescent ceiling lamps dominated the lighting of this commodity exchange. To find the precise filtration needed, the empty room was photographed a few days before the shooting, through different filters (mainly a variety of strengths of magenta). With the test strip of film processed, the best filtration and exposure could be judged, and this was used on the day.

Tungsten lighting

Domestic tungsten lamps are little different in type from the photographic tungsten variety, but the filament does not burn so hotly. As a result, they give a more reddish light; the colour temperature varies from about 2500K to 2900K, and to balance this a bluish filter such as 82C should be used with Type B colour film (itself balanced for 3200K). Accurate colour balance is more important for slide film than for colour negative emulsions, as the latter can be filtered during enlargement afterwards. Some high-speed films, such as Ektachrome 400, give less red results than others. An alternative is to replace existing bulbs with photographic ones (rated at 3200K).

Vapour lighting

While fluorescent lamps have a coating of fluorescent materials to help give a visual white, sodium and mercury vapour lamps do not. As a result, sodium vapour lighting looks and photographs yellowish, mercury vapour lighting looks and photographs bluish. Each emits light in just a narrow part of the spectrum, and while mercury vapour lighting is often close to 'normal', sodium vapour is distinctly coloured and cannot be filtered — using a blue filter to reduce the yellow simply reduces the light, as there is only yellow present. The only practical alternatives are to live with the colour cast, or to use flash. For mercury vapour, a CC30 Red filter may help.

Sodium vapour

Lamps like those used at left in the floodlighting of a cathedral, have a 'discontinuous spectrum' that gives a yellow-green cast on colour film. This cannot be corrected by filtration.

Mixed tungsten and daylight

The orangeness of tungsten lights on daylight-balanced film is usually acceptable when mixed with daylight, as in the interior shot at left.

FLASH

Electronic flash has become the most common form of artificial lighting for photography. Indeed, it is a light source that is uniquely photographic: too brief to be of any use to the eye unaided by the camera.

At the heart of all flash units is a toughened glass tube. This is filled with a rare gas called Xenon that is normally an electrical insulator, like most gases. However, when atoms of Xenon are charged with electricity, the gas becomes a conductor, and a spark jumps between charged electrodes fused into each end of the flash tube. This spark creates a flash of light similar in colour to daylight, and ideally suited to photography.

In practice, operation of a flash unit is a little more complex than this simple description might suggest. One of the two electrodes fused into the tube must be raised to a very high voltage relative to the other. This is done by charging a capacitor with high-voltage electricity produced using a step-up transformer, and a rectifier to turn the alternating current (AC) into direct current (DC). The transformer is powered from the mains or, in portable units, from an oscillator that creates AC from the DC of a battery pack.

To make the Xenon conduct electricity, a thin wire spirals round the flash tube. Passing a pulse of high-voltage current through this ionizes the gas, triggering the flash. The trigger pulse comes from yet another circuit, which, via a second transformer, links the flash unit to the camera's shutter. When the shutter opens, synchronization contacts close, and a small current flows through one side of the transformer. This induces a flow of current at a much higher voltage on the other side — the trigger pulse.

When there is enough power to take another picture, the ready light comes on. This lamp monitors the charge on the main capacitor, and lights up when charging is nearly complete — usually about 75-80 per cent of a full charge.

With portable flashguns, there is a high-pitched whine, too, which cuts out soon after the ready light comes on. This noise is made by the oscillator turning DC to AC. Studio flash units need no oscillator, and are therefore silent in operation.

The power output of a flash unit depends on the characteristics of the capacitor, and the voltage that it stores. The higher the voltage, and the more power the capacitor can store, the bigger the flash. Power of studio flash units is usually measured in joules (also called watt-seconds). A large studio flash unit may have a power of some 4000j, compared with the 25 or so joules of a typical mid-range camera-mounted portable flash.

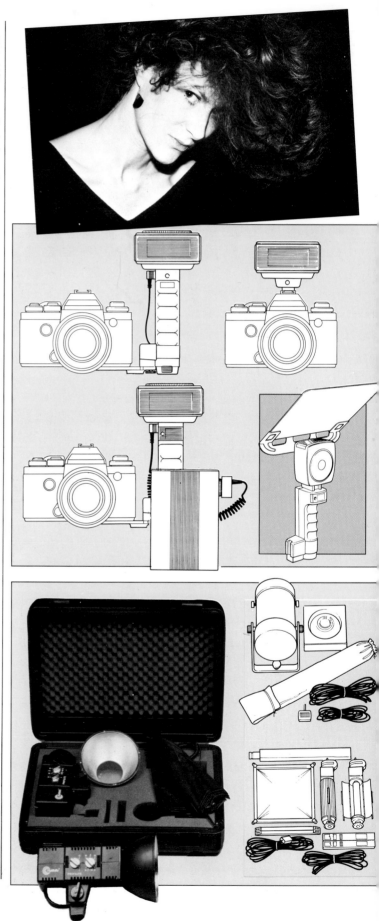

Flash by night
Portable flash can be used simply as a supplement to daylight or other available light, but it comes into its own at night. The darkness of the night covered all unwanted details in this shot (left), leaving just the flash to illuminate the subject and give a very finished, 'studio' look to the shot.

Hammerhead flash
Massive portable flashguns for hand-holding or attaching to a camera bracket may be considerably less manageable than the light flashgun that fits into the hot shoe, but the kind of power this kind of gun can give is needed to exploit the full range of flash techniques to the full. The smaller guns are, in particular, all but useless for bounced flash and may even be of limited value for fill-in flash. But powering large guns calls for considerable power and the grips are designed as much to hold large batteries as to provide a hand-hold. Some high-powered guns have a separate lead-acid accumulator carried in a shoulder pack.

Portable flash units
Clamped to a hand-held camera, a portable flash unit makes the photographer completely independent, and free to photograph anything, at any time, anywhere. The smallest portable flash unit fits neatly into the camera's hot-shoe, and is little bigger than a matchbox. At the other 'end of the scale, a large press flashgun requires a separate power pack, and itself may dwarf the camera.

Compared to their bigger studio-based brothers, portable flash units are electronically very sophisticated. Most are now *automatic*, that is to say, they incorporate a photocell to measure the flash light reflected from the subject. When the unit has emitted just enough light to ensure a correct exposure, the flash is quenched. All the photographer has to do to produce correctly exposed pictures is set a calculator dial to the film speed in use, read off an aperture from a scale, and set this aperture on the camera lens. Within a broad range of sub-

Both of the flash arrangements illustrated here — the ringlight below and the bellows and flash bracket on the right — are suitable for close-up photography and considerably simplify the problems of lighting small, nearby subjects.

Travelling kits for location lighting vary according to the type of shots planned. Shown here are a lightweight travelling flash kit packed neatly into a case, consisting of three 200 joule monoblocs (far left); an extensive basic location kit (near left); and a supplementary kit for flash (left centre, top) and tungsten (left centre, bottom). The basic location kit includes: flexible white plastic; black velvet for shadowless backgrounds; aluminium cooking foil for a reflector; translucent plastic diffuser; clips and grips; extension cable; screw clamps; pliers; insulated screwdriver; plugs and adaptors; lightweight, collapsible lighting stands; white/silver umbrella; translucent umbrella.

ject distances, the flash unit will correctly meter the exposure.

Most units offer the photographer a choice of apertures — sometimes two or three, and in a few instances, six or eight. Some manufacturers add as confirmation of correct exposure a *confidence light* which comes on after the exposure, if the subject was within range of the camera's auto-sensing circuitry. This reassures the feckless photographer that the pictures will be neither too dark nor too light.

A relatively recent innovation is the *dedicated* flashgun that operates exclusively with one particular make or model of camera. A dedicated unit automates certain flash functions — though precisely which functions are affected varies from camera to camera. Most dedicated flash units set the camera's shutter to the flash synchronization speed (usually between 1/60 and 1/250 on 35 mm) but switch the camera back to available-light exposure measurement in the periods while the flash unit is recycling. Some also illuminate a flash-ready light in the camera's viewfinder and this may blink to confirm correct exposure.

The most sophisticated dedicated flash units actually meter the light reflected from the film surface during exposure, using a photocell mounted in the camera's mirror box. The method of metering makes flash exposure virtually foolproof, and is of considerable value in macrophotography. Many recent SLR cameras such as the Minolta 7000 have off-the-film flash metering which further increases reliability.

The smallest portable flash units fit quite comfortably in the camera's accessory shoe, because they need the power of just one or two AA cells. However, higher-power units require more batteries, and larger capacitors and transformers, so their weight may overbalance a small camera. The largest units are invariably in the 'hammer' style — a thick vertical shaft containing capacitors and sometimes batteries, with a flashtube and reflector on top. Two-piece units also require a separate battery-pack attached to a belt or slung over the shoulder.

■ POWER AND POWER SOURCES For simple snapshots indoors, virtually any portable flash unit is satisfactory, but for more advanced photography, small flashguns often prove underpowered. Out of doors, particularly, the reach of a flash unit is cut by anything up to 50 per cent, because there are no walls and ceiling to reflect light onto the subject. Bouncing or diffusing the beam of the flash to soften the lighting also absorbs a lot of power, and with a small unit, this can lead to underexposure, or more likely, severe restrictions on aperture choice and maximum subject distance.

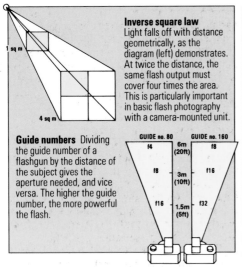

Inverse square law Light falls off with distance geometrically, as the diagram (left) demonstrates. At twice the distance, the same flash output must cover four times the area. This is particularly important in basic flash photography with a camera-mounted unit.

Guide numbers Dividing the guide number of a flashgun by the distance of the subject gives the aperture needed, and vice versa. The higher the guide number, the more powerful the flash.

The flash guide number (GN) is an indication of a unit's power. Dividing the guide number by the camera-to-subject distance gives the approximate aperture that will yield correct exposure. For example, a unit with a guide number of 40 would supply enough light for the photographer to use an aperture of f8 when the subject is five metres away. The guide number can in fact be used to estimate the correct aperture when the flash is used manually, but this involves a short calculation, so it is usually simpler to use in the automatic mode.

Guide numbers are generally quoted for ISO 100/21° film, and either for feet or metres. When comparing flashguns, always check that the guide numbers are quoted for the same film speeds, and that both use the same units — either metric or Imperial.

Guide numbers express only the maximum power of the unit. When there is a choice of several apertures, the various options will progressively cut down the power from this maximum figure.

The smallest portable flash units have GNs of around 15 (metres/ISO 100/21°). This rises to around 25 or 30 for the larger and more versatile hot-shoe mounted units, and to about 50 for a powerful hammer-head flash.

With the exception of the large press units, almost all flashguns now operate from standard-size AA cells. However, these are commonly available in three different formulations. Zinc-carbon cells are the least powerful, giving fewest flashes per set of batteries, and the longest recycling times. Manganese-alkaline cells ('alkaline energizers') greatly reduce recycling times, and last very much longer than zinc-carbon cells. Both types must be discarded when exhausted. Nickel-cadmium cells ('Nicads') on the other hand, can be recharged. They give the shortest recycling times, but need recharging sooner than alkaline cells need

replacing. Since the price of these rechargeable cells is high, their purchase is justified only for frequent users of flash.

High-power units may additionally offer users the option of a shoulder-slung lead-acid accumulator. Though heavy, these power packs give the shortest recycling times and longest life of all. Changing the batteries on a flash unit does not, unfortunately, increase the power of the beam.

■ **USING PORTABLE FLASH** Locked into the accessory shoe of a camera, and pointed directly at the subject, the versatility of even the most sophisticated flash unit is limited. Direct light from the camera position produces harsh, unflattering illumination that is particularly ill-suited to portraits, which are perhaps the most common flash-lit subject.

However, there are several ways to improve flash pictures. The simplest is to direct the flash at a white reflective surface, such as a wall or ceiling, and illuminate the subject by the reflected light. This technique is called 'bounce flash' and to make it easier, many of the more powerful automatic flash units have a tilting head, so that the reflector and tube of the flash can be directed upwards or sideways, while the metering photocell continues to point at the subject. The flashgun can thus continue to function automatically. Units without tilt-heads must be mounted on separate brackets, or hand-held, and exposure must be calculated, which makes the procedure a rather hit-or-miss affair.

Lighting a section of ceiling or wall in this way turns the small source lighting of the flash into a broad source, and this produces softer, more pleasant illumination, as explained on page 86. An additional benefit is that the lighting direction is no longer frontal, so that features in a portrait are more clearly modelled.

Bounce flash can create quite heavy shadows under the chin and nose of portrait subjects, and a few flashguns incorporate a second flashtube and reflector, below the primary tube, to fill in these shadows. An equally effective way of solving the problem when using single-tube flash units is to tape a small piece of silvered card diagonally over a portion of the upward-pointing flash reflector. This spills a portion of the main flash directly onto the subject.

Another way to modify and improve the light from a flashgun is to remove it from the camera's accessory shoe, and hold it to one side of the camera, using a cable to maintain synchronization with the camera's shutter. This makes the lighting less frontal, and yields significant improvement in modelling. However, bear in mind that with the flash moved away from the camera, the unit's sensor will be 'seeing' a view of the

Fill-in flash One of the most useful functions of on-camera flash is to lighten foreground shadows, particularly in scenes containing an element of back-lighting. In the wide-angle outdoor portrait (right), the exposure was calculated for the ambient lighting, and the flash output adjusted so that it would add half the amount that would have been needed if flash were the only illumination. In the bathroom interior (below) the flash output is even less, to give an unobtrusive fill.

Fill-in flash technique With an automatic flashgun, fill-in flash is straightforward — simply a matter of balancing the exposure from the sun and that from the flash unit. The ideal proportion of sun to flash is largely a matter of taste, but is also affected by the exposure latitude of the film, and of the use to which the resulting pictures will be put. For example, colour slide film has little exposure latitude, and the normal ratio is between 4:1 and 2:1 — that is to say that the sunlight is between four and two times brighter than the flash. However, with black-and-white film, the contrast range of the negative can often be adjusted later in the choice of paper grades.

Problems and solutions with fill-in flash (and problems with fill-in flash for pictures of people in particular) are given on page 203.

Direct flash on the camera, while not subtle, can be effective in circumstances where the colours and tones of the subject are distinct and rich, as above. Light from the camera position can give very saturated colours.

limited to a single reflector so that the spread of the beam is fixed. Most flash units produce a beam broad enough to illuminate the field of view of a 35 mm lens on a 35 mm camera. To light the areas covered by lenses with shorter focal lengths, beam spreaders or diffusers are necessary. These usually take the form of Fresnel lenses that fit in front of the flashgun's reflector, expanding the beam to cover the wider area.

In principle, focal lengths longer than 50 mm present no special difficulties with flash, but in practice, much of the light of the flash is wasted, since the unit forms a beam far broader than the field of view of the lens in use. To make more efficient use of the light, it is possible to direct the flash into a reflector to concentrate the light.

Coloured filters which fit over the front of a portable flashgun find occasional use. The most valuable of these is orange-coloured, and converts the light of the flash to the colour of tungsten light. The unit can then be used with tungsten-balanced film.

Perhaps the most valuable flash accessory, though, is the slave unit. This tiny device — half the size of a matchbox — houses a photocell and a cluster of other electronic components encapsulated in resin. At one end there is a female flash synchronization socket, into which the synch cable of the flash unit is plugged. This slave cell then provides cordless synchronization: a flashgun in the camera's accessory shoe will trigger the slave and fire any auxilliary flash unit in the vicinity. This simplifies multi-flash set-ups, and eliminates trailing wires.

subject different from that which the camera records. This can lead to exposure errors, so many flash manufacturers supply a removable sensor that remains in the camera's hot-shoe when the flash itself is removed. Dedicated units additionally need special synchronization cables which relay the extra data between camera and flash.

Multiple flash takes the flash-off-camera technique a step further, permitting quite elaborate lighting set-ups. However, exposure determination when using several portable units can be quite complex unless the photographer uses either a flashmeter or instant-film test.

Portable flash units have a valuable role to play in daylight, as well as in the dark. In bright sunlight, heavy shadows across the faces of portrait subjects create a very harsh impression of the sitter's features. Set to reduced power, an on-camera flash can soften these shadows. This is called *fill-in flash*, or sometimes synchro-sunlight.

■ **ACCESSORIES** Unlike studio flash systems, nearly all portable flashguns are

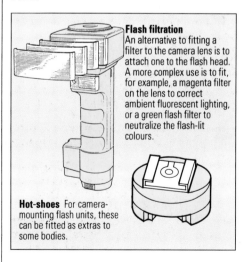

Flash filtration
An alternative to fitting a filter to the camera lens is to attach one to the flash head. A more complex use is to fit, for example, a magenta filter on the lens to correct ambient fluorescent lighting, or a green flash filter to neutralize the flash-lit colours.

Hot-shoes For camera-mounting flash units, these can be fitted as extras to some bodies.

■ **PORTABLE FLASH APPLICATIONS** As the name suggests, the greatest virtue of portable flash is its handiness. Portable flash units are at their most useful on the run: in reportage, social photography, speedy location portraiture, or for the ubiquitous and much maligned family snapshot!

Studio flash

In the studio, portability is not important, but versatility and power certainly are. The smallest studio flash units have a power output of around 100j, as much as the largest portable flashguns. A large studio may have flash units with 200 times this power.

Why is all this power necessary? Because studio photography often involves the use of sheet-film cameras which must be stopped down to minutely small apertures to obtain sufficient depth of field. For example, with 10 × 8in film, an aperture of f90 is by no means unusual. Also, modern studio photography utilizes heavy diffusion of light sources, and this invariably absorbs a great deal of power.

Studio flash units work in broadly the same way as portable flashguns. To cope with the extra power, though, the flashtube must be very much larger than the tube in a portable flash. In studio units, the tube is usually formed into a ring.

In the centre of this circular tube is a tungsten bulb — either a photoflood or, more usually, a tungsten-halogen lamp. The bulb is continuously illuminated, thereby simulating the light of the flash. Called a *modelling lamp*, this tungsten bulb allows the photographer to judge approximately the effect of moving lights around the subject, or reducing their intensity.

The smaller studio flash units resemble overblown portable flashguns, mounted on stands. These *monobloc* units integrate all the components in a single casing, with the flashtube, modelling light and reflector, at the front, capacitors, transformers and control electronics in the middle, and a panel of controls on the back.

Monobloc construction is convenient and inexpensive, and the units are easily portable, making them ideal for location as well as studio work. Into a single fibre case that can be carried by one person, it is possible to pack two monobloc units, stands, all cables, umbrella reflectors and flashmeter. The principal disadvantage of such units is instability. Perched near the ceiling on top of a stand, a monobloc flash unit can sometimes sway alarmingly, and tripping over a cable often has disastrous results.

Monobloc construction is impractical for really powerful studio flash units. Instead of integrating all components in a single housing, these big units are split into two. A box on the studio floor houses the power supply — the capacitors, transformers and other electronic components — and only the flashtube, reflector and modelling light sit at the top of the stand.

The power supply usually has at least two outlets, so that one power supply can run two flash heads. Optional splitter boxes divide the power still further.

Switches on top of the power supply reduce the output progressively from full power down to one-quarter or one-eighth, distribute it among each of the heads in use, and control the functioning of the modelling lights. These can be switched off altogether, switched on at full power, or attenuated in proportion to the power of the flash head in which each is mounted. (This last option gives the truest simulation of the effect of the flash illumination.)

■ **CONTROLLING EXPOSURE** The power output of a studio flash unit is set by the photographer for each picture, and does not change automatically for varying subject distances, as does the power of an automatic flashgun. Choosing the correct camera aperture is therefore not as simple as it is with portable flash.

However, in the controlled environment of the studio, experienced photographers can usually make fairly good estimates of what the correct exposure will be, based on film speed, power routed to each flash head, degree of diffusion of each light source, and other relevant factors. A flashmeter obviously helps in making this initial judgement, but the real work of exposure estimation is usually done with an instant film test. Not only does this allow the photographer to control exposure, it also provides an empirical confirmation that all the equipment is functioning normally, and makes it possible to fine-tune the power output of each of the lights in use. As a final control over exposure, many photographers will also clip-test their films — that is, they make a trial exposure on the first frame of the film, which is 'clipped' off and developed.

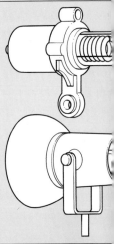

Flash and movement

The high speed of electronic flash is ideal for freezing movement in small spaces — principally studios. A pouring liquid at the distance shown here needs a speed of at least 1/500 second — within the range of even a large, slow mains unit. Nevertheless, the rapidity of the action makes it difficult to time the triggering with certainty, and it is usually necessary to shoot several frames for choice.

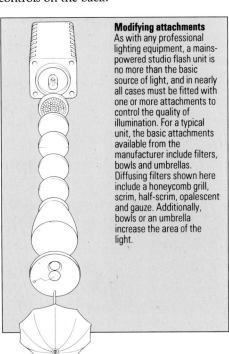

Modifying attachments

As with any professional lighting equipment, a mains-powered studio flash unit is no more than the basic source of light, and in nearly all cases must be fitted with one or more attachments to control the quality of illumination. For a typical unit, the basic attachments available from the manufacturer include filters, bowls and umbrellas. Diffusing filters shown here include a honeycomb grill, scrim, half-scrim, opalescent and gauze. Additionally, bowls or an umbrella increase the area of the light.

Flash head design In studio units, which are mains-powered, the flash head is only ever regarded as a raw source of illumination, and must be modified for nearly all uses. There are two basic types of design, shown at left: a separate head (top) connected by lead to the capacitor and controls, and a monobloc or integral design underneath), which is a self-contained unit. Separate heads are needed for high-output flash (the tube illustrated here can handle 000 joules), but monobloc units are tidier and more compact.

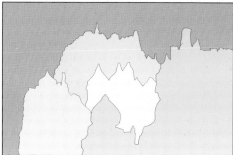

Open flash technique A large space can be photographed with just one small flash unit provided that there is very little ambient lighting. The technique, illustrated here in a large | Burmese cave packed with Buddhas, is to leave the shutter open and fire the flash from several positions.

■ **STUDIO FLASH HEADS** The standard flash head for a studio unit accepts a wide variety of different reflectors, diffusers and other lighting accessories. The studio photographer is not, however, limited to just the one basic head.

High power electronic flash heads have specially lengthened flashtubes, which are wound into a short helix and can cope with the output from several linked power supplies. These heads incorporate a more powerful modelling light, and a cooling fan.

Striplights also have longer flashtubes, but in these heads the tubes are straight, and usually about a metre (3ft) long. Striplights produce a very even light along their entire length, so they are ideal for illuminating studio backdrops. A fluorescent tube next to the flashtube acts as a modelling light.

In ringlights the flashtube forms a wide circle — wide enough to poke a camera lens through. Since the tube totally surrounds the lens, these heads provide the shadowless illumination which is periodically in favour in fashion photography circles.

For applications where the light-source must be concealed, perhaps in a table lamp that forms part of a room set, very small heads are available. These are little bigger than a 150W domestic light bulb, and contain no modelling light.

Bulb flash

Expendable flash bulbs were the ancestors of today's electronic flash systems, and for a few specialized areas, electronic flash still cannot rival bulb flash. Flash bulbs range from bean-sized up to the shape and proportion of an ordinary light bulb. Inside its blue-tinted glass envelope, each bulb carries a charge of magnesium wire or foil, and a small heating coil which is connected to contacts on the base of the bulb. Passing a current through the coil causes the magnesium to burn, giving out a brilliant flash of daylight-coloured light.

Flash bulbs give out relatively massive amounts of power, yet require only a low electric current from a simple circuit for triggering. To produce the same power output as a single flash bulb would require a very large and cumbersome studio flash unit.

Consequently, bulb flash is generally used to light very large spaces such as factories, foundries or aircraft hangars. Multiple bulb arrangements are very common, with each bulb fitted into a lampholder and reflector, and positioned so as to be invisible from the camera position. An electric cable links all the bulb-holders.

Since flash bulbs can be used only once, the photographer must visit all the bulb-holders to change over the lamps between exposures. So bulb flash is best suited to jobs that require just one or two pictures.

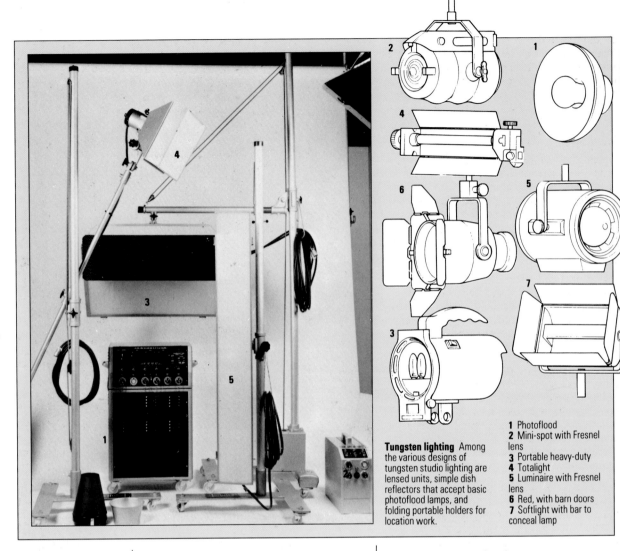

Tungsten lighting Among the various designs of tungsten studio lighting are lensed units, simple dish reflectors that accept basic photoflood lamps, and folding portable holders for location work.

1 Photoflood
2 Mini-spot with Fresnel lens
3 Portable heavy-duty
4 Totalight
5 Luminaire with Fresnel lens
6 Red, with barn doors
7 Softlight with bar to conceal lamp

Area flash lighting The illustration above shows a high-output professional area flash system.

1 The central power unit is a control console with which the 5000 joules from the capacitor underneath can be distributed among six flash tubes or heads. This level of output is needed with large-format cameras, that accept lenses with apertures as small as f45 and f64, and with heavily diffused area-light attachments.

2 A smaller power unit that is relatively portable has an output of 1000 joules. It can be linked in series with similar units, and the modest recycling rate of 5 seconds allows several to be run off one domestic mains outlet.

3 The basic still-life area light in this system is a 600 × 900cm (2 × 3ft) window of translucent plastic fronting a cantilevered box.

4 Small area light on boom arm.

5 Troughlight for backgrounds.

TUNGSTEN LIGHTING

Among professional photographers, tungsten lighting is less popular than electronic flash for most general applications. Nevertheless this traditional light source has a number of special advantages — particularly for the novice photographer who finds it hard to imagine exactly how a brief flash of light will illuminate the subject.

Tungsten lighting can be measured with a conventional camera meter — so even with complex lighting set-ups, it is easy to work out what the exposure will be. It is simple also to see how moving the lights affects the highlights and shadows of the picture.

Compared to flash, tungsten lights are simple, reliable and inexpensive. Since nothing more complicated than a heated wire is involved in producing the light, maintenance is usually restricted to changing blown bulbs.

Finally, photographers can use any shutter speed with tungsten light, rather than being restricted to the totally instantaneous, action-freezing burst of flash.

Lamps, watts and colour

The term 'tungsten lamp' embraces a whole range of light sources, from the smallest 15 W pigmy light bulb, through to giant 300 W floodlights. Photographers, though, generally do not use ordinary domestic light bulbs as primary sources of light in a picture. This is because household lamps are too low in power and give out light that is too yellow in colour. In the colour temperature scale explained on page 114, these small light bulbs fall below 2,500 K and their light needs filtration, even when the camera contains film balanced for use in tungsten light.

For photographic purposes, special types of lamps are manufactured. The cheapest and simplest of these is the photoflood. This looks like an oversize light bulb, and although it will fit into ordinary bayonet light sockets, this practice is not recommended, as the bulbs get very hot in use and there is a risk of fire. Photofloods come in several sizes and give out 275 to 500 W.

Nominally, the colour temperature of photoflood light is 3,400 K, so in principle, an 81B filter is needed to balance the lamps to the sensitivity of tungsten film — which is matched to light of 3,200 K. However, in practice the difference is negligible and diminishes with time, because the lamps yellow gradually in use.

Photofloods burn for only a few hours: usually less than eight. However, photopearl lamps (also called photolamps) have lives 10 or 20 times longer than the photofloods which they closely resemble. These bulbs have other advantages besides longevity — their colour precisely matches the sensitivity of tungsten-balanced film; and they are more powerful — 500 or 1000 W.

Both photoflood and photopearl lamps fit into inexpensive aluminium reflectors and heatproof lampholders, so they are the ideal choice for photographers who want to try their hand at studio lighting without spending a fortune. And because the bulbs themselves are quite large, they produce fairly soft shadows that can be made softer still when the bulb is covered by a metal cap, which is then fitted into a large white reflector.

For day-to-day photography, however, most professionals prefer to use tungsten-halogen lamps. These lamps are extremely compact, have a very long life, and more important, produce light that is a constant colour throughout the life of the lamp.

The beam of a tungsten-halogen lamp has a colour temperature of 3,200 K so the lamps can be used without filtration when the camera is loaded with tungsten-light balanced film. And the lamps commonly have a power output of 250 to 2000 W.

The other light sources occasionally used for photography include lamps 'borrowed' from the theatre and the film industry. For practical purposes, these are very much the same as tungsten-halogen lamps, though they may have higher power outputs.

Lampholders

One of the reasons why tungsten light retains a following among professional photographers is because it can easily be shaped into a tight beam — a parallel or converging beam if need be. With flash, this is possible, but the beam of the modelling light rarely matches the shape of the beam from the flashtube itself.

To make a really well-defined beam, the tungsten lamp must be fitted into an optical system comprising a reflector and lens — rather like a slide projector. The lens at the front is a Fresnel lens similar to that used on lighthouses or below the focusing screens of SLR cameras. Lampholders of this type are called *luminaires* or *focusing spots*. A knob on the housing of the unit adjusts the angle of the beam from broad flood to tight spot, but the beam always casts hard-edged shadows.

Lighting interiors
For the large amounts of light needed for interiors such as this reconstruction of a 19th-century US Post Office and general store (above) tungsten is more convenient than flash, needing only long exposures rather than multiply-tripped flash. Here, 2 × 1000W lamps were aimed from outside through diffusers to simulate daylight.

Miniature tungsten lamps in this model (below) allowed a realism impossible with any other lighting — a 35 minute exposure giving a minimum aperture for maximum depth of field.

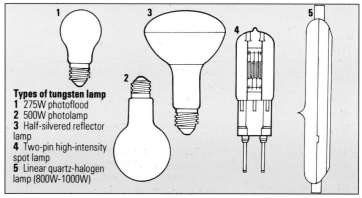

Types of tungsten lamp
1 275W photoflood
2 500W photolamp
3 Half-silvered reflector lamp
4 Two-pin high-intensity spot lamp
5 Linear quartz-halogen lamp (800W-1000W)

Lighting for effect and subject qualities
Lighting can draw out the physical qualities of a subject. Here, a translucent onyx egg is made to glow by aiming a single lamp from beneath, diffused through a milky plastic base and confined by a circular black card mask on the underside.

Using orange window gels One way of dealing with the different colours of tungsten and daylight on location is to cover windows with orange plastic (the colour of an 85B filter), using tungsten lights inside, and tungsten film in the camera. Not only does this match the colour of the light from inside and out, but it also reduces the intensity of the light from the windows. The alternative is to filter the lamps, but this makes the problem of balancing light intensities even greater.

Focused spots range tremendously in size from the giants that are often used to light film sets, down to small mini-spots that provide just enough light for head-and-shoulders portraiture.

Focused spots cannot produce soft lighting, and for this purpose, photographers use a much simpler lampholder. At its most basic, this consists of a tin box with a curving reflector inside. The lamp itself is supported at the focus of the reflector and faces into it, so that only reflected light reaches the subject. This softens the beam, producing very soft-edged shadows.

The broader and less shiny the reflector, the softer is the light. Matt white reflectors form very soft, but relatively weak beams. Shiny silver reflectors are far more efficient, but produce much harder light. Matt silver is a good compromise. These lights are known by a variety of names, such as 'broadlight', 'softlight' and others.

For location lighting, compactness and light weight are priorities, and for this purpose, photographers have adopted lights from the movie industry. A very popular

model is the 'Redhead' — actually a manufacturer's trade name, but now, like Hoover, simply a name attached to almost any lamp of the same type.

The original Redhead has a lightweight, cast alloy frame (painted red) and a fixed reflector inside. A round knob at the rear of the unit moves the lamp within the reflector. Moved forward, the lamp forms a broad beam. Moving the lamp back closer to the centre of the reflector makes the beam narrower. Redheads generally have a power of 650 W, though a larger, fan-cooled version produces 2000 W.

Other similar units have their own unique advantages. Tota-lights are the smallest of all portable units; video lights produce a powerful beam, yet they can be hand-held and even run for half an hour from a rechargeable battery pack.

Tungsten accessories
The range of lighting accessories is more limited for tungsten lights than it is for flash, because the lamps themselves get very hot and cannot be fitted into enclosed spaces as flash heads can. Some types of diffusing material, though, are heatproof and a few accessories are made specially to withstand the heat of tungsten bulbs.

The most valuable of these is the dichroic filter. This heatproof glass plate fits over the front of the lampholder and adjusts the colour of the beam of tungsten light from 3,200 K to 5,500 K — the colour of daylight. So tungsten lamps can then be combined with daylight, using daylight-balanced film. Heat resistant plastic sheets that do the same job are also available, and though these are less robust than the glass filters, some of them combine the function of diffuser and filter. Held a metre or two in front of a powerful tungsten lamp, such a filter/diffuser forms the light into a soft, daylight-coloured window light.

Precautions in use
The greatest risk when using tungsten light is that of fire, burns or scorching. Though the beam can be softened by reflection from a white-painted ceiling, this soon yellows and chars the paintwork, and if continued, can set fire to timber or wallpaper.

Tungsten light also consumes a lot of power, and can easily overload a domestic power circuit causing a fire risk.

Tungsten bulbs themselves must be treated with respect. All types are fragile — especially when burning — and halogen bulbs must not be touched with ungloved hands. They are supplied in cardboard or plastic sleeves so that they can be fitted into the holder without coming into contact with finger grease. The life of the bulb is much shorter if it is inserted with bare hands.

CONTROLLING LIGHT QUALITY

Photographic lamps free the photographer from dependence on available, but unalterable, sources of light — and provide almost complete control over the way a picture is lit. But the lamps themselves are no more than the raw source of the lighting. It is the way their output can be modified by an assortment of fittings that is really important. Yet since certain key fittings depend very much on the type and brand of lamp, the choice between flash and tungsten studio lighting is fundamental.

The advantages and features of each have already been discussed, but here the two different sources are considered in direct comparison. Flash has largely replaced tungsten lighting in still photography studios, principally because of its consistent light output, its action-stopping power and its relative coolness. Certainly, for moving subjects, such as fashion models, flash has a clear advantage, while the low heat output allows the use of attachments that enclose the lamp — such as the area lights illustrated on page 82 that are now widely used in still-life photography. However, the tungsten lighting does provide a *continuous* output of light. This means that you can increase the amount of light reaching the film simply by lengthening the exposure — provided that the subject is static and the camera can be locked down — which is easier than tripping a flash discharge several times. In most photography, flash is limited by its maximum discharge; if more light is needed, multiple flash is the only answer. With small apertures and large-scale subjects, an exposure with tungsten lighting that runs into seconds or minutes is likely to be more practical than firing off flash heads several times (the numbers double for each extra f-stop).

In summary, flash and tungsten compare as in the table below.

Naturalistic lighting
In contrast to the stylized illumination of the egg, opposite, the quality of lighting in the location portrait below was intended to be unobtrusive and to fit in with existing room lighting. A large, diffused lamp was placed to the left of the seated subject, and its output regulated to match the ambient lighting using Polaroid test shots.

Stylized lighting
By contrast with the basically naturalistic style of lighting above, the high-key effect at left was achieved by using a main frontal light with heavy diffusion, a spot from behind, and a soft-focus filter to increase flaring. In addition, the exposure was generous, to further eliminate shadows.

FLASH AND TUNGSTEN COMPARED

	Flash	Tungsten
1	Freezes fast action but cannot give blur of motion.	Can give blur of motion but can rarely freeze fast action.
2	Same colour as daylight so can be mixed with daylight to fill in shadows, and can be used with the wide range of daylight-balanced colour films.	Colour balance can be a problem even with tungsten-balanced film. With daylight colour film, heavy, light-cutting filtration is needed.
3	Needs modelling lights to preview the lighting.	Photographs as it looks.
4	Cool, so comfortable to work with and allows enclosed fittings.	Hot, so cannot be used with delicate subjects such as plants and cold food, and cannot be enclosed without good ventilation.
5	Exposure can only be increased beyond a certain point by multiple flashes.	With static subjects, exposure can be increased by extending exposure time.
6	Relatively costly.	Relatively cheap.
7	Relatively heavy.	Relatively light.
8	Complex technically.	Uncomplicated and easy to repair.

Softening light

Nearly all photographic lamps are effectively point sources of light giving harsh, contrasting lighting and must usually be diffused to give a manageable light. Every method of softening a lamp follows just one principle: it increases the size of the light so that the *effective* source, from the point of view of the subject, is larger. The two main ways of doing this are diffusion and reflection. The best method to use varies with the type of lamp, the conditions and on the precise result the photographer is looking for; each method has a distinctive effect.

Diffusers fit in front of the lamp, and most use some kind of translucent material, such as opal perspex, white fabric, tracing paper or frosted glass. More open screens such as gauze or ray honeycomb do similar work. When light spill from between the lamp and the diffuser is likely to be troublesome, an enclosed diffusion fitting is an advantage. An area light for use with flash heads is designed specifically for this. Otherwise, a free-standing trace frame, corrugated translucent plastic or a translucent umbrella can be used.

With *reflectors*, the light is spread out by reflection from a diffusing surface; the lamp is aimed towards the reflector and bounced back towards the subject. More light is lost through bouncing it off one of these reflective surfaces than shining it through a diffuser, but it is often easier to install a large reflector. Indeed, white-painted walls and ceiling are the simplest of all large reflectors. The most commonly used reflectors are collapsible umbrellas, with a variety of inner linings (white to metallic), but plain sheets of virtually any bright material hung from a frame (or the ceiling) may be quite adequate. The more matt the surface, the broader and more even is the reflected light, but also the more light is lost. Matt white, glossy white, wrinkled metallic foil, matt metal finish and mirror finish comprise the basic range of surfaces.

Concentrating light

Concentrating the light into a narrow beam is not quite the opposite of diffusion — a bare lamp bulb on its own casts strong, hard shadows. The purpose of concentration is to limit the *area* that is lit, and this inevitably means defining a shape. The usual method is to enclose the sides of the light source, channelling the beam through a narrow opening. *Cones, snoots* and *lensed spots* all do this to produce a circular area of light (the latter use a condenser lens to give sharp edges to the circle of illumination). Less extreme shaping of the light is achieved by *barn doors*, which can be swung into the side of the beam of light to concentrate the light on particular areas of the subject.

Direct diffusion and scoop
The most common lighting treatment in still-life photography is an overhead area light, suspended so that it illuminates the objects almost directly from above. When this is combined with a smooth white base, potential shadow areas underneath the objects are automatically filled by reflection. Extending the base — in this case a sheet of Formica — beyond the pool of light causes a gradual shading in the visible background, accentuated by curving the base sheet up (by suspending it or by resting it against a wall).

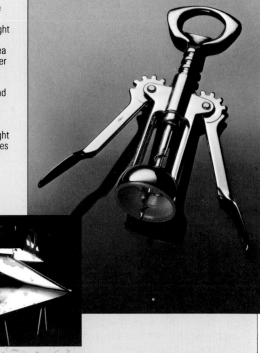

Diffuse reflections
Shiny-surfaced objects are usually best treated by arranging an extra-large light source to be reflected in them. Here, a standard area light is diffused even further by suspending a thick translucent sheet at an angle between the light and the set. The base for this still life is a sheet of dark perspex. Note that the separation between the light and the extra diffuser makes it possible to create a shading effect.

Back-lighting For soft, even back-lighting — the standard treatment for transparent objects such as glass — an area light is aimed from the back, through a diffusing sheet, masked to the edges of the picture to avoid flare. Flare is always a problem with back-lit subjects, cutting down contrast and degrading the image. It is particularly acute with glass, which can catch undamped bright spots and throw unwanted light towards the camera. A careful arrangement of black cards is needed to cut out flare. With such problems, it may seem back-lighting glass is hardly worth the trouble — but back-lighting heightens contrast in the structure of the glass, giving it solidity and weight.

Multiple lighting

While most subjects can be lit efficiently with only one lamp and a few reflectors, using more than one opens up a great variety of effects. Multiple lighting often appears artificial and although this is not necessarily objectionable, it contrasts obviously with the naturalism of single-area lights.

The usual, but not the only, principle in using several lights is for there to be a single main light, secondary fill lights, and secondary effects lights. The idea is to make it look as if there is really only one light source. Fill lights simply alleviate shadows to reduce overall contrast; effects lights are used to pick out edges and add highlights.

Controlling flare

It is a tradition of photography — although not always a justified one — that technical image perfection is an ideal. This means sharpness, freedom from distortion, colour accuracy, and a full tonal range with good contrast. In arranging the lighting, lens flare is the principal danger to these standards, but it can be avoided by shading the lens efficiently from the lamp. This can be done close to the lens in the form of a lens shade, or close to the lamp in the form of barn doors or a *flag* (which need be no more than a black card clipped to a stand). Flare, strictly defined, is non-image-forming light, and avoiding flare means ensuring that no direct light falls on the lens.

Ultraviolet lamps While not normally considered photographic lighting, ultraviolet lamps can be used for interesting coloured effects. The extremely short wavelength lamps that give what is popularly called 'black-lighting', cause fluorescence in certain materials, such as whitened fabrics.

SPECIAL LIGHTING

While the lighting equipment illustrated above is designed to be versatile, and does indeed suit most ordinary lighting demands, there are certain specific methods and sources of lighting for very different effects. The uses to which such special lighting are put are explored under the relevant subject headings in the second section of this book, but the technical basics are as follows.

Base lighting

With base lighting, light is projected upwards through a translucent sheet, commonly opal perspex, just as in a lightbox for viewing transparencies. The applications of this type of lighting are necessarily limited, but it can work well with transparent objects — this is the standard way of making glasses of liquid glow. In combination with normal overhead lighting it provides an extremely clean white background.

BASIC MODIFICATIONS FOR PORTRAIT LIGHTING Some of the permutations of the most common pieces of lighting equipment are shown in the chart opposite featuring a plain phrenological head.

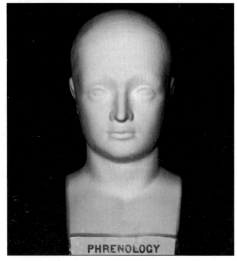

Rim lighting

For rim lighting a single spot is positioned out of sight of the camera behind the subject, pointing towards the camera. The edges of the subject, if textured, catch the light, and against a dark background the effect can be that of a halo. With shiny-surfaced objects, spot lights behind but just out of frame produce a similar effect.

Back-lighting

One method of back-lighting is to place a floodlight behind the subject, usually diffused so as to appear even. With no shadow fill, the result is a silhouette. Two alternative methods are to hang a large sheet of diffusing material (or tracing paper on a

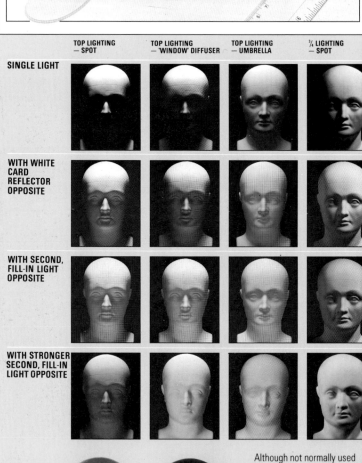

	TOP LIGHTING — SPOT	TOP LIGHTING — 'WINDOW' DIFFUSER	TOP LIGHTING — UMBRELLA	¾ LIGHTING — SPOT
SINGLE LIGHT				
WITH WHITE CARD REFLECTOR OPPOSITE				
WITH SECOND, FILL-IN LIGHT OPPOSITE				
WITH STRONGER SECOND, FILL-IN LIGHT OPPOSITE				

Although not normally used as a portrait technique, back-lighting produces a silhouette effect (left). For this, the light must cover a reasonable area evenly, and can be produced by aiming a light from behind, facing towards the camera and diffused through translucent material on a trace frame.

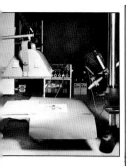

Base lighting For this mixture of opaque and solid objects, two lighting techniques are used: light diffused through a perspex screen from underneath for the transparent objects provides the main illumination; a large area light suspended above the table fills in the shadows on the opaque objects such as the tape.

frame) behind the subject with lights behind that, or to use a white wall or paper background as a large reflector for lights aimed at it from the front. In back-lighting, the base of the set, if visible, can be a problem by appearing as a discontinuity. One method of hiding the edge of the base is to use a highly reflective surface, such as glass or perspex. This appears to merge with the bright background.

Mirrors

All kinds of mirrors can be useful in studio photography for re-directing light. With care, they can give the effect of multiple lighting with only one source. In small still-life sets, dental mirrors are particularly useful, as they can be positioned close to the subject for precise effects.

Axial lighting

Axial lighting takes its name from the *lens* axis, and the principle is to direct the light

along the line of sight from the camera. The usual technique is to place a half-silvered mirror at a 45° angle in front of the lens, and to shine a light towards it from the side, at 90° to the lens axis. The camera can see right through the mirror to the subject but is unaffected by the light. Half of the light shines straight through the glass, and half of it is reflected directly towards the subject, giving completely shadowless lighting.

Lasers

The point of light from a laser is so small that it has no real value as a light source in studio photography. Neither will the kind of low-powered laser likely to be used by the photographer give the striking, intense shafts of light familiar in discos — unless the atmosphere is so dusty or smoky that reflections from particles in the air pick out the beam. However, a moving laser, aided by mirrors and prisms, can be used to create some exotic effects.

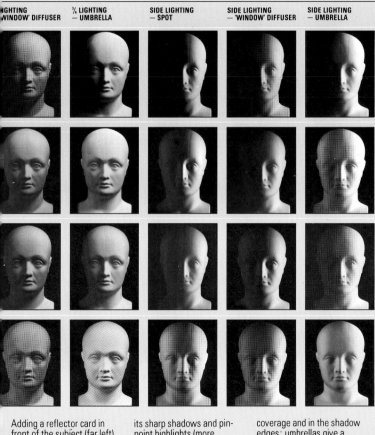

| IGHTING VINDOW' DIFFUSER | ¾ LIGHTING — UMBRELLA | SIDE LIGHTING — SPOT | SIDE LIGHTING — 'WINDOW' DIFFUSER | SIDE LIGHTING — UMBRELLA |

Adding a reflector card in front of the subject (far left) reveals some detail. The more conventional range of methods is shown above. Different types of light and different positions run left-to-right, while increasingly efficient shadow-fill runs from top to bottom. The most contrast light is a single spot, and because of

its sharp shadows and pin-point highlights (more obvious on real eyes and shiny skin than on this model head), it tends to be used only for dramatic effects. The subtle but distinct differences between the two most common lighting attachments — umbrellas and window-like area lights — can be seen in the

coverage and in the shadow edges; umbrellas give a more enveloping light, less obviously directional, and rather softer shadows. The basic methods of shadow fill are passive (reflector cards with white or silvered surfaces) and active (second lights). The effect chosen is very much a matter of personal taste.

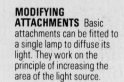

MODIFYING ATTACHMENTS Basic attachments can be fitted to a single lamp to diffuse its light. They work on the principle of increasing the area of the light source.

Filters include, top-to-bottom, a honeycomb design in black metal, scrim, half-scrim, gauze and opal.

Dish and bowl reflectors are available in different sizes, depths and interior finishes (silvered or white, for example).

Bowl and spiller A special design of bowl reflector that gives more diffusion is a shallow white-painted dish with a spiller cap. The spiller hides the bare lamp from view.

Umbrella Apart from the largest area lights illustrated on page 82, the heaviest diffusion is that from a white umbrella, available in different sizes and shapes.

LIGHTING STYLES

The range of lighting equipment available — indeed, the design of the many different lamps and their attachments already shown in this chapter — often depends on something more fundamental than just efficiency. It depends also on the styles of lighting that have become popular in different fields of photography. What tends to happen is that occasional major changes in lighting design made by one or a group of professional photographers catch the imagination of others, including the large amateur market and manufacturers of lighting equipment adapt their range accordingly. This happens particularly when the work is widely published, such as in the advertising and editorial pages of national consumer magazines. In the early days of American fashion photography, for example, the romantic haze and flare created by De Meyer by means of soft, filtered backlighting was very popular. Later, in the 1930s, the sharper, more visually active style of photographers such as Steichen, using large numbers of klieg lights from all directions became the norm.

Sometimes, lighting equipment precedes, or even inspires, a new lighting style. During the mid-1970s a number of photographers adapted powerful ringlights (see page 81), originally designed for medical photography, for fashion work. The brash, frontal effect of ringlighting soon became the vogue for all of the major fashion magazines. The results contrast strongly with the traditional diffuse lighting reflected from large umbrellas. In common with most other distinct styles of lighting, the use of ringflash in fashion was, in fact, a deliberate reaction to existing styles that certain photographers were beginning to find boring. Its popularity, however, proved to be short-lived.

On other occasions, equipment manufacturers have belatedly followed the innovators of a lighting style, and produced commercial versions of lights that had previously been custom built, so both fulfilling a demand and encouraging more use among a much wider group of photographers. An example of this is the window/area/box/soft light, as it is variously known. Exactly when it was 'invented' is unclear, but during the 1960s most professional still-life photographers in Europe and America began using these large, precisely shaped box-like diffusers (illustrated on page 82). Many built their own, while a very few manufacturers of expensive, professional-quality flash lighting produced versions. These lights were developed as tastes in advertising illustration moved towards the clear and simple (at least for product shots), and also because they are a very efficient and uncomplicated way of lighting a basic still life,

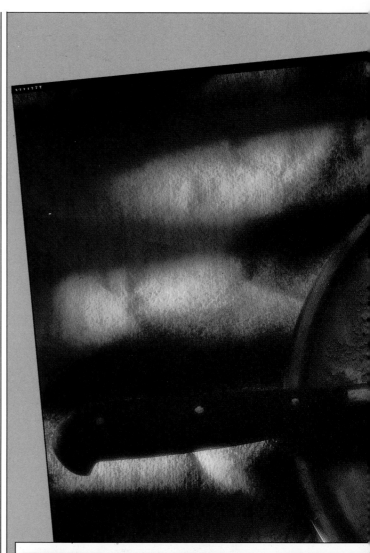

MARLENE DIETRICH in Paramount Pictures

Copr. 1937 Paramount Productions, Inc., Permission granted for Newspaper and Magazine reproduction. (Made in U. S. A.)

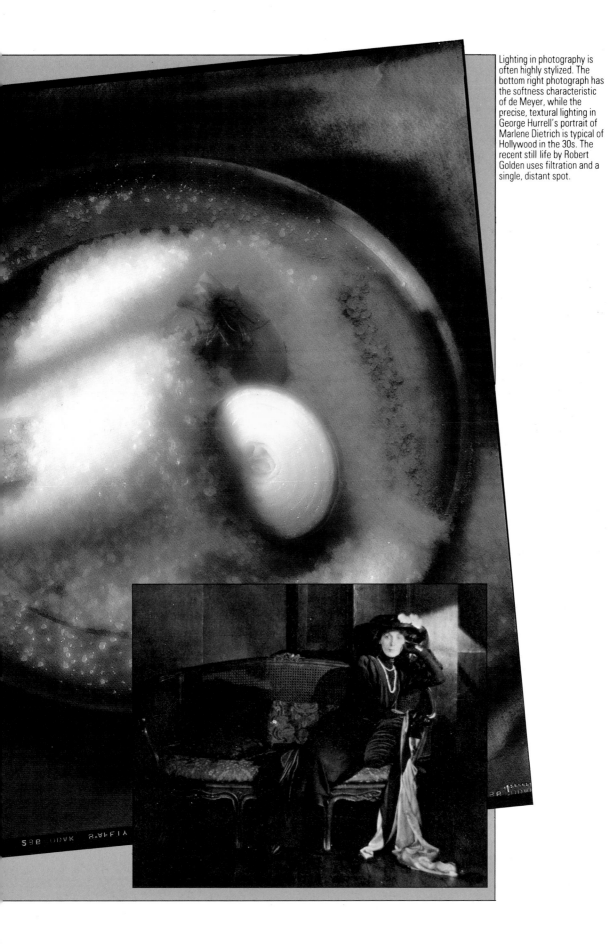

Lighting in photography is often highly stylized. The bottom right photograph has the softness characteristic of de Meyer, while the precise, textural lighting in George Hurrell's portrait of Marlene Dietrich is typical of Hollywood in the 30s. The recent still life by Robert Golden uses filtration and a single, distant spot.

particularly when used overhead. Among mass-produced equipment, however, there was nothing comparable until the mid-1970s, when sufficient numbers of other photographers, including amateurs, had seen and liked the results that appeared in magazines and posters to create a demand.

Not surprisingly, as a fashion in lighting design percolates through the market, some photographers begin to experiment with different techniques. Often, their inspiration may be the renewed interest in a style long fallen out of fashion. For instance, the renewed interest in Constructivism and the Bauhaus that occurred in several areas of design in the early 1980s encouraged experiment with the sharp shadow shapes from naked lamps and spotlights, mimicking the bright, hard utilitarian sense of style of the Bauhaus movement.

Single versus multiple lights

One of the most important stylistic choices is between one and several light sources. The argument for using a single light is partly one of simplicity and partly one of naturalness. Interiors are usually illuminated by daylight streaming through a window; any studio light that imitates this effect (an area light does this the most perfectly) appears generally pleasing, and normal.

The case for multiple lighting, on the other hand, is that a wide range of effects can be created, including a more distinctive style, and that great precision is possible, revealing detail here or enhancing textures there. Multiple lighting can often generate an air of theatricality and lends itself to mannered design.

High-key versus low-key

The overall tone of a picture is another feature in the style of lighting. In most pictures, there is an even range of tones, from dark to light. By deliberately tipping the balance towards the dark tones, a rich, moody, *low-key* effect is created. Tipping the balance the other way, towards the light tones, gives a bright, often delicate, *high-key* result. In both cases, important details of the image can be picked out in the opposing tone — for instance, the eyes and mouth in a portrait that is principally white, or just the outline of a dark object caught against a black background by a light well to the side and behind. The 'key' in this sense of lighting design is not simply a matter of under- or overexposure, but involves constructing both a lighting arrangement and a set or subject that contribute to the effect. A heavily diffused flood of light, for instance, helps to create a high-key effect because it eliminates shadows, while precise spotlights, used carefully, often help to create a relatively low-key image.

High-key lighting gives a lightness and airiness to the still-life above. Generous exposure and light tones enhance the effect.

Area light The window-like effect of an area light gives diffuse but directional modelling, as in the photograph of the necklace (right).

3/4-frontal umbrella This, the most standard lighting style in modern portraiture gives a soft light and good coverage.

Low-key lighting In contrast to the bright appearance of the high-key lighting in the still-life opposite, the low-key style of the portrait above has a predominance of dark tones. In this portrait, the effect is achieved with a single and relatively small light source that strikes the man's face from behind and slightly to one side. There is no shadow-fill, so it is only the outline that defines the shape.

Flat versus contrasty lighting

Another parameter in lighting design is the degree of contrast that the lighting creates. Contrast exists, of course, in the subject and setting themselves, but the position of the lights and the attachments used with them has a crucial influence on contrast. The most extreme contrast is silhouette back-lighting; the lowest contrast is diffused frontal lighting. Strong diffusion or bounced lighting reduces contrast by reducing both the density of shadows and their edges. A small, intense lamp tends to throw sharp, deep shadows and so raise local contrast in a photograph, while any device that limits the beam, such as a lens or a snoot, also increases contrast by darkening the area beyond the edges of its focus.

Precision

When using studio lighting, it is often assumed that the photographer must take meticulous care over the arrangement of the lights. Indeed, the skill of professional photographers is often judged by how well they can control studio lighting. This is usually a fair judgement. Nevertheless, while precision in lighting design is an important aspect of craftsmanship, absolute and pre-determined control in every instance may not necessarily be the most exciting way of making photographs. Some-times, the unexpected results of experi-menting with lights produce more interesting images, gaining in spontaneity what they lose in precision. Portraits in particu-lar may respond to a less painstaking approach.

The instant ease with which today's films produce full-colour images seems far removed from the cumbersome processes used in the infancy of photography more than a century ago. Yet despite the revolutions in materials and processing that have changed photography almost out of recognition, the very basis of image-making has remained largely untouched. Today, just as in 1839 when the first photographs amazed the world, photography is possible only because light causes subtle changes in certain salts of silver.

Even the most sophisticated of today's films relies on this one fact. The change is so subtle that it is invisible to the eye; only when the silver salts are transformed by other chemical compounds does the change in structure become apparent, and the crystals that were struck by light turn to black metallic silver; those which were kept in the dark remain undarkened.

Of course, things have changed since Fox-Talbot and Daguerre made, quite independently, the discoveries on which photography is founded. Nowadays, all films make use of the power of developing chemicals to

enhance the action of light; Fox-Talbot's paper-based 'film' darkened of its own accord — but only after exposure to light millions of times longer than today's fast films require.

Furthermore, the darkening of silver is now only half the story. As sections later in the chapter explain, the silver formed in colour films simply acts as a stimulant to the production of the clouds of dye that make the picture. Once the dye has appeared, the silver is redundant — and is washed away.

Black-and-white film has remained almost unchanged over the years, and the principles of its exposure and development prove the key to an understanding of how all other types of photographic processes work.

19th-century emulsions
Three of the most significant processes at the beginning of photography were the Daguerrotype, the Calotype and the Wet Collodion plate. The Daguerrotype, of which the portrait above left dating from 1840 is a fine example, was the first practical process to be used widely. It could not, however, be reproduced, unlike the paper negative printed Calotype such as the group portrait by Henry Fox Talbot in 1848 above, and the later Wet Collodion plates like the picture at the top by Gustave Le Gray (1855).

BLACK-AND-WHITE FILM
Black-and-white is both the simplest and the subtlest of photographic processes. For the beginner, monochrome offers an economical and easy-to-learn induction to basic darkroom work. Yet paradoxically, perhaps, black-and-white is such a broad and challenging medium that many enthusiasts find in monochrome a lifetime's challenge.

Image formation
The physical structure of black-and-white film is broadly similar to that of other films. The light-sensitive part of the film is contained in a minutely thin layer of gelatin, which is coated onto a flexible plastic base.

Within the gelatin layer are crystals of silver halides — silver combined with chlorine, bromine and iodine. The gelatin holds each crystal in a fixed position, yet swells when wet, allowing processing chemicals to penetrate the spongy structure and reach each crystal. Together, the gelatin and its burden of crystals are called the 'emulsion' of the film.

When the lens projects an image on the film, some of the crystals are struck by light — they are exposed. Exposure causes changes in the crystals at an atomic level, changes that turn the silver halides into metallic silver. The amount of silver formed, though, is far too small to be visible; the silver just forms tiny specks at the most light-sensitive points on the crystal.

After exposure, the film is in a state of limbo. There is an image recorded in the emulsion, but as yet the image is invisible. This image — which will become the photographic negative after processing — is called the 'latent image'.

Development, which is described in more detail on page 122, is essentially a process known to scientists as reduction. During development, the crystals of silver halide that were struck by light are reduced to metallic silver. The specks of silver formed on each exposed crystal grow and expand until the whole crystal has turned black. Additionally, filaments of metallic silver spread to link crystals of silver together in heavily exposed areas of the film.

Development can therefore be viewed as a multiplication or amplification process. Exposure causes very small amounts of silver to be formed, but development increases the amount of silver at each point on the film a millionfold or more, so that even very short exposures yield a visible image. Without development, film can admittedly still form an image, but it is a feeble one and the exposure required to form it is very long indeed — a matter of hours, rather than milliseconds.

After development, another process is necessary before the film can be used for printing pictures. Within the gelatin emulsion there still remain residual silver halide crystals; these are present in areas not exposed to light. If these crystals are not removed, the film will gradually darken when exposed to light. So the film is fixed — soaked in a solution that turns the insoluble silver halides to soluble compounds which can be washed away in running water. This washing, followed by a drying stage, completes the development process.

The developed film is darkest in areas that received the greatest exposure to light. These areas therefore represent the brightest areas of the subject. The shadows cast by the subject create less exposure on the surface of the film,

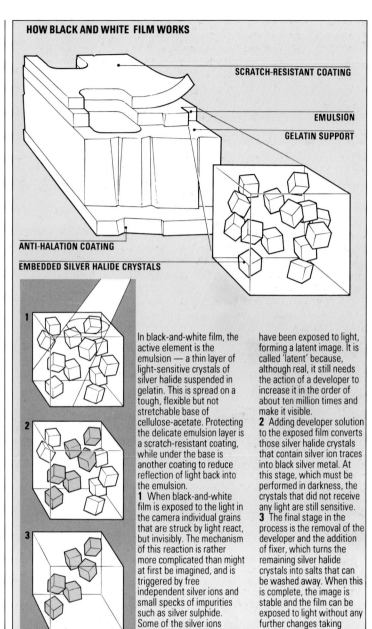

HOW BLACK AND WHITE FILM WORKS

SCRATCH-RESISTANT COATING

EMULSION

GELATIN SUPPORT

ANTI-HALATION COATING

EMBEDDED SILVER HALIDE CRYSTALS

1

2

3

In black-and-white film, the active element is the emulsion — a thin layer of light-sensitive crystals of silver halide suspended in gelatin. This is spread on a tough, flexible but not stretchable base of cellulose-acetate. Protecting the delicate emulsion layer is a scratch-resistant coating, while under the base is another coating to reduce reflection of light back into the emulsion.
1 When black-and-white film is exposed to the light in the camera individual grains that are struck by light react, but invisibly. The mechanism of this reaction is rather more complicated than might at first be imagined, and is triggered by free independent silver ions and small specks of impurities such as silver sulphide. Some of the silver ions collect together at sites that

have been exposed to light, forming a latent image. It is called 'latent' because, although real, it still needs the action of a developer to increase it in the order of about ten million times and make it visible.
2 Adding developer solution to the exposed film converts those silver halide crystals that contain silver ion traces into black silver metal. At this stage, which must be performed in darkness, the crystals that did not receive any light are still sensitive.
3 The final stage in the process is the removal of the developer and the addition of fixer, which turns the remaining silver halide crystals into salts that can be washed away. When this is complete, the image is stable and the film can be exposed to light without any further changes taking place.

LIGHT SENSITIVITY
In their natural state, the silver halide crystals in the emulsion of the film are sensitive only to blue light and ultraviolet radiation. Consequently, films made using these crystals — as the earliest emulsions were — reproduced blue subject areas as white, and other colours in tones much darker than they appeared to the eye. This led to unrealistic pictures — particularly in portraiture, where skin-tones would appear too dark and swarthy.

The situation changed with the discovery that, by mixing very small quantities of dye into the emulsion, it was possible to change the film's sensitivity to coloured light. This process was called *dye sensitization*.
Initially, the sensitivity of film was increased from UV (ultraviolet) and blue light to UV, blue and green light; and eventually, to the full spectrum of colours. Modern camera films give almost equal weight to all colours of the spectrum, though blue subjects still appear a little

too pale. The light sensitivity of such films is described as *panchromatic* ('pan', all; 'chromatos', colours).
Not all of the black-and-white emulsions in use today are panchromatic. Graphic arts films, for example, which are used for copying from one black-and-white image to another, are *orthochromatic* — insensitive to red light. And black-and-white printing paper is sensitive only to blue light and UV radiation.

so these areas darken the least, or not at all. The result is an image which represents each tone of the subject as its opposite — dark areas of the subject appear white on film and light areas, black. This reversed image is called a 'negative'.

To get from the negative a picture that represents the tones of the subject naturalistically, the negative must be copied onto photographic paper. This has a structure broadly similar to film and is processed in similar chemicals. Exposure of the printing paper to the projected image of the negative takes place not in a camera, though, but in a darkroom using an enlarger, as explained on pages 128-139.

Dye-image films

Chromogenic, or dye-image films, are a relatively recent innovation in black-and-white. They borrow the technology of colour negative films and are processed in the same chemicals. Instead of forming a colour image, though, they form a black-and-white one.

The advantages to this approach are considerable. These films have tremendous exposure latitude, and can be exposed at speeds ranging from ISO 100/21° to 1600/33° with no loss of quality. The grain size of the films is very small and can be further reduced by overexposure.

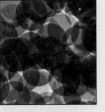

Silver halide v dye image Conventional black-and-white film develops to black silver grains (above left). Chromogenic dye-image film, however, is processed in much the same way as colour film, and the silver halide grains are replaced with a dye 'cloud', with less distinct edges (above right).

Fine grain — slow speed On 35 mm Kodak Panatomic-X, the image remains crisp even when magnified. The silver halide grains are small and spread thinly.

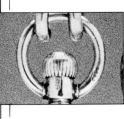

Medium grain — medium speed The price of more sensitivity to light is noticeable graininess in smooth mid-tones. The film is Kodak Tri-X.

Grainy — high speed Ultra-fast film, such as Kodak recording film 2475, has large, clumped grains that give a noticeably gritty appearance.

FILM SPEED
The sensitivity of film to light is of crucial importance to photographers. This is because to give a good picture, the exposure must be adjusted to precisely match the film's sensitivity and the brightness of the subject. A camera's meter measures the subject brightness, but to convert this light reading into exposure settings effectively, the metering circuits must be programmed with the sensitivity of the film loaded.

Light sensitivity is measured on a standard scale — the ISO scale.

The ISO rating of a film is usually written in the form 'ISO 400/27°'. The higher the number, the faster the film forms an image, so the more sensitive it is to light.

Nowadays, the ISO system is almost universal on new films and equipment, but the older ASA (American Standards Association) and DIN (the German industrial system) ratings are still sometimes found. Indeed, the ISO number of a film is simply a combination of its ASA and DIN numbers; an ISO 400/27° film is rated 400 ASA and 27° DIN. When

using ISO numbers, many photographers ignore the DIN component and use the first number (before the oblique line) alone. This makes it much easier to calculate the effect of changes in film speed.

Doubling the speed of a film halves the amount of light that is needed to form a picture. So ISO 100 film needs half as much light to make a satisfactory picture as ISO 50 film and the photographer can set the shutter one speed faster or close the aperture down one stop.

Film speed and quality Since faster film gives the photographer a wider choice of apertures and shutter speeds, it is reasonable to conclude that the faster the film, the better. After all, with a faster film, and therefore a faster shutter speed, the camera can be hand-held in dimmer lighting conditions.

However, there are some drawbacks. Fast film makes up the image from larger grains of silver, and clumps of these grains became quite prominent in prints from fast film negatives. Definition is poorer, too. Slow film, on the

other hand, produces smooth-toned, sharp images.

Dim and bright light The ISO system works well in most conditions, but falls down in very bright light and very dim light. In these conditions, film's response to light does not obey the same rules as in normal lighting, and the film loses some of its sensitivity. This loss is called *reciprocity failure*, and photographers must compensate for it by allowing more exposure than a meter indicates.

Films for different effects
The Florida landscape above
was shot on high-speed
infrared film. The grain has
almost the texture of coarse
sand, while the use of a
visually opaque Wratten 87
filter gives an unearthly
glow to the vegetation and
clouds. In the still life at the
right, the film is a fine-
grained ISO 125 sheet film
— 4 × 5 inches. The
combination of fine grain
and large format gives both
high resolution and a
delicate rendering of tones
and shading.

Compensation is most
often needed in very
dim light, where the film
receives a particularly
low-intensity exposure.
Nevertheless, reciprocity
failure occasionally
causes problems in
extremely intense light,
when exposures are very
short. However, since
problems start only
with exposures of
1/10000 second or so,
difficulties are rare.

BLACK-AND-WHITE FILM	SPEED (ISO)	FORMAT
SLOW, FINE-GRAINED		
Kodak Technical Pan	25	35mm, sheet
Agfapan 25	25	35mm, 120, sheet
Kodak Panatomic-X	32	35mm, 120
Ilford Pan F	50	35mm, 120
Polaroid Positive/Negative	50 (prints)/ 25 (negatives)	Polaroid cameras, holders to fit 120, sheet
Agfa dia-direct	32	35mm
MEDIUM SPEED, MEDIUM GRAIN		
Agfapan 100	100	35mm, 120
Kodak Plus-X	125	35mm, 120, sheet
Kodak Verichrome Pan	125	120
Ilford FP4	125	35mm, 120, sheet
Agfapan 200	125	sheet
Polapan CT	125	35mm
FAST, GRAINY		
Kodak Tri-X	400	35mm, 120, 70mm
Kodak Tri-X Professional	320	220, sheet
Ilford HP5	400	35mm, 120, sheet
Agfapan 400	400	35mm, 120, sheet
Kodak Royal Pan 400	400	sheet
ULTRA FAST, VERY GRAINY		
Kodak Royal-X Pan	1250 (usable in flat lighting up to ISO 2000)	120, sheet
Kodak Recording Film 2475	4000	35mm
DYE-IMAGE FILMS		
Ilford XP1	200-1600	35mm, 120
Agfa Vario XL	200-1600	35mm, 120
SPECIAL PURPOSE		
Kodak High-speed Infra-red	80 (no filter)/ 25 (87 filter)	35mm, sheet

Choosing black-and-white film

Many photographers use black-and-white film just as a matter of personal taste, because they feel it gives them a freer rein to be creative with the camera. But there are other reasons for using monochrome film.

One of these is the rapidity and ease with which black-and-white pictures can be processed and printed — only minutes from exposure to print. Another is the fact that most of the world's daily papers are printed in black-and-white and the wire services, which photojournalists use to transmit urgent pictures down telephone lines, cannot cope with colour pictures. Additionally, black-and-white film is oblivious to small changes in the colour of subject illumination.

Choice of a specific black-and-white film will depend on the application for which the film will be used. Fast film (ISO 400/27° and faster) is ideal for dim light and in conditions in which the photographer must take pictures first, and think later; fast film permits the use of a fast shutter speed to stop action and a small aperture for good depth of field.

Medium speed films (ISO 100/21°-320/26°) are fine for all general-purpose monochrome photography where lighting is good and where very high quality is not a prerequisite. For applications involving considerable enlargement of the negative, though, or for copying, a slow film (ISO 80/20° or slower) is better.

COLOUR NEGATIVE FILM

Of all the photographs taken every year, by far the greatest number are taken on colour negative film. Like black-and-white film, colour negative film does not produce positive images directly. Instead, there is an intermediate negative stage which reverses not only the tones of the subject, as in black-and-white, but the hues as well.

This film type is so widely used that it probably needs no introduction. The orangey-brown negatives that accompany prints returned from laboratories are familiar to every photographer, from the greenest snapshooter upwards. Nevertheless, it is worth looking for a moment at how colour negative film forms images.

Colour pictures in the making

Instead of the single layer of emulsion that is coated onto black-and-white film, colour negative film has several, each one sensitive to a different colour of light. The top layer of the film — the one nearest the camera's lens — is sensitive only to blue light and ultraviolet radiation. Beneath this layer is a second layer, which has sensitizing dyes added so that the emulsion responds additionally to green light. The bottom layer of the film, nearest the base, is manufactured so that it responds to blue light, red light and ultraviolet.

Between the top two layers is a non-light-sensitive yellow filter layer. This layer prevents blue light and ultraviolet radiation from penetrating to the two lower layers. So the film's three layers each respond to just one third of the spectrum — blue (and UV) for the top layer, green in the middle and red at the bottom.

According to the colour of the light falling on the film, a latent image will be formed in one or more of the three layers. White parts of the subject form a latent image in all three layers. Red parts form images in the bottom layer alone. Blue areas are recorded just in the top layer. In reality, of course, few subjects are pure blue or red. Orange subjects, for example, form images in the two bottom layers, because orange light is made up of a mixture of green and red light.

These latent images have no colour themselves; they are similar to the latent image on black-and-white film. The colour is added during processing.

Altering colour and tone in printing
A major advantage in shooting for prints rather than slides for projection is the degree of control possible in the darkroom. Tones and colour can be altered not just to match the original as closely as possible, but also to deliberately create 'distortions' for effect. Negatives allow more control during enlargement than transparencies. Deliberate colour changes are generally most successful with subjects that have no recognizable reference hues (such as flesh tones) — this early morning Burmese landscape was ideal for experiments in colour changes (right).

The versatility of colour negative film Because colour negative photography is a two-stage process — first shooting, then printing — it allows more flexibility than reversal film in exposure and colour. The latitude is greater, making correction of under- or overexposure straightforward during enlargement. Also, strong colour shifts can be corrected: here, the greenish cast from fluorescent lighting in a lecture theatre could be adjusted later — and both colour transparencies and black-and-white prints made without difficulty.

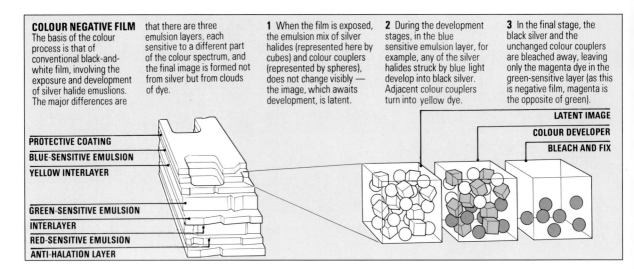

COLOUR NEGATIVE FILM
The basis of the colour process is that of conventional black-and-white film, involving the exposure and development of silver halide emulsions. The major differences are

that there are three emulsion layers, each sensitive to a different part of the colour spectrum, and the final image is formed not from silver but from clouds of dye.

1 When the film is exposed, the emulsion mix of silver halides (represented here by cubes) and colour couplers (represented by spheres), does not change visibly — the image, which awaits development, is latent.

2 During the development stages, in the blue sensitive emulsion layer, for example, any of the silver halides struck by blue light develop into black silver. Adjacent colour couplers turn into yellow dye.

3 In the final stage, the black silver and the unchanged colour couplers are bleached away, leaving only the magenta dye in the green-sensitive layer (as this is negative film, magenta is the opposite of green).

PROTECTIVE COATING
BLUE-SENSITIVE EMULSION
YELLOW INTERLAYER
GREEN-SENSITIVE EMULSION
INTERLAYER
RED-SENSITIVE EMULSION
ANTI-HALATION LAYER

LATENT IMAGE
COLOUR DEVELOPER
BLEACH AND FIX

Processing

Latent images, of course, are of no value to the photographer because they are invisible. Only after processing does a picture appear.

The developer used for colour negative film is rather similar to that used for black-and-white film. The magic ingredient that creates colours is incorporated in the film itself, rather than in the processing solutions.

Incorporated in the three layers of colour negative film are complex organic compounds called couplers. In combination with suitable chemicals, these couplers form brilliantly-coloured dyes. The coupler in the top layer (the blue-sensitive layer) forms yellow dye. The coupler in the middle, green-sensitive, layer of the film forms magenta dye — a purple colour. And in the bottom layer, which is sensitive only to red light, there is cyan coupler. This forms a blue-green dye.

The chemical that triggers the release of these dyes is formed when a silver image develops. So coloured dye is formed in each of the three film layers in amounts proportional to the exposure that each layer received. Where blue light struck the film, yellow dye appears; where the film was exposed to green light, magenta dye appears; and in areas that red light reached, a cyan image is formed.

These coloured dye images are perfect replicas of the silver images that formed them, and after development, the film looks like a muddy, negative picture. The muddiness comes from the silver images, which are then bleached away — leaving just the dye pictures and the unexposed silver halide crystals. This bleaching stage also removes the yellow colour from the second layer of the film. To end the processing cycle, there is a fixing stage (though this may be combined with bleaching) and a wash and dry. The finished negatives are then ready to print.

Printing reverses the negatives back to positive — just as it did with black-and-white film. And again, the paper and chemicals that carry out the reversal of colours and tones have a lot in common with the film emulsion and the chemicals used to develop the initial negative image. For a more detailed description of how colour processing takes place in practice, see page 134-7

Characteristics and applications

Colour negatives have tremendous exposure latitude, particularly to overexposure. For this reason, they are ideally suited to the casual photographer who does not take very much care about setting exposure — or who owns a camera that has no exposure controls. Most of the exposure latitude is to overexposure; the leeway for underexposure is more limited. So many experienced photographers tend to err on the generous side when exposing colour negative film, giving half a stop more exposure than their meters indicate. This technique also reduces grain size and yields better shadow detail, particularly in sunlight.

Just as they are very forgiving of exposure errors, so colour negative films side step problems created by the colour of the light falling on the subject. Within limits, colour casts can be removed at the printing stage. This, again, makes the film ideal for the snapshooter, who is as likely to take pictures in a room lit by fluorescent strip-lights or warm table-lamps as in bright sunlight.

This is not to say that colour negative film is exclusively for the amateur. Professional photographers use negative films for pictures which will eventually be reproduced in the form of colour prints, rather than as reproductions in magazines. Colour negative films are also invaluable in conditions where the exact colours of the light sources are unknown, making the use of transparency film difficult and unpredictable. They may also be useful for situations where an accurate exposure reading cannot be taken — colour negative has far more exposure latitude than slide film.

see page 134-7

Why are colour negatives orange?
The characteristic hue of a colour negative comes from what is called an integral mask. Integral masking is an ingenious technique used to improve the colour fidelity of prints. It is necessary because the dyes produced by colour couplers are not perfect — they have impurities in the form of other colours. To see how integral masking works, consider the magenta dye formed in areas of the negative exposed to green light.

If this magenta dye was perfect, it would transmit blue and red light, and stop all green light. However, the actual magenta dyes used in photography are not pure magenta — they are tinged with yellow. Since yellow parts of the colour negative form blue on the print, this causes green subjects to turn out too blue.

To counteract this tendency, colour chemists choose a magenta coupler which is yellow in colour prior to development. The more magenta dye is formed during development, the more of the coupler is used up. Remember, though, that the imperfect magenta dye formed by the coupler also contains some yellow, and this increases at the same rate as the yellow-tinted coupler is consumed. The net result is that the proportion of yellow colour in the magenta-forming layer of the film remains constant, regardless of the exposure the layer receives in the camera.

The coupler in the film's bottom (red-sensitive) layer

COLOUR NEGATIVE FILM	Speed (ISO)	Format	Process
DAYLIGHT BALANCED (5500K)			
MEDIUM			
Agfacolor XR100	100	35mm, 120	AP-70/C-41
Kodacolor VR100	100	35mm	C-41
Fujicolor HR100	100	35mm, 120	CN-16/C-14
Ilfocolor 100	100	35mm	C-41
3M Color Print 100	100	35mm, 120	CN-4/C-41
Vericolor IIIS	160	35mm, 120, 70mm, sheet	C-41
Konica SR100	100	35mm	CNK-4/C-41
Agfacolor N100S	100	120 sheet	AP-70/C-41
FAST			
Kodacolor VR200	200	35mm	C-41
Agfacolor XR200	200	35mm	AP-70/C-41
Konica SR200	200	35mm	CNK-4/C-41
Kodacolor VR400	400	35mm	C-41
Agfacolor XR400	400	35mm	AP-70/C-41
Fujicolor HR400	400	35mm, 120	CN-16/C-41
Ilfocolor 400	400	35mm	C-41
3M Color Print 400	400	35mm	C-41
Konica SR400	400	35mm, 120	CNK-4/C-41
ULTRA FAST			
Kodacolor VR1000	1000	35mm	C-41
Fujicolor HR 1600	1600	35mm	CN-16/C-41
TUNGSTEN BALANCED (3200K)			
Agfacolor N80L	80	120, sheet	AP-70/C-41
Vericolor IIL	100	120, sheet	C-41
DAYLIGHT AND TUNGSTEN			
Eastman 5247	100-400	35mm	ECN-2
Eastman 5293	400-1600	35mm	ECN-2

is pink in colour, to correct for the impurities in the green dye formed there. Couplers in the film's top layer is colourless, because the yellow dyes used in films are extremely pure.

These two coloured couplers together form the familiar orange hue of the colour negative. Since the orange colour covers the whole frame, it is easily removed, together with the offending impurities in the image dye, by filtration at the colour printing stage, as explained on pages 134-5.

Interchangeability

An image in either form, negative or slide, is not fixed in that form. Just as a positive transparency can be printed on special reversal paper, so a colour negative can be converted to a positive transparency (above), though there is inevitably a loss of quality with every change in state.

Black and white from colour

There is no reason for a colour negative to yield colour prints only — it can be printed on monochrome paper to give a black-and-white print. For good contrast, though, it must be printed on panchromatic paper, such as Kodak Panalure II RC — ordinary paper is not sensitive to the full range of colours.

Choosing colour negative film

The differences between different makes of colour negative film tend to be masked by processing and printing; and the primary distinction between one film and another is speed. The slowest general-purpose colour negative film has a speed of ISO 100/21°, and the quality of most films of this speed is exceptionally good; negatives will enlarge ten times without grain become objectionable.

As the speed of colour negative films increases, though, so the quality falls. ISO 200/24° films are marginally worse than their slower stablemates, though overexposure of the faster emulsion can make the gap between the two barely perceptible. The leap to ISO 400/27° brings a considerable sacrifice in quality, though. Colours appear paler, the picture looks grainy and definition is poorer.

Very fast films — usually ISO 1000/30° — are really suitable only for desperate situations, or for pictures that are going to be enlarged only to postcard size. Nevertheless, it is worth remembering that, poor though the quality of these high speed films may seem today, it is little worse than that of very much slower films only a decade ago.

Choice of negative film will always depend not just on the particular challenges of the individual photo-assignment, but also on taste. Many photographers simply prefer the colours of one brand over those of another, and this is as good a reason as any other for choosing a particular film type.

COLOUR TRANSPARENCY FILM

In applications where picture quality is of paramount importance, photographers usually choose colour transparency film. This film, which is also called colour reversal film or slide film, produces a positive image directly, without the need for an intermediate printing stage. Each time an image passes through a lens, some quality is lost, so a direct-positive system has a lead over a negative-positive system right at the very beginning.

There are other advantages in using transparencies, too. As the text below explains, the grains of silver from which the picture is formed are the smallest grains in the emulsion, so the actual image structure of reversal film is finer than that of a negative film of the same speed. Colours are brighter and cleaner, as well.

Although transparencies are intended mainly for projection, and for reproduction in magazines, they can also be printed by a lab, or in the home darkroom. For the beginner, in fact, it is easier to make prints from transparencies than from negatives, because colour casts are simpler to track down and eliminate.

The reversal process

Colour reversal films closely resemble negative films in their composition. The only difference is that the couplers in slide films are colourless, while those in negative films are coloured. At the exposure stage, the two films act in exactly the same way, with each film layer recording one third of the spectrum. Only in processing do the two paths diverge.

The processing of transparency film is more complex than that of negative film, because extra stages are needed to turn the

Films for low light levels
'Available light' photography is currently popular precisely because fast films are making much of it possible for the first time. Recent developments in film have produced colour transparency emulsions at speeds of up to 1SO 3200 daylight balanced and 1SO 640 tungsten balanced. Hand-held candid indoor photography without flash is now commonplace.

Films for special effects
Not all slide films are designed to reproduce colours accurately; infrared film (picture below) uses false colours to make certain features stand out — usually for scientific and military, though sometimes creative, us

Exposure latitude
This sequence of exposures on Kodachrome 64 demonstrates the tolerance of colour film to under- and overexposure. The scene, although fairly high in contrast, is average in tone, and the indicated TTL Meter reading of 1/30 second at f11 gives an accurate, realistic result (bottom left of this sequence). On either side of this nominal level, the shots have been bracketed, from 3 stops of 'overexposure' to 4 stops of 'underexposure'. Objectively, the range of good exposures is very narrow — little more than one stop — but acceptability is also a matter of personal taste. For many people, slight underexposure may even be desirable, giving greater colour saturation.

1/30 SEC f4 = +3 STOPS

1/30 SEC f16 = −1 STOP

1/30 SEC f5.6 = +2 STOPS

1/30 SEC f22 = −2 STOPS

1/30 SEC f8 = +1 STOP

1/60 SEC f22 = −3 STOPS

1/30 SEC f11 = TTL READING

1/125 SEC f22 = −4 STOPS

negative back to a positive. The first development stage does not create dyes from the colour couplers. Instead, primary development just forms a negative silver image in the exposed areas of each film layer.

The second stage of processing is to chemically fog the whole of the film, forming a positive latent image in each layer of the film. So in the top layer of the film, for example, there will be two images after the second processing step: one of these is a negative silver image of the blue parts of the subject; and the other, a latent image, is the exact opposite of the first — a positive image of the blue parts of the subject.

The step that follows is colour development. At this stage, the developing chemicals act on the newly-formed latent image, producing both a silver image, and an identical dye image. The colours formed are the

Films for fine detail
The relationship between film speed and graininess is the same as in the more basic black-and-white emulsions, although in colour films the actual metallic silver grains have been replaced during processing by less distinct dye clouds. Consequently, for highly resolved images, such as details in nature, a slow emulsion is the usual choice. The film used here, Kodachrome, has the additional advantage of a special process — the colour dyes are not present in the film when it is used (they are introduced later, during processing) and the emulsion layer can be thinner and resolve more detail.

same as with negative film — yellow, magenta and cyan in the layers of film sensitive to blue, green and red light respectively.

The final stages of the process remove the silver that has been formed over the whole of the film, leaving only dye. Since the dyes were formed from positive silver images, the dye images are also positive, as the following example illustrates.

In sections of the film exposed to blue light, a latent image forms only in the film's top layer — and the first stage of development changes this latent image to a silver one. Chemical fogging and colour development then create matching silver and dye images in the areas that were not exposed to blue light — the bottom two layers — and subsequent bleaching removes the silver. The colour couplers in these two layers form cyan and magenta dyes, and mixed together, these two colours form blue. A corresponding process forms all the other colours of the spectrum from differing proportions of each of the film's three dye layers.

An interesting point to note is that it is the grains of silver that were initially *unexposed* which act as templates for the dye images that makes up the picture. Since the largest grains of silver in an emulsion are the most sensitive to light, and therefore the first to be exposed, it follows that reversal images are made up of the film's finest grains. Negative films, on the other hand, form their images from the grains that were exposed first — the largest grains. So compared to negative film, the grain structure of transparency film is far less apparent.

TRANSPARENCY FILMS COMPARED

In normal, non scientific use, colour transparency films can be compared for:
- sensitivity (film speed)
- resolution
- graininess
- colour fidelity
- colour accuracy
- contrast

The slight differences between films are surprisingly hard to spot in isolation, and even side by side comparison of films of similar speed may reveal only small dissimilarities. The most distinctive qualities tend to be graininess, colour saturation, and the rendering of subtle tones such as grey and skin colours.

The most significant difference is between slow and fast transparency films. Kodachrome 25 sets the standard for resolution and several other image qualities. Sharpness and colour saturation in particular are significantly better than Ektachrome 400.

Kodachrome 25 resolution (measured in a way similar to that described on page 29) is 100 line pairs per millimetre; Ektachrome 400 is only 63 line pairs per millimetre.

Controlling tones and colours

Slide film must be exposed with much more care than negative film, because there is no intermediate stage en route to the finished picture where errors can be corrected.

For realistic tones and colours, exposure measurement must be very precise. With some transparency films in bright sunlight, overexposure of just half a stop can ruin the picture. Latitude for underexposure is usually greater, but overall, the exposure latitude of slide film is a fraction of that of negative film.

The colour of the light that falls on the subject is as crucial as the intensity. Most slide films are balanced to give good colour at noon on a sunny summer's day, with a blue sky. Even in overcast weather, filtration is needed to provide correct colour rendition.

In artificial light, the problems are even more severe, with heavy blue filtration necessary when the subject is lit by tungsten light. As an alternative, special tungsten-light balanced films are available, though even when using these in domestic lighting, some fine-tuning of colour with filters may be required. Chapter four explains about this in more detail.

Low light

Dim light causes additional difficulties when using transparency film. Each of the film's three layers has slightly different characteristics, so that the required compensation for reciprocity failure may vary from layer to layer. In practice this means that not only must transparency film receive extra exposure in dim light, but colour correction filters are necessary as well.

Film manufacturers supply data tables that outline how much filtration, and how much extra exposure is required, but these are only a guide. The only way to find out precisely how much compensation to use is to run tests, using several films from the same batch. A typical procedure would be as follows.

Reversal films Widely used by amateurs for slide projection, reversal films are the most important type for professionals whose work is reproduced in print — most photo-mechanical colour printing systems need transparency originals.

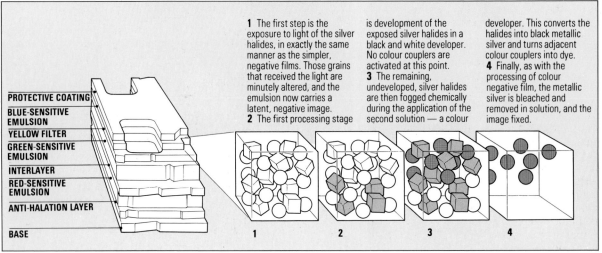

1 The first step is the exposure to light of the silver halides, in exactly the same manner as the simpler, negative films. Those grains that received the light are minutely altered, and the emulsion now carries a latent, negative image.
2 The first processing stage is development of the exposed silver halides in a black and white developer. No colour couplers are activated at this point.
3 The remaining, undeveloped, silver halides are then fogged chemically during the application of the second solution — a colour developer. This converts the halides into black metallic silver and turns adjacent colour couplers into dye.
4 Finally, as with the processing of colour negative film, the metallic silver is bleached and removed in solution, and the image fixed.

PROTECTIVE COATING
BLUE-SENSITIVE EMULSION
YELLOW FILTER
GREEN-SENSITIVE EMULSION
INTERLAYER
RED-SENSITIVE EMULSION
ANTI-HALATION LAYER
BASE

1   2   3   4

First, the photographer makes a series of exposures with the shutter held open for one, ten and a hundred seconds. The pictures are bracketted using the aperture, at half-stop intervals over a range +1/2 to +3 stops. Processing this first roll reveals the necessary exposure compensation, and gives a clue to the colour shift. A second, and perhaps a third test with gelatin colour correction filters on the lens reveals how much filtration is needed for this particular batch of film, at each exposure time, and of what colour.

At very long exposures, correction for reciprocity failure may be impractical, and only with supplementary lighting will colours appear lifelike.

Matching film to task

The differences between different reversal films are more marked, and the range of available speeds greater than with colour negative film. The slowest of slide films — Kodachrome 25 — is legendary for its high resolution, fine grain, and bright colours. However, as the box at right explains, this and other Kodachrome films must be returned to the manufacturers for processing.

At the other end of the scale, the fastest slide films have speeds of ISO 1600/33°, and this can be boosted still further with push processing (see page 113). As might be expected, though, these films produce weak colours and generally poor quality, and they should be used only as a last resort. What these superfast films do offer, however, is the chance to shoot by available light, even in very low light conditions. The loss of quality may be more acceptable than the loss of atmosphere by introducing artificial light.

Between these two extremes, there are progressive trade-offs between speed and quality, and variations between brand to brand in terms of colour rendering. The balance of couplers in one make of film may favour flesh tones — whereas another type may render greys and whites very neutral in hue. Generally, though, the characteristics of films remain relatively constant across film families: the colour balance of Ektachrome 400 bears a family resemblance to Ektachrome 100, but not to Kodachrome

Choice of film depends, as with colour negatives, on personal choice and on the job in hand. Some photographers will use different film for portraits and still-lifes, on the grounds that the requirements are different in each instance.

Ultimately, the only answer is to experiment and pick out the film that has the most personal appeal. Having selected one emulsion, though, it is prudent to use this one film whenever appropriate, and get to know its characteristics as well as possible. Constant changing from brand to brand simply produces inconsistent results.

Workroom films

Certain films designed for use in the darkroom can be deployed in the camera, but their effects are often unpredictable or unimpressive.

Internegative and duplicating films, for example, produce very low contrast images when used in the camera for normal photography. Photomicrography colour film, on the other hand, does the opposite, producing images of extremely high contrast. This film can be used either as a transparency or a negative, depending on processing: C41 processing yields a very high-contrast, unmasked negative; the virtually obsolete E4 process, which this film shares with infrared colour film, produces a transparency.

Movie film is occasionally sold for 35mm still camera use. This film produces a negative from which specialist processing houses will print both projection transparencies and postcard-size prints. The film is balanced for tungsten lighting, and is incompatible with the regular C41 chemicals.

Non-substantive films
Colour couplers are usually incorporated in the emulsions of colour slide films, and such films are described as substantive emulsions. There are two notable exceptions — Kodachromes 25 and 64. These two films contain no couplers in their emulsion layers, so the layers can be made especially thin, leading to very high resolution. Films of this type are called non-substantive.

The colour couplers, necessary for the formation of the coloured image, are introduced during development, making the processing of Kodachrome long and complex. In most countries only Kodak themselves undertake this work, and even then the film may have to be sent abroad to a larger Kodak facility, so involving more delay.

COLOUR TRANSPARENCY FILM

	Speed (ISO)	Format	Process
DAYLIGHT BALANCED (5500K)			
MEDIUM			
Kodachrome 25	25	35mm	Kodak (+ certain independent labs in US)
Polachrome CS	40	35mm	User (rapid)
Agfachrome 50S	50	35mm, 120, 70mm, sheet	Agfachrome 41
Fujichrome 50	50	35mm	E-6
Agfachrome 64	64	35mm	Agfachrome 41
Kodachrome 64	64	35mm	Kodak (+ certain independent labs in US)
Ektachrome 64	64	35mm, 120, 70mm	E-6
Ektachrome 6117	Nominally 64	sheet	E-6
Fujichrome 64	64	35mm, 120, sheet	E-6
Agfachrome 100	100	35mm	Agfachrome 41
Agfachrome R100S	100	120, sheet	AP-44/E-6
Ektachrome 100	100	35mm	E-6
Fujichrome 100	100	35mm, 120	E-6
Ilfochrome 100	100	35mm	RP-6/E-6
3M Color Slide 100	100	35mm	E-6
FAST			
Agfachrome CT200	200	35mm	E-6
Ektachrome 200	200	35mm, 120	E-6
Ektachrome 6176	200	sheet	E-6
Ektachrome 400	400	35mm, 120	E-6
3M Color Slide 400	400	35mm	E-6
Fujichrome 400	400	35mm	E-6
ULTRA FAST			
3M Color Slide 100	1000	35mm	E-6
Ektachrome P800/1600	400-1600	35mm	E-6
Fujichrome 1600	1600	35mm	E-6
TUNGSTEN BALANCED (3200K)			
Ektachrome 6118	Nominally 50	Sheet	E-6
Kodachrome 40	40	35mm	Kodak (+ certain independent labs in US)
Agfachrome 50L	50	35mm, 120, sheet	Agfachrome 41
Ektachrome 50	50	35mm, 120	E-6
Ektachrome 160	160	35mm, 120	E-6
3M Color slide 640T	640	35mm	E-6
DAYLIGHT AND TUNGSTEN			
Eastman 5247	100-400	35mm	ECN-2
Eastman 5293	400-1600	35mm	ECN-2
SPECIAL PURPOSE			
Ektachrome Infra-red 2236	100 (with Wratten 12)	35mm	E-4

Types of transparency film
By shooting the same scene on a variety of films and studying the results side by side, subtle differences can be spotted which would otherwise go unnoticed. For everyday use, almost all of the brands would be acceptable, but there are variations in sharpness, overall colour balance and graininess which can be used to advantage in particular situations. Most films are designed to reproduce *certain* colours well, and photographers will select film based on its intrinsic characteristics and their particular needs for the shot. For example, one manufacturer may aim for a rich blue — good for seaside shots or holiday brochures — and another instead for accurate reproduction of flesh tones.

FITTING THE FILM TO THE OCCASION

Type of film	Brand examples	Best uses
VERY FINE GRAIN DAYLIGHT ISO 25	KODACHROME 25 AGFACHROME 505 FUJICHROME 50	Static or slow-moving subjects, and when detail is important, eg architecture, landscape, still-life, studio subjects.
FINE GRAIN DAYLIGHT ISO 200	KODACHROME 64 FUJICHROME 100 EKTACHROME 100 AGFACHROME 100	General use: the standard films for all except fast action and dimly lit subjects.
MEDIUM-FAST DAYLIGHT ISO 200	EKTACHROME 200 AGFACHROME CT200	Compromise film, giving better grain than the fast films but a speed advantage over standard films. Good for some candid street photography.
FAST DAYLIGHT ISO 400	EKTACHROME 400 3M COLOUR SLIDE 400 FUJICHROME 400	For low light and fast action, eg at dusk, in fluorescent-lit interiors (with fl filter), sports.
SUPER-FAST DAYLIGHT ISO 800-1600	EKTACHROME P800/1600 FUJICHROME 1600	For extremes of low-lighting and fast action. P800/1600 is variable in speed from ISO 400 to 1600 and is becoming the standard fast film for many professionals.
FINE GRAIN TUNGSTEN-BALANCED ISO 40-50	KODACHROME 40 EKTACHROME 50 AGFACHROME 50L	For static interior (tungsten-lit) and studio subjects.
MEDIUM-FAST TUNGSTEN-BALANCED ISO 160	EKTACHROME 160	Moving indoor (tungsten-lit) subjects, especially if lit with photographic lamps. In television studios and on movie sets.
FAST TUNGSTEN-BALANCED ISO 640	3M COLOUR SLIDE SHOT	Candid photography in tungsten-lit interiors. Alternative: super-fast daylight film with 80B filter.
RE-PACKAGED MOVIE STOCK	EASTMAN 5247 EASTMAN 5293	Transparencies and negatives from same film stock. Colour balance unimportant. Good for uncertain conditions.
INSTANT FILM	POLACHROME CS	For testing or when slide is needed immediately.

KODACHROME 25

KODACHROME 64

EKTACHROME 64

EKTACHROME 200

EKTACHROME 400

FUJICHROME 400

FUJICHROME 100

AGFA CT 18

AGFA CT 21

When transparencies are enlarged, differences between makes of film are accentuated. The picture at left is on Kodachrome 25. Kodachrome emulsions are distinctive in that colour dyes are added during processing. As a result they are very sharp and can be enlarged with little break-up of the image.

The picture directly below was shot on Ektachrome 400 — a much faster film but one which works less well in balanced lighting. It has a slightly bluish tint and generally flat colour reproduction.

Ⓒ Michael Freeman

Ektachrome 64   139 L

5 4 5 4 4

Film size and sharpness
Even more important than the choice of brands and film speed is the film format. A large film size needs to be enlarged less, and so the image will appear sharper in its final form. Both the 5×4in sheet film at left and the 35mm transparency above are on ISO 64 Ektachrome. The enlargements of the apple stalk show the advantages of shooting on a large format — the 5 × 4in version is on the left.

INSTANT FILM

Photography has been called 'instant art', and it is certainly true that even conventional photographic processes put effortless creativity within the reach of anyone with a camera. Instant films take this process one step further, so that photographers of all abilities can turn ideas into pictures within seconds.

Instant photography is not just an entertaining way to make pretty pictures, though. Instant film has had a profound effect upon the way that photographers now work. A successful lighting and exposure test on instant film is an insurance that there are no serious problems on a shoot, and the photographer can therefore expose conventional

Integral film cameras such as the Polaroid SX-70 and SLR 680 (left), are principally designed as amateur equipment. Consequently, they are largely automated and have the minimum of controls and adjustments. The lighten/darken control shown here allows 1½ stops' leeway either side of 'normal'.

film with complete confidence. Clients in the professional's studio can see immediately how their products will look on film, and guide the photographer to an ideal result.

Black-and-white instant film

Almost all of the instant film used by professionals is the so-called 'peel-apart' type. After exposure, the photographer pulls a tab at the end of the instant camera or instant-film back, and withdraws two sheets of paper, stuck together with a gooey, alkaline liquid. After a short wait, the two sheets are peeled apart. One sheet — the one on which the image from the camera's lens fell — carries a muddy negative image, and is usually discarded. The other sheet carries the finished picture.

The simplest of the peel-apart films makes a black-and-white picture, and like all instant films, relies on the diffusion of the image from one part of the film to the other. The negative sheet which is exposed to light carries a fairly conventional light-sensitive emulsion. The other sheet, which is not light sensitive, is a piece of specially coated paper. This receives the image after the two sheets are laminated together by pulling through metal squeegee rollers.

Polaroid peel-apart films (above), types 55 and 665, offer a permanent negative as well as a fine-grained black-and-white print, and this is of such high quality that it has certain advantages over conventional negative film (very high resolution, immediate proof of success, and an absence of dust specks and similar blemishes). Before drying, it needs a clearing bath of sodium sulphate — this can be given on location in a special bucket (above right).

These rollers burst a pod of viscous chemicals, which develop the image on the negative sheet. At the same time, a chemical in the 'goo' dissolves away the unexposed silver halides in the areas which must appear darkest on the print. These silver halides are now mobile, and diffuse across to the image-receiving sheet, leaving behind the silver image in the areas that *were* exposed to light.

The receiving sheet contains chemicals that turn the migrating silver halides to silver — forming a positive image which is visible when the sheets are separated.

Black-and-white instant films are available in a wide variety of speeds and types. Some produce line images, but most form conventional continuous-tone pictures. The fastest has a speed of ISO 3000/136°, and of the other types in regular use, one, rated at ISO 75/20°, produces not only a print but a black-and-white negative, too.

Instant colour

This works on a similar image diffusion principle, and again, the most popular professional emulsions are of the peel-apart type.

Like conventional films, the negative sheets of these instant films have three layers, sensitive to blue, green and red light. Laminated between three layers, though, are layers of ready-formed dyes in colours complementary to the sensitivity of the three emulsions. So, linked to the blue-sensitive layer is a layer of yellow dye, and the green and red sensitive layers have associated magenta and cyan dyes respectively.

After exposure, the film is pulled through rollers as before, and the layer of processing 'goo' spreads between negative and receiving sheets. In areas of the negative that were exposed to light, the processing chemicals anchor the dye. In other, unexposed areas, the dye diffuses across to the receiving sheet. Taking as an example an area exposed to blue light only, here the developer will anchor the yellow dye in the layer associated with the blue-sensitive part of the film. Cyan and magenta dyes, though, are not anchored, so they diffuse across, where they combine to form blue.

This peel-apart colour film is widely used for exposure testing, and is rated at ISO 80/20° — conveniently within a third of a stop of the speed of the most popular professional colour films.

Single-sheet films

The more modern types of instant film do away with the messy alkaline goo and the discarded negative sheets that are characteristics of the peel-apart process. These single-sheet films are the type most often used in amateur cameras.

The principles of their operation are broadly similar to those of peel-apart colour films — non-anchored colour dyes migrate during processing from an image-forming layer to a receiving layer. In these films, though, the two layers are integrated inside a plastic envelope, so the processing reagent can never escape.

Extra layers and chemicals are required in these more complex films. For example, in Polaroid instant film there is an opaque black chemical which keeps light out during development. As the process continues, the goo inside the print becomes less alkaline, and in the more neutral environment, the black light-protective chemical becomes transparent, so the image is visible.

INSTANT FILM TYPES

	Availability	Size	Speed ISO
Integral colour print			
Polaroid SX-70	Pack	3½×4¼in (8.7×10.25cm)	150
Polaroid 600 Supercolor	Pack	3½×4¼in (8.7×10.25cm)	600
Kodak PR144	Pack	4×3³/₁₆in (10.5×7.85cm)	150
Kodak Trimprint HS144	Pack	4×3³/₁₆in (10.5×7.85cm)	320
Peel-apart colour print			
Type 809 Polacolor ER	Sheet	8⁷/₁₆×10⁷/₈in (22×27cm)	80
Type 59 Polacolor ER	Sheet	4×5in (10.5×13cm)	80
Type 559 Polacolor ER	Pack	4×5in (10.5×13cm)	80
Type 669 Polacolor ER	Pack	3¼×4¼in (8.3×10.8cm)	80
Type 668 Polacolor	Pack	3¼×4¼in (8.3×10.8cm)	75
Type 88 Polacolor	Pack	3¼×3³/₈in (8.3×8.6cm)	80
Peel-apart black-and-white print (All Polaroid)			
Type 811 (low contrast)	Sheet	8⁷/₁₆×10⁷/₈in (22×27cm)	200
Type 52 (fine grain)	Sheet	4×5in (10.5×13cm)	400
Type 552 (fine grain)	Pack	4×5in (10.5×13cm)	400
Type 55 Positive/Negative	Sheet	4×5in (10.5×13cm)	50
Type 51 (high contrast)	Sheet	4×5in (10.5×13cm)	320 (daylight) 125 (tungsten)
Type 57 (high speed)	Sheet	4×5in (10.5×13cm)	3000
Type 665 Positive/Negative	Pack	3¼×4¼in (8.3×10.8cm)	75
Type 084/667 (high speed)	Pack	3¼×4¼in (8.3×10.8cm)	3000
Type 611 (low contrast)	Pack	3¼×4¼in (8.3×10.8cm)	200
Type 612 (ultra high speed)	Pack	3¼×4¼in (8.3×10.8cm)	20000
Type 87 (high speed)	Pack	3¼×3³/₈in (8.3×8.6cm)	3000
35mm slides			
Polachrome CS	Roll	Standard 35mm frames	40
Polapan CT	Roll	Standard 35mm frames	125
Polagraph HC	Roll	Standard 35mm frames	400
Polalith	Roll	Standard 35mm frames	4
Kodak Instagraphic	Pack	Standard 35mm frames	64

Polaroid single-sheet films are viewed from the side that faced the film during exposure. But on Kodak instant pictures the image appears on the other side — the one that faces away from the lens. Kodak instant cameras therefore incorporate a mirror to flip the image left-to-right. Without this, the pictures would come out the wrong way round.

Instant transparencies

The 35 mm instant transparency film introduced by Polaroid has, paradoxically, most in common with the black-and-white peel-apart film. In fact, the image-forming emulsion on the film is of the same type, and the principle of exposure and processing broadly the same. What makes this film different, though, is that it is overlayed with a regular pattern of red, green, and blue filter bands. Each of these narrow bands filters the incoming light from the camera's lens, and the light-sensitive emulsion beneath the stripe forms an image only of light the same colour as the band above it. When viewers examine the film's black-and-white picture,

they look through the coloured stripes, and these put the natural hues back into the picture.

Development takes place in a special processor. Within this, the film is wound into contact with a stripping ribbon, and covered with viscous chemicals. After the correct time has elapsed, film and stripping ribbon are pulled apart — and with the ribbon goes the unwanted negative silver image.

This method of forming colour pictures — known as the 'additive' principle — sounds fine, but in practice it produces extremely dark transparencies which cannot be projected alongside conventional materials. Big enlargements are impossible, because the pattern of lines show up on the print. Nevertheless, the film can be used in an ordinary 35 mm camera, and is therefore a useful method of making instant proof pictures.

Types of instant film There are currently three different major types of instant film: peel-apart, integral and transparency. Peel-apart film is manufactured only by Polaroid, and is available in four formats. In all peel-apart films the negative separates from the finished print; the range includes a colour print, (right) and, in black-and-white, fine-grain, high-speed high-contrast positive/negative varieties. Integral print films are made by both Polaroid and Kodak (the two Polaroid versions are shown below right); all the chemicals and materials are retained in the packet, and they are designed for use in special cameras. Polaroid also make 35mm slide films, (below and left), which an be used in conventional cameras. They include a colour film, black-and-white film, and a high-contrast black-and-white emulsion.

Instant negatives Polaroid Positive/Negative film produces high-resolution negatives that can be kept permanently for making conventional print enlargements, in addition to the instant positive print.

SPECIAL FILMS

The enormous majority of the available colour films are formulated to give the most realistic tones and colours possible, but for a few specialized photographic tasks, realism is not of primary importance. Although aimed at specific applications, these films can sometimes usefully be borrowed for ordinary photography.

Infrared film

Infrared radiation lies just outside the visible spectrum, and includes wavelengths that most people would describe simply as heat. However, near-infrared radiation can be used to form images in the camera, with appropriate film and filtration.

There are two sorts of infrared film — black-and-white and false-colour film. Both types are sensitive not only to infrared, but

Colour infrared In Ektachrome Infrared, one of the three emulsion layers is sensitive to green light, a second layer to red light, and a third layer to infrared radiation. And each layer gives a false colour. The colour effect depends on both the infrared reflectivity of the subjects, and on the filtration. Here, a red filter (Wratten 25) gave a yellow sky and red vegetation.

Black-and-white infrared Although High Speed Infrared film gives its most unusual effects with a visually opaque filter, even with only a 25 red filter it can give interesting results.

also to visible light, so they must be used with filters if the full effects of the infrared are to be seen.

The sensitivity of the black-and-white emulsion stretches furthest into the infrared portion of the spectrum. This film is rarely kept in stock, and must be ordered specially by photo-dealers. It must be loaded in total darkness, and kept refrigerated before use.

Exposure is rather haphazard, because meters do not respond to infrared. Pictures must therefore be bracketed heavily around the indicated meter reading.

To take full advantage of the film's sensitivity, the camera can be fitted with a visually opaque filter that lets through only infrared wavelengths. Pictures taken using such a filter show sunlit foliage glowing snowy white, and record skin as waxy and mask-like. But the tones are still acceptably natural for many non-living subjects, and black-and-white infrared film can be an effective way of cutting through mist.

Some change of technique is required when focusing, because all ordinary lenses bring infrared radiation to a different focus from visible light. Most lenses are marked with an infrared focusing index, alongside which the subject distance is aligned.

False-colour infrared film forms surreal images which have curious coloration. The film is sensitive to green and red light, and infrared, but all three of the film's layers are also sensitive to blue light. Therefore, to take full advantage of the film's unusual sensitivity, filters must again be used. The recommended filtration is yellow, but for pictorial purposes, other filters give equally interesting effects.

Focusing can be carried out normally with this film, but the lens should be stopped well down if the image formed in the film's infrared-sensitive layer is to be recorded sharply.

FILM CARE AND USE

Colour films are enormously complex industrial products, manufactured in clinically clean conditions, and stored in humidity-controlled packagings. To get the best possible quality out of film, it is important to treat it with respect and care.

Buying and testing film

Film is manufactured in long, wide rolls, which are then slit into narrow strips or sheets and packed ready for use. All the packs of film from one roll are assigned the same batch number, which is printed on the film pack close to the 'use-by' date. All film from the same batch should produce identical results. From batch to batch, though, there is some variation, so for consistent results, it is best to purchase film in multiples of ten or twenty. Multi-roll packs are often cheaper, too.

For professional photographers, consistent colour is essential, so many of them will buy a hundred or more rolls of film from the same batch, and run tests to determine whether the film needs a small degree of over- or underexposure, and whether filtration is needed to create absolutely neutral colour rendering. Testing one roll is enough as the others should produce identical results if stored correctly.

Professional films

Some transparency films are available both in professional and regular versions. Professional film is different in several ways, although the differences are not in manufacture, but in packaging and storage.

Film as it emerges from the coating machine is not ready for use. Like good wine, it must be aged. Amateur films, though, are despatched immediately, on the assumption that they will age on the dealer's shelf, and in the photographer's camera.

Professional films, on the other hand, are retained at the factory in controlled conditions, and periodically tested. When they are in peak condition, they are tested again, so that the manufacturer can overprint the true, measured film speed on the instruction sheet enclosed in the film pack. The tested speed may be up to $\frac{1}{3}$ stop different from the nominal speed on the film box. The film is despatched in refrigerated containers to dealers who put it in cold storage.

Photographers who buy this film therefore catch it at its peak, and they in turn store the film in a refrigerator or freezer until shortly before exposure. After use, they process the film immediately.

Professional films produce superior results only if they are dealt with in this methodical manner. Used in a casual way, pro-designated emulsions will give no better results than ordinary films.

X-RAY PRECAUTIONS

Modern airport-security is in direct conflict with film safety, and this is a matter of real concern to all photographers who travel by air. X-ray exposure affects film; especially ultra-fast film. X-rays are radiations from the same spectrum that includes light, and, although invisible, X-rays fog undeveloped photographic film just as exposure to light does. Unlike light exposure, however, there is no threshold — any X-ray dose can make a silver halide grain developable. In practice, however, the damage depends on a number of factors:

1 The X-ray dose Most airport X-ray machines are designed to give small doses that have no noticeable effect — machines in the USA are required by FAA administered law to give one milliroentgen (MR) or less. Damage usually occurs at over 5 MR for many films.

2 Number of exposures X-ray effects are cumulative. Five passes through a one MR machine has the same effect as a single 5 MR dose.

3 Protection Lead foil bags sold for the purpose of protecting film from X-rays are effective — but only as long as the dose remains low (security personnel may submit the bag to a higher level to find out what is inside).

4 Type of film Fast films are more sensitive than slow, and colour film is more sensitive than black-and-white (one reason is probably that in colour tri-pack construction, the bottom layers must be much more sensitive than the film's overall ISO rating — effectively, the bottom cyan layer of Kodachrome 25 is in the region of ISO 1000). Modern ultra-fast colour films are extremely sensitive, and can be damaged by a single exposure of less than one MR.

5 Orientation of film As illustrated below, 35mm cassette film is least vulnerable when the cassette openings face away from the X-ray, and most vulnerable when the felt lips face towards the source (that is, upwards on an airport machine).

Fogging due to X-rays lowers maximum density and, on colour film, can give a colour cast. X-rays may also cast shadows on the film of the 35mm cartridge rings (and of any other metal or solid objects next to the

VISUAL DENSITY CHANGE IN FILM TO A ONE MR DOSE OF X-RAYS (based on Eastman Kodak Data)

	Density change	No. of passes needed to produce visible effect
Kodacolor 400	0.013	One
Ektachrome 400	0.011	One
Ektachrome 160 (tungsten)	0.006	Two
Ektachrome 200	0.005	Two
Kodachrome 64	0.005	Two
Kodacolor 100	0.004	Three
Kodachrome 25	0.004	Three
Tri-X	0.002	Five

Note: The smallest *Noticeable* change is about 0.01

Storage conditions

Unexposed film is damaged by heat and humidity, and by ionizing radiation such as airport x-rays. The film's original packing keeps out moisture, so do not remove the film from its inner packing until shortly before exposure.

The best place to store film before use is in a domestic refrigerator, though short periods at room temperature obviously do little harm. On location, keep the film as cool as possible, taking particular care to avoid the heat of the sun. In cars parked in the sun temperatures can soar to oven-like levels.

After exposure but before processing, film is just as vulnerable to heat and humidity, so process the pictures as quickly as possible. In damp conditions, it is best to keep film in an airtight tin, along with some silica gel crystals, which dry out the air. Failure to observe these precautions can lead to colour casts and lack of contrast.

X-rays are extremely harmful to film, and damage is more likely with faster emulsions. At airports, always ask for a hand search of baggage, and carry film separate from other

A prominent label is a useful precaution for camera cases travelling by air. If film is unavoidably subjected to X-ray examination, the direction the cassettes are facing may influence the amount of damage.

Storing processed film
High temperatures and high relative humidity will speed the deterioration of negatives, especially colour ones. Even properly processed black-and-white negatives will deteriorate gradually in time. Chemicals and solvents can also damage the emulsion — even apparently harmless items like sticky tape can cause stains and fading. Humid conditions cause transparencies to stick together or to photographic

ilm). 1985 tests by Fuji showed that with colour negative emulsions, a low 0.3 MR dose showed visible effects on ISO 1600 film after only one pass, on ISO 400 film after 10 passes (3 MR), and on ISO 100 film after 30 passes (9 MR).

The best protection, therefore, is to avoid X-rays altogether, but knowledge of the screening procedures at specific airports is important. If it is known that hand inspections will be allowed (mandatory by law in the USA), carry film in hand baggage and remove from the bag for hand inspection. Carry the film in a transparent plastic bag so that it can be removed and seen easily by security personnel. If, however, a visual inspection cannot be guaranteed — many French and Swiss airports for example, will not co-operate — carrying the film by hand will usually leave no option — there may be insufficient time to return the film to the checked baggage. In these circumstances, it is safer to pack the film in a lead-foil bag in the checked baggage. Although there is occasionally a risk of the baggage being X-rayed, it normally is not.

There is, as can be seen, no ideal universal solution.

envelopes, and may even encourage the growth of mould.

To safeguard against this many photographers keep some silica gel which acts as an excellent dessicant. A little kept in the storage containers with the slides avoids condensation problems. For long term storage, colour negatives must be kept refrigerated at a temperature of about 2°C (36°F). They should be removed at least one hour before printing.

luggage to make this easier. Avoid at all costs having film x-rayed repeatedly; for while a pass through an x-ray machine may do no harm, multiple passes will.

After processing, film is not as liable to damage, but will still fade in the course of time unless properly stored. Certain sorts of plastic including PVC give off damaging vapours which can affect colour, and even mothballs and wood-glue can damage transparencies, prints and negatives. Heat, damp and light reduce permanence, too, so ideally photographic materials should be stored in dark, dry conditions on polyethylene storage shelves, or in the containers in which they were returned from processing. A few companies now supply archival storage media which is ideal for the purpose.

Altered use of film

Most colour films are processed in completely standardized chemicals, to a rigidly followed time schedule. The two processes used — designated E6 for reversal, and C41 for negative films — were designed specifically for machine processing, and the high temperatures and short process steps are difficult for the home darkroom enthusiast to maintain with sufficient accuracy.

Nevertheless, on occasions there is good reason to depart from the rigidly defined guidelines for film processing, either to control film density to a high standard of accuracy, or else to manipulate the colours and tones of the film.

■ PUSHING AND PULLING The density of transparency film is related not only to the exposure received in the camera, but also to the length of the first development step. Prolonging this step makes film paler, whereas abbreviating the first development time makes pictures darker.

Within limits, then, it is fair to say that changing development time changes the speed of the film. If the film is processed for longer, the photographer can anticipate lighter pictures, and give less exposure — perhaps in order to obtain a faster shutter speed in dim light.

Prolonging development time is called 'pushing' or 'uprating' the film. It is a service many labs which cater for professional photographers will carry out — sometimes for an extra fee, but often at the standard charge. If a photographer requests a 'one-stop push', the lab will increase the first development time by a time that corresponds to a one stop increase in film speed.

Increasing the film speed has obvious benefits, but labs will also pull film — reduce its speed. Photographers use this service to fine-tune the density of their pictures, using a sample sheet or roll of film, or a 'clip-test'. A clip-test is a short length

of film clipped from the end of the roll. This is processed normally (or perhaps at a specified push or pull) and the photographer then examines the result before deciding whether to push or pull the rest of the roll. As long as all pictures were taken at the same exposure setting, pushing or pulling will trim the density of the pictures to the nearest 1/3 stop. Photographers using sheet film process a single sheet in advance of the rest for the same reason.

PUSHING AND PULLING COLOUR POSITIVE FILM

Underexposure and overexposure can, to a certain degree, be compensated for during developing. Pushed processing means giving underexposed transparencies additional development time, and pulled processing means giving overexposed transparencies less development time. Compensation processing (using E-6) is as follows:

Camera exposure	Adjustment of development time
−2 stops (×4 normal ISO)	+5½ min
−1 stops (×2 normal ISO)	+2 min
Correct exposure	6 min
+1 stop (½ normal ISO)	−2 min

All steps after development are timed as normal.

Colour negative film cannot be pushed or pulled in this way, because changes of development time have a slightly different effect on each of the film's three layers. Pushing or pulling therefore leads to colour casts that are impossible to correct when printing.

■ TRANSPOSED PROCESSING The structure of transparency and negative film is broadly similar, as explained on page 98, and it is perfectly feasible to make negatives from slide film, and vice-versa. All that is required is to process each film in the 'wrong' chemicals — negatives in E6, and transparencies in C41.

Of these two techniques, the latter is most successful. It yields a negative that lacks the familiar brown mask of C41 films, but when enlarger filtration is adjusted to take this into account, quite reasonable prints can be made. They will, however, be high in contrast, and distorted in colour. The technique is therefore best considered as a special effect, rather than as everyday routine.

Other similar techniques provide rather different effects — negatives can be processed in E6 chemicals, but they will be lacking in contrast, and have a pronounced orange-brown colour cast. This can be removed if the slide is printed onto reversal paper.

FILTERS

The action of the human eye and the action of the camera are often compared and it is certainly true that the two have a lot of features in common. Each has an adjustable lens; each forms an inverted image; each houses a light-sensitive medium at the rear of a darkened chamber. Unfortunately, the comparison breaks down when the process of human vision is compared with the process of photography.

These two ways of seeing — with the eye and the camera — have separate and quite distinct characteristics, as anyone who has tried taking pictures by the light of a table lamp knows. Photographs often bear only slight resemblance to the scene we pointed the camera at. In the table lamp example, we remember seeing our friends' faces in their normal hues; but on the photographs, the portraits come out as sickly orange/yellow masks.

Fortunately, filters can help to correct the distortions that the camera introduces and bring photography more into line with vision. They can do other things, too, helping the photographer to introduce deliberate distortions, or to enhance reality — perhaps to show portrait sitters as they would like to be seen, rather than as they are. Of all the filters used in photography, though, the most valuable are those that match the colour of the light source in use to the spectral sensitivity of the film. One of these filters would restore the true colours to our portrait taken indoors by the light of a table lamp.

Colour balance

Unlike the eye, which can adapt to light of all colours, photographic film only works perfectly in light of just one colour. Most films are formulated to give correct colour rendering at noon on a sunny summer's day; a few films, though, are balanced to give ideal results in tungsten light. Using films in lighting conditions other than those for which they are manufactured will create colour casts — the pictures will seem washed over with a single hue. *Light-balancing* filters eliminate these colour casts.

There are numerous light-balancing filters and it is not always easy to decide which one to use. To simplify things, the colour of each different light source can be measured and a filter picked to match the light source to the film. Photographers specify the colour of each light source using a scale called *colour temperature*. There are two different measurements of colour temperature.

The commoner of the two scales is called the Kelvin scale. On this scale, light sources are assigned a Kelvin value, which runs from about 2,000 Kelvin for deep reddish-coloured light sources such as candles, up to 20,000 Kelvin for the light from a clear blue

sky. Summer sunlight has a value of 5,500 on the Kelvin scale and requires no filtration with normal film. Other light sources with higher or lower colour temperatures need filtration if they are to give accurate colours on film. This filtration can go either on the camera lens, or between the subject and the light source.

The filters most widely used to balance the colours of light sources to the sensitivity of films are the Kodak Wratten series. These filters — about 20 in number — range from deep blue through to deep yellow. The yellow filters, which are designated series 81 and 85, are used when the colour temperature is too high. For example, if the subject is sitting in summer shade, lit only by blue sky, a Wratten 85 filter fitted over the camera lens would give correct colour rendition. Without this filter, pictures taken on transparency film will come out tinged with blue. (With negative film, this and other colour casts can be at least partly corrected during printing.)

Blue filters — series 82 and 80 — are used when the colour temperature is too low, as it is when tungsten light illuminates the subject. Photographic floodlights, for example, will give correct colour rendering with daylight-balanced film only if a Wratten 80A filter covers the camera lens or studio lights.

In the same light, tungsten-balanced film requires no filtration, but when this film is used in daylight, an orange 85B filter must

Fine-tuning colour balance Absolute neutrality of colour balance is a widely accepted ideal in studio photography. To achieve neutral colour balance a studio photographer must take into account such factors as batch of the emulsion (there are frequently colour differences in manufacture), diffusing material placed in front of the light, and the age of the lamp. Normal procedure is to test variables by comparative shots. Colour differences are most easily judged on a standard colour separated guide, neutral greys and flesh tones.

be fitted over the camera lens. The chart opposite shows precisely which filters are needed in a wide range of conditions.

■ **MEASURING COLOUR IN MIREDS** The disadvantage of the Kelvin scale is that one filter shifts the colour of each different light source by a different number of Kelvins. So it can be difficult to tell which filter will make precisely the right adjustment to the colour of the light. The alternative Mired system gets round this problem, as explained below, and is simpler to use with colour temperature meters.

The two scales are related. Mireds are simply Kelvins divided into one million. In practice, though, it is rarely necessary to convert between the scales.

Mired filters are calibrated with *Mired shift* values, because they shift the Mired value of all light sources by the same fixed amount. Generally, Mired shift filters are supplied in values of plus and minus 15, 30, 60 and 120. To determine which filter to use, the photographer simply subtracts the Mired value of the light source from the Mired value of the film in use. The result is the Mired shift value of the filter that must be used. For example, daylight film has a Mired value of 182 and used in combination with tungsten-halogen spotlights, which have a Mired value of 312, the Mired shift is −130. The photographer would probably use the nearest approximation — a −120 and a −15 filter in combination. (Mired shifts of less than ten are undetectable to the eye.)

When Mired shift filters are unavailable, Wratten series filters can be used instead, though their Mired shift values are not convenient round numbers. The table below gives the Mired value for each filter.

Mired shift values for Kodak filters		
Filter (*yellowish*)	Shift value	Approx. f-stop increase
86A	+111	⅔
85C	+81	⅔
86B	+67	⅔
81EF	+53	⅔
81D	+42	⅓
81C	+35	⅓
81B	+37	⅓
86C	+24	⅓
81A	+18	⅓
81	+10	⅓
Filter (*bluish*)	Shift value	Approx. f-stop increase
82	−10	⅓
82A	−18	⅓
78C	−24	⅓
82B	−32	⅓
82C	−45	⅔
80D	−56	⅔
78B	−67	1
80C	−81	1
78A	−111	1⅔
80B	−112	1⅔
80A	−131	2

Filtering colours into tones
Each of the four distinct colours in this still-life are susceptible to alteration by filters. With no filter used, the over-sensitivity of normal black-and-white film to blue and its under-sensitivity to red give pale tones to the cigarette packet and a too-dark version of the red Dutch cheese on the left of the picture. A yellow filter lightens the yellow cheese and darkens the blue design on the cigarette packet. An orange filter performs a similar function to the yellow, but more strongly. A red filter dramatically lightens the red cheese and darkens the blue packet. A blue filter turns the yellow cheese almost black. A green filter lightens the tone of the apple, but makes the red cheese appear black.

NO FILTER

WRATTEN 8 YELLOW

WRATTEN 16 ORANGE

WRATTEN 25 RED

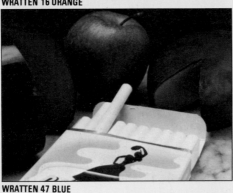

WRATTEN 47 BLUE

WRATTEN 58 GREEN

Filters for black-and-white film

Although today's panchromatic black-and-white films produces a strictly lifelike interpretation of the scene in front of the camera, this is not always what the photographer is seeking. For example, the flowers of many types of plant are more or less the same tones as the leaves of the same plant. To the viewer looking directly at the plant, there is no problem in distinguishing bloom from foliage, because they are different colours. But to panchromatic film, colour is irrelevant, and so the camera records all parts of the plant in the same shade of grey.

Such an even-handed response to colour therefore causes problems for the photographer who is seeking to make the blooms of the plant appear distinct from the leaves. Fortunately, though, the problem can be solved using filters.

A filter absorbs coloured light from part of the spectrum. A red filter, for example, absorbs green and blue light. By fitting a red

FILTER MATERIALS
Filters are made from many different types of material, but not all of these are suitable for use over the camera lens. The most common optical-quality filters are made of glass, gelatin or resin.

Glass filters are the most resistant to scratches and marks, but are also quite expensive. They are round and mounted in threaded brass rings. These filters screw into the front of the lens, so a different size of filter is needed for each different lens size. Fortunately, though, lenses from each manufacturer now have standard-sized filter threads, so photographers using, say, Nikon lenses with focal lengths between 20 and 200 mm need buy only 52 mm filters.

Resin filters are unmounted rectangles of plastic. They slide into plastic filter holders, which can be fitted with several different adapter rings; so one holder fits several different lenses. Resin filters are of poorer quality than glass or gelatin and though many special effects filters are available, there are few light-balancing filters in the manufacturers lists and the colours of those that are available are not accurately controlled.

Gelatin filters are optically the best of all, because they are thinner than glass or resin and therefore introduce less distortion to the photographic image. However, they are quite expensive, easily damaged and virtually impossible to clean. They must either be

taped over the lens, or mounted in a special holder.

A few filters are not intended for use over the camera lens. Dichroic filters are made from heat-resistant glass, tinted blue with a thin film of evaporated metal. Used over tungsten lights, these filters convert the beam to daylight-colour.

Coloured acetates and gells are designed for the same purpose. These filters, though, are not as heat resistant as glass, though most are now non-flammable

Speciality filter systems
The popularity of effects filters — such as graduated and soft-focus filters — has encouraged some comprehensive and sophisticated filter systems, (right).

filter over the camera lens, a photographer can increase the film's sensitivity to red light, and decrease sensitivity to other colours. This means that red parts of the subject will appear lighter on the print and other colours, darker.

Returning once more to the garden, it is clear that filtration can aid the photographer of flowers. When photographing red roses, a red filter will darken the leaves and lighten the petals, thereby separating the two parts of the plant. A green filter would have the opposite effect, making leaves lighter and bloom darker.

Other colours of filter affect the tones of black-and-white film in different, but equally valuable ways. The most useful ones are orange and yellow. Yellow filters reduce the film's slight over-sensitivity to blue light, so that the film renders tones closer to how the eye sees them. Orange filters have a more pronounced effect and are particularly useful for darkening blue skies, so that clouds stand out more clearly. Used for such pictures, red filters turn blue sky almost black, creating dramatic, if tonally distorted pictures. All three filters increase contrast in sunlit scenes.

For portraiture, orange and yellow filters will hide blemishes on faces, and the cooler colours — green and blue — make complexions more swarthy.

All of the filters used for black-and-white films are very much brighter in colour than the light-balancing and colour correction filters used with colour films and the two types are more or less incompatible. However, the bright colours of monochrome filters can occasionally be used to produce extreme colour distortions with transparency or colour-print films.

Used for their intended purpose, filters form an important control for the photographer using monochrome film, and make it possible to alter, adjust and manipulate the reproduction of colours for corrective or creative purposes.

Controlling haze and reflection

All film is sensitive to invisible ultraviolet radiation, but the two lower layers of film, sensitive to green and red light, are protected by a yellow layer that absorbs UV and blue light. However, the upper layer of the film, which makes a record of the blue light from the subject, is not protected. Consequently, in scenes that reflect a lot of UV radiation to the camera, this top layer receives more exposure than it should.

The practical effect of this is that pictures taken in a high-UV environment come out too blue. The cure is simple — just fit a piece of UV absorbing glass over the lens. This is the function of UV and skylight filters. Made from almost clear glass, these filters take out the blue tint from pictures taken at high altitude and near the sea, where UV radiation is a hazard.

Since such filters have no material effect on pictures, other than removing UV, many photographers leave them in place as lens protection at all times.

Polarizing filters

On reflection from most shiny surfaces, light undergoes a change. Normal daylight is made up of waves of light vibrating in all directions, but reflection from a surface cuts out some of these vibrations, so that the reflected light waves are vibrating in a single plane. This reflected light is said to be polarized.

CONTRAST CONTROL
There are more opportunities for controlling contrast in black-and-white than in colour. The basic options are:
1 Use a high- or low-contrast film
2 Use fill-in lighting or reflectors
3 Shade concentrate, or diffuse, the light source
4 Alter the processing: overexposure and underdevelopment reduces contrast, underexposure and overdevelopment raises contrast.
5 Reduce contrast by pre-exposing the film to a featureless light surface (such as the sky) then giving at least three stops less exposure than the meter reading.
6 Use degrading filters such as fog or diffusing filters to reduce contrast.
7 Use a coloured filter, as shown on the opposite page, to alter relative values. In particular, outdoors, a blue filter increases the effect of haze and usually reduces apparent contrast, while a red filter will tend to deepen shadows under a blue sky.
8 Treat a negative in a reducer or chromium intensifier.
9 Print on a soft or hard grade of paper.

Polarized reflections
Reflections from windows often limit the view inside, and reducing them is a common use of a polarizing filter. The pair of pictures below show the difference.

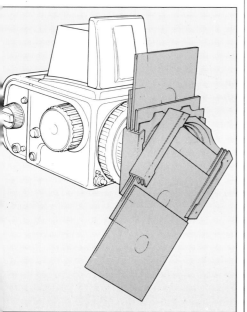

To understand this concept more clearly, think of a child turning a skipping rope. One end is tied to a tree and the rope passes through vertical iron railings. At the other end, the child's arm makes circles. This sends spirals down the rope as far as the railings. But here, the left-to-right movements of the rope are stopped and only the up-and-down movements continue.

The significance of polarization becomes apparent on trying to photograph through a shop window, or a similar reflective surface. Reflections of the street outside obscure the view on the other side of the glass. A special kind of filter, called a polarizing filter, can cut these reflections out.

In skipping-rope terms, a polarizing filter is like a second set of iron railings, through which the waves in the skipping rope — the polarized light — must pass. When the second set of bars is vertical, the waves continue on to the tree. Turning the bars through 90°, though, blocks all movement of the rope.

In a similar way, turning a polarizing filter in front of the camera lens cuts out the reflection from the window. In one orientation, the reflections are clearly visible, but with the filter turned 90°, reflections vanish.

In a more homely form, polarizing filters are familiar to millions of motorists. Polaroid sunglasses are simply sheets of polarizing material with the axis of polarization vertical. Since glare from the setting sun on a wet road is polarized horizontally, the sunglasses remove the glare without blocking out the other unpolarized light.

Polarizing filters work best when the lens axis is at about 60° to the reflecting surface; the reflecting-cutting power is more evident with telephoto lenses; and they do not work at all when the shiny surface is metal — such as chrome work or polished silver.

However, polarizers have another important function besides cutting reflections. Foliage, paintwork and other common photographic subjects reflect glaring highlights which dilute and weaken colours. Polarizing filters, correctly orientated over the lens, can remove the glare and intensify the hues.

Blue sky is partly polarized and a polarizing filter will darken and enrich the sky colour. The area most affected runs in a band across the sky, in a plane at right-angles to the sun. A handy rule is to make a fist, with the index finger and thumb sticking out. Pointing the index finger at the sun, a twist of the thumb points out the arc of sky most darkened by a polarizing filter.

Haze polarizes light to a small extent, so a polarizing filter has some value in cutting through haze. The effect is limited, but clearly visible on turning the filter in front of the eye.

Special-effects filters

Reality is frustratingly imperfect. Idyllic rural scenes are criss-crossed by power lines, and the faces of many portrait subjects are equally marred, by lines of a different sort. Special-effects filters help to gloss over things that are not quite right. Used with skill and restraint, they can make an interesting picture out of boring or mundane subject matter.

■ SOFTENING THE EDGE By far the most popular types of filter are those that diffuse or soften the image. This has an obvious value in portraiture, where a sitter may not wish to be reminded of the effects of time on their features. By softening the edges, these filters also produce images which many people feel more closely resemble images in our memory than do the unmanipulated products of the camera. So softening filters are frequently used to create a nostalgic or 'times-past' mood.

Though each works in a different way, all have one thing in common — they spread the picture's highlights into the shadows, reducing contrast. Where solid blacks are an important feature of the picture, the lens should be used unfiltered.
● *Mist filters* are usually etched with lines or scratches to spread the lighter parts of the pictures into the shadows.
● *Fog filters* have a similar, but more pronounced effect than mist filters.
● *Diffusion filters* simply soften fine detail, with less spreading of highlights. Diffusion, fog and mist filters are available with clear centres, so that only the periphery of the picture is affected.

Diffusing filters There are several types of these, each giving a slightly different visual effect. The fog filters used in both the pictures immediately below soften contrast overall, diminish sharpness slightly, and give slight flare effects around highlights.

Combining near and far Often stopping down a lens gives insufficient depth of field to render both foreground and background sharply.
A split-field close-up lens can solve the problem, as here, where a close wildflower and distant church tower appear focused together. Such filters are essentially half-lenses: half of the mount contains a close-up lens while the other half is empty. To conceal the dividing line, it helps to use a wide aperture and a camera lens that has a normal rather than a short focal length. Also, natural dividing lines in a scene, or featureless areas such as sky, help to disguise the trick. Split-field close-up lenses are available in ranges similar to conventional supplementary lenses, graded by diopters.

■ **TINTING HALF THE PICTURE** Gradated filters are coloured at one side and clear at the other, so they affect only one half of the image. The change from coloured to clear is not abrupt, but takes place over several millimetres, so that the join is not obvious.

Though gradated filters are available in many colours, each in two densities, and in mist, fog and diffusion forms, the most useful gradated filters are neutral grey. Positioned over the horizon, these darken the sky, intensifying colour. The paler of the two is virtually undetectable, but prevents washed-out sky areas — particularly on transparencies, which cannot be burned-in as can prints. Other colours tend to look gaudy and artificial on film, except where the light itself is brightly coloured. At sunset, for example, a red gradated filter helps reduce contrast, enhances sky colour, and retains extra foreground detail.

■ **MULTIPLYING THE IMAGE** Putting a multi-faceted prism in front of the lens creates several images instead of one. These heavy prisms, though, only rarely produce images that do not look hackneyed and dated. Best reserved as a last resort, prism filters may work with light subjects on dark backgrounds, such as spot-lit stage performers.

■ **ADDING SPARKLE** Twinkling nightlights never seem to sparkle quite as much in photographs as they did at the time of pressing the shutter release. *Starburst (or cross-screen) filters* redress the balance, creating brilliant rays around each light source.

These filters are etched with miriads of

Graduated colour filters
Although graduated filters are more conventionally used in neutral grey versions to control the tonal balance in a photograph, coloured varieties can be used for a more obvious pictorial effect, as for the pictures at left and below.

Starburst filters These have a crossed pattern of etched lines on the glass. This etching interferes very little with most of the image, but produces a characteristic pattern of rays from bright, specular highlights. The number and angle of the rays depends on the etched pattern. The effectr is enhanced at small apertures.

The effect of apertures
All effects filters produce different images at different apertures, so it is wise to preview the picture using the camera's stop-down control. Even this gives a limited idea of what the final effect will be, so a sensible precaution is to make pictures at several different apertures, adjusting the shutter speed to keep exposure constant.

lines which spread light out. The simplest just have etched parallel lines, and make two-point starbursts. Etching square patterns on the filter makes four-point stars — and so on, usually up to 16-point stars.

The effect of starburst filters varies considerably with the size and intensity of the highlight and the darkness of the surrounding scene — streetlamps at night give dramatic starbursts. Starburst effects also vary with the lens aperture — narrow apertures give the most pronounced star points.

Diffraction filters additionally turn each spark of light into a rainbow of colour. More brash than starburst filters, these are often useful in scenes that have little inherent colour of their own — such as snowscapes.

■ **PARTIAL STREAKING** Another design of special effects filter overlays a streaking effect in one direction only, so that the basic image remains undistorted but has the appearance of movement — as if a flash exposure and time exposure had been combined.

DARKROOM PROCESSES

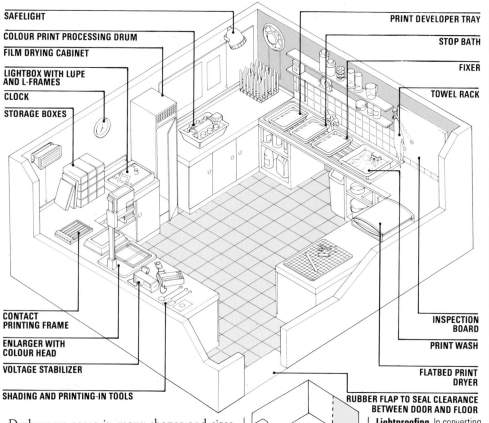

SAFELIGHT
COLOUR PRINT PROCESSING DRUM
FILM DRYING CABINET
LIGHTBOX WITH LUPE AND L-FRAMES
CLOCK
STORAGE BOXES
CONTACT PRINTING FRAME
ENLARGER WITH COLOUR HEAD
VOLTAGE STABILIZER
SHADING AND PRINTING-IN TOOLS

PRINT DEVELOPER TRAY
STOP BATH
FIXER
TOWEL RACK
INSPECTION BOARD
PRINT WASH
FLATBED PRINT DRYER
RUBBER FLAP TO SEAL CLEARANCE BETWEEN DOOR AND FLOOR

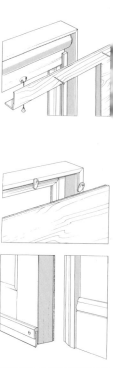

Darkrooms come in many shapes and sizes, from a cramped cupboard under the stairs to luxury purpose-built complexes. The basic requirements of a darkroom depend on the kind of work undertaken. For those photographers who simply want to process their slide films, for example, a well blacked out wall cupboard, or even a wardrobe used at night, will be quite adequate. Here the film can be loaded; the wet process is carried out in the light. Colour printing need not be too space-consuming as the two main items, an enlarger and a colour print processing unit, do not need to be in the same place.

Colour enlargers must be used in the dark, but the processing unit can be used elsewhere. The only part of processing that needs to be carried out in the dark is loading exposed print into the tube.

Black-and-white printing takes up the most room as prints are processed in trays. Laid out in a row they will need at least four feet of 'wet' bench, unless the trays are stacked in tiers which saves space.

Although the kitchen and bathroom are often suggested as temporary spaces because they have running water, any room will do. All the water needed is a bucket or two to put fixed prints into; these can be carried out later for proper washing.

There are points worth considering when setting up in a temporary location. Avoid dusty rooms, and deal with any chemical splashes on walls or carpets immediately.

Wet and dry Accidental contamination is an ever-present danger in a darkroom, and the greatest risk is of splashing onto dry materials. To minimize this risk, a normal precaution is to separate wet and dry processes in the room.

Lightproofing In converting a room into a darkroom, the two areas that need special attention are the window and door. One way of light-proofing a window, is to fit a wooden board into the frame, holding it in place with clips (above right, centre). Alternatively, a special darkroom roller blind can be fitted (above right, top); the blind is made of black fabric and runs in a trough. To seal the gaps around the door, rubber flaps and black foam strips will usually be adequate.

■ **WET AND DRY BENCH** It is a cardinal rule of darkroom layout to separate 'wet' and 'dry' operations as far as possible. This helps to ensure that fresh paper and negatives are not affected by chemical splashes, helps separate electrical apparatus such as the enlarger from water and other liquids and makes the darkroom much easier to keep clean. In many darkrooms, the 'wet' bench, containing all the process chemicals, is a shallow sink that can be swilled out completely at the end of the day. If the enlarger and the chemical solutions have to occupy the same worktop, a free-standing dividing unit made out of plywood helps to prevent splashes from the trays going anywhere near the enlarger.

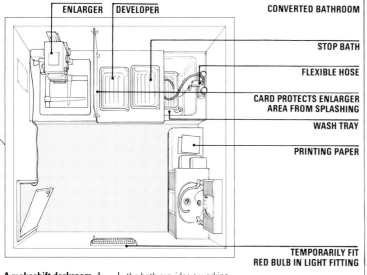

CONVERTED BATHROOM

ENLARGER   DEVELOPER

STOP BATH

FLEXIBLE HOSE

CARD PROTECTS ENLARGER
AREA FROM SPLASHING

WASH TRAY

PRINTING PAPER

TEMPORARILY FIT
RED BULB IN LIGHT FITTING

A makeshift darkroom A bathroom has certain advantages for temporary conversion: plumbing large water containers, and disposal. In the conversion above, a board over most of the bath provides a working surface. Print washing takes place underneath, in the bath itself. Power for the enlarger should be taken from outside the bathroom, for safety reasons.

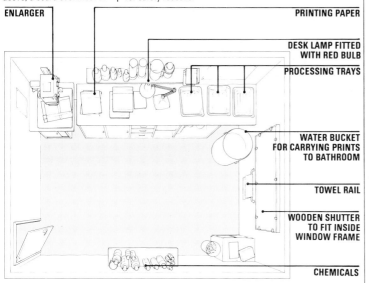

CONVERTED STUDY OR OFFICE

ENLARGER

PRINTING PAPER

DESK LAMP FITTED
WITH RED BULB

PROCESSING TRAYS

WATER BUCKET
FOR CARRYING PRINTS
TO BATHROOM

TOWEL RAIL

WOODEN SHUTTER
TO FIT INSIDE
WINDOW FRAME

CHEMICALS

■ PERMANENT DARKROOMS Few people have a spare room that can be fitted out permanently. But many people do have a shed, garage, attic, cellar or large cupboard under the stairs that can be turned into a permanently equipped darkroom. Large-scale darkrooms with running water can be expensive to fit out but offer tremendous scope for all kinds of work. A small bedroom with an existing sink is ideal. Kitchen units can be fitted down two walls for enlarging and print finishing, while a long, shallow sink can be fitted under the taps.

Special plastic sinks can be bought, into which four processing trays fit, allowing all the 'wet process' to be done in them. Three taps are useful in the darkroom — one cold

A converted study A slightly more sophisticated type of conversion, yet still temporary, is of an office or study. Even if there is no plumbing, processing solutions can be mixed and brought in from the bathroom, while a plastic bucket can be used for taking fixed prints out for washing. The room can be lightproofed with a wooden shutter than fits tightly into the window frame, and felt or rubber flaps around the door (see lightproofing methods on the opposite page).

tap can have a hose permanently fitted for washing films or prints while the other cold and hot ones can be used for mixing solutions or washing hands and equipment.

Darkrooms should be painted a light colour so that the safelight (see page 131) is well reflected around the room. A black section should be painted in around the enlarger, however, to prevent light from the lamphouse being reflected onto the paper in the easel.

Two safelights are a good idea in an average-sized room, one for general illumination hanging from, or reflected by, the ceiling, and one over the wet bench or sink to allow inspection of the print throughout the process.

A properly blacked out room may well be airtight, and good ventilation must be provided. Fumes from colour chemicals can be unpleasant and, without a supply of fresh air, working in the darkroom gets very tiring. An electrical fan incorporated into a light baffle is ideal.

The room should be laid out in working order so that all the major facilities are within easy reach. Worktops should be very stable, particularly the one which supports the enlarger. It is worth strengthening the support of free-standing units by screwing the back into the wall with a batten in between.

All working surfaces should be non-porous and 'wipe-clean' to avoid chemicals getting into the surface — chemicals lodged in the surface may contaminate subsequent operations. Floors should also be washable but splashed water on vinyl or PVC floor coverings can be slippy and dangerous and a less slippery surface, such as quarry tiles, is better.

It is a good idea to have all the power sockets in one place. Four or five will come in useful and they should be wall mounted at bench level. All plugs should be labelled so that they can be read under safelighting.

■ HEATING It is far easier to keep the solutions at the right temperature if the room temperature is warm and steady. Attics, sheds and garages are hard to keep warm in winter and to keep solutions warm every tray may have to have its own heater and every solution be kept permanently in tempering baths.

Darkrooms should also be comfortable to work in and the printer's own need for warmth is just as important as that of the processing solutions'. Electric bar fires are not a good idea as they give off light which will fog panchromatic materials. Fan heaters cause too much dust and oil heaters give off unpleasant fumes. A small electric radiator is ideal if the location does not already have central heating.

FILM PROCESSING

Behind nearly every successful photographic print is a properly exposed and correctly processed negative. The processing of any film, black and white or colour, is a simple sequence which, if followed correctly, will always lead to predictable, and consequently successful results. And yet there is still considerable scope for varied and individual treatments.

The fundamental approaches to processing both black and white and colour films are very similar. There are one or two extra stages in the process for colour films, and the timing and temperature controls traditionally needed to be much more precise than for black and white. However, recent developments in the field of colour processing and printing have simplified matters considerably and it is now almost as simple to work with colour materials as it always has been with black and white.

Black and white film processing

There are four basic steps to producing a black and white negative from exposed film: development; stop bath; fixing; washing and drying.

■ DEVELOPMENT The idea behind development is to convert the 'latent image' in the exposed film to a real image. When the picture is taken, the silver halide crystals exposed to light change, but the change is invisible. Development converts these changed crystals to black silver, eventually bringing the dormant image to life.

The way in which the image develops depends on a fine balance between the intensity of development (governed by developer strength and temperature — see below) and the film. For complete control over development time, many photographers use a 'stop bath' after development to cut short the process abruptly. The stop bath neutralizes the developer and also helps prevent the contamination of the third bath, the fixer, helping to prolong its active life.

■ FIXING Even after development, the image is not actually visible. This is because the unexposed silver halides are still present in the emulsion which now has an opaque 'milky' appearance. The fixing bath loosens these unexposed halides and makes them soluble in water so that they can be washed away to leave the visible silver image.

■ WASHING The final washing of the film removes any traces of unwanted halides and residual chemicals. Most photographers prefer to add a small quantity of 'wetting agent' at this stage to reduce drying marks on the film.

PROCESSING BLACK-AND-WHITE FILM

Materials and equipment

The basic equipment for black-and-white processing is, shown at right: developer, fixer, stop bath and wetting agent, with a graduate, funnel, thermometer, developing tank and reel, timer, rubber hose for washing, clips for hanging rolls to dry, scissors for cutting the film, and a squeegee for wiping off excess water.

1 Begin development by preparing sufficient volume of developer at 20°C (60°F).

2 Pour the developer into the tank (loaded with film), and start the timer.

3 Keep the developer at a constant temperature in a 20°C (68°F) bath.

5 Pour made-up solution of stop bath into the tank. Agitate as before.

6 After about 30 seconds, empty the stop bath, conserving it for future use.

7 Pour in fixer solution, set the recommended time, and agitate as before.

9 With the top of the tank removed, wash the film on its reel with a filtered hose. Place the hose deep into the tank and keep the flow gentle.

10 After washing for the recommended time, add a few drops of wetting agent to the remaining water, and agitate gently.

11 Remove the reel from the tank, gently attach a hanging clip to the free end, and withdraw the film carefully from the reel.

Agitation Regular agitation of the developing tank is needed to ensure that all the film receives equal chemical action. Follow the manufacturer's advice.

4 Empty the tank so that it is drained just as the development time finishes.

8 Empty the fixer when the time is complete, and briefly inspect the film.

12 Just before hanging to dry, draw the rubber squeegee tongs gently down the length of the film, to remove drops.

Altered processing Black-and-white film can be given less or more development than normal very easily, and this treatment can be used to control contrast. In the examples at left, the same shot was made on three separate lengths of film. One was given normal development, another underdeveloped by one-and-a-half stops (the exposure was increased to compensate) and the third overdeveloped by the same amount (and underexposed). Underdevelopment gave low contrast, over gave high.

■ **DRYING** Films are usually hung up to dry in a dust-free place, sometimes using warm air to speed up the process. A weighted clip on the bottom end of the film keeps it straight during drying. Without a weight, the film will curl and this can cause problems at the printing stage.

Developers

Four factors control the development of film: time; temperature; agitation; and developer activity. For predictable results, development must be exactly timed. If development is cut short some of the latent image is left undeveloped and the resulting negative looks thin and pale. If development goes on too long, the subtle variations in silver density are lost; the negative is contrasty, dense and hard to print.

The temperature must also be consistent — usually around 20°C (68°F) for black and white films. Higher temperatures mean a more rapid reduction of the silver halides, and consequently a denser film. If the developer is too cold the recommended time produces a weak negative.

Developer quickly becomes 'spent' as it works on the emulsion, so agitation is necessary to make sure that 'active' developer comes into contact with the emulsion throughout the process. Failure to agitate the developer at regular intervals through the process will result in weak negatives, and sometimes dark and light 'waves' in the emulsion.

■ **DEVELOPER TYPES** The most economic type of developer is called 'universal'. This can be used to develop both films and papers. However, it is very much a compromise; a universal developer cannot supply the optimum quality with all the various films and papers available. Each film has its own recommended developer, which is usually supplied by the same manufacturer. Most black and white films can be developed in a variety of developers, however, some of which produce quite different results with the same film.

In general, the manufacturer's recommended developer will provide a good tonal range for their film's speed or light sensitivity. Other developers will alter some of the characteristics of the final negative, thus making it possible for photographers to 'fine-tune' their working methods and materials to produce a negative which suits their own style of photography.

Typical promotional claims for developers are: increased film speed; finer grain; high contrast; and high definition. However, these characteristics cannot all be achieved with just one developer. For example, increasing the film's speed will normally result in coarser grain and the

developers which provide the finest grain normally reduce the film speed.

■ **FINE GRAIN DEVELOPERS** Many developers are termed 'fine grain' and these offer a good contrast range without speed loss. These developers are especially suitable for enhancing textures in the subject. Very fine grain developers are available too but these require a sacrifice in film speed. On the whole, fine grain developers can be used with any speed of film, and most general-purpose film developers are now termed fine grain.

■ **HIGH ENERGY DEVELOPERS** These are designed for use with fast films for 'pushing': they allow an increase in film speed without increasing contrast, therefore they are suitable for low-light, high contrast subjects.

■ **HIGH DEFINITION DEVELOPERS** For use with slow or medium speed films, high definition developers increase the apparent sharpness of the negative. Sometimes known as high acutance types, these developers create hard edges between areas of high and low density in the negative, helping to define an image crisply.

■ **CONTRAST** Many films are able to be fined-tuned during development to suit the two basic forms of enlarger, the condenser or the diffuser type. Often development times for film are given twice, one for normal contrast and one for higher contrast. If the negative is to be printed in a condenser enlarger then the normal contrast time is used. If a diffuser enlarger is to be used however, then the higher contrast range from the longer development time will be more suitable.

■ **CHARACTERISTIC CURVES** The type of developer used affects the range of tones in a negative. Some developers give equal emphasis to the complete tonal range, while others reduce highlight contrast, or emphasize mid-tones. The type of tones a developer gives a particular film is often expressed as a graph called a 'characteristic curve'. In simple terms, the density is measured in the upward direction of the graph and the exposure along the bottom. The developer controls the density that a certain exposure will give. The single upwards-sloping line indicates how the tonal range of the film appears in the negative. The steeper the slope, the higher the contrast in the negative.

The bottom part of the slope is called the 'toe' and this denotes the shadow areas. The top part is called the 'shoulder' and this represents the highlights.

■ **MIXING**   Developers come as dry chemicals or concentrated solutions. The dry powder forms must be mixed by the photographer and stored, usually in quite large quantities. These 'stock solutions' are then either further diluted and used just once, or used at full strength; they can then be reused to develop subsequent films. Amended development times are then needed to take account of the loss of activity which each developed film causes in the solution.

Many photographers, though, find it more convenient to use concentrates, which do not need lengthy preparation and are used in small quantities to make enough solution to process a few films, or a single film at one time.

In general, concentrates take up less storage space, can be bought in smaller amounts and are less complicated to prepare than powder types which need careful preparation and storage.

It is essential to store chemical solutions correctly to avoid shortening their effective life. Special 'collapsible' bottles are useful to keep the solution as airtight as possible. If the developer is exposed to air for a prolonged period, it becomes oxidized and consequently less active, thus causing poor results.

■ **DEVELOPING EQUIPMENT**   Most methods used to develop films involve some form of developing tank. The most common type of tank, and certainly the most popular with photographers who don't have a permanent darkroom, is the daylight 'universal' tank. Although these must be loaded in the dark, all other parts of the film process, from development to washing, can then be carried out in daylight.

Loading a tank
A small tank for up to two films can be loaded in a changing bag — a light-tight, zippered bag with elasticated arm holes. However, tanks are available for loading up to eight or more 35mm films and five or six roll films. For this number, a properly blacked out room or large cupboard is usually necessary for comfort and efficiency.

Films are loaded onto spirals which allow developer to circulate freely over all the emulsion surfaces at the same time. The cap of the tank prevents light coming in but allows solutions to be poured in and out.

Instructions on the base of the tank give the amount of solutions to mix in order to cover the film properly. Insufficient solution will result in part of the film being above the surface of the developer causing uneven development and ruined negatives.

Besides a tank, there are several useful and necessary items used in processing films.

| In the print, this girl would be cropped out to improve composition. | The key tones are the faces and the arms of the girl. | Care must be taken in printing to avoid blocking highlights in these areas. | The shadow detail in the eyes needs to be retained. |

Timers come in many forms, from a simple wrist watch with a secondhand to expensive digital timers with LEDs that make a noise when the sequence is over. The only requisite is that it must show the time in seconds to allow for consistent timing of agitation and the beginning and ending of each step.

A thermometer is also essential. For black-and-white processing a simple spirit thermometer is adequate; colour processing demands the precision of a digital or mercury thermometer.

A tempered water-bath, kept at a constant temperature by a small heater and a thermostat is useful for keeping solutions up to temperature during the process. Even in black-and-white processing, fluctuations of temperature between baths of more than 5°C should be avoided. This includes the wash, for plunging into cold water can cause 'reticulation' — crazy paving cracks in the emulsion.

Some means of measuring out solutions is also essential. Graduated measuring cylinders are normally used for measurement as well as for keeping the prepared solution warm prior to filling the tank.

NEGATIVE CHARACTERISTICS
A close inspection of the negative through a magnifying glass can indicate just how it will print. The qualities to look for are:
Density A negative with shadows too thin (light) or highlighs too thick (dark) will print badly.
Tonal range is the contrast between the maximum and minimum densities.
Sharpness should be checked in areas of fine detail.

Film developers
By matching films with certain developers, different negative characteristics can be enhanced (below).

Film developer combinations

Film Example: Ilford	Normal speed (150)	Developer	Effective speed (150)	Characteristics
FP4	125	Perceptol	64	Very fine grain
HP5	400	Perceptol	200	Very fine grain
FP4	125	Microphen	200	Good tonal range, sharpness, increase in speed
HP5	400	Microphen	500	Good tonal range, sharpness, increase in speed

Greater film speed increases can be achieved by extending development time in Microphen, with some loss of detail in shadows and highlights and an increase in grain size.

COMMON FAULTS

Most processing faults in black-and-white or colour can be traced to one source: the operator. The two commonest faults are over- or underdevelopment.

Overdevelopment gives a dense negative which prints as a very contrasty image. It is caused either by leaving the film in the solution for too long or by too high a temperature for the developing bath. (NB Do not confuse over-developed negatives with overexposed ones. These are more evenly dark and do not print contrasty images [near right].)

Underdevelopment is caused by low temperature, too short a development, or weak or exhausted developer. This type of negative looks thin, although unlike underexposed negatives they do have shadow detail (far right).

Drying marks Dirty patches or 'runs' on the film side, caused by chemical deposits; they mean that the film was not washed properly (below).

Crescent-shaped marks This is a particular problem with roll-film which is harder to fit into the spiral. It is caused simply by 'kinking' or creasing the film during handling before it is developed (below).

Fogging in camera If light gets onto the film while it is in the camera, or just the film cassette, opaque areas may be visible at the edges of the film, though the middle should be clear.

Scratching Parallel scratches indicate grit either on the film cassette mouth or in the squeegee used to dry the film.

Fogging Opaque areas that should be clean and clear, almost certainly due to light reaching the film while loading into the tank. All-over density throughout the film could also be fogging of a different sort. This could be the remains of silver halide still in the emulsion which has not been 'cleared' by fixing. A re-fix can cure the problem.

Undeveloped strip down one side of film, caused by insufficient developer in the tank. All the film must be immersed under the developer. If one film is developed in a two spiral tank, it is possible for the single spiral to move upwards during agitation. Use the securing device supplied with the tank.

Colour film processing

As in black-and-white film, a latent image in silver halide forms colour negative and colour transparency films on exposure to light. However, colour films have three layers of emulsion rather than one, and each layer records one of the three primary colours. During processing, the three latent silver images must be converted to three dye images in magenta, cyan and yellow. Then the unexposed silver halides must be removed as well as the images in black silver.

In colour negative film, the latent silver images are converted to negative dye image so dye forms exactly where the latent image is developed. In colour slide film, however, the dye image is positive and must form wherever the latent image is not. In other words, the latent image must be 'reversed' during processing. So colour negative and colour slide film each require quite a different processing approach. Two things both have in common, though, are an added complexity and a need for absolute precision in both time and temperature control — though this is less true than it used to be.

■ COLOUR NEGATIVES Most colour negative films can be processed by the C4I process. This has six chemical stages, although a number of recently launched kits have just three or four. The normal stages are: developer; bleach; water rinse; fixer; water rinse; and finally stabilizer followed by drying.

During development, not only are the three latent images converted to metallic silver, but also colour couplers form dye images in each of the three emulsion layers. Since the dyes are in complementary colours, the colours formed are the exact opposites of those in the original scene, just as the image forming silver halides show a reversed 'negative' image. Thus, wherever there was blue in the original scene, there is yellow in the negative. Another way of looking at it is to say: yellow appears in the negative wherever it did not appear in the original. When the negative is printed, the colours are 'reversed' to show once again the original colours of the subject.

After the negative has been developed it is immersed in a bleach. This particular bleach removes all the silver image, by 're-halogenizing' it (turning it back into its unexposed state). After a wash, the film then goes into the fix, which removes any unexposed areas of silver halide by turning them into soluble chemicals which can easily be washed away. Fixing also removes the re-halogenized silver, thus leaving an image made up of just coloured dyes.

The final bath is a stabilizer, which helps to protect the dyes against fading.

1 With the chemicals ready, pour colour developer into developing tank, and start timer. Agitate as necessary.

2 Near end of development time, pour developer back into its container. Add next solution and reset timer.

3 Add fixer in same way, and wash with hose and water filter. The bleach can be carried out with the tank lid removed.

5 The most widely used reversal processing kit is Kodak's E-6, shown here. Start by pouring developer into the tank. Start the timer.

6 Follow the recommendations for agitation. Empty the tank so as to finish at the end of the 7 minute development time.

7 Wash for two minutes with a hose and filter, or else simply add water, agitate and drain, twice.

9 After returning the reversal solution to its container, add the colour developer. After six minutes, replace with stop bath.

10 Return the stop bath to its container after two minutes. Add bleach for seven minutes, and then fix for four minutes.

11 Wash for six minutes and then soak in stabilizer for one minute. Remove the film to dry.

PROCESSING: TIME AND TEMPERATURES

'Kodak Ektachrome' Films (Process E-6)		
Processing step	mins*	°C
1 First developer	7†	37.8±0.3
2 Wash	1	33.5—39
3 Wash	1	33.5—39
4 Reversal bath	2	33.5—39
5 Colour developer	6	37.8±1.1
6 Conditioner	2	33.5—39
7 Bleach	7	33.5—39
8 Fixer	4	33.5—39
9 Wash (running water)	6	33.5—39
10 Stabilizer	1	33.5—39
11 Drying	10—20	24—49

'Kodacolor 100' and 'Kodacolor 400' Films (Process C-41)		
Processing step	mins*	°C
1 Developer	3¼	37.8±0.15
2 Bleach	6½	24—40.5
3 Wash	3¼	24—40.5
4 Fixer	6½	24—40.5
5 Wash	3¼	24—40.5
6 Stabilizer	1½	24—40.5
7 Drying	10—20	24—43.5

*Includes 10 seconds for draining in each step
†See instructions for using solutions more than once

Left Equipment shown here is (left to right): squeegee tongs, funnel, collapsible chemical container, film reel, developing tank, rubber hose, timer, graduate and thermometer, processing kit and drying clips. Commercial processing kits are available for small quantities of film, which suits most amateur use, although for convenience many professionals use custom labs to develop their film.

4 Some processes require film to be soaked finally in stabilizer. After this, hang to dry in dust-free atmosphere.

8 Drain the water, then add the reversal solution for two minutes. Re-check the temperature of the colour developer.

12 Dry by hanging in a dust-free atmosphere. Replace the stabilizer in its container.

COLOUR TRANSPARENCY PROCESSING FAULTS
Image too dark, red cast Inadequate first development time, **Temperature too low** Overdiluted or exhausted developer. **Entire roll black** Developers in wrong order. **Film too light, blue cast** First developer contaminated with fixer. **Colours pale, blue or cyan cast** Short colour development, temperature too low, weak developer. **Green colour cast** Reversal bath exhausted.

■ **COLOUR TRANSPARENCIES** There are several different types of colour reversal film. However, the most common ones are based around the E6 process. This has nine stages, as follows: first developer; water rinse; reversal bath; colour developer; conditioner; bleach; fixer; water rinse; and stabilizer.

Transparency film reacts to exposure in just the same way as negative film. A black-and-white type developer is used first to form the black negative silver image without affecting the colour couplers. In contrast to colour negative processing, the development of the latent silver images (first developer) and the creation of coloured dye images (colour developer) are separated in colour slide film processing. And in between comes a reversal bath which chemically fogs all areas of the film which were not exposed when the picture was taken. (Some reversal film processes require fogging by exposure to light rather than by chemical.) This creates *positive* latent images complementing the already developed silver images. The colour couplers in the emulsion are only activated in the next, colour development stage. Since colour couplers are activated by the by-products of a developing latent image, the coloured dyes form exactly where the positive latent images created by the reversal bath are being developed. So the coloured dyes give a positive image, corresponding to the colours in the original scene — though this cannot be seen because silver now covers the entire film.

After a 'conditioning bath', a bleach re-halogenizes all the silver, thus allowing it to be removed during fixing and washing, leaving the image formed by coloured dyes only on a clear background. Some manufacturers of processing kits make a bleach and fix that can be used at the same time (blix), which cuts out one stage in the process.

Finally, a stabilizer is used after a water rinse, as in colour negative processing.

COMMON PROCESSING FAULTS

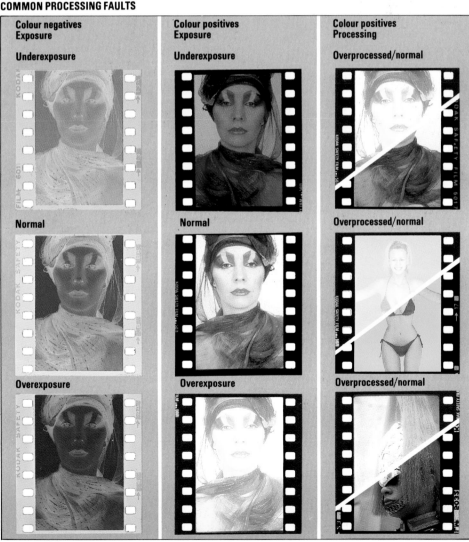

Colour negatives
Exposure

Underexposure

Normal

Overexposure

Colour positives
Exposure

Underexposure

Normal

Overexposure

Colour positives
Processing

Overprocessed/normal

Overprocessed/normal

Overprocessed/normal

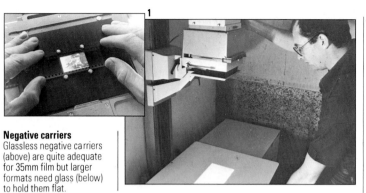

Negative carriers
Glassless negative carriers
(above) are quite adequate
for 35mm film but larger
formats need glass (below)
to hold them flat.

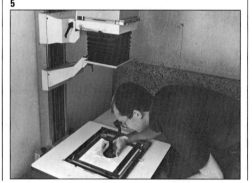

BASIC PRINTING With a
black-and-white negative
follow these steps:
1 If the enlarger is designed
to take different formats of
negative, check first that the
correct condensers are
fitted, and/or that the
picture area is illuminated
evenly (do this with an
empty carrier).
2 Clean the negative with
compressed air and/or an
anti-static brush.
3 Adjust the size of the
printing easel to take the
paper format and picture
size selected.
4 Using a sheet of white
paper for a brighter image,
focus at full aperture.
5 Use a focusing magnifier
for the sharpest image.
6 Place a ruler as a position
guide for the test strip.

BLACK-AND-WHITE PRINTING

Black-and-white prints are essentially photographs made in a darkroom, and the process has many similarities to taking a photograph in a camera and processing the film. The negative is projected onto light-sensitive printing paper by an enlarger. The image is then focused, exposure is calculated and the paper is exposed. The exposed paper, bearing a latent image, is then developed to turn the exposed silver halides in the paper emulsion to black, forming a positive image.

Any unexposed silver halides are dissolved in a fixing bath, leaving a permanent representation of the original subject in tones of grey ranging from black through to white. Because the whole darkroom is normally the 'camera' (though special enclosed enlargers do exist) the process must be carried out in semi-darkness.

7

8

9
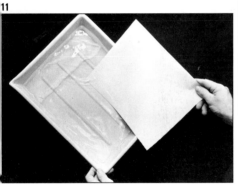

10

11

12

7 Select the lens aperture. With a negative of average density, the best resolution will be at about two f-stops less than maximum.
8 Under a safelight, cut three strips from a sheet of normal-grade printing paper. Place the first alongside the positioning ruler on the easel, and expose for the estimated correct time. Then expose the second strip for half of that time, and finally the third for double the time.
9 Develop all three test strips together for 90 seconds to two minutes (according to the paper and developer in use) at 20°C (68°F).
10 After development and a stop bath fix the strips for the recommended time (resin-coated papers need less than fibre papers). Then examine the tests under bright room illumination and note the best exposure. If the contrast is too high, select a lower-number grade of paper; if too low, choose a higher-number grade.
11 Finally, with the necessary adjustment made to the timer, expose and process a full sheet of paper. For smooth development, slide the paper into the liquid quickly and smoothly, and rock the tray gently but continuously during the development. Fix and wash as recommended.
12 Dry the print as appropriate to the paper type and the effect required. Resin-coated paper can be dried in a rack or laying flat exposed to the air. Fibre papers can be dried between heavy photographic print blotters or in a flatbed or rotary dryer.

Selecting the negative

Take care to select the best negative if there is a choice of exposures. A contact strip sheet is a useful selection guide and makes an at-a-glance file reference, but use a magnifying loupe when making the selection. Having chosen what seems to be the best frame from the contact sheet, make a more critical examination of the negative itself.

■ **ENLARGER** An enlarger is a little like a slide projector. Its function is to project the miniature negative image onto a larger sheet of printing paper to produce a reasonably sized 'viewable' image.

The basic design of most enlargers includes a head which contains a light source; an optical arrangement for passing light through the negative; a carrier to hold the negative flat and parallel to the baseboard; a lens; and a focusing device for getting a sharp image of the negative on the baseboard or printing easel.

The head is usually mounted on a vertical column which allows the head to be moved up and down. The further away from the baseboard, the greater the degree of enlargement.

The column is usually fixed into a baseboard which balances the weight of the head and provides a smooth parallel surface to focus on, and a flat base to put the paper or the easel on.

There are variations in enlarger design which are worth noting. The major variation is in the method used to transmit light through the negative. There are two basic systems: condensers and diffusers.

The condenser type is very popular for black and white enlargers. The condenser is a system of lenses that concentrate the light from the lamp onto the film plane, producing crisp, contrasty images and reducing exposure times. However, condenser enlargers tend to highlight any scratches or dust particles on the surface of the film, and those show up clearly on the print.

With diffuser enlargers, the light is scattered, usually by some form of opal Perspex screen, before it hits the negative. This

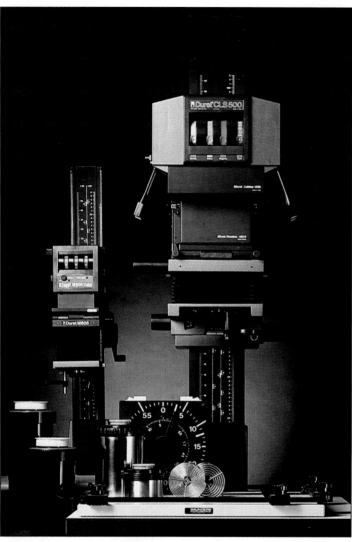

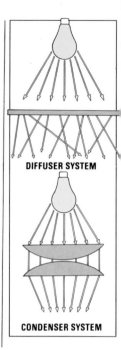

Colourheads on modern colour enlargers, such as these two Durst models (left), the three colour filters and the light intensity can be adjusted by dials on the head.

Enlarger light sources
The two alternative systems are diffusion and condenser, and each produces a distinctive quality of image. In a diffusion head, the light source is made even by a translucent screen; in the condenser system, two lenses focus the beam. Condensers deliver a slightly more contrasty result with black-and-white film but reveal defects. Diffusers are normally preferred for colour.

DIFFUSER SYSTEM

CONDENSER SYSTEM

Film carrier types include an adjustable mask for different film formats (**1** below), a glass carrier to hold thin film flat (**2**), and a hinged plate (**3**).

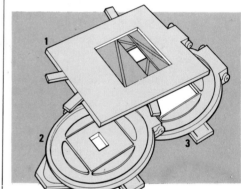

results in a softer image which does not show up blemishes to the same extent.

Enlargers are available for printing nega tives from all sizes between 110 and 10×8. No enlargerers can print all film formats properly, but most 35mm enlargers will also print 6×6cm negatives with a change of lens and an adjustment to the position of the condenser.

■ TIMERS AND THERMOMETERS The exposure of the paper and the development both have to be timed accurately. Many enlargers now have electronic timers as integral parts of their system. These can be pre-set to switch the enlarger on and off for accurately controlled periods ranging in length from one second to 99 seconds. The latest types have LEDs which flash the time and emit an audible signal on completion.

Like many other items of darkroom equipment, thermometers are available in electronic forms as well as the traditional mercury or alcohol type. The electronic

types have a probe which remains in the developer and a separate display which shows the temperature. If the temperature falls below an acceptable level, an audible warning is emitted.

Traditional mercury thermometers are perfectly acceptable, but they should be able to accomodate the very high temperatures required by colour processes.

■ EXTRA EQUIPMENT Washing trays or tanks for prints provide a constant flow of water to carry away chemicals. Generally they have a hose at the bottom connected to a tap and an overflow pipe which runs into a sink. Compromises based around this principle are often used, however, especially if there is no supply of water nearby.

Other items of value in the darkroom are a print easel and a focusing magnifier. Print easels sit on top of the baseboard and hold the paper by its edges to ensure a perfectly flat and stationary surface for the image to fall on.

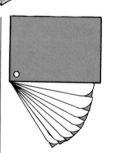

Printing filters For enlargers that lack dial-in filtration, a set of acetate colour printing filters is needed. The standard set of Kodak CP filters includes the four colours cyan, magenta, yellow and red, each in four strengths (5, 10, 20 and 40), with an additional CP2B, the UV-absorbing equivalent of a Wratten 2B.

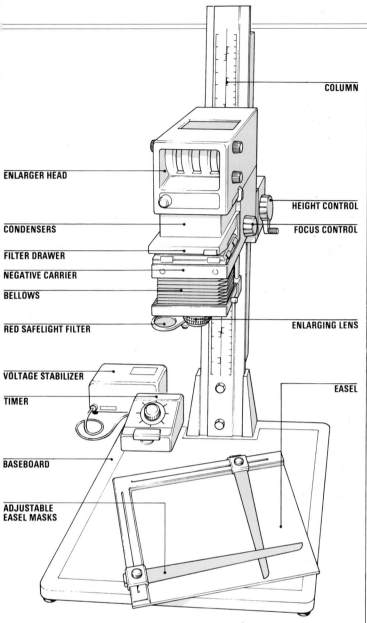

- COLUMN
- ENLARGER HEAD
- CONDENSERS
- FILTER DRAWER
- NEGATIVE CARRIER
- BELLOWS
- RED SAFELIGHT FILTER
- HEIGHT CONTROL
- FOCUS CONTROL
- ENLARGING LENS
- VOLTAGE STABILIZER
- TIMER
- EASEL
- BASEBOARD
- ADJUSTABLE EASEL MASKS

■ **DRYING** Resin coated prints (see below) can simply be hung up to dry. Warm dryers are available which can do the job quickly. Fibre-based papers, though, take much longer to dry because they absorb more moisture. If left to dry naturally, fibre papers curl dramatically. To avoid this a 'glazer' is traditionally used. This is basically a heated metal box with a polished and curved metal top. The print is laid flat onto the warm metal, emulsion side down for a high gloss finish or upwards for a matt finish. A tensioned canvas blanket is then stretched over the print and fastened to flatten the paper while it dries

■ **LENSES** The lens used with an enlarger is as important as the one used to take the original picture. A 50mm lens is the standard for the 35mm form format and an 80mm for 6×6cm negatives. The more expensive lenses have a wider maximum aperture, which provides a bright, easy to focus image on the baseboard.

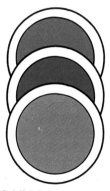

Safelighting
A standard red filter (top) can be used for black-and-white printing paper, dark green (middle) for slow panchromatic materials (indirectly), and amber for Ektacolour and similar papers.

Some easels allow an adjustable border of unexposed paper to be made around the printed image, which can be useful, for presentation as well as for easy cropping of unwanted details on the edges of the composition, or for drastic changes of shape of the final image.

Focusing the negative on the easel unaided is often difficult, particularly if the negative is very weak or too dense. A focus magnifier placed on the projected image acts as a type of microscope, enlarging the actual grain structure of the image, thus allowing it to be focused precisely.

■ **SAFELIGHTS AND DISHES** Black-and-white printing need not be done in total darkness — 'safelights' can be used to illuminate the darkroom. Unlike black-and-white film and colour paper, black-and-white paper is not affected by yellowish/orange light. So it is possible to work in quite bright lighting conditions, providing that the light is of a 'safe' colour. Most brands of paper have a recommended colour of safelight written on the pack.

Most safelights contain a bulb and a coloured filter, although there are a few which are simply light-emitting diodes (LEDs). Some safelights can be screwed into existing light sockets, although ordinary coloured household bulbs are not safe.

The size and type of safelight will be determined by size of darkroom and the layout of the working areas. However, most photographers prefer a light over the trays for inspection and one close by the paper storage and cutting areas.

As total darkness is unnecessary, the print processing can be carried out in rectangular dishes rather than tanks. This allows you to see the developing image and decide development time visually.

Three dishes or trays are used for print processing, although a fourth is often used for washing. The three trays are for developer, stop bath (or simply a water bath) and fix. Trays may be plastic, stainless steel or enamelled. They come in sizes to fit each standard size of paper, although the tray used is usually at least one size larger than the paper size in use, to allow for easy handling. Trays are sometimes sold in sets, with each one a different colour to allow for easy identification of the solutions each one contains.

Developer in trays quickly becomes oxidized due to the large surface area. Fingers also cause a more rapid deterioration of developer and so print tongs are useful to lift prints out of the developer into the stop bath. Tongs are also valuable for the fix to keep hands clean and thus prevent accidental contamination of the print paper or negative.

Black-and-white print papers

Black-and-white papers may be either resin coated (RC) or fibre-based.

Fibre papers are the traditional type and come in two thicknesses, single and double weight. Single weight is suitable for all purposes although some photographers use it only for making contact prints, preferring the durability and better appearance of the thicker papers for exhibition or portfolio prints.

RC paper has a plastic base with a very thin coating of emulsion on the surface. RC papers require less chemicals to process them, and they also have shorter processing, fixing and washing times. RC paper is far more convenient to use. However, it is more expensive and the final product is often considered to be less attractive than the fibre print.

Both types of paper are available in the same standard sizes and similar surface finishes. Typical paper sizes are 7×5, 10×8, 14×11, 16×12 and 20×16. Other sizes are available but less common.

The surface appearance of both types of paper can vary, too, and is usually chosen according to taste. Some common types in both RC and fibre papers are as follows:

● Glossy: smooth, brilliant shine on RC, less so on fibre unless glazed during drying.
● Lustre: finely stippled or textured surface low shine
● Semi-matt: smooth dull finish
● Pearl: very fine texture, low 'satin' gloss.
● Pearl and fibre glossy have a similar appearance from a viewing distance and these are the two most popular surfaces.

■ CONTRAST In terms of control over final print quality the most significant variable is paper contrast or 'grade'. All black and white printing papers come in a selection of grades from soft (low contrast) to hard (high contrast), often numbered from 0 to 5.

Although each brand of paper has its own grade system, as a rule the higher the grade number the harder the contrast. One manufacturer's grade two will not necessarily be the same as another's.

These grades are designed to accomodate the variety of contrast ranges found in negatives. Usually, a paper grade is chosen to enable the widest possible range of tones from a given negative to be reproduced in the final image. However, individual styles and tastes are the final veto on image appearance. As a rough guide, however, a high contrast or dense overdeveloped negative needs to be printed onto a low grade (soft) paper if the maximum number of tones from the negative are to be recorded. Conversely, a weak, low contrast or under-developed negative needs printing on a harder, higher grade paper to separate highlights and shadow areas from the mid-tones.

With experience, a darkroom worker will aim to produce standard negatives which will always produce pleasing results if printed on one particular grade of paper — usually the normal grade. This is a more economical approach as well as more efficient, as only a single grade need be stocked to accommodate fluctuations in negatives.

An alternative to stocking several papers with different grades, is to stock papers which offer several grades on a single sheet with the use of different coloured filters in the enlarger. These variable contrast papers (see box) are economical and give very fine contrast controls, even allowing more than one contrast range in different areas of the same print.

Local exposure control
It is quite common for certain sections of the print to need more or less exposure than the general time calculated by the test strip, especially in bright highlights and deep shadows. But localized exposure controls (dodging and burning) are quite simple in black and white printing. Many photographers use their hands or a black card mask to prevent light reaching the paper on a particular part of the image, simply by interposing them between the paper and the projected image during exposure.

■ COLOUR The image is ostensibly black and white, but print papers can actually vary considerably in colour. Most black and white papers have a bromide composition and these provide neutral black tones. There are a few papers still available called chlorobromide, which have a warmer (brown) black. Certain paper/developer combinations can provide blacks ranging from very cold, blue to warm, brown blacks.

■ CHEMICALS Although a 'universal' developer gives acceptable results with either RC or fibre papers, it is usually better to use the right developer for the paper.

Paper fixer is the same as film fixer but used at a different dilution. If care is taken in storage and during processing, fixer will keep for long periods and will work on many prints. It is particularly useful to use a stop bath for this purpose, for apart from its obvious use it also prevents too much contamination of the fixer with surplus developer from the print.

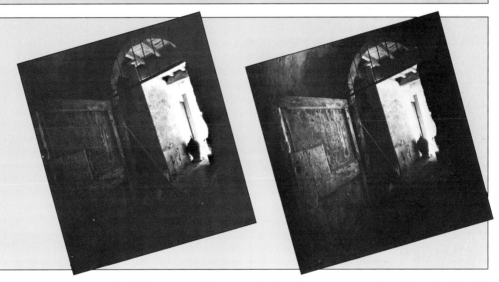

Highlights so bright that they do not record any detail at the same exposure as the rest of the print can be 'burnt-in' — given extra exposure — while a mask shades the rest of the print. Shadows that would become too dense at the whole print exposure can be dodged (masked) to hold back exposure at the right level while the rest of the print is given the full exposure. The pair of prints on the right show how local exposure control can bring detail into over-bright highlights even when contrast in the negative is high.

Print faults Correctable but common faults that occur in printing are those that involve particles or deposits on the negative. Because of the degree of enlargement in most printing, particularly from 35mm film, blemishes that easily pass unnoticed when holding the negative up to the light can involve considerable retouching and spotting later on the print. Some of the most common effects are (right) fingerprints and hairs from anti-static brushes, and (below right) dust. Basic precautions are to inspect the negative with a loupe before printing, and then to hold it at a sharp angle to an intense light (underneath the enlarger lens, for example). With scratches in the film, it may be possible to minimise the effect by printing the negative wet, in glycerine, between two sheets of glass.

COLOUR PRINTING

Colour prints can be made from either negatives or slides with any enlarger that has some facility for controlling the colour as well as the intensity and duration of light. The colour of the light is altered by filtration, whether the filters are simple glass slides held just above the enlarger lens or special 'dichroic' filters that can be dialled into the light path in a colour head.

Colour printing papers are similar in construction to films. There are three layers sensitive to blue, green and red which after processing give complementary coloured dyes — yellow, magenta and cyan — in the respective layers. As colour materials are sensitive to all colours of light, they must be handled and processed in complete darkness. So, unlike monochrome prints, colour paper is processed in lightproof drums, like film developing tanks, not in open dishes.

The procedure for processing colour papers is almost identical to that for processing colour film. However, there are alternative systems for making prints, such as image transfer (Ektaflex) and image diffusion (Agfachrome-Speed) as well as the more sophisticated dye transfer techniques.

Processing tube For convenience, and to avoid performing all steps in darkness, a print tube can be used for colour papers. This makes economical use of the more expensive colour chemicals, and is designed to be rotated through a bath of water thermostatically controlled at a constant temperature.

There are two basic procedures for normal colour printing from negatives or slides, the 'subtractive' and the 'additive' methods.

Most colour enlargers are equipped for the subtractive method, which uses three sets of filters in the subtractive primaries: cyan, magenta and yellow. These filters are moved or dialled into the light path to alter colour balance either singly or in combinations of two — combinations of three block out all colours of light and so act simply as a neutral density filter.

The additive method uses filters in the three additive primaries, red blue and green, or three separate light sources in these colours. Light is thus *added* to create the right colours in the print; in subtractive printing, the filters subtract colour from white light to achieve the same result. Colour balance is controlled in additive printing by increasing and decreasing the brightness of the light or the duration of exposure through each filter.

In a perfect world, a perfect colour negative or slide projected onto colour paper would give a balanced representation of the original. However, colour balance in the original is often less than perfect — especially with colour negatives — and the dyes used in film and papers are rarely a perfect match, due to variations in batches, light sources and the quality of materials. Indeed, colour negatives have an inbuilt colour cast created by the amber colour mask (see page 100). So for almost every

Filter factors The density of a colour printing filter depends on both its colour and strength, as the tables below show (yellow has little density at any strength). Use the filter factor to calculate any change in exposure: divide the originally calculated time by the factors for any filter that is removed; multiply if the filter is being added.

Filter	Factor	Filter	Factor	Filter	Factor
05 Yellow	1.1	05 Magenta	1.2	05 Cyan	1.1
10 Yellow	1.1	10 Magenta	1.3	10 Cyan	1.2
20 Yellow	1.1	20 Magenta	1.5	20 Cyan	1.3
30 Yellow	1.1	30 Magenta	1.7	30 Cyan	1.4
40 Yellow	1.1	40 Magenta	1.9	40 Cyan	1.5
50 Yellow	1.1	50 Magenta	2.1	50 Cyan	1.6

COLOUR PRINT PROCESSING

With a tube, all actions can be performed in ordinary room lighting once the paper has been loaded. This means, for instance, that the exposure sequences can be undertaken in a dry darkroom, and development elsewhere. Although many of the steps shown here resemble those for processing black-and-white film (pages 122-3), timing and temperature are more critical.

colour film image, the colour of the enlarger light must be individually adjusted by filtration to produce an acceptable print — although the same filtration may well be applied to a number of similar images on the same film.

As a starting point, most new packs of paper will have a suggested filter combination to correct any colour bias which that batch of paper was found to have before it left the factory. This filter combination might be written as 20Y 0M 0C. This stands for 20 units of Yellow, no Magenta and no Cyan. By dialling in this amount of filtration or building up a filter pack in the right combination, the light source will be altered to suit the balance of the paper. However, subsequent adjustments normally have to be made to get the colour absolutely correct for each picture.

Colour analyzers give an objective measurement of colour balance, once calibrated, and can save time and materials. Aesthetic judgements are up to the printer.

The choice of colour balance is inevitably subjective in part. Some photographers might prefer to see a slightly warmer colour range in the final print than actually appeared in the original scene, for instance. Absolute accuracy is often less important than a visually pleasing picture.

Judging which filters should be added and which removed to correct a certain cast can be difficult. But with colour negatives, the paper reproduces colours in reverse. So a cast is corrected by increasing the strength of filtration in the same colour as the cast, or by reducing filtration of the cast's complementary colours.

In colour slide printing, the colour correction is more obvious because the paper reproduces the same colours projected on it. So a colour cast is corrected by reducing filtration in the same colour, or increasing it in the cast's complementary colours.

When printing from a negative, then, a yellow cast is corrected by adding yellow filtration, or by cutting down magenta and cyan. But when printing from a slide, correcting a yellow cast means *cutting* yellow filtration or *adding* magenta and cyan.

Processing colour prints

Print processing in colour follows a similar pattern to colour film processing, and the controls, time temperature and agitation, are just as critical. It is because of the need for precision and because colour prints must be processed in complete darkness that they are normally processed in print processing tubes — unlike black-and-white prints, which are usually processed in open dishes. Processing tubes are very similar to film developing tanks, in that they are light-proof but have an opening which allows the various process chemicals to be poured in and out. However, the print paper is not held in a spiral, but wrapped around the inside of the tube.

The drum fits onto a base which should ideally contain a tempered water bath, as the temperature of the chemicals must not fluctuate during processing. Some bases are motorized so that the drum is turned constantly, maintaining an even distribution of chemicals over the surface of the print during processing. This operation can be done by hand, however, and a number of units have a manual crank handle — some are designed to be rolled across the bench.

Printing colour negatives

The reversed colours and heavy orange mask make a colour negative hard to assess visually and it is advisable to make a contact sheet. Two contact sheets are usually made. The first one will be to judge the correct exposure time and the second the colour balance. The first will also give some idea of

Filter	Factor	Filter	Factor	Filter	Factor
05 Red	1.2	05 Green	1.1	05 Blue	1.1
10 Red	1.3	10 Green	1.2	10 Blue	1.3
20 Red	1.5	20 Green	1.3	20 Blue	1.6
30 Red	1.7	30 Green	1.4	30 Blue	2.0
40 Red	1.9	40 Green	1.5 -	40 Blue	2.4
50 Red	2.2	50 Green	1.7	50 Blue	2.9

1 Fill the print-loaded tube with warm water to bring the contents to the recommended temperature.
2 Discard the water and add pre-warmed developer, starting the timer.
3 Roll the tube by hand or on a motorized cradle to ensure evend evelopment.
4 Towards the end of the recommended time, discard so that the tube empties as the timer comes to a stop.
5 Add the bleach/fix, roll the tube as in 3, discard and refill with warm water.
6 Open the tube, pull the paper carefully out by its edge, and wash as recommended. Clean the tube.
7 When the wash is complete, gently sponge excess water off the print.
8 Hang the print to dry in a room that is free from dust. Drying can be accelerated with a hairdryer.

of what major colour casts are to be dealt with. Unlike black-and-white paper, colour papers only come in one grade, so no decisions about contrast need be made. There are other aids, however, which may provide a good compromise, helping the inexperienced printer who does not want to rely on an analyzer to decide on the filtration needed. One very useful and direct method is to use print viewing filters made in percentages of cyan, yellow, magenta, red, green and blue. These give an idea of the effect of adding or subtracting specific percentages of particular colours, simply by viewing the test print through them.

Comparative exposure and filtration corrections

Print	Pos/pos paper	Neg/pos paper
Too light	Reduce exposure	Increase exposure
Too dark	Increase exposure	Reduce exposure
Small area dark	Burn in	Shade
Small area light	Shade	Burn in
Too yellow	Reduce yellow filters	Add yellow filters
Too magenta	Reduce magenta filters	Add magenta filters
		Add cyan filters
Too cyan	Reduce cyan filters	
Too blue	Reduce magenta + cyan filters	Reduce yellow filters
Too green	Reduce yellow + cyan filters	Reduce magenta filters
Too red	Reduce yellow + magenta filters	Reduce cyan filters

There are two important points to consider when making decisions about colour filtration. Firstly, the colour of the ambient light — that is, the light in the room where the print is being assessed must not be allowed to prejudice judgement of colour values. Daylight is the correct light for checking your prints; household lights are the wrong colour temperature and will affect the way the print is perceived. Special 'colour corrected' fluorescent bulbs which operate at around 5500 K are ideal for viewing; ordinary fluorescents make the print look green and household bulbs make it look yellow.

The second important point is to make assessments mainly by looking at neutral areas of the print. Greys, pale colours, and skin tones are the best indicators of subtle colour casts. If there is a cast, these colours will show it.

Colour reversal printing

Printing from colour slides goes by a number of names, including colour reversal printing and 'pos-pos' (positive to positive) printing. And unlike the colour negative process, there is a choice of print materials. There are, for instance, reversal papers, such as Kodak Ektaprint R14, which are like negative papers in as much as their colour dyes are formed during development. There are also dye destruction papers (Cibachrome) in which the dyes are already present and are destroyed during processing in proportion to the projected image. There are even the rapid print processes working on the dye transfer or dye diffusion principles, such as Ektaflex and Agfachrome-Speed.

Yet despite this range, the basic procedure for exposure and colour balancing is the same as for colour negatives — though filtration values are reversed. Only the processing differs substantially.

In many ways, getting the colour balance right with slides is actually much easier because the image is clearly visible in the light colours on the enlarger baseboard, and there is always the original slide for comparison. But there are extra points to consider in pos-pos printing. Weak slides will rarely provide a good print but underexposed, well saturated slides print well. Very contrasty slides are also difficult without some form of highlight masking. Highlight masking is a complex process which involves making a weak negative copy of the slide which is then sandwiched with the original during printing.

Reciprocity law failure is also more common with reversal papers. Very short or long exposure times will result in colour shifts in the paper. It is better to standardize on an average exposure time such as twelve

Colour reversal print processes

Reversal paper	
Process	Time at 30°C
Pre soak	½ min
First developer	3 min
Wash	3 min
Colour developer	3½ min
Wash	2 min
Bleach/fix	3 min
Wash	3 min

Image transfer	
Process	Time at room temp. (approx 20°C)
Soak in activator	20 secs
Migration of image	10 mins

Image diffusion	
Activator	1½ min
Wash	5 min

Dye destruction	
Process	Time at 24°C
Pre soak	½ min
Developer	3 min
Wash	½ min
Bleach	3 min
Fix	3 min
Wash	3 min

Chromogenic black-and-white film

Most black-and-white films form images in metallic silver, but some variable speed types such as Ilford's XPI 400 form the image in coloured dyes, like colour films — the word 'chromogenic' simply means 'dye-forming'. The dyes in chromogenic black-and-white film are neutrally coloured. Like colour film, they also have three emulsion layers, although each layer is sensitive to all colours. Like colour negatives, chromogenic black-and-white films begin with silver, link up with a colour coupler and finally form the image by a series of dye 'clouds' rather than actual grains. This accounts for the grainless quality of prints made from chromogenic black-and-white negatives.

The chemical process for this type of film is very similar to C4I. Indeed, a colour negative kit can be used to process one of these films, although the manufacturers recommend that the proper developer be used for optimum results.

RAPID PRINT SYSTEMS

Neither the image transfer nor diffusion system require complicated processing sequences and critical control over time and temperature, and for this reason, both systems have obvious advantages for the beginner.

Ektaflex

This system can be used to print either slides or negatives. Exposure and colour tests are made in the normal way using the Ektaflex colour photo colour transfer film in the easel. After exposure the PCT film is soaked in an activator solution in a special printmaker. After a short soak the film is laminated in the print-maker with a sheet of PCT paper. That is the end of the process.

The two sheets are peeled apart ten minutes later or slightly more if the room is cooler than 20°C (68°F) and the image is revealed complete.

Agfachrome-Speed

This system is for making prints from colour slides only. The exposed seconds, and increase or decrease the intensity of light via the enlarger lens apertures rather than increase or decrease times.

Colour reversal papers take roughly 20 minutes to process at a fairly high temperature while dye destruction papers take about 13 minutes at a slightly lower temperature. The dye transfer or diffusion processes such as Ektaflex and Agfachrome-Speed take much less time and require far less control over time and temperature. But once again the decision as to which process provides the most desirable results is personal.

■ RINGAROUND Many printers make their own customized colour cast identification chart called a 'ringaround'. This is a series of prints at different, known filtrations made from a very well exposed negative, with good tonal range and a selection of bold colours and a neutral area or two such as a pale grey wall or well lit portrait.

To make a ringaround, start off with a 'perfect' print from the chosen negative, then make a series of prints, changing the filtration by units of ten progressively up to 30 or 40 units in each of the filter colours, including red, green and blue. Mark each print on the back for reference, ie 10 Y, 20 Y, 30 Y, and ensure that the exposure time is adjusted to keep the density of each print the same.

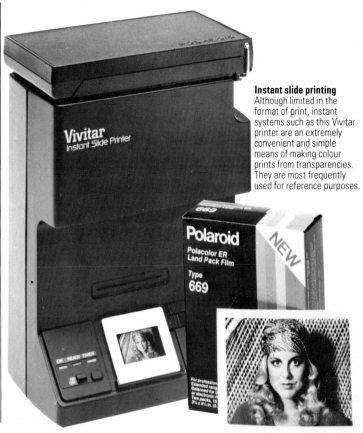

Instant slide printing
Although limited in the format of print, instant systems such as this Vivitar printer are an extremely convenient and simple means of making colour prints from transparencies. They are most frequently used for reference purposes.

Agfachrome-Speed material is 'developed' in an activator solution, either in a drum or a tray for 1½ minutes at room temperature. This is followed by washing for 5 minutes and that is the end of the process.

Both systems work in much the same way, in that there is a migration of the dye image from the exposed part of the sheet to a receiver layer. The main difference between the two is that the Ektaflex system has a separate sender and receiver while the Agfachrome-Speed combines the two elements in one sheet.

No laminating machine is required for the Agfa system, so a larger range of sheet sizes is available. The Ektaflex papers are restricted to 10 × 8 by the need for the processing machine.

Unlike any other colour printing medium, Agfachrome-Speed can have its contrast modified, simply by altering the strength of the activator solution.

For softer contrast a recommended amount of

potassium bromide is added, and for more contrasty results water is added.

Alternative routes
There are many pathways to a colour print. For example, a colour negative can be used to make a transparency and a transparency can be printed via an internegative onto colour negative paper. This procedure, sometimes known as 'C' type printing — as opposed to 'R' type printing directly from the slide. The internegative is ideal for high quality repeat prints from a slide. The internegative is made by contact printing the slide onto special low contrast internegative film, which is processed as normal colour negative film. The low contrast quality of internegative film reduces the high contrast sometimes found in a transparency and ultimately provides a better result.

Colour negatives can be printed onto special film with a transparent base which can be used either as a projection slide or for displays.

Colour negatives can also

be used to make black-and-white images by printing onto special paper. Normal black-and-white paper is only sensitive to blue light, so you won't get an accurate tonal range from a colour negative. The mask will also cause low contrast.

Special papers such as Kodak Panalure are sensitive to all colour (panchromatic) and so will give an accurate reproduction of the colour negative. Due to its panchromatic characteristics the paper must be treated as colour is and handled in the dark.

Stick all the various colour progressions in sequence around the ideal print on a sheet of card and use this to help assess subsequent work. If each print is labelled with the amount of filtration it was given, then it is a simple task to compare the print in progress with the ringaround to see how much of any particular colour must be removed to get the print back to neutral.

Judging colour balance is an acquired skill, although there are various aids on the market to help you along. A colour analyzer is an electronic device for measuring the colour of light transmitted through the negative. However, to use an analyzer you must have already made one 'perfect print' for reference. The information about filtration gained from making this print is then used to calibrate the analyzer for making subsequent 'ideal' prints on the same batch of paper. This certainly helps in achieving consistent results, and may save time making test prints.

However, the very objectivity of colour analyzers can tell against them, for many printers feel that each print must be individually, and subjectively, matched to each negative. Some prints will have colours that need to be enhanced or subdued to give the most pleasing effect. All the electronics can do is tell what filtration to use for prints with identical colour balance every time.

SPECIAL EFFECTS

Conventional developing and printing techniques can be experimented with to produce creative or 'special' effects with either black-and-white or colour originals.

■ **COMBINATION PRINTING** Two more negatives can be printed onto the same sheet of paper to create surrealistic images or simply to add interest from one negative to a dull area of the other.

Landscapes with featureless skies but interesting foregrounds can have dramatic clouds added to them to create more interest. The original scene is printed and left in the enlarger easel. The negative is removed and the cloudscape is put in. With the red filter under the lens to prevent further exposure of the paper, the sky is positioned roughly to cover the area of empty space in the original image. An overlay with a rough outline of the horizon is often used as a compositional aid.

During the second exposure, a mask with one edge cut to resemble the shape of the horizon is held over the already exposed area of the print, thus preventing further exposure.

■ **HIGH CONTRAST** Images formed solely from black-and-white with no intermediate tones can be quite dramatic. The simplest method of making a high contrast image is by using lith film. Lith film can be handled like black-and-white paper under a red safelight. But it requires lith developer, two stock solutions which are mixed for use immediately prior to development. To create a positive high contrast image, the continuous tone negative must be copied onto lith film to make a film positive. This is usually done by contact printing the original onto 'line' film, processing it and then contacting the line positive again onto another sheet of lith film to give a high contrast negative. This can be cut out to fit into the enlarger and printed onto ordinary black-and-white paper or, through coloured filters, onto colour paper.

Composite printing To print the image of trees hanging over a seascape, five separate exposures were made onto one sheet of paper: one of the seascape, one of the nearer tree and another of its 'roots', and finally the same pair but smaller.

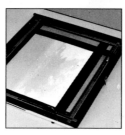

Composite printing:
1 Select the negatives
2 Block out unwanted areas
3 Sketch the images onto a sheet of paper on the easel
4 Make the first exposure
5 Store the sheet
6 Load the second negative
7 Position the second image
8 Expose on original sheet

Bas relief The negative was contact-printed onto line film and weakly developed. The two pieces of film were then printed slightly out of register.

■ **BAS RELIEF** This term stems from certain types of low profile sculpture, which is hung on a wall and lit from the side to enhance its three-dimensional quality.

The hallmark of a bas relief print is an illusion of 3D. A weak positive image is made on film by contact printing with the chosen negative. The two images are then sandwiched together on a light box. The negative and positive images should match up exactly, but the effect is produced by moving one or the other slightly to the left or right.

When the two images are very slightly out of register, hard shadows and highlight will appear around solid shapes in the picture. When the best effect is achieved, the two bits of film are taped together along the sprocket holes and printed to produce an illusion of 3D.

■ POSTERIZATION This type of image is half way between a continuous tone and a high contrast picture. There are tonal changes but they are abrupt rather than gradual, giving solid areas of tone or colour rather than gradations.

Posterizations are made by making several copies of an original in varying densities on lith film and then printing them in register on a single sheet of paper. Lith negatives must be the same size as the required final image as these will be contact printed, each one providing a tone of grey which will build up to a complete image in solid areas of black, grey and white.

■ SABATTIER EFFECT The visual qualities of the Sabattier effect are the result of chemical reactions. An ordinary print is exposed and partly developed, but at some point in the development it is very briefly re-exposed to light — usually a normal household bulb held over the print.

The bright areas of the print will still contain some unexposed silver halides after the first exposure under the enlarger. The second exposure turns these to metallic silver; the result is a darkening of what would have been highlight areas. Further manifestations of the effect appear as light lines between dark and light areas.

COLOUR FROM BLACK-AND-WHITE
Colour prints can be made from black-and-white negatives by printing through filters onto colour negative papers. Prints can be made either in a single colour or in various colours by selective masking, filtration and exposure. A normal test strip helps decide exposure times; a second with different filtrations shows the effect of different colours.

Colour pape
with filters to m
flat colour rather
essential for the
usually done with
bars. Registration h
edges of the lith ne
pins on a bar corr
the film are fitte
locate the lith fil
ment, the bar with the p
to register each sheet of fil
exactly the same position.

■ SANDWICHES Two negatives can be printed simultaneously by sandwiching them together in the negative carrier of the enlarger. The idea is usually to sandwich two negatives which have opposing light and dark areas, that is, where one has a shadow area (a clear area on film), the other should have some interesting detail with plenty of highlights (dense areas on film).

■ SCREENS Combining a special texture screen negative with an ordinary negative can create interesting graphic effects. The screen and the image are printed together like a sandwich and the texture is super-imposed all over the actual image.

Proprietary texture screens come in many forms, from fine parallel lines to grainy 'etched' effects, but home-made screens can easily be made by photographing interesting textures and developing a weak negative to cut out and use as a sandwich.

LOW DENSITY LINE POSITIVE

MID-RANGE LINE POSITIVE

HIGH DENSITY LINE POSITIVE

DENSITY NEGATIVE

MID-RANGE LINE NEGATIVE

HIGH DENSITY LINE NEGATIVE

ORIGINAL CONTINUOUS-TONE NEGATIVE

Posterization The first step is to make a series of tone separations. The original negative here was first contact-printed with line film at different exposures to give three line positives at different densities. These in turn were contact-printed with line film to produce three corresponding line negatives. Different combinations of these six pieces of film gave a variety of separated tones, each of which could be printed normally (either at different densities on black-and-white paper for a posterized version in greys and black, or through different filters on colour printing paper). From a basic set of line conversions a large number of interpretations is possible.

Photograms are images made without optics — by placing objects directly onto a sensitive emulsion and exposing to light. They are, in effect, shadow-pictures, and can be made on printing paper or film, in colour or black-and-white. The photogram at left is of a flower placed directly onto 5 × 4 inch colour reversal film and exposed under an enlarger. Any light source can be used, from a flashlight to the room light, but an enlarger allows precise control for repeatable results.

DUPLICATES AND CONVERSIONS

Making accurate duplicates of transparencies and negatives and converting one to the other are essential skills. The principal uses of duplicating and converting are:

Safety Any original photograph is susceptible to damage and deterioration and if only one piece of film exists of an important image, a copy is useful insurance. Duplication is also an important archival technique, particularly with colour film, because the coloured dyes are less stable than the silver in black-and-white film — colour images can be converted into three black-and-white silver images, called 'separations'.

Simultaneous use In professional photography in particular, a picture may be needed for reproduction by more than one publication at a time.

Different use An image shot on negative stock may be needed for slide projection, or the photographer may want to use a negative colour printing process for a photograph that exists only as a transparency.

Correction Image values such as contrast and colour balance can be altered relatively easily during the process of duplicating.

Post-production techniques Techniques such as retouching, toning and dyeing, which may include some risk of irreversible damage, are more safely performed on a copy than on an original. Additionally, such techniques may be easier to perform on an enlargement.

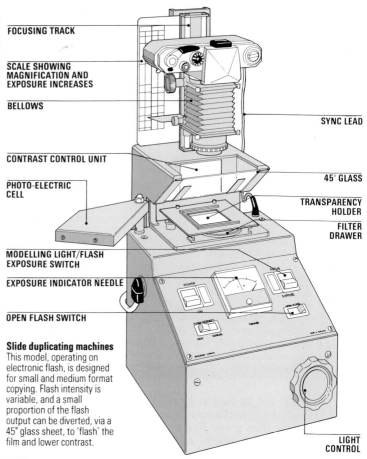

FOCUSING TRACK

SCALE SHOWING MAGNIFICATION AND EXPOSURE INCREASES

BELLOWS

CONTRAST CONTROL UNIT

PHOTO-ELECTRIC CELL

MODELLING LIGHT/FLASH EXPOSURE SWITCH

EXPOSURE INDICATOR NEEDLE

OPEN FLASH SWITCH

SYNC LEAD

45° GLASS

TRANSPARENCY HOLDER

FILTER DRAWER

LIGHT CONTROL

Slide duplicating machines
This model, operating on electronic flash, is designed for small and medium format copying. Flash intensity is variable, and a small proportion of the flash output can be diverted, via a 45° glass sheet, to 'flash' the film and lower contrast.

Copy negative procedure
Using an enlarger, negatives can be copied up to the size of the required print on Direct Duplicating Film, and this copy negative can then be contact printed. Place the original negative in the carrier just as for normal printing, and focus and frame the image in the same manner. Under red safelighting, make test strips, remembering that longer exposures produce a weaker image. Develop for two to two and a half minutes in Kodak D-163 or similar developer.

DUPLICATE TRANSPARENCIES

Film	Format	Type of copy	Comments
Ektachrome Slide Duplicating Film 5071	35mm 46mm 70mm	Colour transparency	E-6 process; tungsten-balanced
Ektachrome SE Duplicating Film SO-366	35mm	Colour transparency	E-6 process; balanced for electronic flash
Ektachrome Duplicating Film 6121	4 × 5in 8 × 10in 11 × 14in 12 × 15in 16 × 20in	Colour transparency	E-6 process; tungsten-balanced
Kodachrome 25	35mm	Colour transparency	Increases contrast, but very sharp results

SEPARATION NEGATIVES

Film	Format	Type of copy	Comments
Kodak Separation Negative Film 4133	18 × 24in 24 × 30in 30 × 40in 40 × 50in 50 × 60in	Set of three black-and-white negatives, recording red, blue and green images	DK-50 or DG-10 developer

INTERNEGATIVES

Film	Format	Type of copy	Comments
Vericolor Internegative Film 6011	35mm	Colour negative	C-41 process; tungsten-balanced
Vericolor Internegative Films 4112 and 4114	4 × 5in 5 × 7in 8 ×.10in	Colour negative	C-41 process; tungsten-balanced

Copy negatives

Negative materials reverse the tones of an image, while copying is a positive process. Consequently, special direct copy films are needed in order to make a duplicate of a negative. For black-and-white copy negatives, Kodak's Professional Black-and-White Duplicating Film and Rapid Process Copy Film are ideal, but for colour negatives the choice is less satisfactory: transparency duplicating films will do the job, but without the orange masking in conventional colour negative stock, and printing may not be easy.

As with most copying and converting, there are a number of methods of duplicating negatives: loading the film in a camera and using a slide duplicating machine or simple slide holders; contact copying in a glass frame; or by projection in an enlarger. In-camera copying, using the 35mm Rapid Process Copy Film is convenient and makes it possible to reduce different negative formats to a common size. Enlarger copying is useful in allowing shading and other fine controls, as well as making detailed retouching possible. Also, if the copy is made to the size of the intended print, the printing can be made by contact, so saving some loss of image quality.

Contrast control is one of the major problems in copying. Altered processing (see page 113), shading and printing-in during enlargement, and sandwiching a weak mask with the original are just some of the ways of reducing contrast. Shading and printing-in can be performed in the same way as for regular paper printing (see pages 132-33), except that the tones are reversed: this is a positive process, so that to make part of an image darker in the print, it must be weaker in the copy negative, and needs *less* exposure.

Duplicate transparencies

Transparency duplicating can be performed with the same equipment as the copying of negatives: slide duplicating machine, enlarger or contact printing frame. However, as the greatest demand is for 35mm slides for projection, in-camera use with a slide duplicating machine is often the best method. Some slide duplicating machines have a tungsten light source compatible with Ektachrome 5071 slide duplicating film, but most use electronic flash and for these Ektachrome SO-366 is the best film. Such specialist duplicating films contain their own masks to reduce the build-up of contrast that is normal in duplicating. The table includes Kodachrome 25, for although duplicates are likely to be contrasty, the film gives the sharpest results.

For all the films, careful filtration is essential for colour fidelity, and as the colour balance varies from batch to batch, it is best to buy in bulk, test one roll to discover the filter pack needed, and freeze the rest for future use. Standard test transparencies containing

COPY NEGATIVES

Film	Format	Type of copy	Comments
Kodak Professional Black-and-White Duplicating Film (formerly SO-015)	4 × 5in 5 × 7in 8 × 10in	Black-and-white negative	D-163, DPC or DK-50 developer
Kodak Rapid Process Copy Film	35mm	Black-and-white negative	DX-80 developer has blue-tinted base
Any duplicate transparency film (see below)	35mm 46mm 70mm 4 × 5in to 16 × 20in sheets	Colour negative, but lacking orange mask	Reversal processing: E-6 if Ektachrome

NEGATIVE TO POSITIVE

Film	Format	Type of copy	Comments
Eastman Fine Grain Release Positive	35mm	Black-and-white positive transparency from black-and-white negative	D-163 or HC-110 developer
Vericolor Slide Film 5072	35mm	Colour transparency	C-41 process; tungsten-balanced
Vericolor Print Film 4111	4 × 5in 8 × 10in 16 × 20in	Colour transparency	C-41 process; tungsten-balanced

Film suitability Use these four tables (above and opposite) to select the most suitable film for the type of original that must be copied. Note that professional duplicating films are not always the best choice, as they are designed for specific techniques that may involve equipment that is unavailable.

recognizable colours (such as flesh tones) are useful. Filtration will vary according to the dyes in the original transparency. Kodachrome and Ektachrome, for example, will need different filter packs.

Internegatives

Although transparencies can be printed directly, using Cibachrome and similar processes, the more traditional technique of printing from colour negatives offers more fine control over image values. An internegative is simply a negative copy of a transparency. Internegatives can be made on the films listed above in the same way as negative copying and transparency duplicating.

Separation negatives

For dye transfer printing, and also for archival storage, colour transparencies are converted into three black-and-white continuous-tone negatives. Each is copied through a different primary colour filter — red, blue and green — using respectively Wratten 25, 47 and 58 filters. The colour information, carried in permanent metallic silver, is thus separated, hence the name. Separation negatives must be made in perfect register and with highly accurate exposure. Step wedges are usually copied alongside the image as controls and measured with a densitometer.

CONTRAST CONTROL One of the inherent problems in copying an image from one piece of film onto another is the build-up of contrast, tending to wash out highlights and causing the shadows to block up — in both cases, detail will be lost. Only if the original lacks contrast will there seem to be an improvement.

In duplicating, there are three standard ways to treat this problem. One is to use a professional duplicating film, which contains its own inbuilt masking to reduce contrast. For conventional films, some slide duplicating machines contain mechanisms for fogging the emulsion very slightly (see illustration opposite). Thirdly, the development time can be reduced to lower contrast.

POST-PRODUCTION TECHNIQUES

The photographic process can be divided into three distinct areas: shooting, the dark room and the work room. Each is physically separate, but photographs are often planned with the later stages in mind. For instance, a photographer may shoot a high-contrast interior without fill-in lighting, knowing that the shadows can be opened up by printing controls in the darkroom. To an even greater extent minor miracles of alteration and adjustment are possible in the work room *after* the final image has been processed and fixed. These post-production techniques range from the minor cosmetics of spotting a black-and-white print to the kind of manipulations and additions that create an entirely new image. Because of the wide range of post-production techniques it helps to plan the work at an early stage, deciding at which point — negative, print or transparency — particular action is needed.

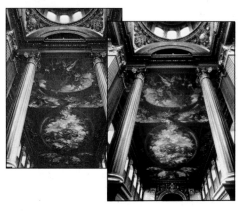

Gold toning Gold chloride is not only useful as an archival toner (to increase permanence), but also produces a range of attractive colour tones.

Bromide prints tend to go blue-black, unless they have first been sepia-toned in a sulphide bath, in which case they will be warmer (above right).

BLEACHING, TONING AND DYEING

Black-and-white prints can be subjected to various kinds of chemical treatment and to baths that add or remove tone or colour. These can simply be corrective techniques, such as retouching (see pages 145-146) but they can also be used to enhance the appearance of the picture more dramatically — to alter the overall colour of the picture, for example. Certain kinds of toning also increase the permanence of the image, and are standard archival treatment.

Bleaching

The standard bleach is *Farmer's Reducer*, a two-part solution of potassium ferricyanide and sodium thiosulphate. The strength of the solution determines the speed of working, but if concentrated can get out of

control. To lighten the entire print, submerge it completely in the bleach bath, but to brighten the highlights alone, use a cotton wool swab soaked in reducer on a *dry* print, quickly washing it when the desired lightening has been reached.

Toning

There are a number of different toning formulae, each giving a subtly different hue, but all add a colour to the developed areas of a print, and some also give protection against any atmospheric contamination. Aesthetically, there is a major difference between the generally modest effects of toners such as selenium, gold and sepia, and the more strident and colourful results of multi-toners that use colour couplers.

The two most generally useful are *selenium* and *gold*. They are popular because they significantly increase the life of the print. The colour each gives varies considerably with the brand of printing paper. But this is not a problem, since the photographer can stop the process when the colour is right because both are single-solution toners. Selenium toning usually takes between one and ten minutes, and must be watched carefully. Sometimes split-toning occurs, with only the darker tones affected. Gold toning (with a gold chloride solution) can take up to 20 minutes. On bromide paper the effect tends towards blue-black, on chlorobromide paper, towards orange-brown. As with selenium, continuous monitoring is important.

Sepia toning gives a more distinctive colour, reminiscent of old prints. Most photographers use a two-bath solution to sepia-tone prints. The print is soaked in the first bath, a bleach bath, until the image has all but disappeared, and then rinsed. The second bath restores the image in brown. Less bleaching gives a darker brown result.

Dyeing

Toners work only where there is developed silver in the print, so that in white highlights their effect is negligible. But dyes can be applied all over the print, and their effect is particularly pronounced in light, undeveloped areas. So by careful planning, the colouring of a black-and-white print can be split between toners and dyes.

Photographic dyes are transparent, and can be applied in a variety of ways, from an undiscriminating bath, which gives even coverage, to swabs, brushes and airbrushing, for controlled results. Dyes are soluble in water, so that, at the time of application they can, to some extent, be removed quickly by a thorough wash. However, because dyeing is primarily a retouching technique, it is dealt with on the following pages.

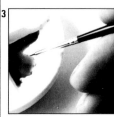

Retouching For the basic brush retouching of spots and blemishes from a black-and-white print:
1 Mix different tones of the retouching colour until the colour of the print is matched as closely as possible.
2 Dilute the mixed colour with water.
3 Pick up some colour on the brush, twirling the brush for an even soaking.
4 Draw the brush against your thumbnail to remove excess retouching colour. Ensure the brush is not so full that it leaves a pool.
5 Build up colour on the print in small touches until the density of the retouched area matches the surrounding print precisely.

Hand-colouring These hand-coloured prints by Sue Wilks demonstrate that in this area of retouching restraint is important. The delicacy of effect in the colours is achieved by building up the dyes very slowly. As the added colour increases the density of the image, the original print must be lighter than in those areas that will be coloured. For the top picture, the base print shown was made with a deliberately low contrast range and the head especially was held back in tone.

RETOUCHING

The techniques of retouching are essentially those of an illustrator, including brushwork, airbrushing, shaving the emulsion with a knife, and various other means of adding and removing dyes, pigments and silver. The uses of retouching however, vary from the simplest tidying up of the picture to creating new images in the form of artwork. The key to successful retouching, though, is to blend retouched areas imperceptibly into the base photographic image. If the retouching is noticeable, it has not worked.

Retouching should be avoided if at all possible and it is worth taking time at earlier stages in the photographic process to reduce the need for retouching to a minimum. In particular, take care not to allow dust particles to reach film that is drying (inspect carefully), keep the enlarger clean.

Black-and-white prints

A maxim of retouching is that the larger the scale the easier it is. Because of this print, retouching is usually the simplest, and has the added advantage that opaque can be applied as well as transparent dye. Black-and-white prints are far easier than colour prints to retouch. There are four basic techniques, and if more than one is to be used, they should be performed in this order:
● bleaching
● emulsion removal
● dye application
● opaque application

For local bleaching, pre-moisten the print to avoid hard edge-marks, and apply with a swab or brush, washing off between applications.

Pre-mix the dye from different colours (such as brown-black and blue-black) to match the exact colour of the monochrome image. Apply dye to the print gradually, starting with it very dilute and building up the colour slowly.

Airbrushing

Airbrushing is a skilled technique, which can be used for dye and opaque application, and requires an investment in equipment. But it has remarkable advantages for photographic retouching. The ability to shade large areas smoothly from one tone to another matches the photographic effects of both softening focus and graded lighting. Moreover, the spray pattern can often be adjusted to match the pattern of graininess in the photograph exactly.

An airbrush works by regulating a flow of compressed air to blow out a fine-controlled spray of colour that has been loaded into a small reservoir. Used in broad, overlapping strokes, airbrushing can add large, even areas of tone or a smooth tonal gradation. Used freehand, the edges of the airbrushing are soft, but masking with a *frisket* (painted or stuck down over the parts of the print to be left unsprayed) gives hard edges. Intermediate edges can be achieved by holding a card or some other material at a slight distance above the print while spraying.

Hand-colouring black-and-white prints

Once, hand-colouring was the only way of adding colour to a photograph. Now it is used as an artistic device without any attempt at realism and the range of styles and method is considerable. Transparent dyes blend in with the underlying image, but opaque, and even oil-paint, can be added on top of the image. Because tone and colour are being added, it is generally easier to work on a print that is lighter than normal. If the print already has a full range of tones, the usual answer is to bleach and sepia-tone it.

To avoid edge-marks and brush-marks, pre-moisten the surface of the print, so that colour application will merge smoothly at its edges. It is easier to make several dilute washes and to build up the colour slowly than to attempt one concentrated application. Over-colouring is a common fault.

Black and white negatives

If the fault lies in the negative, it may sometimes be better to try retouching the negative rather than every single print made from it. However, for detailed work, a sheet-film size negative is needed, and if the original negative is 35 mm format, it will need enlarging first (see copy negatives page 141). A negative can be prepared for retouching by local reducing and intensifying (see page 143) with a swab in a dish. Knifing is possible, although risky if the negative is an original. An abrasive reducer is easier to apply, rubbing gently in overlapping circular movements.

As the actual colour of *added* tone is unimportant, dyes, opaque or pencils can be used, but in many ways a sharpened black-lead retouching pencil is easiest to use. It is safer to apply the pencil on the base of sheet film rather than the emulsion side.

Colour prints

Unlike the single silver layer on a black and white print, colour prints have three layers, making etching impossible. Indeed, scratches require colour retouching — the top layer of an Ektacolor print, for example, is cyan, under which lies the magenta, followed by the yellow, and the depth of the scratch determines its colour. The three standard techniques for colour retouching are liquid dye retouching, dry-dye retouching, and opaque retouching. If combined, they should be performed in this order. *Liquid dyes* penetrate easily, and are good for small blemishes. For large areas, however, *dry dyes* are easier to apply smoothly, and have the additional advantage that they set with moisture, so that they can be removed, if needed, during the early stages of the retouching. The disadvantage of both is that they can only *add* tone to the print. Bleaching is unsatisfactory with most colour prints, and to lighten areas, *opaque* is needed.

Apply liquid dye diluted and nearly dry on the brush. Dab dry after each application and build up to the desired intensity.

Apply dry dye by breathing on the cake in the jar and picking up a quantity on a ball of cotton wool. Rub this onto the print and then buff smooth with a clean cotton ball. Set the colours by steaming, over a boiling kettle. Dry the print thoroughly before adding any more dye. Opaque is applied the most smoothly with an airbrush.

Colour negatives

The more retouching that can be done on the colour negative, the easier life becomes when printing. This, however, is only practical when the negative is large, and is not worth attempting on 35 mm. An alternative for small-format film is to make an enlarged duplicate onto sheet film.

As with all colour emulsions, the separate dye layers make etching impossible. The standard techniques are with black-lead and coloured pencils. The best side of the film to retouch depends on the make, Vericolour II sheet film, for example, can be retouched on both sides. Working on both sides makes denser application possible. A black-lead pencil lightens the area of the picture without a colour change; coloured pencils also lighten, but add a colour cast that is the *opposite* of their own colour. The effect of a particular colour is therefore very difficult to judge, and only tiny blemishes should be retouched in colour on a negative.

Colour transparencies

As with colour negatives, it is only worth attempting to retouch very *large* transparencies. Colour transparencies are usually retouched with three dyes — cyan, magenta and yellow — and a buffer solution to dilute

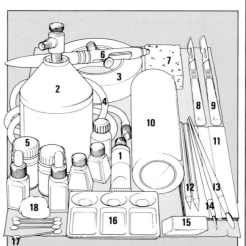

AIRBRUSHING Because it can give smoothly graduated tones, the airbrush is in many ways the ideal instrument for retouching photographs. The following comprises the basic kit (a compressed air can is shown as the inexpensive alternative to the electrically-powered compressor that a professional airbrusher would use):

1 Colour and black-and-white dyes
2 Compressed air supply
3 Masking tape

4 Airbrush hose
5 Photo-opaque
6 Airbrush
7 Sponge
8 Scalpel for pointwork
9 Scalpel for shaving
10 Masking film
11 Absorbent paper
12 Crayons and pencils
13 Broad brush
14 Fine brush
15 Eraser
16 Mixing palette
17 Cotton buds
18 Cotton swab

Preparing a mask A transparent mask is used to outline each area to be sprayed:
1 Peel the masking film from its backing.
2 Lay the adhesive film over the dry-mounted print, covering the whole picture area.
3 Cut around the area to be sprayed lightly (avoid cutting into the print).
4 Peel away the unwanted film very carefully.
5 Alternatively, paint masking fluid over the area to be protected, and allow to dry completely.

Using an airbrush
Practice on discarded prints
is essential before tackling a
fine print:
1 With pigment, dilute with
water for a milky
consistency. Liquid dyes may
not need dilution.
2 Fill the reservoir with a
brush or a dropper.
3 Press the button down to
start the flow of air.
4 Pull the button back to
start the flow of colour.
5 Test on a spare print. For
smooth tones, sweep from
side to side, extending
beyond the area of the
mask.

them. Most slide films are processed by the E-6 process, and only E-6 retouching dyes should be used if the picture is to be printed. E-6 dyes penetrate well into the film base, although dye can be applied to both sides of the film. Transparencies cannot be etched.

First mix small quantities of the dyes to achieve the exact hue. Add all three for black, cyan and yellow for green, magenta and blue for red, and magenta and cyan for blue. Pre-moisten the surface with Photo-Flo. Apply the dye dilute, building up to the required colour with several applications. This takes longer but is easier than trying to remove too much dye.

Dark shadow areas and dark spots can be bleached, and then retouched if necessary. There are total dye bleaches, which affect all three dye layers, and selective dye bleaches, which work separately, on the cyan, magenta and yellow layers. As these bleaches are applied to the emulsion side, the film must be dried before the effect is judged. Dye bleaches are generally unstable, and are supplied in separate solutions. Two methods of application, therefore, are possible: the solutions can either be pre-mixed, or, for more control, used one after the other. For large areas, the transparency can be covered with a waterproof frisket, which is cut to expose the areas to be retouched, and then soaked in the bleach. After bleaching, wash in running water for at least 10 minutes, preferably with at least three separate baths, and finally rinse in stabilizer before drying.

SPECIAL EFFECTS
Although the image can be manipulated in various kinds of ways at the different stages of photography, from the moment of shooting onwards, it is usually more convenient, for a number of reasons, to work with 'straight' photographs that have already been taken and processed. There is a wide choice in post-production special effects and having a regular original for experiment allows different effects to be tried out at leisure. Also, performing effects in the workroom allows and demands much greater precision than is possible during the actual shooting.

Montage
Montage is the simplest of all ways of combining different photographic images. Different prints are simply cut out and laid over a base to create the new combined image. The main problem is making a satisfactory visual. The technique works with both colour and black and white prints, and the progress of the work can be checked continuously.

A basic print is prepared — the background to the final image — and dry-mounted on board. The image that is to be added as an overlay is then printed, on *single-weight* paper if possible, and cut out with the tip of a sharp craft knife. If the combination is to look real, the separate elements of overlay and background must match in overall tone, contrast, colour and the apparent lighting. The chief difficulty at this stage is to hide the edges of the overlay; this is why it should be on thin paper and the edges should be chamfered at the back with fine sandpaper. The overlay is then stuck down in place on the base print. To help the illusion it is usually better to rephotograph the finished montage, and possibly retouch the edges of the join or add shadows where necessary.

Sandwiching
An extremely simple, but effective, method of combining images is to take two transparencies together. The pre-requisites for a successful sandwich are that the originals are over-exposed (so that the combined base density appears normal, with fairly bright highlights), and that the position and tone of the subjects complement each other. There should, in other words, be sufficient pale areas (such as sky) in each for the darker subjects of the other to show clearly. Surprisingly effective combinations can be made simply by laying out a number of stock transparencies from the files on a lightbox and trying them out.

Masking
Masking is a technique used in a whole range of special effects, of which photo-composites are just one. Masks for special effects are basically the same as the contrast-control masks used in slide-duplicating (see page 140) but the contact copy of the original is made not on normal 'continuous-tone' black and white film but high-contrast line film, developed in high-contrast lith developer. The result is a solid black mask that can be sandwiched with the original to completely block out either shadows or highlights, depending on whether the original was a positive or negative — copying the copy will reverse the mask. Sometimes, retouching may be necessary to ensure the mask is solid black, and a skilful retoucher may be able to add or take away areas from the mask. The contact-copy can be made on the same size film as the original, but many photographers prefer to enlarge the original on to sheet film first by printing and then make the contact-copy as sheet film too. This bigger image is much easier to work on. The problem with all masking techniques though, is ensuring that the mask is held precisely 'in register' with the original when sandwiched together. Some registration techniques are illustrated on page 149.

STORAGE

No photograph will last for ever, but its life can be considerably extended by good storage — and shortened by poor storage. Good storage should also make pictures easy to find, identify, and enjoy. The element of enjoyment is often forgotten. It may be 'efficient' to stack everything tightly in rows, but it is likely to make more sense visually if the photographs can be pulled out for easy display. Proper presentation of photographs is as important as organization.

Nevertheless the need to *preserve* the photograph remains the main priority in storage. For a number of reasons, a photographic image, on film or a print, can deteriorate slowly over the years. To begin with, some of the materials of which photographs are made are not permanent. Although the silver in a black and white negative or print *is* very stable and can be made even more permanent by toning, many colour dyes are not. Moreover, the ordinary action of light tends to cause fading in the image and sometimes discolouration of a print's paper.

These are, in a sense, inevitable problems of conservation, but there are ways of tackling them. Most of the archival treatments in photography, however, are aimed at more easily preventable sources of deterioration. The chief of these is contamination from the chemicals actually used to create the image. Ideally, in a black and white negative or print, all that should remain in the emulsion after processing is metallic silver. Fixer ought to remove the last traces of silver salts in the unexposed areas of the picture, but in practice some residue is normally left, together with a little of the fixer itself. Alone, the fixer can tarnish the silver image, and combining with the silver salts can discolour the whole photograph.

Additionally, pollutants in the atmosphere take their toll, and many substances, such as paper and card, that come into contact with film and prints contain harmful acids.

Archival techniques

These problems of deterioration may take years to appear noticeably, but by then it is likely to be too late to repair the damage. Prevention is the best treatment, and there are certain established archival techniques to preserve photographs. Most, however, apply to black and white rather than colour materials, as dyes in the latter are inherently less stable than metallic silver. The only sure method of guaranteeing the permanence of a colour photograph is to go to the trouble of having black and white separation negatives made from it; the resulting image is then preserved in silver. The life of black and white materials can be extended by taking the steps outlined in the box at right.

Personal computers are ideal for cross-referencing of picture data, and their capacity for storing information makes it easy to expand entries to show, for example, the occasions on which a picture has been used, or the printing instructions and filtration for a negative. A basic inventory program can be adapted for this, or any of a growing number of special programs designed for photographers.

Maintaining a sequence
When presenting sequences of slides to a client, the order in which they are seen may be important. One simple way of ensuring that they stay in order is to mark the edges with a diagonal line as shown on the left.

COPYRIGHT STAMP

NAME STAMP

SELECT STICKER

FRAME NUMBER

SUBJECT INFORMATION

LOCATION STAMP

ROLL NUMBER

DATE STAMP

Ⓒ Michael Freeman

United States WHITE SANDS, NEW MEXICO.

3403

ARCHIVAL TECHNIQUES

- Remove residual silver salts from black-and-white negatives and prints with two fixer baths.
- Remove all residual fixer with a hypo clearing agent and archival washing.
- Coat with a protective toner. Dry gently.
- Store or mount in acid-free materials.
- Do not expose for long periods to fluorescent light or strong daylight.
- In humid conditions, keep the storage area dry. Do not use fungicide.
- Keep photographs separated individually.

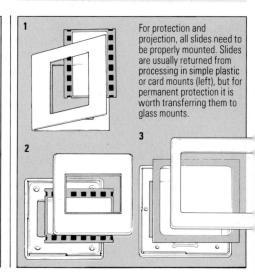

For protection and projection, all slides need to be properly mounted. Slides are usually returned from processing in simple plastic or card mounts (left), but for permanent protection it is worth transferring them to glass mounts.

The picture agency This storage system is used in one of the major international stock agencies, Bruce Coleman Ltd. The storage and viewing room is conventional, with filing cabinets and a large lightbox for visiting picture researchers to make selections (right), but downstairs a computer terminal gives access to all the transparencies in the files, the information on each shot stored on tape. Rapid location of picture requests is at least as important as the storage. The computer files might cross-reference pictures by date, location or subject, for instance, so that a picture to fit a particular request can be found within minutes from among thousands of slides.

Slide labelling When slides are stored, stamps or printed labels are convenient for standard information, such as the photographer's name. A typical arrangement of caption information is shown left.

Safe storage and display

Archival materials: use these

Acid-free paper and board (100% cotton rag)
Achival linen tape
Cellulose acetate
Polyethylene
Polyester sheets and leaves
Aluminium
Stainless steel
Anything coated with baked enamel
Glass
Porcelain
Acrylic

Non-archival materials: avoid these

Brown wrapping paper
Paper with high sulphur content
Cardboard
Uncoated wood
Ordinary glue
Glassine envelopes
Ink
Rubber bands
Insecticides
Fungicides
Polystyrene

Containers and mounts for filing

One of the basic needs, which becomes more and more important as time passes and the volume of photographs grows, is a logical and convenient system for filing. There are three criteria:
● Physical protection for the film or prints
● Space-saving
● Easy access and viewing

Negatives are an intermediate step in the production of a picture, and so are most commonly stored in strips. These can be kept in acid-free translucent paper sheets or cellulose acetate sheets, which themselves can be stored loose or in a ring binder. An alternative, which takes up a little more room but which allows each negative more protection, is a card transparency mount.

Transparencies are used for projection, and direct reproduction. Small and medium-format transparencies can be mounted individually in card, plastic or metal — necessary for slide projection and a sensible precaution if they are to be handled regularly. Card mounts, which adhere when the two halves are pressed together, are the simplest, but for extra protection may need a cellulose slip-over cover. Plastic mounts are available with and without glass; the case *for* glass is that it protects the transparency, the case *against* that it can trap damaging particles inside and is liable to break. Metal mounts are hermetically sealed with a special mounting device. Large format transparencies are usually kept in individual cellulose acetate envelopes and even small and medium format slide film can be kept in these clear sheets.

Prints are more liable than film to physical damage, particularly scuffing at the corners and edges. For this reason, a simple precaution is to make enlargements with an adequately large boarder, so that the picture area itself is not damaged. Because bulk is often a problem, prints tend to be stacked in drawers, but it is much safer to separate them individually. One method is to slip each into an acid-free paper envelope, another to mount each print with an over-mat, first. If separate envelopes are not used, interleave the prints with cellulose acetate or polyethylene terephthalate.

Filing systems

There are two equally important considerations in filing photographs: a physically safe and convenient arrangement, and a method of locating a particular photograph quickly. The two are linked, but inevitably some cross-referencing system is essential. For large numbers of photographs, some kind of cabinet design is normal: the choice then is usually between fairly shallow drawers in which films and prints can be stacked, or deeper drawers with runners that will accept sheets attached to hangers. Ideally, alongside the filing cabinets, there should be a space for viewing: a lightbox for slides and negatives, a desk with an overhead lamp for prints, or a space for a projector.

The storage conditions are important for preservation. Ideally, the temperature should be between about 16°C-21°C (60°F-70°F), at a relative humidity of 30 to 50 per cent. The temperature should not fluctuate daily by more than about 4°C (7°F).

SLIDE PROJECTION

35mm transparencies are too small to look at unaided; to be seen and appreciated, they must be magnified. The most effective way to do this is with a slide projector, which enlarges the image to mural proportions.

Simple one-projector slide shows are only the starting-point. Using two or more projectors, it is possible to build a presentation that has more in common with cinema than with still pictures.

Projection hardware

Compared to a 35mm SLR, a slide projector is a very simple piece of equipment. It consists of: a light-source (usually tungsten halogen) with a reflector behind; one or two condensors — simple lenses — to turn the diverging beam of the lamp into a parallel beam; a slide carrier, to support the 35mm frame in its two-inch-square mount; a projection lens, to throw the image onto the screen; and a mechanism for focusing the lens.

Of these components, only the slide-changing mechanism and the lens focusing system vary substantially between the cheapest and quite expensive projectors. Premium models, though, offer substantially better quality and greater reliability.

The more expensive a projector is, the more sophisticated will be the slide advance mechanism and the focusing system. The most elementary slide-changing mechanism is a sliding rack behind the lens, that supports two slides. While one is projected, the other is changed by hand.

A more convenient arrangement found on slightly more costly models is to pre-load the slides into a magazine. Slides are changed and the rack advanced either with a push-pull slider, or electrically, using a remote handset.

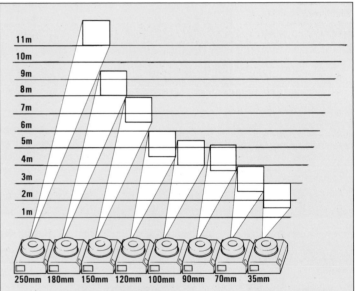

250mm	180mm	150mm	120mm	100mm	90mm	70mm	35mm

As editing a show involves many slides, easily viewable storage is important. Transparent sheets are common, but a selected sequence can be packed in boxes. Once edited, slides can be kept in the drum.

Slide Projectors The two standard designs of 35mm slide projector are the revolving drum magazine type (such as the Kodak Carousel on page 150) and the sliding tray type, such as the Leitz Pradovit and Rollei.

Image size The size of the projected image is influenced by both the focal length of the projector lens and the distance from the screen. In the chart below left, the different projection distances are shown for a variety of focal lengths to give a constant 1.5in (5ft) screen width. The chart directly below shows variable image widths with different lenses at different distances.

Similarly, focusing mechanisms vary in sophistication. If all slides are in the same type of mount, focusing is usually just a 'once per show' activity. But mixtures of different thicknesses of mount may need constant refocusing. On simple slide projectors focusing is a matter of turning a knob or rotating the lens. Middle-price projectors, though, have motorized remote focusing, and the best models have fully automatic focusing which readjusts focus if necessary as soon as the slide appears on the screen.

Audio-visual (AV) projectors have special inputs that permit the use of slide fading and synchronization equipment. Additionally, these units are more robustly built, but they only really justify their high cost in a multi-projector show.

Back-projection screens are translucent, rather like tracing paper. They are stretched tight on a frame, and the slide projector stands behind the screen, instead of in front among the audience. Back-projection screens are useful in projection areas where space is limited, but they absorb some of the projector's light — so a more powerful lamp is required.

Mounting slides

Many slides are returned ready-mounted from the processing lab. Usually these mounts are plastic, and are fine for rough and ready storage. However, other types of mount may be better suited to individual applications. The relative merits of the three main types are discussed in the panel below.

Slide format 24 × 36 mm

Projection distance*	1m	1.5m	2m	2.5m	3m	4m	5m	6m	7m	8m	9m	10m	12m	14m	16m	18m	20m	24m
(focal length mm)	**PICTURE WIDTH IN METRES**																	
35	1.00	1.48	1.96	2.34	2.80	3.65	4.50	—	—	—	—	—	—	—	—	—	—	—
60	0.58	0.87	1.16	1.46	1.75	2.33	2.92	3.50	4.12	—	—	—	—	—	—	—	—	—
85	0.39	0.60	0.80	1.01	1.21	1.62	2.03	2.44	2.85	3.26	3.71	4.15	—	—	—	—	—	—
90	0.37	0.56	0.76	0.95	1.15	1.54	1.93	2.32	2.61	3.10	3.51	4.06	—	—	—	—	—	—
100	0.32	0.50	0.68	0.85	1.02	1.37	1.72	2.07	2.42	2.77	3.12	3.88	4.24	—	—	—	—	—
150	0.19	0.31	0.43	0.55	0.67	0.91	1.14	1.38	1.62	1.85	2.09	2.33	2.80	3.28	3.80	4.24	—	—
180	—	0.24	0.34	0.44	0.54	0.73	0.92	1.12	1.31	1.50	1.70	1.89	2.28	2.66	3.05	3.46	3.85	4.22
250	—	—	0.23	0.30	0.38	0.52	0.66	0.80	0.95	1.09	1.23	1.38	1.66	1.95	2.23	2.54	2.82	3.15
70	0.49	0.74	0.99	1.24	1.49	1.99	2.49	2.99	3.49	3.99	4.49	—	—	—	—	—	—	—
120	0.27	0.43	0.58	0.73	0.88	1.17	1.47	1.77	2.07	2.37	2.67	2.97	3.56	4.20	4.80	—	—	—

*Distance between front of the projector and projection screen.

SLIDE MOUNTS
There are three main types of slide mount:
Card or plastic mounts are the simplest and cheapest and are popular with professionals because they can be sent through the post, unlike glass mounts. But they offer little protection to the slide.
Glass mounts offer the best protection but cannot be sent through the post. If left for long in a warm projector, colour fringes called 'Newton's rings' may form where the slide curls and almost touches the glass.
Register-punch mounts provide perfect registration of multiple images but can only be used with slides taken in a camera with the right back.

Screens

White-painted walls make convenient screens for impromptu slide-shows, but purpose-built screens are more satisfactory. They are more reflective and accumulate fewer marks than does a wall.

Additionally, screen surfaces can be chosen to suit particular projection requirements. In totally dark rooms, simple matt screens are acceptable. They reflect a sharp image of the slide, and can be seen through a wide angle — viewers do not need to sit close to the projection axis.

In quite bright projection areas, high-gain screens are a better choice — they reflect more light back to the audience. These screens have a narrow viewing angle, though. Lenticular and beaded screens produce images that are almost as bright, but beaded screens need careful use and have an equally restricted viewing angle — people at the side of the room see a very dim picture. Beaded screens also make the picture look less sharp.

Making titles

Putting titles on slides, or making slides that carry text instead of pictures, adds a professional touch to any slide show. For titles to be effective, though, they must be carefully lettered and photographed systematically.

Commercial laboratories can make title slides for a fee, but the process is not difficult, and can easily be carried out at home. The starting point is to plan where in the frame the lettering is to appear, then letter the text using black rub-down lettering on a piece of white cardboard the same proportions as a 35mm frame. The lettering is photographed using lith film, such as Kodalith, and processed using lith chemicals. This yields a slide with white lettering on a black ground.

From this basic title slide, it is easy to make other types, and to add colour, as follows.

For coloured lettering on a black ground, this basic slide should be re-photographed onto colour transparency film, with coloured filters over the light source. Contact-printing the basic slide onto lith film prior to this copying stage yields coloured letters on a white background.

To drop black lettering onto an existing slide, the basic white-on-black title must be contact printed onto lith film to make black letters on a white background. Then this title slide can be sandwiched with the image and the two re-copied together.

For white or coloured lettering in the dark area of another slide, a white-on-black title slide is the starting point. This is copied onto colour transparency film, (using a coloured filter if the letters are to appear in colour); then onto the same frame a second exposure is made of the slide on which the lettering is to appear.

Editing a slide show

The first step is to sort through all the pictures scheduled for inclusion and remove all that are out of focus, blurred by camera shake, or wrongly exposed. Ideally, there should be some theme to link the pictures together. This could be chronological, or it could be literally thematic, composed only of extreme close-ups of flowers, for example.

The way each slide follows on from the previous one is important and sudden changes of tone and colour should be avoided. Try not to mix vertical and horizontal slides for the same reason.

Finally, time the show and prepare a commentary. An upper time limit of 20 minutes is reasonable; it is better to leave an audience calling for more than to make them bored and tired.

AUDIO-VISUAL PRESENTATIONS

An audio-visual presentation is not simply a slide show with sound, it is a distinct medium in its own right. It involves not only shooting the pictures, but also preparation of a script and elaborate editing. Scripting does not necessarily imply dialogue, but it does concern both the addition of sound and the *planning* of a sequence of images. Editing A-V is much more involved than selecting; it is a skill relatively fresh to photography that has most in common with, and most to learn from, film-editing. In other words, many of the creative possibilities in A-V production have some connection with cinematic styles and techniques.

However, before embracing film-editing methods whole-heartedly as the creative guide for handling sequences of still images, it is worth looking at the limitations of A-V presentation. There are effects to which it is ideally suited — sometimes better even than film — but others that cannot be created without very strained results. Basically, juxtaposition is the forté of A-V sequences, while anything involving continuous action tends to suffer badly.

Standard equipment for audio-visual slide shows includes a matched pair of projectors, tape player and speakers, all linked by a console. This version from Kodak — their AV Presentation Unit — has most of its functions built into one unit. Operating two Carousel projectors, it can record and replay the slide and audio programme on either impulse or digital mode, has a dubbing facility that enables tapes from different sources to be mixed on to the cassette tape, a public address facility, and a built-in monitor speaker that an operator can use if screened from the audience.

Production methods

With an A-V show, thorough organization is vital. Whatever production method is adopted — and there are several — it has to ensure that the different elements of script, slides (sometimes specially shot), soundtrack and programming, are all handled in a logical sequence. The basic alternatives are:

● Prepare a script first to include voice, sound effects and/or music, with an idication of picture needs and timing. The degree of detail incorporated at this stage depends very much on personal preference and on the motives and specifications of the show. A commercial presentation is likely to need very full scripting in order to get client approval to the next stage. Equally, an A-V show intended to make a specific point or argument may call for a detailed script in order to present the case step by step.

● Prepare a shot-list first. If the general subject is known, but the details are not, it may be better to note all the kinds of photograph that might be useful, before shooting. This can mean shooting pictures that prove to be unnecessary, but it ensures that none of the vital shots are missing. For instance, in producing an A-V show on 'a day in the life of an airport', a shot-list might include such pictures as overall establishing shots of the airport at dawn and dusk, comparison shots between an empty and thronged concourse, close-up details of baggage tags, and so on. Note that shooting for A-V use calls for both variety (different views of the same subject) and continuity.

Editing is usually best performed with a plentiful supply of material:

● Work directly with available material. Spreading out all the possible transparencies on a lightbox may be better suited to certain A-V shows, particularly if there is a large amount and wide range of material. It may, of course, be the only practicable method — if the subject is, for example, a trip that has already been completed.

● Shoot to a broad script outline, tightening up the details as the work progresses. This may be less efficient, but it is also likely to leave open more opportunities for changing ideas and being imaginative.

Principles of picture editing

Editing is the important new skill that slide programmes bring to photography. It is, essentially, the organization of photographs into sequences that make some kind of sense, and performs, in time order, the same kind of job that the editing of a picture story does in a printed publication like a magazine (see pages 188-203). Although a large part of editing is concerned with the practicalities of making a sequence flow smoothly and be understandable, editing can be used more creatively, sometimes even to jolt the audience and make them see something in an unexpected way.

As an A-V programme is organized in a sequence of time, one extremely useful, but not always recognized, function of editing is to alter the perception of time. By appropriate cutting, the passage of time in a story can be made to seem longer or shorter than it would really be. For instance, the tension in certain dramatic moments can be increased by spinning out the time of the event, and an easy way of doing this is to cut from one related piece of action to another, but at each cut beginning a few seconds earlier. Imagine, for example, someone searching a building for a hidden bomb that is about to explode. The slide sequence could cut from the search to the clock-face on the bomb's timer, but going back each time *before* the real time, so as to telescope time. Such a sequence could last as much as double the real time elapsed without seeming odd.

Conversely, time can be compressed by cutting out the tedious, if logical, bits of action. To show someone walking out of a house and getting into a car across the street, for example, it is not necessary to show the person walking between the two. A cut from closing the front door of the house to starting the engine of the car will do just as well.

The three most important techniques of editing — continuity, timing and montage — are now dealt with individually.

■ **CONTINUITY** Simply thrown together, a number of slides is not a sequence, but a jumble of images. Continuity is the process of smoothing the flow of pictures, story and information, and comprises the following set of techniques. One caution, however; just making a sequence flow may not make it interesting, and dramatic editing may need on occasion to ignore continuity. Techniques for ensuring continuity are described in full in the box on the previous page.

■ **TIMING** The length of time that each slide is held on the screen, and the exact moment of cutting or mixing from one to another is something of an art. Although it can be improved upon, a sense of timing can only be inherent. A fraction of a second can make a big difference to the flow or dramatic effect of a cut. A music track, suitably selected, can suggest the timing of the cuts, but in any event it is important to be aware of the rhythm of a sequence. Successful editing is often paced to create an emotional response — for example, a gentle, regular pace for a lyrical sequence, or an accelerating pace towards a dramatic climax.

■ **MONTAGE** In montage sequences, A-V shows probably come closest to film. Famous film montages, such as the shower sequence in Alfred Hitchcock's *Psycho*, or the passage-of-time sequences in Orson Welles' *Citizen Kane*, are essentially well-chosen shots cut so quickly together that each is almost a single, if not quite still, image. A-V slide programming is obviously ideally suited to this form, as there is usually a substantial stock of slides from which to select. It is quite distinct from narrative programming, and if used in conjunction with this is usually best kept short and 'identified' (with, for example, a distinct difference in the soundtrack). Montage gives full scope for juxtaposing images to make graphic, emotional or intellectual points.

Sound editing

The principles involved in sound-editing are a little different from picture-editing, in that we perceive sounds in a highly selective way. In other words, to mix together all the sounds in many everyday situations would sound hopelessly confusing. We normally edit out much background noise in our mind — the sound of traffic, for example, or the ticking of a clock.

Sound can help continuity considerably. One method, described above, is to overlap the sound with the visuals. Another is to use obvious establishing sounds to do the work of a slide; for instance, a close-up of a man at the steering wheel of a car with a track of heavy surrounding traffic eliminates the need to *show* the traffic in long shot. Sound can also, as already mentioned, be a tempo anchor for the pace of cutting.

Certain sounds, such as the ring of a telephone or an alarm bell, produce a definite emotional response — often better than could a picture. Indeed, action that would be limp or impossible visually, such as an explosion, can be carried very successfully off-screen in sound. In addition, music virtually always has an emotional content, and a well-chosen music track can contribute a great deal to an A-V show.

Sound is normally classified as effects, voice and music. Sound effects are commercially available on record (but check performing rights restrictions) or can be recorded oneself. Rather than run the risk of ruining one track by making a mistake in overlaying another, mix all the sound from individual tapes onto a master. Then copy this for performances.

Multiple-screen programmes

Very elaborate effects are possible by using more than one screen, as the configurations opposite show. Nevertheless, there is as much opportunity for overdoing the imagery and producing a kaleidoscope of pictures that merely confuses, overwhelming the capacity of the viewer to absorb all the information being presented. For clarity, it is best to have a good reason for using multiple screens. Some of the uses are shown in the box below.

MULTIPLE SCREEN EFFECTS
1 The dramatic introduction of a large image. If the show begins on a single screen, at a certain point one large photograph can suddenly be introduced, covering all the screens. To preserve the picture quality, this is usually best shot on a large film format which is then copied in sections corresponding to the arrangement of screens. **2** The width of a triple screen can, like widescreen formats in the cinema, preserve a dramatic 'distance' between characters and elements of the action. **3** Similarly, a triple screen gives good panoramic views. **4** Several screens can deliver a high density of information in the form of a montage, although whether the audience can cope with it is another matter. **5** Concurrent events or sequences can be shown on different screens — an alternative to cross-cutting.

BASIC PROGRAMMING GUIDE
Complete audio-visual presentations need careful planning. Particular care is needed to ensure a smooth and easy transition from one slide to the next. Obvious things to avoid include mixing formats, unless it is for deliberate effect. Changing from horizontal to vertical is a common mistake and destroys the flow of images. The very method of changing from one image to the next introduces a completely new element. Some of the basic slide changes are outlined in the pictures on the right. Clearly these techniques, as all audio-visual are virtually impossible without at least two projectors and a proper dissolve unit. Pacing is important, and it is a mistake to mix, say, ultra-slow and fast dissolve too freely.

Ultra-slow dissolve Between six seconds and about 12 seconds, a dissolve is almost imperceptible. This can be especially effective with a match-dissolve, for example from one image to another of the same size and shape.

Slow dissolve At around four seconds, the rate of dissolve can be used to create a relaxed and tranquil mood, well-suited to many landscapes, for instance. As an experiment, take a well-known piece of music, such as Vivaldi's 'Four Seasons', and, using appropriate scenic transparencies from stock, match the rates of change to the music.

Fast dissolve This is the workhorse of slide programming. Fast dissolves create a sense of urgency and immediacy, and are the programmer's answer to fast music and themes involving action. Many events that include people, such as a conversation, require this treatment. Also, to show a large quantity of slides in a limited space of time, this may be the only solution.

Animation By oscillating the slider on a manual control backwards and forwards, *without* hitting the change switches at either end, the two pictures can be made to flicker. If the images show repetitive action — for example, a hammer hitting a nail — this useful trick will convincingly animate the sequence.

Exponential dissolve If you start slowly, gradually increasing the speed of the change, you can introduce an element of surprise into the dissolve. You can make effective use of this if, for example, you are changing from one picture with the focus of attention on the left to a picture with the focus on the right. The slow start to the dissolve is not noticed immediately, but the rapid end to the change snaps the viewer's attention across the screen.

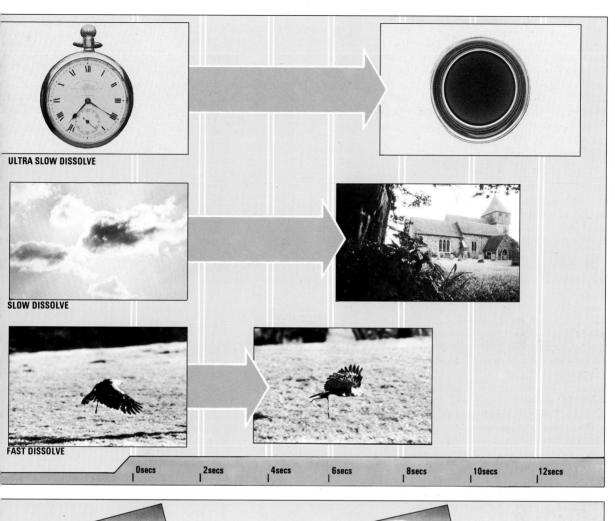

ULTRA SLOW DISSOLVE

SLOW DISSOLVE

FAST DISSOLVE

0secs   2secs   4secs   6secs   8secs   10secs   12secs

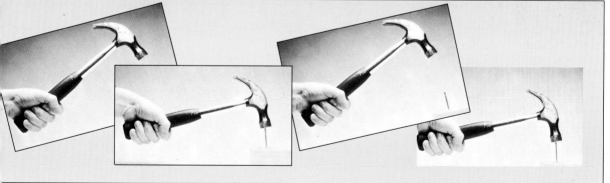

PRINT DISPLAY

The two traditional ways of displaying a photograph are in a mount and in a frame. Both share some of the same techniques. The advantages of a plain card mount are that it can be sized and cut to suit the individual photograph, that it is the least distracting of displays, and that it can be used as basic protection when storing. Frames provide extra protection through their acrylic or glass cover, and add a sense of value and importance to an image.

Mounting

For archival permanence, refer to the precaution on page 146. The two main parts of a mount are the backing board and the overmat. Both should be identical in size. The ideal material for the backing is museum board, although it is often only available in white; it can be bought from most artist suppliers. The print can be attached permanently to the backing board by means of dry-mounting, or it can be made removable by using corner mounts. Dry-mounting will hold the print perfectly flat against the board, although whether this is needed or not will depend on the size of the print and the type of paper (resin-coated paper normally lies flat, and the overmat will also help to prevent edge curling).

Dry-mounting *can* be performed with an ordinary iron, but as the temperature, evenness and length of time of pressing are all critical, it is much better to use a heated dry-mounting press. The principle is straightforward. Dry-mounting tissue is cut to the size of the print, tacked on it in several places with the tip of a tacking iron, and then the print, tissue and board all heated together.

A loose-fitting alternative is to use corner mounts, or diagonal corner slits cut into a backing sheet of acid-free paper. The mounts should be acid-free, and can be made easily by folding strips of archival paper. Then, the mounts or the backing paper can be stuck to the board with archival linen tape.

On top of the print, a second sheet of board is placed, cut with a 'window' a little larger than the image area. This is the overmat, and serves the double function of providing a raised protection for the print, and setting it off with an attractive surround.

Framing

As a frame encloses the print, special care should be taken to avoid contaminating materials. Aluminium, stainless steel and baked enamel frames are the safest. Check also the composition of the backing board in a proprietary frame. Either acrylic or glass is suitable for the front cover; both give UV protection, but acrylic is more effective.

Making a frame
Frames can be made with lengths of moulding from a framing shop using basic wood-working tools — but a mitre clamp is vital.
1 Use the clamp to hold the moulding while you make 45° cuts with a tenon saw.
2 Glue the exposed ends and press together in the clamp.
3 Drill small holes and hammer in pins at a shallow angle to secure the joint.
4 When the joints are secure, rest glass, print and backing in place. Hammer in brads just above to secure.
5 Alternatively use heavy-duty stapler.
6 Cover the edges and backing board with strong sticky tape.

The choice of frame is obviously largely aesthetic but there are strong arguments for simplicity. Unlike many oil paintings, for example, most photographs have no significant surface texture; black-and-white prints, in addition, have at most a subtle colour component. Few photographs, therefore, tend to go well with ornate or dominating frames — plain metal or else clips on a simple block are the most generally successful.

The size of the frame relative to the print, its shape, and the *position* of the image within its surround all need careful consideration. As the examples (opposite) show, these choices can make subtle but important differences. A small print within a large frame tends to concentrate attention and add a sense of specialness to the image; a narrower print border tends to increase the importance of the centre of the image.

Prints for exhibition need to be presented properly if they are to have maximum impact. This does not only mean taking time and care over mounting; it means designing the mount in relation to other pictures in the exhibition — so that the exhibition as a whole has the desired effect. Also important are such considerations as caption information. For the pictures on the left, a broad space was left between the captions and the picture, so that the text did not distract attention from the picture.

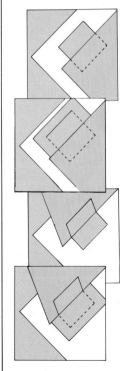

Types of hinge (above, top to bottom): pendant hinge; pendant hinge on paper; folded hinge; folded hinge on paper.

Viewing conditions

The lighting and hanging conditions are important in the appreciation of displayed prints. A high ultra-violet content will promote fading, and prints should be hung away from windows and fluorescent strip lighting. Also, direct sunlight can cause expansion cracks in the emulsion.

The lighting should be as uniform as possible over the area of each print. This means that the light should not be close to the photograph. Ceiling-mounted spots are very suitable. To diminish reflections from the surface of the print and the glass, spot-lights should be directed at a sharp angle.

black to pure white, through many other subtle tones. Printing ink and paper, though, can reproduce only two colours — the colour of the ink and the colour of the paper the picture is printed on.

To simulate shades of grey using only black ink and white paper, the printer uses what are called half-tones. The picture is split up into a myriad of tiny black dots, which are clearly visible on examination of a newspaper photograph. The larger the dots in any one area of the picture, the blacker that area appears to be. Since we rarely scrutinize printed pictures too carefully, our eyes are deceived into thinking that clusters

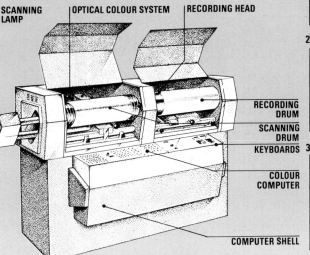

Electronic scanners are now the normal way of obtaining the four-colour separations needed to reproduce colour photos in print. These machines have two connected rotating drums—one for the original and one for separations (**1**); and computerized colour control panel (**2**). The compact scanner shown here needs only one operator (**3**).

SCANNING LAMP | OPTICAL COLOUR SYSTEM | RECORDING HEAD

RECORDING DRUM
SCANNING DRUM
KEYBOARDS
COLOUR COMPUTER
COMPUTER SHELL

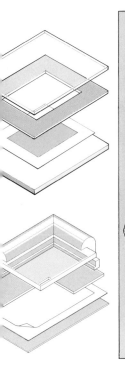

Types of frame
One of the easiest ways of mounting a print is a simple block frame (above, centre). This can be bought in kit form, or more cheaply, made from scatch. The main components are a thick backing board, a sheet of glass of identical size, a mount cut from rag fibre and the print itself. The corners can be secured by one of three types of clamp (above, top): spring clamps; special double clamps that are tied together with stout nylon cord; and metal corner clamps secured with screws. These frames do not provide perfect protection from dust, but they are cheap to make and look neat — which is why they are so popular for exhibition. Ultimate protection is provided by a shadow box frame (above).

The overall tone of the background also has an effect on viewing. For the most accurate translation of tonal values, a mid-grey background is the most suitable; if the walls are of a different value, one method of achieving this is to hang prints on larger grey panels. The precise effect of this, and of the association of other prints nearby is best judged by experiment, trying out different positions and layouts within the room.

Graphic reproduction

To reproduce a photograph in a magazine or book, it is totally impractical to make prints in the conventional way, with one print per edition of the publication. So pictures in print are reproduced in the same way as the printed word — using black or coloured ink on white paper.

In a conventional black-and-white photograph, the image is made up of many shades of grey, ranging from the deepest

of larger dots represent darker shades of grey — especially at a distance.

With colour photographs, the situation becomes more complicated, because the picture must carry not only tonal information, but hues, too. The reprographic techniques described below enable the printer to turn the continuous tones of a print or a transparency into a picture on the printed page or poster.

Printing plates for black-and-white are usually made by rephotographing the original picture through a screen engraved with a regular pattern of dots. Colour printing plates though are created by a more sophisticated process.

Colour pictures are reproduced using four colours of ink — yellow, cyan, magenta, and black. The first four of these are the same colours as the dyes formed on a colour transparency, and indeed, the colours on the printed page are built up in a similar way. The fourth colour, black, is added because the pigments or dyes in the other three do not together produce satisfactory dark tones on the printed page.

These four colours are laid on the page one by one on the printing press and a separate colour plate must be made for each colour to be printed. The plates which lay the ink on the paper are in their turn made by contact printing from black-and-white film negatives. Since each of these negatives represents a separate colour, they are called colour separations.

These film separations are generally made using a scanner. The transparency to be reproduced is locked to a rotating glass cylinder, and four sheets of black-and-white film are fixed to a corresponding cylinder rotating about the same axis. As both cylinders spin, a spot of light scans the transparency. Three photoelectric cells then analyse the amounts of red, green and blue at each point struck by the spot of light. This data is then analysed by a computer, and a separate record of each colour is made on three of the sheets of black-and-white film. The fourth, the black separation, is taken from the yellow channel, with some modification.

In the course of scanning, the picture can be enlarged, reduced, made more or less contrasty. Even made to look sharper!

Print methods
Transfer of ink to paper is carried out in one of three ways. *Letterpress* printing resembles a rubber date-stamp: the higher parts of the plate pick up ink and transfer it to the paper. On a printing press, the plate is made of metal, not rubber, but the principles are broadly the same.

Litho printing relies instead on the fact that ink — which is itself greasy — will stick to oily areas of a flat printing plate but be repelled by areas that are

20% HALFTONE OVER BLACK

40% HALFTONE OVER BLACK

et. So areas of the plate
at are to print white on the
ge are made to absorb
ater, and repel the oily ink.
Gravure, the most high-
ality process of the three,
a relief printing process,
e letterpress. But in
avure printing, it is not the
sed parts of the plate's
lief that get inked; instead
s the hollows of the plate
at retain the printing ink
the high parts of the
ate are wiped free of ink
st before plate and paper
e pressed together.

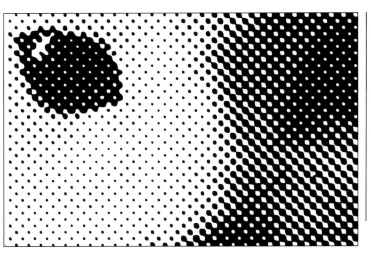

Halftone screens The seemingly continuous range of tones in a printed photograph is actually an illusion that depends on the limits of the eye's ability to resolve detail, as the image of the kitten (left) shows.

Duotones A duotone is, as its name implies, printed from two plates. One is the black plate, which underlies all the examples below. The other plate is for a colour which is used to create all the middle tones. The colour plate can be printed at different percentages.

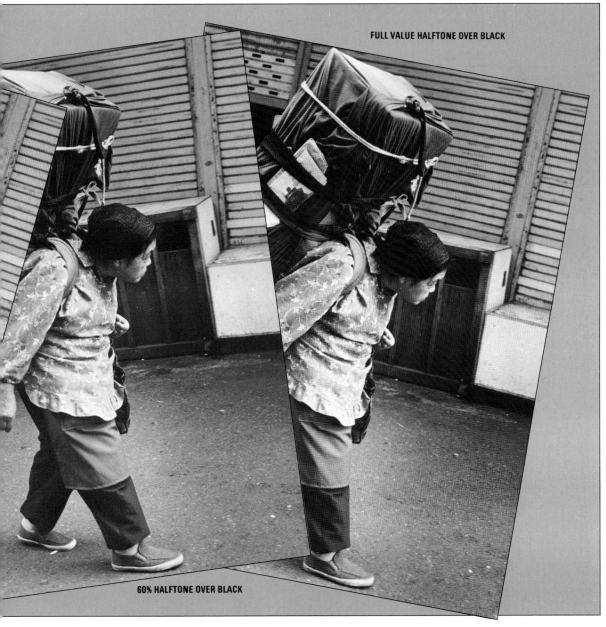

FULL VALUE HALFTONE OVER BLACK

60% HALFTONE OVER BLACK

PART TWO: SUBJECTS AND TECHNIQUES

Technological improvement has had a profound effect on the types of photography undertaken. We can see certain subjects and areas of interest as the products of their times — photographs made possible, or at least made easier by the improved capabilities of equipment and film. Candid photography, once almost exclusively the province of professional photojournalists, is now practised widely by amateur photographers for their own pleasures. Whereas two decades ago a photojournalist would have to work quite hard to overcome the limitations of slow colour film and a limited range of fast lenses, most modern 35mm SLRs can produce pictures of guaranteed technical accuracy in an instant, easily and in poor light if necessary. Available light photography in particular has been opened up through combined improvement in film speed and lens speed. Also, what were formerly real specializations — notably underwater and wildlife photography — are gaining ground in popular use simply because the necessary equipment is now widely available at a price that can be afforded by non-professionals.

The range of possible subjects increases as the technology improves. In the early days of photography only well lit and more-or-less motionless subjects could be photographed. Now even the very dimly lit and fast moving subjects are within the scope of the camera.

Photography in the 1980s shows an interest and emphasis unique to our time, and the structure of the following chapters reflects this. Notably, the photography of people on location, candid and otherwise, receives more space and attention than any other single subject, in keeping with its modern importance. Landscape photography in the 80s is very different from landscape photography in the 50s — though just as much through style and acceptability as changes in equipment and film. Urban landscapes are now a distinct subject in their own right, more accessible than natural landscapes, and to many photographers more relevant.

Nevertheless, although the modernization of equipment, materials and processes has influenced subjects and their treatment, it is always a mistake to see the practice of photography as mainly a technical process. Although knowledge of and proficiency in the mechanics is a necessary foundation, photographs are taken for what they show and for the form of the images. Fast colour film, for example, may open the door to low-light photography, but it meets an existing demand rather than suggests new kinds of pictures. This is the reason for separating subjects and techniques from the equipment, materials and processes — practically speaking, knowledge of the subject, organization, design and imagination are at least as important as the mechanics of photography, and in many cases more so.

In terms of approach, there is a major division between photography that is used to document and report, and photography that is used to construct pictures from the imagination. The difference is between circumstances beyond the photographer's control and those that can be manipulated, and as this division mainly falls between location photography and studio photography, these are the two main subject areas treated here.

LOCATION PHOTOGRAPHY

More than any other graphic art, photography is used to record and report — to capture images of the world as it is rather than how it should be. It is bound to reality in a way that illustration and painting are not, because in ordinary use, unless specially manipulated, it records the actual appearance of things. There is still room for variety of approach, but the raw material of photography on location is the visual record of real objects, places and people.

This simple fact has ensured that photography on location is influenced as much by the circumstances as by the photographer's preferences. The situation always makes certain practical and technical demands that must be met regardless of how any photographer wants to interpret the subject. Wildlife photography, for example, depends on a knowlege of the habits of the animals and on using various techniques for getting in close.

Photographers may take a passive or an active role, but in either case they are observers and hardly ever directors. The passive role is to watch and record while trying not to influence the course of events. In the active role, the photographer becomes involved in the situation, perhaps to provoke a reaction — possibly because that is a way of gaining a sharper insight. Nearly always, however, it is the progress of events that rules the photographer, not, as happens in the studio, the other way round. The scale of most of the subject matter is simply too large to allow substantial alteration without great effort and expense. The ethos of most location photography, therefore, is towards the realistic rather than the imaginative.

From candid photo-journalism to carefully planned and organised outdoor sets, location photography contains great variety of both subject material and style of imagery. The common denominator is the influence of the setting on the approach of the photographer.

NATURAL LIGHT

Most photographs are taken by natural light. Natural light is, essentially, light from just a single source, the sun. But that single source provides an almost infinite range of different lighting effects. Even simple direct sunlight varies enormously with the season of the year, the time of day and the orientation of both the subject and the camera. And the atmosphere always adds even more variation, even when the sky is crystal clear, for the air itself modifies and reflects the sun's light in different ways. On a bright day, with no pollution or haze and visibility of many miles, the sky performs pictorially as a huge blue dome surrounding the intense, concentrated light from the sun. It appears blue because the photons from the sun are scattered by collision with the molecules in the atmosphere, and the shorter, bluer wavelengths are scattered more readily.

This same scattering that gives a blue colour to the atmosphere away from the sun is responsible for the sun appearing orange or red at sunrise or sunset — the scattering pushes the bluer, shorter part of the light spectrum away from the direct view of the sun's disc, and what remains is, therefore, more red.

A clear sky is the simplest of all the conditions of natural light, but even so, it has great variations in the way it models

NATURAL LIGHT CONDITIONS

CONDITION	GENERAL FEATURES	EFFECT ON CONTRAST	EFFECT ON SHADOWS	FAVOURED SUBJECTS
High sun	Difficult to add character to a shot	Low with flat subjects, high with subjects that have pronounced relief	Tall and angular subjects cast deep shadows underneath	Subjects that are graphically strong in shape, tone, pattern or colour, eg some modern architecture
Low sun	Great variety, depending on direction and weather; may be unpredictable; warm colours	High towards sun, medium-low facing away	Strongest with sun to one side; least with sun behind camera	Most subjects suitable, particularly scenics
Twilight	Low light level only distinguishable when sky is clear	High towards light; low facing away	Shadows usually weak	Reflective subjects, eg automobiles
Haze	Enhances aerial perspective, weakening distant colours & tones; bluish over a distance	Slightly weakens contrast	Slightly weakens shadows	Some landscapes, some portraits
Thin cloud	A mild diffuser for sunlight	Slightly weakens contrast	Slightly weakens shadows	Some portraits, some architecture
Scattered clouds	Dappled lighting over landscape, causing changing local exposure conditions	Slightly weakens contrast	Fills shadows slightly	Many landscapes
Storm	Unpredictable	Variable	Variable	Landscapes
Snowfall	Low light level; dappled, foggy appearance	Weakens contrast considerably	Weakens shadows considerably	Landscapes, natural & urban
Moonlight	Very weak light, but quality similar to sunlight	As sunlight	As sunlight	Many subjects that would look too familiar in daylight

High, direct sunlight does not always have the same effect, as the two photographs far left show. In the upper picture of a desert highway close to California's Salton Sea, the flatness of the scene produces a generally low contrast range. In the lower picture, taken in an Andean town, the scene has relief, and so shadows that create high contrast — the effect is completely different.

Through the day, sunlight continually changes the way a scene looks. The sea-arch off the Spanish coast demonstrates the sheer variety of natural light in clear weather in any one place at different times of day (left and above). Notice how the texture and colour of both the rock and the sea change quite dramatically from one hour to the next.

its subjects and in colour. When the sun is high, shadows pool directly underneath and visually the light seems very intense — often more so than it actually is — and the general effect is, to most people's aesthetic senses, rather harsh and unattractive. If there is strong relief in the scene — say, tall buildings or closer views of people — the lighting usually seems to be contrasty, with over-bright highlights above and impenetrable shadows underneath. If, on the other hand, the scene is flat, such as a stretch of grassy plain or desert, the effect seems lacking in contrast. In photography that sets out to be attractive, high tropical sunlight is one of the most difficult conditions to work with.

The psychology of attractiveness, which has a strong bearing on lighting with photography, is both interesting and poorly understood. There is a consistency in what is considered to look good by most people, and this applies to conditions as much as to the subjects. This general opinion may change slowly with time, but at any particular moment it tends to be firm. Currently, mass aesthetics favour the unusual and exotic in natural lighting, which is to say that most viewers of photographs seem to prefer scenes shot under conditions that they would think themselves fortunate to have seen. In other words, a landscape photographed in a storm, with a spectacular shaft of light illuminating just a part of it, or photographed at dusk, tends to draw a more favourable viewer response than the same scene shot in the middle of the day, in bright sunlight.

Now, viewer reactions of this type are made more with certain subjects and types of photograph than with others. As a general rule, the more inherently compelling the subject, the less important are the conditions under which it is photographed. This in itself is not too surprising; a portrait of an interesting face will always be less dependent for its photographic success on the type of natural light than will be an expansive landscape. However, it does introduce a new area

KELVINS

2000	CANDLELIGHT
	DOMESTIC TUNGSTEN
3000	
4000	PHOTOFLOOD
	MEAN NOON DAYLIGHT
6000	
10,000	BLUE SKYLIGHT
20,000	

of value judgement — that certain photographic subjects carry a kind of weight of interest — and that this influences the amount of photographic effort that is usually put into them. From the point of view of lighting, it means that, in practice, photographers tend to go to greater lengths to arrange the best conditions with some subjects rather than others — notably landscapes and other long views.

The reasons for this probably stem from a mixture of different influences. One, undoubtedly, is the desire, even at a mild level, for visual sensation — a desire to see things in a different, even idealized form. Photography, with its massive published output of images, certainly encourages the search for the new. The lighting conditions that are most familiar are those that last the longest, in the middle of the day, and as such are generally regarded, when they are thought about at all, as undistinguished. Sunrise, sunset and storm light, to name the more obvious of prime photographic conditions, are short-lived and generally unpredictable in the form that they take. They have acquired a corresponding value. An allied influence may be that the unusual natural lighting condition is a kind of evidence that the photographer has either been very lucky, or has put effort into the picture; in either case, it has external worth. These influences are overlaid with editorial intervention — published photographs have always been edited and selected by professionals, who have a more sophisticated interest in pictures than the average viewer, and who will reinforce or shape public taste.

For all these reasons, however they are combined, most professional photographers working on location spend considerable effort avoiding the obvious. The obvious in this case is epitomized by high, bright sunlight or flat, overcast cloud. A professional assignment that must be shot by natural light tends to encourage a practical attitude towards the weather.

From this practical point of view, the most generally useful conditions for many subjects are the few hours around sunrise and sunset. The orange disc hanging on the horizon could hardly be a better example of visual cliché, with its associations of postcard view and subjectless photographs, yet this

Low angle sun All of these photographs were taken within an hour of sunset or sunrise, yet the range of lighting effects is enormous. Changes in the atmosphere make the sun itself look different at every sunrise or sunset. So even on pictures of the sun itself, such as the view of an Indian fishing boat (bottom right), there can be immense variety. The variety of modelling and labour in scenes lit by a low sun is even greater, as the pictures here show.

Sunset or sunrise?
There is no objective visual distinction between sunrise and sunset, and to a viewer unfamiliar with the geography, any of these photographs could have been taken at either time — in fact, only the scene at the bottom centre, of Holy Island off the northeast coast, was photographed at dawn.

bad reputation tends to hide the fact that a low sun provides enormous *variety* of lighting within a range of directions and a short space of time. The time of day, the season of the year, and the latitude all determine the angle of the sun. Ignoring, in other words, the direct view of the rising or setting sun, this time of day offers cross-lighting, back-lighting, frontal lighting, broad overhead lighting (at dusk), interesting skies, and the choice of rapid change within an hour or so.

If the sky is clear, shadows are sharp, distinct and long. The colour of the light is warmer the closer the sun is to the horizon, due to scattering, but in fact there is considerable variety from yellowish to red, reflecting the range of possible atmospheric conditions. With the sun behind the camera, few shadows are visible, and the lighting is even for the sides of hills, buildings and other tall objects. Colours appear warm, rich and saturated.

Against the light, contrast is high, and subjects can even appear strongly silhouetted, either against the sun and sky or against bright surfaces such as water, which pick up the sun's reflection intensely. Shooting into the light often produces flare, and under the right circumstances this can create a strong sense of atmosphere, the whole image suffused with orange. The colours in this direction are much less intense than with the light, and photographs on colour film may even be monochromatic.

As cross-lighting, a low sun can be seen to cast long, distinct shadows, which give a three-dimensional modelling effect. Even virtually flat landscapes display some relief, and fine textured detail, such as rocks and grass, is picked out sharply. As the sun sinks lower in the evening, only a few high points remain lit.

Interesting and useful as low-sunlighting may be, there are very few locations and times of the year when it can be relied upon. The lower the sun, the more possibility there is of clouds, haze or mist hiding it. Nevertheless, this unpredictability usually makes it worth waiting for, and the photographs on pages 166-167 illustrate better than any description how much can be done with this condition of natural light.

Nightfall

Before sunrise and after sunset twilight offers a lighting condition that, though dim, has unique qualities. If the sky remains clear, then in the direction of the sun both the tones and colours grade upwards from the horizon. Again, the atmosphere creates variety. At the horizon line, the sky may be anything from white, through gold, to red, violet or blue. Above the horizon, the sky becomes smoothly darker, as if a white wall had been carefully airbrushed. For any reflective subject, be it water or an automobile, this smoothly graduated lighting gives a gentle modelling. The low light levels may call for fast film, or a tripod and time exposure, or both. If the light meter is not sensitive enough at the ISO setting of the film being used, it helps to adjust it temporarily to a higher film speed, making a mental allowance for the difference. In other words, turn the meter setting until a reading is registered; then use *that* setting *plus* the number of f-stops added to the meter setting.

When the last trace of twilight has disappeared, the only light sources are the moon, stars and the glow from the lights of any nearby town or city (this last is stronger when there are low clouds to reflect it). The moon appears roughly the same size as the sun, but even when full is about 400,000 times less bright. Exposures are usually impossible to meter, and vary according to how clear the sky is, the phase of the moon and the reciprocity failure of the film being used (see page 97). As a starting point, ISO 64 film could be exposed for 20 minutes or more at f2.8 for a moonlit landscape (Kodachrome) and ISO 400 film for about three minutes. Wide bracketing of exposures is recommended. A darker-than-daylight result may in any case look more realistic.

Weather effects

Clear skies, even if sought after, are by no means the most common condition, generally speaking. Weather modifies the lighting, and its variety is enormous.

Haze is caused by microscopic particles suspended in the atmosphere, and is particularly noticeable in hot, humid con-

Low light photography
Because night-time exposures are almost invariably long — at least a few minutes — a high-speed film is not necessarily an advantage. Even with a high-speed film, a timed exposure on a tripod is essential, so a slower film may be a better choice, giving a finer-grained picture as in the pre-dawn Arizona landscape (top).

Haze can often be attractive, as in the picture above, but it tends to reduce contrast and definition. A UV filter or, if the sun is to one side, a polarizing filter may help to cut through light haze. In the triplet at right the difference between no filter, UV filter and polarizing filter is marked.

ditions and after a day or so under a stationary anticyclone. Being so small, these particles tend to scatter the shorter wavelengths, blue and ultraviolet, more than others, with the result that a distant view through haze generally appears bluish on colour film. Regular film is more sensitive than the human eye to ultraviolet, hence the common use of ultraviolet filters in landscape photography. The effect is most noticeable with a long focus lens used on a distant scene, as its narrow angle of view tends to eliminate the foreground. As sunlight is polarized, the effect of this haze scattering can be cut even more with a polarizing filter — provided that the view is more or less at right angles to the sun. Conversely, haze can be exaggerated in a photograph by using no filter, by shooting into the sun, and, with black-and-white film, by using a dark blue filter.

Mist and *fog* are also made up of particles, but being mainly water these are much larger than haze particles. As a result, there is no tendency towards blue and ultra violet, and the blanketing effect is much stronger. Generally, mist and fog are more interesting conditions, as they often shift rapidly, covering and uncovering different parts of the landscape. Early morning mist hanging low over wetlands and meadows can look very appealing, and as the rising sun begins to clear, it offers a choice of images from vague silhouettes to clear but soft pastel pictures.

Mist and fog are made up of suspended droplets that are larger than haze particles, and so cannot really be filtered out. But with a careful choice of viewpoint, mist can make atmospheric photographs. Early morning is the most common time of day for these conditions, particularly close to water or over marshy ground. Both of the photographs below were taken shortly after sunrise: over water-meadows in the east of England (bottom) and on Lake Dal in Kashmir (below). But exposures need wide bracketing since light meters can be fooled by the whiteness of mist into underexposing, rendering the mist neutral grey.

Clouds and colour temperature Colour film is notoriously sensitive to slight variations in colour temperature — or rather, the human eye sees colours differently according to the colour of the light, while colour film's response is constant. As a result, film picks up the 'coolness' of scenes under a cloudy sky that would not be noticed at the time. This can usually be corrected fairly easily with an 81 series warming filter over the lens. The landscape at right in the English Lake District was photographed with no filter (left) and with an 81B filter (right) — an 81A would have less effect, an 81C would have more.

Clouds are the main component of skies, and come in a wide range of forms and at different heights. Thin, high stratus can appear much the same as haze, giving just a slight softening to the sun. The thicker and lower the cloud cover, the greater the diffusion, just as with the diffusing materials used in a studio. With this diffusion, which reduces the intensity of shadows and softens their edges, comes a lowering of the light level; thin, high cloud may reduce the light by the equivalent of one stop or less, but the effect of a very low continuous cloud cover that would be described as 'overcast' might be three stops or more. Because these clouds diffuse the light not only from the sun but also from the blue sky, colour temperatures in this weather tend to be rather high, and a slight warming filter, such an 81A or an 81B may be needed to restore the appearance of 'neutral' lighting.

In much location work, the photographer simply treats the scene and its lighting as one complete subject, designing the shot accordingly. In this sense, there are no preferences involved — the lighting is as it is and the subject appeals to the photographer or is ignored. However, if there is time to wait and return, and if the photographer has in mind a particular image, then some value judgements about the suitability of the lighting are inevitable. This is especially true in those areas of professional photography when the specific subject comes first. Then, the photographer has to decide which of the likely conditions of natural light will suit the subject best. In this respect, cloud cover tends to play two conflicting roles. By diffusing the sun's light, it provides softer modelling and shadow fill, which to a degree can help angular shapes that need to be shown clearly. As far as clarity is concerned, a portrait is easy to make in light that is partly softened by some cloud — strong, direct sunlight creates contrast problems, and harsh, unflattering shadows.

A cloudy sky gives a soft light that reduces the modelling on subjects and so is often dull, but it is good for scenes with complicated shapes, details and textures, like the forest view below.

Clouds can make dramatic visual elements in the landscape, as the top right picture shows — a polarizing filter may enhance contrast between clouds and a blue sky.

The other side of the coin is that heavy diffusion tends to produce a lack of distinction in the lighting; modelling is reduced as shadows are reduced, variety of direction of the light is masked, and a sameness can settle on pictures shot in overcast weather. Moreover, views split by a horizon line generally show uncomfortably high contrast between the cloudy sky and the ground — on transparency film in particular; an experiment that is ideal for one of these areas is not likely to suit the other. This last problem can usually be solved by using a gradated filter over the lens (see page 119). A neutral gradated filter, aligned so that the darker area coincides with the sky, will balance the picture. Gradated filters are normally available in two strengths, and the dark section adds approximately one or two stops to the exposure in this area. They can also be used with clouds either to give a hint of tone or to give an impression of storminess and threatening rain.

Perhaps it is the general effect of overcast weather on leisure that gives it such a bad reputation for photography. In the end, however, these *are* value judgements, and there is complete freedom of choice on aesthetic grounds. Decisions as to the suitability of natural light fall heavily into the area of controlled location photography (see pages 204-205).

While cloud cover is essentially a lighting condition, being mainly featureless, other cloud forms can be subjects as well.

Rainy days have a poor reputation for photography, because the light is so dull. But they can be very atmospheric, as in the shot of a tropical downpour above.

Stormy weather with heavy black clouds can be spectacular, if unpredictable, as in the view (right) of the ancient ruins of Monte Alban in Mexico.

This is particularly so when the cloud shapes are distinct, as with fair-weather cumulus or the remnants of a storm at sunset, and when the clouds touch the ground, as often happens in mountains. Scattered clouds against a blue sky can be enhanced by a photograph by means of filters. With black-and-white film, an orange or red filter will darken the sky and heighten its contrast with the clouds, while with colour film a polarizing filter will perform much the same thing (as long as the sun is at 90° to the camera).

More extreme weather can create obvious problems — unpleasant conditions and damage to equipment, for instance — but it carries some special advantages. Since it is often avoided by photographers, it can have, for many subjects, a visual freshness. *Storms* are marked by their unpredictability, but may contain, as the photograph (above) shows, moments of special beauty.

The usual product of storms is rain or snow, and both create their own particular lighting conditions. *Rainfall* at a distance appears much as a mist, and as the light levels are usually low and the shutter speeds needed slow, tends to photograph much as a mist as well. Individual raindrops are likely to appear at best as streaks (against a dark background), and for a more definite impression the necessary conditions are backlighting from a direct sun, a shutter speed of at least $1/_{125}$ second, and a dark background. If the sun does break through during rainfall, the chances are good for a rainbow. Since rainbows are optical effects, they appear to move as their observer moves — a useful thing to know if the composition of rainbow and landscape needs to be improved.

Lightning is a spectacular but tricky subject. The standard technique for photographing lightning is to work at night, leaving the shutter open until one or more flashes have occurred. The exposure settings are not critical, for the flash is so bright that it will register at any aperture — yet its effect on the surroundings will be minimal. As a guide-line, with ISO 64 film, use an aperture of about f4 for strikes at a great distance, f5.6 for 2-10 miles (3-16km), and f11 for any closer. Distance is easy to work out by timing the difference between flash and sound; for each five seconds' difference, assume about 1 mile (1.6 km). Of course, it can be difficult knowing exactly where to point the camera. A wide angle lens improves the chances of catching the lightning flash in the frame. But the picture must still be carefully composed.

High altitude

As there is less atmosphere at altitude, there is less screening effect. As a result, light levels are generally a little higher in mountains, contrast under a clear sky is higher than at ground level, and ultraviolet radiation is stronger. A basic precaution for normal photography is to fit a strong (yellow-tinted) ultraviolet filter to the lens.

Polar light

The low angle of the sun at the poles (maximum 40° in mid-summer) means that light levels are lower than in temperate latitudes and colour temperatures are generally lower also. In the summer, there is sufficient light for photography for most of the day and night though at night a tripod may be needed. But winters are dark. Snow and ice increase reflectivity, particularly with blue skies in clear weather.

Tropical light

At low latitudes the sun rises higher (directly overhead at some times of the year) and therefore sunrises and sunsets take less time. This has an important bearing on location photography, as lighting conditions in the middle of the day are less attractive for many subjects. Sunrise and sunset are close to six o'clock in the morning and six o'clock in the evening respectively, but from mid-morning until mid-afternoon the sun is at its brightest. This leaves little time for low-sun photography.

During the day, shadows are most pronounced under objects. This gives both high contrast with tallish subjects and low contrast with flat landscapes. Unfamiliarity with tropical light often encourages exposure mistakes, and the meter should be followed very closely.

Exposing for snow scenes
Without a clear idea of how the picture should appear, it can be hard to expose snow scenes well. TTL and other direct-reading meters indicate the exposure for an *average* mild-grey tone, while snow is white and should appear in a picture as white. So a direct reading uncorrected would give an underexposed picture. In a scene such as the New England winter landscape at right, the most realistic exposure would be between one and two stops more than the TTL reading. Bracketing of exposures is a worthwhile precaution since recording the fine crystalline texture of sunlit snow needs exposure accurate to within a third or half of a stop.

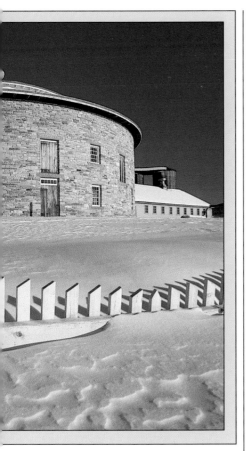

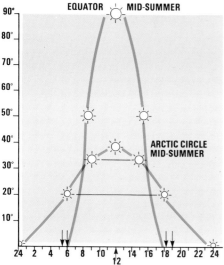

Reflective surroundings

A number of conditions provide strong or noticeable reflection, filling shadows and generally raising the light level sometimes by about one stop. Snow, light sand, water and bright clouds are the chief natural reflectors. They may be so bright that the lens will need shade protection against flare.

Snow in particular can cause exposure problems. If it appears in the picture, it usually looks more realistic when reproduced just white enough to show a hint of texture. A straight meter reading from clean snow will indicate an exposure setting that will make it seem grey in the photograph (see pages 58-59). To avoid this, take an incident reading, measure an average subject, or take a direct reading from the snow and add two stops to the exposure.

Tropical light is notable for its extremes: from high, brilliant sunshine in the middle of the day (left) to the brief but frequently spectacular twilight (below). Because the sun rises and sinks so quickly during a 12-hour day, the useful shooting times in early morning and the evening are very short, and high sun occupies most of the day.

At high altitude (left), the air is thinner and so ultraviolet light from the sun penetrates more easily than at sea-level. Although this extra ultraviolet light will not be perceptible to the eye, it will register on film, giving a generally blue, overexposed effect on colour film. UV filters help reduce this effect.

The path of the sun through the sky varies with latitude (above). At the equator, the sun rises and sets rapidly, but is little brighter at midday than in mid-morning or mid-afternoon. In the polar circles, the summer sun's course through the sky is much shallower. During winter there is little and, for some time, no daylight at all.

People are the principal subject of photography, both amateur and professional, and although a significant number of portraits are made in studios, most photography of people is on location, showing them as they appear and behave in normal life. In particular, they are the main concern of reportage photography, and this mainly professional field has a powerful influence on all photographers.

Reportage photography is essentially journalistic, and so usually searches for effect, impact and summation. The almost universally accepted ideals of reportage photography are that it should be visually strong, and so catch the viewer's attention, and that it should, within a single picture, concentrate as many as possible of the subject's qualities.

CANDID PHOTOGRAPHY

A major technique of reportage, candid photography makes the most of photography's unique ability to freeze movement, catching fleeting glimpses of people at their most natural and revealing. The photographer remains unobtrusive, recording events without ever getting involved. This is not the same thing as appearing to be unaware, as frequently happens in involved reportage, where the presence of the camera is known but accepted. The great value of candid photography is that it allows situations to be recorded naturally, without the inevitable distortions in behaviour and expression that occur when people become self-conscious and start to worry about their appearance.

Dr Erich Salomon used the Ermanox camera with its fast lens, to pioneer the 'candid' style of reportage, typified by his 1928 shot (above) of statesmen at the League of Nations conference. Although the camera still had to be mounted on a tripod, the Ermanox's fast lens meant exposures could be brief enough for unposed pictures indoors. In the 19th-century, long exposure times made such shots impossible — the shot of a boar being transported in China (right) had to be posed.

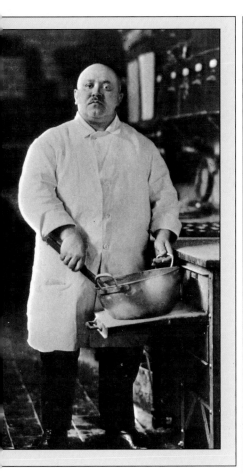

Henri Cartier-Bresson This 1948 photograph (above left) of the pandemonium that followed the Kuomintang decision to distribute gold in China shows just why Cartier-Bresson's close-working style had such a powerful influence on photojournalism.

Formal reportage Another stylistic direction in reportage photography was pioneered by Auguste Sander. His photograph (above) of a pastry cook is in the formal, objective tradition of documentary photography.

Influential cameras

The history of candid photography is linked intimately to the history of photographic equipment and materials. Faced with a low light level or a poor view-point in most other areas of photography, the photographer can often find a way of adapting, but this usually takes time. In candid photography, however, the technical capabilities of the equipment must be up to the demands of the immediate situation.

Candid photography was impossible in the early days of photography. Indeed it was not until the introduction in the 1880s of smaller cameras that could be held in the hand, that the idea of the photographer as the unobtrusive observer, first emerged. Paul Martin, for instance, used to wander the streets of Victorian London with his camera concealed in a brown paper parcel or in his briefcase. Jacob Riis was not unobserved when he took his photographs, but his use of the newly invented powder flash allowed him to photograph people and places as he found them, regardless of the prevailing light.

Nevertheless, while exposures were long or needed flash, photography could never be really candid in the modern sense. The breakthrough was the launch of the German-made Ermanox plate camera in 1925 with its incredibly fast f1.8 lens — the fastest in the world at the time. Dr Erich Salomon caused a sensation with his candid pictures of the statesmen at the League of Nations conference in 1928, taken on an Ermanox. But even with the Ermanox, exposures indoors were so long that Salomon had to use a tripod, fitting a silent Compur shutter and firing it with a long air release to remain as discreet as possible. And the need to change plates after every exposure was a major drawback for on-the-spot reportage.

The rise of candid photography stems from the introduction of first the Ermanox (right) with its fast lens and then the Leica (above) which used 35mm film.

This was where the Leica, the first 35mm camera, giving 36 exposures on a single roll of film came into its own. The camera had been invented in 1925 by Oscar Barnack to take 35mm movie film, but it was not until Leica brought out their Model C, which took interchangeable lenses, and the introduction of fast (ISO100/21°) 35mm film in 1932 that the Leica movement really took off. With the Leica and the similar Zeiss Contax, a whole new style of candid 'photojournalism' emerged, making the names of photographers such as Henri Cartier-Bresson, Alfred Eisenstaedt and Bill Brandt whose picture stories were featured in new picture news magazines such as *Picture Post* and *Life*.

The Leica was such a well-designed instrument, and improved regularly with deference to its professional user's requirements, that it became the standard and well-loved camera of the first generation of candid photographers of whom Henry Cartier-Bresson is the archetype. The reputation of these people has influenced successive generations, with the result that not only is the Leica's original influence felt today, but the camera itself remains the tool of choice for many modern street photographers. In particular, this has meant that one approach to candid photography has historically dominated all others: the method of working in close and using a special demeanour to remain unobtrusive. The principal reason for this is that at the time of the invention of the Leica in the 1920s the technology for combining reflex viewing and bulk film was not available and there was instead a separate viewer with rangefinder focusing. Now, a separate viewing system is only practical with standard or short focal lengths, and even wide-angled lenses pose problems (of parallax).

The option of a more distanced method of shooting was possible only with the development of compact 35mm SLR cameras that have built-in through-the-lens metering. The Nikon, though by no means unique, is strongly associated with the more varied reportage techniques.

Candid approaches

Over the years, a number of distinct approaches to candid photography have evolved. But they all involve the photographer keeping a low profile, biding time until the right situation occurs.

■ CLOSE WORKING Working close to the subject — within a few feet — has a strong tradition, influenced strongly by Henri Cartier-Bresson and others of his generation. Working close yet remaining unnoticed means dressing and behaving discreetly — using a camera that is light, quiet, simple, familiar and unobtrusive, and using a fast lens and fairly fast film. It also includes presetting the camera controls for instant shooting — anticipating focus and exposure settings, constantly checking that there are sufficient frames left in the camera, having spare film and alternative lenses to hand (if likely to be needed). Automatic exposure systems can be useful. Composition and design sense must be developed to the point where they become almost instinctive, so that no time is wasted adjusting the framing.

Familiarity with people and the way they behave is fundamental. The more that is known about what is occurring — say, an argument in the street — the easier it is to anticipate what might happen next. Anticipation, even if only of something as undramatic as a change of facial expression, helps the photographer preset the camera controls correctly and frame the shot a fraction of a second ahead of time.

There are some subsidiary techniques within the close working method. One is the use of wide-angle lenses. Their depth of field is generally sufficient to make precise focusing not absolutely necessary, which gives an advantage in working quickly. Also, if the design of the photograph can be arranged so that a subject close to the camera is off-centre in the frame, the photographer can appear to be aiming in a slightly different direction. Another distinction in technique is between a 'one-shot' situation, in which the desired result is a single image, and 'continuing' photography, in which the photographer wants to stay with the subject, hoping to improve the image by working on it. In the first case, surreptitiousness is only important up to the point of shooting. In the second case, however, the photographer has to remain unobtrusive; quiet camera operation is vital.

■ TELEPHOTO METHODS A completely different candid technique is to shoot from a distance through a telephoto lens. This technique depends on SLR camera technology, for not only is reflex viewing necessary for accurate framing and

Wide-angle disguise Under certain circumstances, the broad coverage of a wide-angle lens can be exploited to include people in the foreground of a shot without their being aware. In the picture above, at a bathing ghat in India, the photographer could hardly avoid being conspicuous (right), but the broad coverage of the 24mm made the figure on the left assume the shot was being taken over his shoulder.

Bystanders Using a wide-angle lens increases the chance of including in the picture someone staring at the camera.

Eye contact in street photography

In a situation where there is really no possibility of concealment and every chance of being noticed as a photographer, the following procedure may help to get a natural shot — or at least, one in which the subject is not staring at the camera:

● avoid looking directly at the subject before shooting

● shoot quickly, with a pre-set camera

● immediately after shooting, look *beyond* the subject, as if you had been photographing something else.

The last can help to preserve the situation in case you want to try for other shots; in particular, it is useful in places where a subject can be expected to react adversely to being photographed.

Cultural reactions

Different cultures, societies and groups of people have varying responses to photography in general, and being the subject of candid shooting in particular. These reactions may manifest themselves in any way from mugging for the camera to actual aggression. To some extent it is possible to generalize (in an Indian city, for example, people are usually very easy-going and often *too* eager to appear in shot), but many reactions are highly specific. For example, a street hawker in a particular location may be hostile because he is selling illegally and does not want to be identified. It is a sensible precaution in an unfamiliar place to have a short briefing from a friend or acquaintance who has good local knowledge.

Lenses for candids A wide-angle lens, with its wide coverage and depth of field, is suitable for shots glimpsed while passing a doorway, as in the hashish shop (second left). A telephoto — 180mm in the pair of shots on the left — is good for long shots but obstructions can be a problem.

Equipment and film
Within a range of personal preferences, cameras used for candid photography are lightweight, relatively small, and easy to use quickly. Both 35mm rangefinder and 35mm SLR models are used, the former with standard and wide-angle lenses, the latter with telephotos as well. Popular focal lengths are 24mm, 28mm, 35mm and 50mm for close working methods; 135mm, 150mm and 180mm for working at a distance. Zoom lenses are sometimes preferred for speed of altering the framing, although they are relatively slow lenses.

Automatic exposure is used by some photographers for speed of response, although others prefer to have manual control and be able to bracket exposures so as to deal with non-standard lighting conditions.

A motor-drive or automatic winder is useful for speed and for allowing greater concentration, but is noisy and adds weight.

In black-and-white photography, an ISO 400/27° film such as Tri-X is normally used. In colour photography, however, preferences vary, between the fine grain but slow speed of films like Kodachrome 64, and fast but grainier films like Ektachrome 200 or P800/1600. One or two camera bodies may be carried. A small, drab shoulder bag is used more than other types.

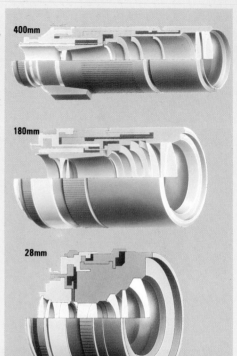

Three types of focal length that have special value in candid photography are the long telephoto, the medium telephoto, and the wide-angle lens — all for different reasons. Long focal lengths of around 300mm and more allow completely concealed photography (as the downward-looking shot at left, taken from an upper balcony of the Pompidou Centre in Paris). Lenses of around 180mm are useful for across-the-street shots, while wide-angles lenses can be used among crowds.

focusing, but TTL metering is important for rapid exposure measurement at a distance. Fewer demands are placed on the photographer to behave inconspicuously, but camera techniques must be sound. The camera must be held firmly, for the maximum aperture is usually smaller than for shorter lengths, and this tends to reduce the usable shutter speed. The problem is compounded by the increased chance of camera-shake with lenses of long focal length. Focusing, too, is more critical and, as the working distance is greater, there is more chance of people and objects in front of the subject getting in the way. It may be necessary to shoot with both eyes open, one looking out for obstructions passing in front of the camera.

The popular lenses are 135mm and 200mm for 35mm cameras. Longer lenses, such as 400mm, call for a slightly different technique. The working distance is greater, which often makes it possible to continue shooting for as long as wanted, but long lenses are difficult to hold steady for long periods. For these reasons, a concealed camera position is often used, such as a doorway or a balcony (people in streets rarely look up).

■ CONCEALMENT Another, less common, approach to candid photography is disguise. The photographer, for instance, may shoot with an SLR from waist-level with the prism removed or pretend to tinker with the camera while viewing the image, again with the prism removed. More extreme is to hide the camera under a coat or in a bag with an opening made just large enough for the lens.

The value of pre-setting camera controls — that is, focus, exposure and shutter speed — is that the unexpected can be caught on film rapidly. Furthermore, when working close to in a market like this (above) a wide-angle lens increases the chances of including all the important ingredients of a situation. Here, even a 24mm lens only just manages to include the petty theft unnoticed by the market women.

A medium telephoto lens makes it possible to work comfortably some distance away for full-length shots of small groups of people. The photographer usually has sufficient time to wait and observe without being conspicuous as in this shot of Smithfield Market, London (far left).

A direct but unposed portrait works better than a candid approach in many street situations. The evident good nature of the people in the welding shop in Athens (left) was an opportunity too good to miss.

Most photographs with depth in the subject contain some areas that are out of focus, but this can be turned to good effect. In *Terror of War, Biafra*

(below) Romano Cagnoni has focused beyond the obvious first point of interest in the scene and the result, like the subject, is disturbing.

Styles

Historically there have been two main polarizations of style in candid photography. One follows the principle that there are certain points in the flux of human activity that are particularly telling or elegant, and that it is the skill of the photographer to identify them and catch them. This was articulated first by Henry Cartier-Bresson as the highly influential concept of the 'decisive moment'. The other main movement is in many respects a reaction to the great hold that the 'decisive moment' has had in the field — it is the photography of the casual, un-special moments that can be argued to be truer to life. Robert Frank and Gary Winogrand are strongly associated with this interest in the commonplace. Robert Frank's book of photographs called *America* was extremely influential.

INVOLVED REPORTAGE

Clearly there are limits to what can be achieved with a candid approach, for it is both unpredictable and difficult to sustain for any length of time. The alternative to a candid approach is 'involvement', which may range from a simple announcement of intention to detailed arrangements to ensure the full co-operation of the subject.

The type and degree of involvement depends on the preferred working method of the photographer, familiarity with the customs and language of the people and on the amiability of the subjects.

There are many situations where it is simpler just to go straight ahead and begin taking pictures rather than going into the ritual of discussing it in advance and asking permission. The photographer can often assume a right to shoot, although clearly, some charm and warmth helps, and the photographer has to be able to play the situation on the spot and sense if anyone minds. An alternative is for the photographer simply to ask permission to take pictures there and then. For certain kinds of impromptu portrait — say, a stallholder in a market — this is the obvious approach. Although the result can be something that looks similar to a candid shot, there is likely to be eye contact, and professionally this tends to draw mixed reactions. One school of opinion holds that eye contact in an unplanned reportage photograph destroys any sense of authenticity by showing that the camera was having an effect. The opposite view is that to insist on avoiding eye contact is only looking for a spurious reality, and that there is a frank honesty in admitting the presence of the camera. It is only fair to say that these are the extremes of

Extended coverage By spending time with a group of people, a degree of intimacy can often be achieved. For this assignment — a week spent documenting the life of one family in Normandy — familiarity with the photographer allows the subjects to relax and continue their normal activities.

The 'head shot' (below) is the most common of all types of portrait to maintain attractive facial proportions; a long focal lens is used.

Person and product Another standard treatment (bottom) is to combine the subject and the things they want or are involved with.

opinion, and many photographers and editors would not bother to discriminate on these grounds.

More involved still is a full request for co-operation, made in advance. Here the advantages lie in being able to arrange the shoot for the best condition, and this is one of the most common professional approaches. There is often a formal chain of commands for such requests, involving the press or public relations office of an institution or business corporation. At a parade, a political conference, or a festival, for example, formal arrangements for accredited press representatives are nearly always made. Typically, this will at least provide a convenient shooting position for photographers, as well as a schedule of events and the possibilities of arranging certain special shots. Where no channels exist for making arrangements, yet an extended coverage is needed, the photographer may have to invest some time in gaining the confidence of the subjects. This is especially true if the plan is to work at some depth in a very structured community or social group, such as a family, a religious sect or a tribe. In order to be able to reach the stage of complete freedom of action and not attract special interest, it may well be necessary to spend a little time with the people first without attempting to take pictures.

Finally, at the furthest point possible from candid photography, the involvement of the photographer may be such that a shot is virtually created. Stage-managing a photograph can be useful where the action does not need to be spontaneous in order to be authentic, and where the accuracy is easy to check. A common example of a reconstructed shot is of people at work. This kind of shot needs considerable organization and time, and demands full co-operation from a subject unaware of just how long it can often take to set up a shot.

Portraits on location, particularly those intended for publication, tend to fall into two categories: pictures of what people look like and pictures of what they do. But there is an enormous variety of ways in which each can be treated. The subject can be one person alone, or any number up to a very large group. The method can be direct, with eye-contact between the subject and the camera, or informal, with the subject appearing to pay no attention to the camera. The picture may be framed tightly on the face, or show more of the setting than the person, and the subject can be shown in relation to other people or relevant objects. The location, if it appears at all in the shot, can be indoors or outdoors, with or without additional lighting.

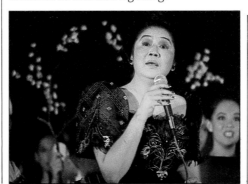

Organized events Official functions demand the use of official press channels. Even so, unusual moments, such as the impromptu singing performance by Mrs Marcos during the state visit of the Japanese Prime Minister to the Philippines (left), can only be hoped for.

Single portraits

For single portraits, the choice in composition is generally between four scales: a head shot in which the framing is sufficiently tight to exclude the background; a head-and-shoulder shot; a three-quarter shot showing the torso more or less from the waist up; and a full-length shot in a setting.

In many situations, the choice of scale is simply a reflection of the photographer's own taste. Sometimes, however, there are specific advantages for a particular viewpoint. A head shot concentrates attention on the eyes and mouth, and so on facial expression, while the tight framing is useful if the available settings are distracting, unattractive or irrelevant. Head-and-shoulders shots often give the most recognizable views of a subject. A three-quarter torso shot allows some of the background to enter the picture, without dominating the composition. And shots showing the setting are a useful way of placing the subjects in context or showing what they do — typically, a craftsman surrounded by the tools of his trade, or a businesswoman at her desk. In addition, if the portrait is only one part of a picture story, the photographer may choose a particular scale to balance accompanying photographs. For instance if the setting is distinctive and is shown elsewhere, the portrait will be more tightly framed.

The more of the picture area occupied by the face, the more thought needs to be given to the pose. Full face, three-quarter profile and profile are the most common, and the choice is often influenced by the lighting (see below). A close portrait introduces the risk of some distortion of the features, and for proportions that look right — and flattering — a longer focal length is necessary. Commonly used 'portrait' lenses on 35mm cameras range from about 85mm to 200mm in focal length.

People and objects In the two pictures at the top of this page, a similar compressed treatment is used to deal with a disparity in size. In the pearl photograph, the object is much smaller than the man, but both are shown clearly by very tight framing with a medium telephoto lens. In the famous photograph of Isambard Kingdom Brunel by Howlett, the same technique is used in reverse, with the heavy chains cropped tightly as a background.

Consistent backgrounds When portrait photographs from different locations need to look similar, the simplest technique is to carry one backdrop from place to place. The four photographs of milkmen (above) were part of an advertising campaign that involved hundreds of similar shots all over the country. A standard set-up of background and lighting, transported to each new location and arranged in any convenient room, provided consistency.

Context shots

Shots showing the subject in context are a stock-in-trade of the photojournalist because they tell you succinctly about the subjects and why they are being featured. There is a wide variety of possible treatments, but two or three tend to be more popular.

Typical of the style of colour magazines is a wide-angle shot from a distance of a metre (3ft) or so, showing a range of artefacts laid out in front of the subject. The wide-angle lens gives the depth of field needed to keep both subject and artefacts sharply focused — though a small aperture may still be needed to give enough depth of field and this type of shot

Group portraits Normally much more attention to the composition of the image and the arrangement of the subjects is needed with groups of people rather than with individuals and couples. In order to make the image cohesive, as in the picture of a large Colombian family (right), the group must be compact.

Work-related portraits Two alternative portrait treatments, shown below, involve arranging for the subject to be busy with some relevant project, even if only for the sake of the camera. Simulating work in progress, as in the photograph of a university professor undertaking research in a library, is legitimate if the activity would normally appear that way. The more formal 'man-with-his-wares' approach, as in the photograph of a French chef, is more suited to activities that have tangible and interesting end-products — in this case, *nouvelle cuisine* dishes.

People at work Shots of people involved in their work can be virtually candid. For a clear view, working close with a wide-angle lens is probably the most common method, as in the photograph of the Indian fishermen (right) and a bell foundry (bottom). Where the location permits, however, a high camera position from a distance can be used with a telephoto lens, as in the shot of a council meeting in the City of London (below).

often calls for extra artificial light. The wide angle also has a useful visual effect, for the exaggerated perspective gives the artefacts more prominence, minimizing the scale difference between artefacts and subject.

A wide-angle lens can also be used to minimize the scale difference between the subject and a much larger background. An oil sheikh, for instance, can be photographed right up against the oil well that brought him his wealth.

An alternative approach is to use a telephoto lens to compress perspective and exaggerate scale differences, with a man dwarfed by a mighty engineering construction for instance.

If, however, there is nothing relevant in the background, then advantage may lie with a setting that is plain, or at least visually uncomplicated. Continuous tones, colours and patterns all make good potential backgrounds of this kind. Indoors, as in the subject's home or place of work, a safe, though unexciting approach is to hang a backdrop of paper or cloth. This is virtually studio photography, and uses the techniques described on page 258.

Group shots

Organized group portraits require different techniques. Composition is important simply because it is usually essential to see every face — the larger the group, the more care must be

Work sequence Certain types of work, which involve a sequence of actions, may need several pictures rather than one. In the Parisian fashion house of Chanel, shown here, a medium dress-making shot, a close detail of stitching and a picture of the finished product are the smallest set of shots that can show the range of activity.

taken. A high camera position helps to prevent the faces of people behind being obscured by those in front, as does an arrangement of standing, sitting and squatting rows. As facial expression is important in portraiture, and as it can rarely be fixed in advance, the chances of one person blinking, grimacing or looking away at the moment of exposure are increased in proportion to the number of people. Good direction and management by the photographer are needed.

People at work

People at work make up one of the largest single subjects, if 'work' is loosely interpreted. Professionally, this kind of picture is in regular demand because so much reporting concerns what people do for a living and the way in which things are produced. At an amateur level it is not only interesting for these same reasons but it offers an easy way for both the photographer and the subject to conduct the session; the photographer may be relieved of the responsibility of suggesting poses and backgrounds, while most people feel at ease and unselfconscious when concentrating on their regular activity. Tenseness of expression in a reluctant subject is also avoided. The actual treatment of people-at-work shots varies according to the activity, and there are few useful generalizations. There are nearly always opportunities for several different pictures within one working situation, including, for instance, a wide-angled shot that takes in the work environment as well as individual actions in the foreground, and a 'hands-on' shot of close, detailed work. This variety often suggests a photo-essay approach.

Parades and events

Another popular human activity for reportage photography is the special event, which can include the public appearances of famous people, parades and festivals. Visually, such events usually contain special attractions, with costumes, displays and large numbers of people, which provide good opportunities for colourful, exotic images. Most are organized to a degree, and this makes it possible to plan the photography in advance. As events attract crowds, good shooting positions are at a premium, and best arranged in advance, either through the help of the event organizers, or by reaching them early. Crowds and organization also usually hinder free movement during the event, so that a single camera position may have to suffice. Passes and permissions to move through restricted areas may be available for professional photographers. The best views of a parade are likely to be head-on, as from one side of a bend in the road, but a view that seems clear in rehearsal or on a reconnaissance may be either restricted by the police or blocked by crowds later.

If the event has a central moment or feature of interest, this is an essential shot — no coverage of the Lord Mayor's Show, for example, would be complete without a picture of the Lord Mayor. Identifying this and other key shots is a crucial element of the photojournalist's task. Apart from the centrepiece, photojournalists may look for shots setting the entire scene ('establishing shots'), individual tableaux in a parade, crowd shots, costumes, individual spectators, behind-the-scene activity, and the occasional odd, unpredictable moments that make it important to stay alert.

Variety in one event In a parade or similar public celebration, there are many opportunities to take a variety of pictures — as here, in three shots from the Hong Kong Bun Festival, including the main event and spectators.

Rock concerts are usually a good source of strong images, but pose specific problems with lighting and viewpoint. Lighting during a concert varies greatly in colour, contrast and brightness. To cope with low levels, it is best to use a fast lens and high-speed, tungsten-balanced film.

There are two basic alternatives to access, as shown here: a long shot from the back (right) or a tight shot of individual performers from the photographer's pit in front of the stage (above). For both, a medium telephoto is the most useful lens.

Circuses and other performing arts are colourful and lively as these pictures (above, above left) demonstrate — both were taken at the 1977 Circus World Championships in London. But it is essential to make sure that there are no restrictions governing the use of cameras.

REPORTAGE PHOTOGRAPHY IN USE

The way in which the media use photographs has an importance out of all proportion to the number of pictures taken, and published photography strongly influences approaches to photography. Photography is a very public activity, and the standards of taste in this popular field are largely set by what people see in magazines, newspapers, books, posters and to some extent on television.

Magazines and newspapers are the major media for reportage photography, but each makes different demands on photography. Newspapers use normally single images, poorly reproduced in black-and-white. This picture must be newsworthy rather than necessarily high-quality. So the emphasis is very much on capturing that single potent image and despatching it to the newspaper in time for printing deadlines.

Capturing a single image that sums up a story is a demanding task, and press photography is a specialist field. Being on the spot at the right time is often as important as photographic technique. As Robert Capa once said, 'If your pictures aren't good enough, you aren't close enough.' Press photographers are renowned for their courage in getting right into the thick of the action.

But quick reactions are also at a premium and photographers often preset camera controls — typically to $\frac{1}{250}$ second at f4, focused at 3m (10ft). With many photographers often working alongside each other, the difference between a picture not even used by the local paper and one syndicated

Early picture story: Mussolini Stefan Lorant was one of the pioneer European Art Directors of the pre-war years, and responsible more than anyone else for the birth of the photographic picture story. In this classic short picture essay, published in the *Weekly Illustrated* of the 4th August 1934, Lorant displays his skill in making the most of his material.

In picture magazines like this, photographs were for the time used as powerful elements in their own right: the combination of one large picture spreading across the magazine's 'gutter' (the clip where pages meet), an overlapping picture to the left and a strip of four smaller photographs has a visual impact lacking in the more traditional layouts of same-sized photographs in a design of box-like regularity. The long shot is a natural for the main photograph, but Lorant has turned the other, smaller pictures into one principal portrait and what appears as a sequence.

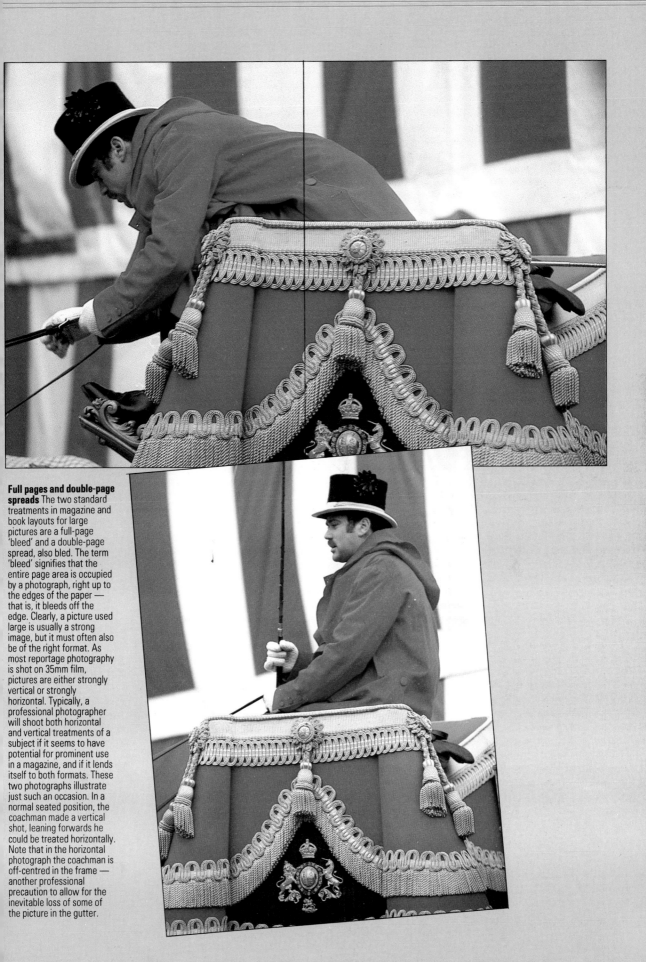

Full pages and double-page spreads The two standard treatments in magazine and book layouts for large pictures are a full-page 'bleed' and a double-page spread, also bled. The term 'bleed' signifies that the entire page area is occupied by a photograph, right up to the edges of the paper — that is, it bleeds off the edge. Clearly, a picture used large is usually a strong image, but it must often also be of the right format. As most reportage photography is shot on 35mm film, pictures are either strongly vertical or strongly horizontal. Typically, a professional photographer will shoot both horizontal and vertical treatments of a subject if it seems to have potential for prominent use in a magazine, and if it lends itself to both formats. These two photographs illustrate just such an occasion. In a normal seated position, the coachman made a vertical shot, leaning forwards he could be treated horizontally. Note that in the horizontal photograph the coachman is off-centred in the frame — another professional precaution to allow for the inevitable loss of some of the picture in the gutter.

(simultaneously published) in newspapers right across the world is often a matter of fractions of a second. The press photographer must be continually aware of the editorial demands of his or her particular newspaper. Some newspapers, for instance, might relish a picture of a union leader caught in a militant, aggressive stance; others may prefer a picture showing a more conciliatory, friendly pose. Press photographers will be constantly on the watch for moments that guarantee their picture will be used.

News photographers have produced some of the most memorable photographic images of modern times. Pictures such as Eddie Adams's 1968 photo of a Vietnamese police chief summarily executing a Vietcong officer with a bullet to the head, and Huynh Cong Ut's picture of a young Vietnamese girl running screaming and naked from a napalm attack have played a major part in the public's awareness of the horrors of the war in Vietnam.

Whatever the quality of the picture, however, it must reach the newspaper quickly if it is to have news value. Films must be processed rapidly, or the photographer must use high-quality instant picture materials to bypass the processing stage. In the future, more and more photographers may use the electronic still cameras based on video technology, such as the Canon cameras used at the Los Angeles Olympics in 1984. These enable the picture to be phoned directly to a newspaper's picture desk seconds after it is taken.

Magazines and layout
Magazines encourage a different approach from the photographer. Pictures must be of higher quality and generally in colour, and the photographer has far more time to take the pictures. Commonly, magazines will use a series of pictures to illustrate a story, rather than just a single image. It is the

A Lake of Pink and White

Gatefolds The purpose of a gatefold is to add visual drama to a magazine and to use photographs as large as possible. To work well in this form, a photograph must not only be suitable for cropping to the long format, but must also offer some surprise as the second and third pages are folded out. In the example here, of flamingo on Tanzania's Lake Ngorongoro, the surprise i one of sheer numbers. The photograph at top right, of southern Indian rice field, typical of pictures that hav such large areas of even tone that they can carry headlines and type right o the image without illegibil

Double-page spreads and gatefolds
The largest regular display space in a magazine is a double-page spread — two facing pages. In most magazines the spread is rectangular in the proportion of approximately three to four. A single 35 mm frame fits neatly into these proportions with the minimum of chopping in the horizontal format, leaving a little space for text. Unfortunately, binding inevitably hides part of the middle of the picture, where the pages join, known as the 'gutter', this can ruin some photographs where the focus of attention is exactly the middle (portraits suffer particularly in this respect). Consequently, there is a tendency for designers, to choose, if available, a picture in which the main point of interest is *off*-centre, shifted to right or left. Many professional photographers, knowing this, deliberately shoot off-centre designs.

Gatefolds, as their name implies, fold out to give extended space and although they add to printing costs, can be spectacular if handled well. They may be used for a dramatic photograph which benefits from being both long (typically about five to two in proportion) and reproduced large. Massed shots, as of an enormous crowd of people or animals work particularly well as gatefolds. Because they must be opened by the reader, gatefolds contain an attractive element of surprise in revealing the full picture inside.

Full pages
As the double-page spread is the largest normal display for a horizontal picture, the full page is the largest regular use of a vertical shot and is used more often. One of the reasons for its popularity is that it is a big presentation that still allows plenty of space, (the facing page) for text. So, while the natural way of using a 35 mm frame is horizontally, all other things being equal, reportage photographers tend to include vertical treatments of subjects where possible for full page use.

Subsidiary pictures
One principle in layout design is pacing — to maintain visual variety. Spread after spread of large photographs can become tedious, and a designer often needs pictures that are just as effective used small or large. More often than not, simplicity works best in small images — compositions that are obvious and direct at a glance, with strong shapes, lines and colours. There is a natural correspondence in these and 'point' pictures discussed below.

Openers and closers
For both design and editorial reasons, many picture stories are presented so that they open and close with a powerful picture. The opening picture is often the largest of all and this 'lead' picture may take up a whole spread. Closing photographs are more likely to be full pages than double-page spreads, as it is the end of the text that marks the end of the feature most obviously, and it helps if this is on the same spread as the last picture.

Covers
The strongest picture of all needs to be on the cover, for it is this that sells the magazine. But the choice of shot is restricted by the vertical format and the need to include title, price and so on as well, and also by the magazine's established style of cover. Titles or 'mastheads' normally run along the top which usually favours photographs that have unimportant space above the main subject so that the title can be run over the picture. A few magazines such as *Audubon* deliberately run a horizontal photograph round the back cover as well. The front cover is then the righthand half of a horizontal image.

'Type-over' areas
Cover shots are not the only type of picture that may need bland areas over which type can be set. This may apply, for example to a double-page spread over which a caption is run and the smaller the type, the plainer its background must be. In advertising, the areas for type are often calculated precisely before shooting.

India

Michael Freeman

FLAMINGOES, NGORONGORO, TANZANIA

5 7 6 1

Opening shots This close view (right) of Aldermen of the City of London was actually given a similar layout treatment in a German feature magazine (*Geo*). It works in this form because such a detailed shot is striking when used large and because the miniature Tower of London (in fact, a mace) is eyecatching. A full-page treatment (below) could open or close an article.

London's Square Mile

Mosaics Sometimes known as a mosaic or collage, a composite arrangement of pictures that have a similar visual appearance is often surprisingly successful as a design. There is something about sets and collections of similar things that is inherently appealing, and although individually the photographs may not be striking, as elements in a larger picture they often acquire visual interest.

Wrap-around cover shots must meet some very specific requirements, particularly if titles and other type are to run over the picture. The photography must not only work full-frame and horizontally, as the original colour transparency below, but also, its right-hand half must work as a vertical shot. In addition, plenty of featureless space in the upper right of the overall picture will keep the title clear. Note that type can be set so that it fits into this picture — the subtitle is arranged so that it fits neatly in between the trees in the cover picture (right).

The Author

SALLIE MORRIS gained a domestic science diploma at the Edinburgh College of Domestic Science. Since then she has taught and written on the subject regularly. In particular, she spent a number of years living and teaching in both the Far East and Africa. She is the author of *Herbs and Spices* and has also contributed to two other books, *Home Freezer Cookbook* and *Cooking for Today*. She has written for the cookery section of various magazines, including *Woman*. She is married and has two children.

Cover photographs by Michael Freeman

CHARTWELL BOOKS, INC.
A Division of
BOOK SALES, INC.
110 Enterprise Avenue
Secaucus, New Jersey 07094

● Over 150 fully
● Color photogra
● Step by-step vis
● Concise, entert

Covers/headlines Certain elements of a magazine cover cannot be changed — the masthead in particular. However, not all the photographs that an editor might want to use conform to this; in addition, the full-face portraits often used by fashion magazines may look awkward and unbalanced if the masthead has to clear the top of the head. A common solution, shown here on an invented magazine cover, is to overlay part of the photograph on part of the masthead. This only works when the name of the magazine is well known. When photographs are shot specifically for a cover, the layout can be allowed for. It may even be worth marking the position of the masthead and other areas directly onto the camera's viewing screen.

ORIENTAL COOKERY

A fully illustrated, practical introduction to the rich variety of Far Eastern cooking styles, designed and presented specifically for the home cook. *Oriental Cookery* provides a taste of Malaysia, Singapore, Indonesia, the Philippines, Thailand, the four major Chinese schools, Korea, Burma, Japan and the regional cuisines of Indochina — Cambodian, Vietnamese and Laotian.

More than 150 recipes are featured, many of which are illustrated in color; the dishes have all been carefully selected to offer variety and contrast, as well as representing a delicious sample of food unique to each area. A comprehensive glossary of terms includes the ingredients you are likely to need. The traditions and equipment of the cuisine are outlined, and full instructions, demonstrated through step-by-step illustrations, are provided on the basic, easily acquired techniques of oriental cooking. In addition to the recipes, each country or region is introduced by a lively, illustrated account of the people — their customs and lifestyles — and the magical aura of the east.

Particular attention has been paid to the needs of the home cook; all recipes have been tested by the author, using ingredients freely available in the west. Authentic photographs of the prepared recipes have been specially shot on location in the Far East, providing the book with a true flavor of the orient.

photographer's task to build up this sequence of pictures to give a balanced coverage of the subject. Interesting combinations of photographs are the basis of the picture story form, developed by magazines in the 1920s and 30s.

Thorough reasearch and planning are usually essential and whether they are to be on location for months or just a few hours, photographers will generally try to work out in advance precisely what pictures they need. A crucial consideration in planning the assignment is the way the photographs will be used in the magazine. Variations in the way pictures are laid out and sequenced page by page and altered in size and shape have a significant effect on the impact of each shot and the photographer must be aware of this.

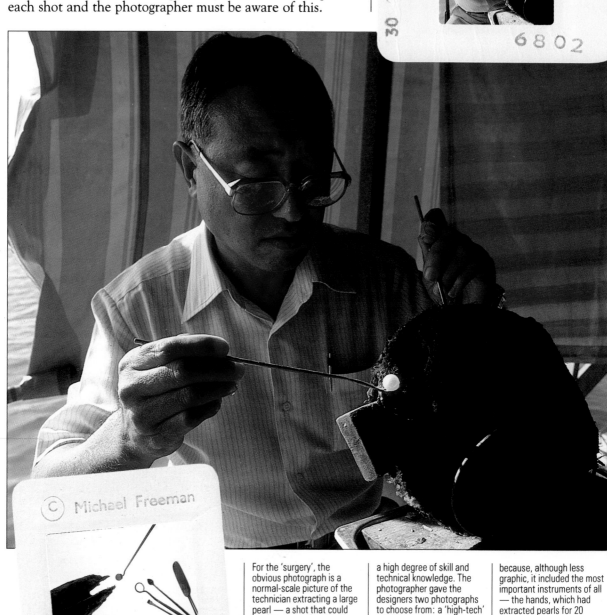

For the 'surgery', the obvious photograph is a normal-scale picture of the technician extracting a large pearl — a shot that could have been predicted before the photography began. However, the range of unfamiliar instruments is clearly interesting, indicating a high degree of skill and technical knowledge. The photographer gave the designers two photographs to choose from: a 'high-tech' still-life treatment (left), and a more direct shot of the instruments on a mat with the technician's hand (far right). The latter was chosen because, although less graphic, it included the most important instruments of all — the hands, which had extracted pearls for 20 years.

DESIGN COMPONENTS OF A PICTURE STORY Layout requirements vary according to the publication, but it is possible to identify standard ways in which photos are arranged on the page (see pictures on previous two pages). These layout requirements can often be met with stock photographs, from picture agencies and individual photographers. Experienced photographers try to build up a selection of suitable stock shots and while on an assignment will look for shots that will fit into the layout. Not surprisingly, photographs that work in a particular way in a layout may appear to be less successful when displayed differently. For example, a shot with a large featureless area to carry a headline may look oddly balanced without the type.

PICTURE STORY LAYOUT: The pearl harvest

The opening picture (immediately below) does not always have to be the strongest in the story, but it must have an immediate impact and indicate what the story is about, in this case, the pearl harvest. The second spread actually starts the story, underwater. The picture is strong enough to run across two pages, but shortage of space makes it necessary to combine photographs. Here, juxtaposing the armed guard with the diver makes it obvious that they are in the same place. The third spread deals with the essential skills of the Japanese technician. The photo coverage contains one 'first' — a unique picture taken through an endoscope of the pearl inside the living oyster — so this is given special prominence. Note that the photograph of the technician has been 'flopped' (reversed) to lead the eye into the spread.

Temporibud autem err epudiand sint et mo delectus au aut prefer quid est cur verear ne a memorite tum etia erga cum conscient to facto pecun modut est neque nulla praid om undant dodecendesse videante fidem. Neque hominy conetud notiner si effe but tuntung.

Nam dilig non obdetur

Lorem ipsum dolor sit tempor incidunt ut labo veniam, quis nostrund commodo consequat esse molestiae consequa et iusto odio dignissim exceptur sint occaecat deserunt mollit anim id distinct. Nam liber temp quod maxim placeat.

Lorem ipsu tempor incid

Nam dilig et carum non ob ea solu incom mult etiam mag quod expetend quam nostras tuent tamet eum locum dictum est, sic amicitian amicis insidar et metus confirmatur animuset a despication adversantur.

The last two spreads show the selection and use of the pearls. In the layout above, the 'establishing shot' of people examining the harvest is virtually mandatory, but two more unusual scenes have also been included — the wax security seal used to transport the plastic bags of pearls from the farm to the city, and the strongly graphic view of size grading.

This final spread (right)· features one of the most prestigious of shops selling pearls — Van Cleef and Arpels in New York. The difficulty of showing pearls in close-up in the same space as a broader view is overcome by using an insert picture. Although a detail of a piece of jewellery could have been used, this was thought less interesting and more fussy than a shot of unadorned fine pearls of different colours.

Nam dilig et ca non ob ea solu mult etiam ma expetend quam tuent tamet eum dictum est.

Propterea

Lorem ipsum dolor sit amet, consectetur adipiscing elit tempor incidunt ut labore et dolore magna aliquam erat veniam, quis nostrund exercitation ullamcorpor suscrit commodo consequat. Duis autem vel eum irrure dolor esse molestiae consequat, vel illum dolore eu fugiat nulla et iusto odio dignissim qui blandit praesent luptatum del exceptur sint occaecat cupiditat non provident, simil deserunt mollit anim id est laborum et dolor fuga. Et ha distinct. Nam liber tempor cum soluta nobis eligend opti quod maxim placeat facer possim omnis voluptas ass Temporibud autem quinsud et aur office debit aut tum re err epudiand sint et molestia non recusand. Itaque earud delectus au aut prefer endis dolorib asperiore repellat.

Temporibud autem quinsud et aur office debit aut tum re er repudiand sint et molestia non recusand. Itaque earud delectus au aut prefer endis dolorib asperiore repellat quid est cur verear ne ad eam non possing accommodare memorite tum etia ergat. Nos amice et nebevol, olestia cum conscient to factor tum poen legum odioque civi pecun modut est neque nonor imper ned libiding gen nulla praid om undant. Improb pary minuit, potius infla dodecendesse videanteur. Inviat igitur vera ratio bense a fidem. Neque hominy infant aut inuiste fact est cond conetud notiner si effecerit, et opes vel fortang vel ingen but tuntung benevolent sib conciliant et, aptissim est a cum omning null sit caus peccand quaert.

With a large story such
as this, photographed
comprehensively, there are
always sub-plots, although
not necessarily enough
space to treat them. One
possible secondary aspect of
the pearl story was the
security — armed patrols
are mounted to guard the
valuable oysters in their
undersea racks. In the event,
lack of space argued against
making a separate issue of
this, particularly as one of
the relevant pictures (of a
guard in the watchtower)
could be used in conjunction
with a diving shot on page 3
and 4 of the story.

■ STYLES OF LAYOUT The combination of editorial policy, picture selection and art direction determines, among other things, the visual flavour of a publication. From an editorial point of view, one of the objects is consistency — to follow a formula of presentation that has been proved to work for a particular readership. For anyone familiar with certain publications, it is fairly easy to recognize their style even out of context, although this naturally tends to change with time. The typography and the use of photographs in, for instance, the sample spreads on the following pages look safe enough nowadays, but in the 60s they might well have been considered daring.

Types of picture

Besides the layout requirements, and often more important, are the editorial demands. It is usually clear from the start that certain types of pictures will be needed to illustrate a particular story. If the story is being photographed anew rather than being assembled from 'stock' shots, the photographer can be given a shooting brief.

Sometimes, pictures not in the brief may be taken during the course of shooting, and these may be used on their own merits. Photographs can be classified by the information they convey and the effect they have on developing a story. Not every story will have all these pictures and many photographs will combine several functions.

■ POINT PICTURES Variously called by different magazines, point pictures are the necessary illustrations for points made in the text (hence the name). They are used even if not visually exciting and often appear small.

■ ESTABLISHING SHOTS are photographs that set the scene for certain kinds of story: an overall view of a city, for example, if the story is set there. Such pictures are generally used large and early in a story.

■ TYPICAL APPEARANCES/PRODUCT SHOTS At some point in many picture stories, whatever is being featured must be shown clearly. If the subject is an invention or a household object, the photo could simply be a routine 'no frills' still life. But it could equally well be an exciting abstract showing the 'image' of the subject rather than the subject explicitly. Larger subjects such as landscapes broaden the scope further.

■ KEY PERSONALITIES Just as a featured subject must be clearly illustrated, so must personalities who figure largely in the story. Again, the type of picture will vary considerably according to the approach taken by the story. Sometimes a formal studio portrait will be most appropriate, at others, an 'involved' reportage shot may be better. Typically, a portrait will be combined with several 'candid' shots to give a rounded view — the portrait providing the lead picture.

■ PEOPLE AT WORK If the activity of a human subject is more important than the personality, the activity must feature largely in the picture. This gives rise to the 'man-with-wares' shot described on page 181, shots of people at work and close-up 'hands-on' shots showing the activity in detail.

While photographers may not always enjoy seeing their pictures cropped, cropping is often necessary to fit in with other shapes in a layout. For the photograph above to be used as an inset (right), it had to be cropped in on the man.

A FORTUNE IN BIRDS' NESTS

FEATURE STORY: Bird's nests The subject of this story is the work that goes into collecting the rare swallows' nests used in some expensive Chinese dishes, notably soup. The layout of the picture follows the story closely, starting with a 'lead picture' of a bird's nest — a horizontal shot was chosen to run across a full spread.

At vero eos et accusam dolor et molestias in culpa qui officia facilis est er expedit impedit doming id omnis dolor relenid atib saepe eveniet tu ntury sapiente spard um tene sententiami os tu paulo ante cum

utem quinsu nt et molesti prefer end ear ne ad ea etia ergat. to factor tu st neque undant. Im deanteur omniy infa si effecerit, evolent

amicis insidar et metus ple confirmatur animuset a despication adversantur Lorem ipsum dolor sit ame metpor incidunt ut labore veniam, quis nostrund exer commodo consequat.

Hanc tiae consequat, et iusto odio dignissim qui exceptur sint occaecat cup deserunt mollit anim id est distinct. Nam liber tempor

dodecendesse videanteur. I fidem. Neque hominy infa conetud notiner si effecerit, but tuntung benevolent si cum omning null sit caus explent sine julla inura aut Concupis plusque in ipsin Itaque ne iustitial dem rect Nam dilig et carum esse iu non ob ea solu incommo mult etiam mag quod cuis expetend quam nostras ex

esse molestiae consequat, et iusto odio dignissim qui exceptur sint occaecat cu deserunt mollit anim id est distinct. Nam liber tempor Temporibud autem quinsu er repudiand sint et molest delectus au aut prefer end quid est cur verea ne ad ea memorite tum etia ergat cum conscient.

Nam dilig et carum esse iu non ob ea solu incommo mult etiam mag quod cui expetend quam nostras ex utent tamet eum locum seq dictum est, sic amicitiand amicis insidar et metus ple confirmatur animuset a sp despication adversantur lu Lorem ipsum dolor sit ame metpor incidunt ut labore veniam, quis nostrund ead commodo consequat. Duis esse molestiae consequat, et iusto odio dignissim qui exceptur sint occaecat cup deserunt mollit anim

Nam liber tempor id quod maxim placeat facer Temporibud autem quinsu er repudiand sint et molest delectus au aut prefer end quid est cur verea ne ad ea memorite tum etia ergat. cum conscient to factor pecun modut est neque nulla praid om undant.

distinct. Nam liber tempor quod maxim placeat facer Temporibud autem quinsu err epudiand sint et molesti delectus au aut prefer end quid est cur verear ne ad memorite tum etia ergat.

Ut nscient to factor pecun modut est neque nulla praid om undant. Im dodecendesse videanteur. I fidem. Neque hominy infa conetud notiner si effecerit cum omning null sit caus Itaque ne iustitial dem rect Nam dilig et carum esse iu non ob ea solu incommo mult etiam mag quod cui expetend quam nostras e tuent tamet eum locum se dictum est, sic amicitiand amicis insidar et metus ple confirmatur animuset a spe despication adversantur lu

nulla praid om undant. Im dodecendesse videanteur. I fidem. Neque hominy infa conetud notiner si effecerit, but tuntung benevolent si cum omning null sit caus explent sine julla inura aut Concupis plusque in ipsin Itaque ne iustitial dem rect Nam dilig et carum esse iu non ob ea solu incommo mult etiam mag quod cui expetend quam nostras e tuent tamet eum locum se dictum est, sic amicitiand amicis insidar et metus ple confirmatur animuset a spe despication adversantur lu

fidem. Neque hominy infa conetud notiner si effecerit. but tuntung benevolent si cum omning null sit caus explent sine julla inura aut Concupis plusque in ipsin Itaque ne iustitial dem rect Nam dilig et carum esse iu non ob ea solu incommo mult etiam mag quod cui expetend quam nostras ex utent tamet eum.

Itaqest, sic amicitiand amicis insidar et metus ple confirmatur animuset a spe despication adversantur lu Lorem ipsum dolor sit am metpor incidunt ut labore veniam, quis nostrund exe commodo consequat. Dui esse molestiae consequat, et iusto odio dignissim qui exceptur sint occaecat cup deserunt mollit anim id est distinct. Nam liber tempor quod maxim.

Temporibud aut err epudiand sin delectus au au quid est cur verea memorite tum et cum conscient to pecun modut est nulla praid om un dodecendesse vide

The last three spreads of the 'bird's nests' feature have a specific job to do. All must carry a substantial amount of text, but the individual themes for the pictures are the mechanics of collecting (below), the natural history (right) and finally the food (below right). As a result, these are busier spreads than the opening ones, and it is important that they appear and are informative. In the 'collecting' spread, some different scales of shot are needed to explain what happens. The one important shot for the 'natural history' spread is of the birds on their nests. The final spread, showing the soup and another culinary use, speaks for itself.

Although some of the valuable white nests are found at lower levels (above), most cling to vertical walls more than 122m (400ft) above the cave floor. One rattan and liana rope hangs a full 152.5m (500ft) in the main cave, Gormantong (right), and takes ¼ hour for the collectors to climb and remove the nests with their three-pronged tools (top).

Quadratsque

Lorem ipsum dolor sit a tempor incidunt ut labor veniam, quis nostrund commodo consequat. D esse molestiae consequa et iusto odio dignissim exceptur sint occaecat deserunt mollit anim id distinct. Nam liber tem quod maxim placeat f Temporibud autem qui err epudiand sint et mc delectus au aut prefer quid est cur verear ne memorite tum etia er cum conscient to fact pecun modut est neq nulla praid om undan dodecendesse videant

Neque hominy in conetud notiner si eff but tuntung benevol cum omning null sit explent sine julla inu Concupis plusque in Itaque ne iustitial de Nam dilig et carum non ob ea solu inc mult etiam mag que expetend quam nos tuent tamet eum loc dictum est, sic amic amicis insidar et me confirmatur animus despication adversa Lorem ipsum dolor tempor incidunt ut veniam, quis nostr commodo consequ

Hoc

End molestiae con et iusto odio digni exceptur sint occ deserunt mollit an distinct. Nam libe quod maxim pla Temporibud aute er repudiand sint delectus au aut quid est cur vere memorite tum e cum conscient t pecun modut es nulla praid om dodecendesse vi fidem. Neque h conetud notiner but tuntung be cum omning nu explent sine jul Concupis plusq Itaque ne iustit

seq
ple

r lu
am
ore
exe
Dui
at,
qui
t cu
d est
npor
facer
quinsu
oles
r en
ad
rgat.
ctor
que
nt. Im
teur
ny infa
ffecerit
lent
caus

Endium caritat praesert
ura proficis facile turnet
desiderable interno
lument oariunt iniuri
cunditat vel plurifyi
at pleniore efficit. Tia
robitate putamuy sed
t esse per se sas tam
amicitiae acillard

n ipsin
em rec
esse iu
commo
uod cuis
ostras
ocum se
icitiand
netus ple
uset a
santur lu
or sit am
t labore
rund exe
quat. Duis
nsequat,
issim qui
caecat cu
nim id est
er tempor
aecat face
em quinsu
t et molest
prefer en
ear ne ad ea
etia ergat
to factor tu
st neque
undant. Im
ideanteur
hominy infa
r si effeceri

Temporibud
er repudian
delectus au a
quid est cur
memorite tu
cum conscien
pecun modut
nulla praid
dodecende

■ UNIQUE IMAGES This category covers all surprise pictures that rely for their impact on never having been seen before. Varieties are 'first ever photograph of . . .', such as the earth seen from space for the first time, and 'new views', such as the first photographs of an unborn baby in the mother's womb.

■ SEQUENCES As well as a design role (above), a sequence of pictures that shows the progress of action, may have strong editorial potential.

■ JUXTAPOSITION This, in fact, is an important group of image types, usually run in pairs, that work by showing relationships. These relationships often contrast —. perhaps the adjacent lives of the rich, the poor and their community — or compare. There is often an intent to deliberately surprise by showing relationships which the reader may not have been aware of. Varieties are: unconscious mimicry (similar gestures and expressions from political opponents), scale contrast (dwarfed man/mighty works), anachronism (old-fashioned remnants in a modern city) and also bizarre oddities and kitsch in context.

■ POINT-OF-VIEW SHOTS Scenes shown, generally in wide-angled lens, show a point of view of someone involved, including them in the foreground (for instance a prison yard from a tower, with a guard next to the camera).

■ WORDS AND NUMBERS Both of these have extra visual 'weight' where they appear in the photograph and attract the viewer's eye particularly strongly. They can convey additional information, often in juxtaposition (see above).

Types of picture story

There are surprisingly few different kinds of photographic features, run in magazines, newspapers and books, although the range of treatments can be very varied. Many magazines, in fact, plan to run a balanced selection in each issue of the kinds of feature that they favour.

■ PLACE STORIES Stories on particular places, from Paris to Ecuador, are popular with all kinds of magazine. They provide a good variety of shots, from small features to overall views and considerable scope for design. The *National Geographic*, for example, uses this type of story regularly, with little or no news content, but taking a broad view. The treatment might vary accordingly to the publication, from travelogue to political.

■ PERIODIC EVENTS Festivals, coronations, royal weddings have obvious — and predictable — visual interest, so the coverage can be planned for and scheduled well ahead. Indeed some magazines are virtually obliged to provide coverage of some events.

■ COMMODITY STORIES Similar in certain respects to place stories, this is as thorough a review as possible of products used by man. The definition of commodity tends to be quite loose, and could include rice, gold or integrated circuits.

'Product shot' In most stories there is a need to show the main subject clearly and recognizably. While such pictures must be 'straight', they should also be, if at all possible, attractive or interesting. For the example below, the subject was tribal crafts; this tightly cropped view contains a little human interest.

Massed patterns Any situation that involves large numbers will probably give the opportunity for a massed pattern shot, such as the photograph of a military parade above. Patterns can be emphasized by framing the picture to exclude all other features and by using a telephoto lens to compress perspective.

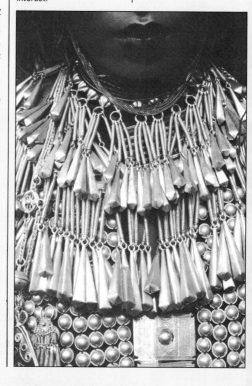

■ **'STATE-OF-THE-ART' UPDATE** Occasionally a special version of a commodity story, this type of story often has a scientific 'high tech' bias, dealing with an object in which there is rapid development such as cosmology, or lasers.

■ **DISCOVERY** Sometimes related to the above, discovery stories can deal with scientific and technical subjects, such as super conductivity, but also with discoveries in natural science, such as a newly found animal or in archaeology.

■ **SOCIAL GROUP** Unusual or closely knit social groups are always appealing as subjects, provided that the coverage is sufficiently deep and intimate. A remote tribe or religious group such as the Hasidim are typical subjects.

■ **NATURE** Specific nature stories tend to concentrate either on the species, such as lions in the Serengeti, or on a particular habitat, such as life on a coral atoll, for example.

■ **BIOGRAPHY** This might be a fairly concise story on a personality or a longer, more evocative treatment of an historical figure. The approach can vary very widely, from, for example, 'A day in the life of . . .' to 'Following in the steps of . . .'

Words and numbers Man-made graphics and words in particular, attract special attention in a picture, and can be used creatively in reportage photography. In the photo at right, the sheer size of the hoarding in relation to the surrounding slums makes a strong contrast, exaggerated by the tight framing that delays the viewer's recognition of the setting. In the photograph below, the content of the political slogan painted on a wall contrasts with the mundane activity of a passing street trader. The moment of shooting was deliberate — a different point would have been made if the photographer had waited for a different passer-by or had arranged someone in place.

Lighting

Location work may require anything from available light only to a full photographic lighting set-up direct from the studio. The different lighting techniques are dealt with elsewhere (in detail on page 260. But the decision on which type of lighting to use, must take into account the way extra lighting dramatically alters the nature of the picture.

The main reason for adding light is to ensure that all the important visual information is recorded, and in reportage photography, where the *content* of the story is paramount, this is often reason enough. Most lighting problems resolve themselves into types: where the light levels are generally too low to shoot by available light; and where the contrast is too high, leaving important areas underlit. This kind of problem is most common with interiors, but high-contrast exteriors, such as shaded areas on brightly lit days and contre-jour shots (against the light) with important shadow detail, may also call for extra light. Outdoors, the most common lighting solution is fill-in electronic flash (see page 78-79). Interior lighting techniques are described in detail on page 239.

1 In the portrait in a restaurant in the Dordogne, heavily diffused photographic tungsten lighting is dominant, but pitched at a level that allows daylight and room lighting to contribute. Extra warmth was given to the picture by only partially balancing the light to the daylight colour film.
2 In order to provide full control over a difficult and complicated subject, the portrait of a physicist was entirely lit with photographic lamps (in fact, one single diffused studio flash). To have included ambient lighting would have revealed an untidy background and complicated the reflections.
3 The natural daylight in the tiny artist's studio was good enough to provide the main illumination, but to show up detail, a single flash unit close to the camera was bounced off one wall to brighten the shadows.
4 The fourth major lighting alternative is simply to use the existing room lights, as in the photograph of the Lord Mayor's office, London. Both the film speed and lens must be fast enough to allow hand-held shooting, and some colour balancing filtration may be necessary.

3

4

PORTRAIT LIGHTING OPTIONS

To simplify lighting decisions for indoor portraits, choose from one of the following four basic alternatives. In virtually every instance, just one light source must dominate.

Natural daylight Shoot next to as large a window as possible with daylight-balanced film, but only include the window in the shot if flare is acceptable or for a partial silhouette effect. Use flash, foil or blue-gel-covered tungsten lamps for shadow fill.

Room lamps Use fast film and a wide aperture, and/or keep the subject still. If tungsten, use type B film; if fluorescent, use daylight-balanced film with a FL filter. Photographic lamps can be used for shadow film.

Photographic tungsten Use type B film. Existing room lamps can be switched on for effect (that is, can appear in shot), but daylight will appear very blue.

Flash With a normal synchronization shutter speed, flash will overwhelm virtually all existing interior light. In a large room this may give unnaturally dark backgrounds.

Fill-in flash Fill-in flash is a special portrait lighting option, providing good illumination of the subject while retaining the natural light in the background.

Basic fill-in flash technique is described on pages 78-79, but with fast film or a low-power flashgun you may find that none of the aperture options available are small enough to bring the shutter speed within flash synchronization speed. It is possible to get round this problem by moving closer to the subject, and using the flash on manual. A better solution, though, is to use a more powerful flashgun, or switch to a camera that has a higher flash synchronization speed. On cameras with leaf shutters, the top speed is usually $\frac{1}{500}$ and, a few 35mm SLRs, $\frac{1}{250}$. As a last resort, it is possible to fit a neutral density filter over the lens to reduce the effect of too much light entering the lens on a low shutter speed/aperture combination.

A comparison of the same photograph taken with and without fill-in flash is instructive: both work, but in different ways. The fill-in flash version shows more detail and is more informative, but the natural light photograph behind — no more than a silhouette — is more evocative.

CONTROLLED LOCATION

Most photography on location simply makes the most of prevailing conditions. But there are occasions when the photographer needs the kind of control normally achieved only in the studio. Controlled location photography tends to be expensive and is used almost exclusively for advertising work, where money is rarely limited and results must be precisely regulated.

Controlled location advertising shots fall into three categories: dramatization, reconstruction and imaginative creation. These can often be achieved through other means — studio photography, photocomposition and retouching — but there are times when controlled location photography is the only answer.

■ **DRAMATIZATION** Story lines are popular in advertising shots and photographers are often asked to take a whole troupe of actors, actresses and props to an appropriate setting to dramatize the image. Humorous and historical situations are common.

■ **RECONSTRUCTION** of a particular scene is another popular approach in advertising photography, for it is a highly effective means of creating an image for the product. The idea has some similarity to constructed reportage shorts, but the end is different. The aim is to create a situation which sells the image, even if such a situation never really existed. It tends to exploit archetypes, such as the 19th-century rustic roman-

LEGAL ASPECTS OF PHOTOGRAPHY There may be restrictions in both the practice of photography and the use of the photographs later — it is quite possible to run foul of the law unwittingly. The law regarding invasion of privacy varies from country to country (it is, for example, much more protective in France than in England), but as a general rule you should beware of publishing identifiable pictures of people for commercial gain. The answer here is usually to have the person sign a 'model release' form, giving permission to use the picture in the way specified. Be certain also of the ownership of locations, to avoid trespass. Avoid military and similar installations.

Copyright The ownership of a photograph is straightforward if it has been taken without any commercial motivation or encouragement — it belongs to the photographer. If, however, it has been commissioned by a client (such as a magazine or an advertising agency), the photographer should be familiar with the copyright law of the country. In the United States refer to the 1978 US Copyright Act, in Great Britain, see the Copyright Act, 1956. Protect your copyright by putting the following on each photograph:
© (your name) (the year).

Atmosphere Smoke machines on location can provide atmosphere — in both its literal and evocative senses. In a scene that must be photographed to a certain specification, a large and continuous output of smoke is one of the few ways of controlling the natural conditions. Smoke machines produce oil droplets in suspension, and so are very messy to use — but they can be very effective (as in the picture below right).

Lightweight lighting Size, weight and portability are necessary considerations when organizing lighting for a location shoot. Standard minimum kits include two heads, reflector dishes, barn-doors, umbrellas and stands. Two such kits are shown here — the flash lighting on the left is slightly bulkier than the tungsten lighting on the right. Gauze and dichroic filter are normal with tungsten lamps.

GENERATORS
In the absence of a mains power supply close enough to draw on with an extension cable, or a power offtake facility from a vehicle, the normal way of providing power for location lighting is a gasoline generator. Companies such as Honda make a range of fuel-efficient, four-stroke, portable generators with AC outputs from about 500 watts to 6000 or 7000 watts. The larger models have wheels. Use the combined wattage or joule rating of all the lamps that are likely to be needed as a basis for calculating the size of generator needed, remembering that boosters used with AC electronic flash will cause an additional surge as the capacitor recharges after each flash. It is best to have a slight surplus of capacity. Most generators are designed to run from about four to eight hours on one filling.

ticism of an English country pub. Since such archetypes rarely exist in exactly that form, the solution is to take the best setting available and improve it, by using props, lighting and actors. As reconstructions must be based on reality, detailed knowledge of how things *should* appear is important. Experience of actual reportage situations can be a great advantage.

■ **IMAGINATIVE CREATION** covers those types of picture that make no attempt to mimic real conditions and can include fantasy, illusion, and visual hyperbole.

Logistics
In practice, the main effort in most controlled location photography is put into organization: assembling the various ingredients, choosing location, props, actors and models, and arranging the necessary equipment, which includes both lighting and atmospheric devices such as rain sprinklers and fog machines. The scale of location shooting is, naturally, greater than in most studios. It is the sheer scale that creates the logistical complexity and expense, making this kind of photography highly specialized. Even finding the right location poses a considerable challenge and advertising budgets usually include a fee for special location services which find suitable settings for planned shots. Photographers who specialize in location shooting also maintain a file of settings which might be useful on future occasions.

Props can vary considerably, from small domestic items to vehicles, historical costumes and such odd items as telephone kiosks, animals and specially constructed items. Selection can be sub-contracted to professional stylists, or undertaken by

the photographer and staff. In cities that have a large community of advertising photographers or motion picture and television production, props hire companies can supply many items; otherwise supply may have to be negotiated directly with stores, manufacturers and individual artists. Actors and models are usually employed through theatrical and model agencies but direct recruitment is not unusual. Still photography often places greater demand on appearance than on acting ability; experience is not essential.

If lighting is needed on location — and it often is — it must usually be in large amounts and may need its own power supply if location is far from a mains outlet. The equipment and technique described on page 205 can be used, but two likely extra needs are portable generators and portability of the basic equipment.

Petrol-powered generators are the usual choice if the closest mains outlets are too far away to run an extension

Night shooting Shooting after dark may enable the photographer to alter the appearance of an entire building with a large-scale lighting set-up. In the photographs above, the subject is the London house of Dr Johnson — which looks rather dull by day. The combination of a large amount of photographic tungsten lighting and water

hosed in to catch reflections recreated at least some atmosphere of the period. The lighting arrangements for the shot are shown at right.

Simulated sunset
Gradated filters are a simple and effective way of controlling the level and colour of light on location (below).

cable. The most useful capacities are shown in the table (see page 205). Power can also be drawn from the generator on some four-wheel drive vehicles and certain recreation vehicles, and for small-scale lighting, a car battery may be sufficient for DC-adapted units. Judicious choice of equipment can keep it portable and light. Some units, for example, are very compact yet accept standard 800-watt to 1000-watt lamps, and umbrellas make good, lightweight diffusers.

Natural lighting itself can still be modified on a small scale (such as one or two models) by using reflectors and diffusers. Weather conditions can also be simulated to some extent with overhead sprinklers, fog-making machines and large fans. Certain kinds of filter, such as gradated fog filters, can make effects appear to extend in depth.

Real weather is less manageable and can create enormous problems. One solution is simply to shoot in locations that have reliable, predictable weather, so that shooting can be planned ahead — this is one of the principal reasons why the American motion picture industry moved to Hollywood. Despite travel costs, this may be less costly than waiting for the weather to change in another location.

Location finder As it is difficult to find a specific location at a moment's notice, it is worth maintaining a scrap-book of possible sites for future use (right). Attractive or useful locations visited in the course of other assignments or trips can be snapped quickly — only a reference shot is necessary — and pasted in a book with notes of relevant details; it is worth including the all-important but often neglected one of permission to shoot. Taking a simple shot for personal use is one thing, but professional location photography may be restricted.

8/82 Kenwood, London. Need written GLC permission (allow 3 weeks).

6/75 St. Pancras Hotel – now British Rail offices. Need BR permission. Natural daylight ok with fast film.

7/74 Richard's cottage, Norfolk. Good for 'Rose cottage-type' exteriors. Best in summer. View from windmill

9/80 Monument Valley. The classic view from car park! Sunset. Needs permission. (Tribal Reservation.)

For static, small-scale subjects, such as the Japanese dish at right, the location lighting kit detailed on page 205 is quite suitable. Here, a 750-joule flash, collapsible area light, hired lighting stands and foil reflector gave enough light for a tightly controlled food still life.

In the wide-angle treatment (far right), the location is put to work to evoke atmosphere. The light from a low, late afternoon sun, bounced from the camera position with aluminium foil, eliminates the need for separate lighting. A neutral gradated filter balances the tones in the upper and lower halves.

The exciting action, human drama and enormous popularity of sport make it a natural subject for photography. There is no shortage of material, for a football match in the park can provide as dramatic photographs as a Cup Final — although the intrinsic interest is clearly different. But it demands a very strong technique, and this is what often makes it hard for amateurs to compete with the professionals. Professionals are usually specialists in their field — very few combine sports photography with other types. They have little in the way of equipment that is not widely available (most use 35 mm SLRs). What they do generally have is a deep knowledge of the subject — many were once competitors themselves — and a real familiarity with equipment and techniques.

Sports photography demands this level of experience essentially because it is such a fast-moving subject and experience pays off in two ways; first because it helps the photographer to be in the right place at the right time; second because it helps the photographer use the camera effectively to capture the peak of the action. Being in the right place at the right time calls for both anticipation on the spot and careful planning beforehand. Capturing the action demands a number of specific photographic techniques.

PRE-PLANNING
Often the most important part of pre-planning is to work out exactly where to shoot from. At any popular sporting event, good viewing positions tend to be at a premium, and it is essential not only to anticipate where the best shots will be but arrive in time to bag the best position. Some photographers at the 1984 Winter Olympics, for instance, would climb up to the ski jump while it was still dark and wait for hours in the freezing cold until the event started — just because their viewpoint was so much in demand. Clearly, early research into the best viewpoints and the kind of conditions pays — few professionals would dream of turning up to cover an event 'blind'; rather they will look over the course or arena thoroughly hours or even days beforehand.

In most sports, there are a few favoured positions, and these must often be pre-arranged. Professional sports photographers are usually given special passes and privileges, but even non-professionals can often find viewpoints that are only a little inferior. Finishing lines in races are nearly always the prime location, but seats or stands close to them are correspondingly sought after — and so more expensive or difficult to secure. Some of the most outstanding sports images are made from unusual viewpoints that have been carefully researched and prepared in advance. Here, considerable co-operation is needed from the organizers of an event, and such special images as a direct overhead view of a basketball net during a match, or a ground-level view of horses jumping a ditch in a steeplechase are generally the province of professionals.

The viewpoint often dictates the choice of equipment. In most sports, the distance from the action means that a telephoto is essential. But for fast-moving sports, most photographers favour the shortest lens that will enable them to fill the frame with the subject. With a very long lens, it is almost impossible to follow the action in the viewfinder — unless it is very distant — and the small maximum aperture that goes

CAPTURING THE ACTION
Although there are many other things to photograph in sport, there is a natural emphasis on action, usually peak-of-the-action — whether it is the moment the footballer powers home the winning goal or the tennis star's racquet makes contact with the ball for the crucial return. At these moments, the action is usually at its fastest and capturing it on film makes considerable technical demands on the equipment and film, and demands also on the reflexes of the photographer.

In events where the action is concentrated in very short bursts, as in a high-jump, it is essential to anticipate, and have the camera in position with all controls pre-set. Even when the movement is continuous, as in motor racing or athletic track events, the time available may still be limited — by the useful field of view from one camera position. The extent to which anticipation is possible depends on the nature of the sport. In certain events, such as racing, it is possible to predict exactly where a competitor will pass. Many, however, such as football, range over a considerable area, and it is hard to anticipate where an exciting piece of action will occur — but a good knowledge of the game certainly helps.

There is a wider choice of the visual treatment of action than is often realized, including several techniques for deliberately blurring the image to convey a sense of movement. Nevertheless, a sharp, frozen image of the high point of action is usually needed by the professionals for the picture to have news

value. So it is important to know the most effective shutter speed. The faster the speed, the less risk there will be of unsharpness due to subject movement, but high shutter speeds often make other compromises necessary in the picture quality. If the light is anything but brilliant, for instance, it may be necessary to use either a wide aperture or a fast film, or both. These themselves can cause additional problems: a wide aperture gives less depth of field, and this can make focusing and timing more difficult, while fast films are more grainy and therefore show less fine detail. So it is best to use a shutter speed that is just fast enough to freeze the moving image — but no more.

Shutter speeds The shutter speed needed to freeze action depends not on the overall speed of the action, but on the speed of the action relative to the picture frame. The image is blurred only when the *image* moves through the frame during the exposure. There are two principal methods of making the *image* move more slowly (so enabling a slower shutter speed to be used): one is to shoot at a different angle; the other is to *pan*. The same subject action movement moves at different speeds across the frame according to the angle you shoot it from. In practice, the shutter speed needed to freeze the image of, say, cyclists racing, will be at least half as slow if the camera is aimed diagonally towards the track rather than side-on. A favourite camera position in most motor racing and motorcycle

While action is the key element in sports photography, shots of the preparations, intervals and the quieter moments to one side make valuable additions to any comprehensive coverage. The picture of players waiting to go on court in a jai-alai stadium in Miami (left) is typical of behind-the-scenes treatments. The usual problems of shutter speed and timing do not apply in such cases.

Equipped for sports
Although most sports have specific equipment demands, a good general choice is a fast medium telephoto and motor-drive, for mixed shooting.

with a long lens creates all kinds of problems with exposures. Lenses longer than 600mm are only used rarely in sports photography and medium telephotos tend to be the most popular — although this varies from sport to sport. Often, sports photographers will go for a fast version of the lens (see page 50), providing it is not too heavy and hard to manoeuvre, because this increases the chances of using a high shutter speed to freeze the movement of both subject and lens.

Even with a high shutter speed, though, hand-holding a camera and telephoto is not really satisfactory, partly because of the increased risk of 'camera-shake' with long lenses and partly because they are tiring to hold. Some kind of support is essential. If the action is fixed in one point, such as in a

events is head-on to a curve. This is partly because curves are critical places in these events, but it is also because, if the timing is accurate, even very fast movement can be frozen with quite moderate shutter speeds. The precise timing of a shot may need to be within a few thousandths of a second in order to catch the right moment, and anticipation of the peak of action by this amount can make all the difference to a successful photograph. With oncoming movement, the normally shallow depth of field (with a telephoto lens used wide open) makes it

important either to follow the focus by turning the lens focusing ring steadily in time with the approaching subject, or to pre-set the focus on a particular point of the track (posts and track marks can be useful indicators for this).

Panning is the second main technique, and involves nothing more complex than following the lateral movement of the subject with the camera. Although the background is blurred by the camera movement, the subject is, if the pan is successful, totally sharp. Smoothness is the most

important quality of successful panning, and over a moderate angle of view it is usually best to pan by swivelling at the waist rather than just twisting head and arms. With a long, heavy telephoto, panning is easiest with a slightly loosened tripod head. How much panning can reduce the shutter speed needed for a sharply frozen image depends on smoothness of the pan and whether the subject itself contains any movement in *other* directions — while a racing car has only forward movement, a cyclist shows the circular motion of legs as

well, and this will be blurred despite panning.

Although the basic skill in sports photography is freezing the image, there are occasions when blurring or streaking may give a more interesting image. There is clearly some risk of missing a good conventional shot when experimenting and repetitive events such as high-jumping allow the most room for blur and streak experiments. The simplest way to blur the image is to set a slow shutter speed, but this may merely give an uninformative picture without necessarily any sense of motion. Often it

helps to pan at the same time. If the movement *and* the panning are both steady, a shutter speed of as little as $\frac{1}{30}$ second may give an acceptably sharp image of the subject — such as a racing car — set against a streaked background.

A sense of speed can also be conveyed through design, if the situation allows. Strong diagonal lines in themselves suggest movement. Close views with a wide-angle lens — such as a trackside shot of a car on a curve — can be impressive. And tilting the camera in the direction of movement can often give a dramatic effect.

Shutter speed The choice of shutter speed depends largely on the desired effect. A fast shutter speed will freeze movement and may reveal movements too quick for the eye to take in clearly, as in the shot of horses falling at a novice race at Newbury (left, by George Selwyn). When the action is predictable or continuing — and so less interesting — the photographer may prefer to blur the action deliberately with a slower shutter speed, as in the racing car shot above.

cricket match or jumping event, a tripod is quite adequate. But if the action can be anywhere, and the photographer needs to follow it around, a monopod or pistol grip is better.

Motor-drives are often associated with sports photography, but their prime value is not to 'machine-gun' the action in the hope of getting at least one good shot. Instead, they allow the photographer to keep his or her eye glued to the viewfinder and finger poised on the shutter button; winding on manually may be so distracting that the photographer misses the crucial moment. For peak-of-the-action shots, a single manual exposure is more reliable than a motor-drive sequence.

A second camera body, already loaded with a fresh roll of film, is a useful precaution against missing action. When the end of the roll is reached with the first camera, the second can be brought immediately into use, and the first camera reloaded at leisure during a quieter moment later. Nevertheless, the photographer must always carry enough film for the entire event, and also a range of alternative films to guard against changing light conditions. Particularly useful are fast films that can be push-processed if necessary, giving, in effect, a range of film speed options. Ektachrome P800/1600 is one of the first such to be designed for variable processing: the photographer chooses the speed rating to suit the circumstances, from ISO 400 127° to ISO 3200 136°.

1

THE SPORTS
Good reflexes, organization, motor-drives and long lenses apart, nothing contributes more to the success of sports photography than a feel for and an intimate knowledge of the particular game or event. Each sport has its own rhythm and good photographs. Because all sporting events follow a certain pattern and take place in known locations and at known times, most of the *types* of sports photography have already been tried, but within these parameters there still remain an unlimited number of powerful images to be taken.

Football As a field team sport, football's action can range over a considerable area, so that shooting opportunities are difficult to predict. Most of the important action is likely to be concentrated close to either end. In soccer, the goal mouth will attract the critical action, but a camera position right behind, favoured by many professionals, actually has a restricted view. Goals and touchdowns are important for professional photographers, but a photographer shooting for his own pleasure may find

more opportunities from a midfield touchline position. Less important and friendly games give more open access to photographers. As the distance from the action is unpredictable, and varies, a zoom lens (such as 80-200mm) can be useful, or else a combination of two cameras, one with a medium telephoto (such as 100mm or 150mm), the other with a medium-to-long telephoto (300mm to 400mm).

In virtually all circumstances, it pays to follow the ball. A ground-level position often gives the least complicated views with a telephoto lens, setting players against the unfocused background of stands and spectators. A motor-drive is useful.

Baseball Most of the action takes place at known points — the bases and the batting plate — but distances are great, and a 300mm or 400mm telephoto is usually necessary. Floodlit games at night are common, and call for highspeed film and, ideally, a wide maximum aperture. One of the classic baseball shots is of a player sliding into a base in a cloud of dust. This is best caught with a ground-level position. Pre-focusing on the base may help.

Cricket The distances over which cricket is played are even greater than in baseball, and a 600mm lens is ideal. Because of its weight and the long periods of waiting between action, a tripod is virtually essential. Changes in the placing of fielders will suggest where a catch is most likely to occur — or to be attempted. Shooting from almost directly behind the batsman will give good on-coming pictures of the bowler. Minimum shutter speed, as with most other sports, should be $\frac{1}{500}$ second.

Track athletics Key positions are the start and finish, but head-on to a bend from outside the track gives opportunities for shots of bunched athletes. The field is most closely packed at the start, although the most exciting action usually occurs later in the race (from the start of the last lap onwards in a long race). For head-on shots of short distance events, such as 100m, make sure that the combination of lens focal length and camera position gives a *wide* enough view of the runners at the finishing line, or else have a second camera ready with a more moderate telephoto. An inside position on the track

gives the most freedom of movement, but will require permission. A telephoto lens from a distance allows more time for shooting than a standard or wide-angle lens from close to the track. Shutter speeds of at least $\frac{1}{500}$ second are needed. A motor-drive is useful.

Field athletics These vary considerably in the opportunities they offer for photography, but in most there are exact places, such as the bar of a high-jump and the take-off point for a long-jump that can be pre-focused on. How close a camera position is allowed depends largely on the status of the event, and it is best to check beforehand, as this will determine the focal length of lens that is needed.

Swimming Races are confined in lanes, and this makes it relatively easy for follow-focus. As most of a swimmer is submerged, it is usually important to time the shot for when the head breaks clear of the water — this can be anticipated after watching only a few strokes. Most events are indoor, calling for fast film and a fast lens. A medium telephoto is likely to be the most useful focal length unless access to

the poolside is restricted. Underwater shots are an interesting alternative, especially at the turn at one end — these would have to be staged rather than taken during a competitive event.

Golf The distances in golf involve a considerable amount of walking. The best opportunities are likely to be powerful drives and putts, but at the latter in particular, the noise of a camera may be unwelcome, a motor-drive or winder should not be used. The split-second *after* contact is made with the ball is often the most effective moment to shoot — shooting earlier than this may put the golfer off the stroke.

Horse racing Opportunities depend on how much access there is to the track. Under special circumstances, it may be possible to rig a remotely controlled camera with motor-drive and a wide-angle lens close to a jump, for example, for very dramatic shots. Ordinarily, however, head-on shots of a bend or panning shots side-on to a straight are the usual positions.

Motor racing For safety and security, access is usually restricted, and it is worth

aking considerable trouble
o obtain a photographer's
ass, for it will allow access
o camera positions on the
nside of the track, and close
o it. Most races last a
ufficient time to allow
novement between
ifferent camera positions.
A grid start always has
ossibilites of excitement,
while parts of the track that
re known to be likely
assing places are also
worth watching. A long
elephoto can give good
ompressed views head-on
o a curve. Panning shots,
ven at slow shutter speeds,
re another alternative.

**ailing and power-boat
acing** The best camera
osition is nearly always on
boat, and one or more of
hese may be available for
hotographers and reporters
t a major event (although a
pecial pass will usually be
eeded). A variety of lenses
s useful, as are waterproof
ags and some provision for
rying and cleaning
quipment in the event of a
pray soaking. An
mphibious camera held at
he waterline close to a
ailing boat can give
nusually dramatic pictures.

1 The classic steeple-
chasing shot shows the
horses clearing a jump, in
silhouette. To take this shot,
George Selwyn set up his
camera before the race,
using a wide, 24mm lens
and Kodachrome 64. He fired
the shutter from a distance
using an infrared trigger
(see page 63).
2 The clack of an SLR's
mirror can put a golfer off his
stroke, so the standard shot
shows the moment after the
stroke. Shooting from a
distance, as in this shot of
Severiano Ballesteros,
through a 300mm lens,
reduces the chances of
distracting players.
3 Zooming the lens during a
long exposure — here 80 to
200mm at $\frac{1}{4}$ second —
gives a dramatic, though
uninformative, view of a
tennis player.
4 Ski events offer few good
viewpoints. Perhaps the best
view of a downhill race is
facing a turn, where the
skier has to slow down. But
high shutter speeds — here
$\frac{1}{1000}$ second — are essential.
5 Like most watersports,
windsurfing looks dramatic
from close to the water line
— a waterproof housing is
clearly vital. For this shot,
Clive Boden used a Nikonos
IV, from a small boat.

LANDSCAPES

Landscape photography has been one of the principal and most clearly defined uses of the camera, with a history of development as old as that of photography itself. Just as the landscape in art has been a consistent theme through eras and movements, so, over a shorter period, it has been a continuing interest in photography. As such, it has at times clearly reflected changes in the style of picture-making and in general taste, covering such obviously different treatments as the impressionistic and lyrical pastoral scenes of André Martin, the cool and clearly delineated views of Western America by the Westons, and the high drama of Yoshikazu Shirokawa. It has also acquired the features of a general artistic discipline.

The easy availability of the landscape scene as a subject is only a part of the reason for its popularity and its importance in photography. It certainly offers more immediate opportunities than most subjects. It has great variety, depending on viewpoint and the weather, and is permanently available — but its attraction goes deeper. Even without a camera or other means of expression, natural and rural landscapes of a certain type have a broad emotional appeal. This can range from a feeling of relaxation to one of inspiration, but the general sensation is one of pleasure at being surrounded by, and even being at one with, the environment. Then, too, the practice of landscape photography can be carried on alone and at the photographer's own pace, allowing time for reflection.

Ansel Adams is probably the most famous landscape photographer. The photographed grand scenery with great sensitivity, always displaying the image with considerable craftsmanship. The view, as

Landscape styles

George Davison's gravure print, *The Onion Field* (left) was taken in about 1890. At the time, the deliberately fuzzy image created a storm of controversy, but now it seems to promote a comfortable, pastoral view.

Meanwhile, landscape photographers like Carlton Watkins (picture below) were photographing the dramatic scenery of the cities of the American West. He and other photographers did much to encourage governmental protection of wilderness areas.

Later, a plainer approach evolved, as beautifully exemplified by the work of Edward Weston. He never lost sight of the typical in American landscapes, as in the un-mannered picture of a farmhouse in New Jersey, taken in 1941 (below right).

Because landscapes are among the least controversial and most enduring subjects, they have shown changes in photographic approach only slowly. At any one time, it is often seen that the basic appeals are unchanging. As a result, landscape photography has acquired some of the formal aspects of a discipline — defined methods of working, of composition, of tonal arrangements, and so on.

For example, the Zone System, which formalized the judgement of exposure (see page 55), was applied more to landscapes than any other subject, because that was the main interest of Ansel Adams, its chief publicist. In the process of bringing a logical system to the matter of the tonal arrangement of the photograph, Adams's own system also assumed a basic rightness to a full, rich tonal range of landscape view. Unchallenged for a long time, this belief can now more easily be seen as just one of several alternative approaches — the recent development of other types of landscape photography put it in perspective.

These newer areas of interest are in a less idealistic and more sharply pointed vein, like the work of such committed environmentalists as Robert Adams, and in a re-definition of the contents of the landscape which has physically changed over the last few decades in many areas. Many younger photographers would argue that not only had Ansel Adams and others of his generation shown all that is possible of the grand natural landscape, but that a depressing reality is the layer of additions made by man — the landscape of the freeway and the gas station. Landscape photography has slowly reflected the changing values of photographers, and continues to do so. At this point, the values of many photographers who might at other times have been identified with

this sunrise over Mount McKinley, is romantic in concept, but not in its surface treatment.

gentle and ordered rural scenes, or with wild and momentous 'Nature', have changed so much that it makes more sense to distinguish between the natural and urban landscapes in photography. Here, natural landscape photography is dealt with as an associate of wildlife photography — the appeals are very close — while urban landscape photography is considered separately, as a new field (see pages 242-249).

STYLES
Approaches to landscape photography fall into three main areas: straight descriptive (with objective clarity as an ideal), impressionistic (using various techniques to give atmosphere) and abstract (with a compositional emphasis on tone, colour, and line). Each of these is used differently by photographers as they pursue the various styles of landscape photography.

Romantic
Romanticism has for many years been the most widely popular style of landscape photography. There is, nevertheless, some resistance among many photographers to the romantic approach, and personal definitions vary considerably. Within the romantic style, there have been many different individual approaches more or less in vogue at any one time.

Early pastoral approaches, such as that of George Davison followed painterly influences and still find favour with some photographers. A certain amount of softness in the image quality is often deliberately introduced, by a number of means. Soft-focused and diffusing lenses are an obvious method (although *too* obvious for many tastes) but others include deliberately induced flare through back-lighting and longer lenses, shallow focus, soft printing, use of fast film for

Triangle A clever visual pun, John Pfahl's photograph is a landscape joke which refreshingly jars with all the traditional concepts of the field of photography. Although not in any way similar to other original work, Pfahl's 'altered' landscapes have in common with a number of other modern photographers a challenge to accepted notions of fit subject matter. Most landscape photography has always been a fairly serious, considered activity — and probably always will be — but iconoclasm like this, however short-lived, is a valuable antidote to pretension.

Graphic/abstract Two conditions make it easy to turn landscapes into graphic designs — unusual shapes and features, and high contrast. In the photograph below left, the unlikely shape of a tapering rock pillar makes a dramatic shape in silhouette against a late afternoon sun, far removed from the normal, representational treatment. The photograph above left is even less recognizable. Sandbanks in a meandering river in the Swat valley were photographed from a nearby mountainside to catch the reflection of a setting sun. A 400mm telephoto lens further isolated the meanders, thereby making what seems an almost graphic design.

Compressed and wide field The foreshortening effects of long-focus lenses have helped create a very distinctive type of landscape photograph, as in the mountain view below. Here, a 400mm lens restores some of the massive scale of the mountains, so that they appear to loom high over the nearer forested ridge. The massive depth of field of a wide-angle lens can be exploited to create an entirely different effect with a camera position close to interesting foreground details. In this view of an island off the Washington coast (bottom), shot on a 20mm lens stopped down to f22, the depth of field extended from the horizon to as close as 0.6m (2ft).

its graininess and of the qualities of some optical designs such as mirror lenses. The subject matter tends to be comfortable, familiar and rural rather than wild and unusual.

Drama and grandeur are other versions of the romantic theme, and are generally more acceptable to modern tastes because they appear to be less contrived and dominated by technique than lyrical pastoral photographs. Yet the apparent impression of spontaneity is often false. Ansel Adams, for instance, visualized his photographs as closely as possible before taking them. This is evident in both the timing and the precision of his composition, which tends to exploit the dramatic potential of views to the full. He often went to considerable lengths to make the exposure at just the right moment of weather and light. A more extreme presentation of drama in subjects (such as mountains and deserts), lighting (low sun, dusk and dawn), and design (extreme focal length and high sky-to-land ratios) is common in modern magazine photography.

Descriptive

Straight descriptive landscape photography uses fewer identifiable techniques and is less insistent as a style than the romantic approach. One of the features that sets it apart from casual record shots, however, is attention to detail, with careful craftsmanship and design — as Edward Weston's landscape work shows. Weston, indeed, was one of the founders of what he called 'straight' photography. Lack of artifice and visual manipulation is one of the appeals of this essentially formalist style, and it has been adopted by many of the American photographers who developed the theme of urban landscape photography in the late 1970s and early 1980s (see

page 249). Large-format cameras and careful, studied technique are common.

Graphic/Abstract

At times verging on the romantic, at others using constructivist principles, the graphic/abstract style places even more emphasis on design over content than does descriptive formalism. Extracting graphic simplicity from a landscape can be a display of the photographer's visual abilities, and there is a typical emphasis on presenting the unexpected and unusual. Minimalist design often features strongly, and there is a preponderance of exotic subject matter (for instance, deserts, geothermal springs and rare land forms) because of the extra possibilities that they offer.

Environmentalist

Perhaps reflecting growing concern over protection of the environment from man-made pollution and destruction, some recent landscape photography has avoided the idealization that is common elsewhere. Environmentalist concern itself is not new, particularly in the United States, and the Sierra Club and Audubon Society have been active proponents of this style for many years. Nevertheless, the publications of both these organizations have mainly presented images of natural beauty that ought to be preserved rather than the much less attractive views of what has already happened in some landscapes. Arguably this *is* more effective politically, but a few photographers, notably Robert Adams, have taken a serious look at landscapes that are already undergoing change. There are stylistic links here with some modern urban landscape photography.

Manipulative

Less traditional still is the recent style of photography in which objects are added to a landscape image — as virtual props — or in which juxtapositions are made with existing man-made things, or in which alterations are later made to the image. Although one of the least common styles, it contains great variety, from the visual puns of John Pfahl to the surrealistic, multiple images of Jerry Uelsmann.

Controlled

While natural landscapes do not suggest themselves as subjects that can be altered and rearranged, lighting can be added with a certain amount of effort. In attempts to find more interesting and unusual ways of seeing landscapes, a relatively modern style is to shoot at dusk or night, using portable flash. With foreground and medium-distance features, such as trees and large rocks, this is not so difficult as might be imagined. Landscapes are static, so the camera can be left on a tripod with the shutter open, and a flash fired from various concealed positions as the photographer walks around the scene.

CAMERA TECHNIQUES

Because landscapes are large-scale subjects and naturally lit, they often require the minimum of technique. Over such large distances, depth of field is often irrelevant and, outdoors, the light level is sufficiently high to allow a fairly

The hand of man Although most traditional styles of landscape photography have treated their subject as pristine Nature, avoiding man-made scars and intrusions, some recent approaches are less preconceived. Both the photograph at left and below delicately include evidence of human presence — the shadow of the photographer in one case, the visual pollution of graffiti in the other. The validity of such treatment rests on the fact that fewer and fewer natural landscapes can exist without active preservation.

fast shutter speed. Nevertheless, while landscape photography can be managed perfectly with simple equipment, photographers looking for distinctive images often use either long focal lengths or large-format cameras, or both. The choice of lens is particularly important, as there are few other ways in which the photographer can directly influence the appearance of the landscape.

Wide-angle lenses give a special flavour to landscape photographs in two ways: they produce a sense of the panorama; and they can combine the foreground and distance in one image. Both of these have much to do with the pleasure that most people derive from simply looking at a landscape: the broad, expansive vista from a viewpoint, and the relationship between the large features of scenery and its more intimate details. The panoramic sense can be enhanced by cropping the picture to produce a narrower, more horizontal image, or by using a panoramic camera (see page 26). To make the most of the foreground/horizon technique, a wide-angle lens is generally used low enough to include small

Long telephoto techniques
The apparently compressed perspective given by very long focal lengths makes them especially useful in landscape work. Steadiness on location is, however, a problem, compounded by wind vibration and by the need for small apertures to give better depth of field (and so slower shutter speeds). A second tripod is often needed to support the front of the lens. Since lenses are not fitted with tripod bushes at the front, the simplest method of attachment is a strong elasticated band. Lock up the mirror on an SLR to reduce vibration still further.

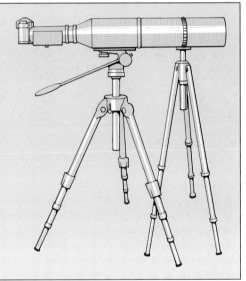

details such as plants, and a small aperture for the maximum depth of field. This may well call for a shutter speed so slow that a tripod is necessary.

Long-focus lenses give a more selective view, and careful choice of viewpoint can sometimes produce quite unusual images. The apparent perspective is compressed, especially with very long lenses, and in a scene that contains a variety of relief, such as a view of a series of mountain ranges, the graphic effect can be that of stacked layers. With telephotos, though, the camera must be handled carefully to avoid flare and camera-shake and if the depth of field is important, or in low light, a tripod may have to be used.

Large-format photography is quite popular for landscapes as the image can record extremely fine detail. Bulk and weight are the obvious problems, and a tripod is virtually essential. Lightweight (often wooden) field cameras have an advantage. Tilts and swings give great control over foreground/distance sharpness in the way shown on pages 18-19 and 218.

Variety from one viewpoint
Panoramic viewpoints, which in scenic areas are often well known, usually offer more than one broad sweeping picture. There may only be one, or possibly two, wide-angle shots, but longer focal lengths can be used to probe for alternative views. From Zabriskie Point, overlooking a part of Death Valley, one camera position yields a number of different photographs, using lenses ranging from 20mm to 40mm (right and below). Note that the changing angle of the sun, from dawn to about one hour after sunrise, affects the composition of the different pictures.

Large-format landscapes
View cameras have a special place in landscape photography, following in particular the tradition of American photographers such as Ansel Adams and the Westons. The two most obvious advantages of a large-format camera are the wealth of detail recorded on the film, and the possibility of using camera movements to adjust the distribution of sharpness in the picture. The scene above in the Canyonlands of Eastern Utah was photographed with a 4 × 5in studio view camera, and the picture demonstrates both virtues. Not only is the quality superb, but the lens is tilted forward to ensure that everything from the foreground to the horizon is pin-sharp.

Control

A few landscape views are virtually tailor-made for easy photography. Certain viewpoints in national parks offer such ready-made scenes and the basic design of the image tends to fall naturally into place. The photograph on the right is an example. More often, however, the components of a landscape are not in any obvious arrangement. Although the potential may seem to be there from a glance, the basic problem in most landscape photography is to co-ordinate all the different elements into a coherent image. The components include not only the solid features of the landscape — mountains, rocks, trees and rivers, for example — but also the quality of the lighting and the weather.

As subject material, landscapes are probably the least amenable of all to control. The addition of artificial lighting, as shown on page 204, as a stylistic approach, is clearly very specialized and restricted in its application. The two principal ways of exercising visual control open to a photographer are viewpoint (combined with choice of lens and composition) and timing.

Experience counts considerably in choosing the camera position, because it is useful to be able to visualize the possible views from different places. If a wide-angle lens is being used, even moving a few feet may make a profound difference to the image.

None of this can be judged in isolation from the conditions of lighting and weather which dramatically alter the balance of tones and colours. A dark, thundery sky, for instance, will have more compositional 'weight' than light clouds, and if a low sun picks out a rocky outcrop much more brightly than its surroundings, it will naturally become a focus of attention. Waiting for the right light may seem to be an extremely passive type of control, but it is, by and large, the only one.

© Michael Freeman

United States

© Michael Freeman

© Michael Freeman

United States

United States

6 1 5 1

© Michael Freeman

5 2

United States

6 1 5 1

While the photography of natural landscapes is principally concerned with overall form on a fairly broad scale, nature photography looks at the detailed structure: the plant and animal life, both individually and in the way they are related to the environment. There is an essentially factual basis to this kind of photography, and while there is a wide variety of possible treatments, the need for close observation and special techniques tend to give it a documentary and often scientific flavour.

The general increase in environmental concern has encouraged more photographic interest in nature than ever before, and it is now an extremely popular field among amateurs. Improvements in cameras, lenses, lighting and film have had a particularly important effect, simply because many nature subjects do make heavy technical demands. Optically, the important special need in nature photography is magnification: close-up enlargement for the large numbers of small subjects such as flowers and insects, and the magnification of distant views for full-frame pictures of wary animals. The development of relatively inexpensive macro and telephoto lenses has made more nature subjects accessible to more people. Electronically, automatic metering and more sophisticated flash units have simplified exposure and lighting, while mechanically, motor-drives make it easier to deal with active subjects.

Trees and smaller plants are technically among the easiest class of nature subject, and as a result are both popular and open to a variety of interpretative treatment. Some specialized knowledge may be needed to find good specimens, but the photographer still has considerable scope for experiment. Documentary realism is not the only approach; flowers in particular can make attractive abstracts.

Trees

The complex shapes and outlines of most trees, and the fact that most grow together, makes it generally difficult to produce clear, simplified designs in photographs. Even pictures of trees *en masse* usually benefit from a definite visual structure — in a woodland interior view, this means the photograph must have a distinct focus of attention. An important first stage therefore is to find good and accessible specimens, whether individual trees or complete stands, and for this some knowledge of natural history is useful. At the least, it helps to be able to judge the standard and condition of a particular species.

For individual specimens, a clear view is valuable, and some means of isolating it visually. This isolation may be through viewpoint (against a relatively plain background), setting (a tree standing apart from the edge of a forest), or lighting (for example, sunlight picking out one individual).

For masses of trees, shooting across an open space, such as a river or from one hillside to another, is a standard procedure. In this kind of shot, the texture and pattern is more important than the shapes of individual trees and the whole effect is almost graphic. Lighting and colour are therefore key ingredients. Forest interiors are more difficult, but often helped by overcast light (which reduces the contrast) and a wide-angle lens. A tripod and time-exposures may be necessary in such low light conditions.

Gardening In wildflower photography there is often very little choice of specimen and if, as in the case of this orchid in a Borneo rain forest, there are no other good specimens nearby, the surroundings may need a little 'gardening' to give a clear view. 'Gardening' needs care and discretion, not only because of the risk of making an unnatural picture, but because removing surrounding foliage may expose a shade-loving plant to direct sunlight.

Isolating with light and weather With trees and many other plants, a basic problem in photography is to isolate clearly enough to show their shape. In both of these photographs, it is the light that helps reveal the outline of the tree clearly. In the picture at left, the conditions could be anticipated — under a clear sky, the moment at which the sunlight would just leave the slopes of this death valley crater could be predicted. The photograph below, however, could not be planned; instead the photographer exploited mist over an East Anglian water meadow.

Wildflowers and small plants

Photographing small plants, fungi and flowers involves mainly close-up techniques, and a macro lens, or at least a close-focusing lens, is the most common equipment. At this scale, movement of the subject can be a problem but the plant can be protected from gusts of wind by makeshift shielding. So time-exposures are quite feasible. Unlike insect photography, which also needs close-up methods, the choice of flash lighting can be made for its visual effect rather than from necessity.

Photographing flowers by natural light usually calls for long exposures both because many flowers grow in the shade, and because very small apertures are often needed for good depth of field close-up. A tripod is essential but as most small plants are ground-dwellers, the most useful types of tripod are a pocket tripod, a regular tripod with wide-spreading legs, or a regular tripod with a reversible centre column. With colour film, long exposures cause colour shifts due to reciprocity failure, and the appropriate colour compensating filters are part of a field photography kit for flowers.

Flash can be used to simulate sunlight, to fill in shadow detail in a natural-light shot, or simply to provide basic, over-all lighting. In conjunction with a tripod, one or more flash units can be used off the camera with cable extensions for a variety of lighting effects. Holding the flash over the plant imitates sunlight; aiming it through a sheet of diffusing material gives more even lighting with softer shadows.

Fungi Although visually similar, fungi grow faster than most flowers (some in only a few hours) and damage more easily. Many are seasonal (late autumn in temperate woodlands is a prime time), and specimens stay in good condition for a very short time indeed. Many are so delicate that they can be spoilt even by touching. Particular care is needed, therefore, to achieve a striking shot like the one on the right. Early morning is often a good time to look for fresh fungi.

Masses of Trees Although the clustering of trees in forests, woods and thickets tends to disguise the shapes of individual trees, the very density of foliage can sometimes make graphically interesting photos. A clear space between camera and forest edge is essential, but attractive lighti[ng] careful composi[tion] important, as the photographs here[...] views of the yello[w] in Colorado (far rig[ht] the tropical gallery (right) were taken fr[om] distance through a t[ele] lens — the aspens a[...]

Forest light Interior forest views are among the most difficult to carry off successfully. One obvious difficulty is that the tangle of density of vegetation tends to produce a messy and confused image, but this is compounded by the high contrast from bright sunlight. The chiaroscuro effect obscures detail and, for a typical scene such as that at far right, colour film has insufficient contrast range to keep shadow and highlight detail (printing controls and a soft paper grade give a slightly better result with black-and-white film). In this kind of light, the usual technique is to expose — and compose also — for the brightly lit areas, leaving the shadow areas black. Often a framed view, looking past dark, silhouetted branches and trunks to a path of sunlight (right), is the most successful. Easier still, however, is to photograph on a cloudy day, when the contrast range is lower, and more even colour and tone help to blend the different elements of trees, shrubs and so on (near right)

lake and the tropical forest from a river. The telephoto helped to compress perspective and give a compact view of the trees. The clear blue sky in the background of the trees in the Florida swamp (below), however, meant that a wide-angle shot was possible.

The most common types of plant photograph taken on location are full-frame portraits, very close details of parts of the plant, and 'environmental' shots of plants in their wider settings. Consequently, although a standard close-focusing lens is basic, different focal lengths have their uses.

INSECTS AND SPIDERS

The sheer abundance of insects makes them, and other groups of small creatures, such as crustaceans and arachnids, one of the easiest animal subjects to find. The principal specialization called for is close-up technique. Recent electronic improvements in the integration of flash and camera circuitry have made this considerably easier.

■ FINDING AND HANDLING A diligent search on a nature walk should reveal quite large numbers of species in most habitats. Generally speaking, the more variety of micro-habitats, as in a forest, the more species, and high summer is the peak period in a temperate seasonal climate. Forest litter, such as dead leaves and rotting wood, are particularly likely places for searching. At low temperatures, insects are more sluggish; early morning is a good time to photograph species that would otherwise take flight easily.

Alternatively, insects can be attracted to a particular site. A sugar mixture, such as one made of beer, treacle and rum, will attract butterflies and moths. Salt licks can also be used, and at night a lantern behind a white cloth will net large quantities of winged insects.

Using baiting and luring techniques, it may be easier to collect insects and photograph them later under controlled conditions, with some of the natural vegetation.

■ CLOSE-UP EQUIPMENT Most insects and spiders in temperate habitats are so small that they need a magnification of at least $\frac{1}{2}$x for an image that fills a reasonable area of the frame. Supplementary close-up lenses are rarely powerful enough; a close-focusing macro lens with a selection of extension rings is usually needed. Extension rings are more sturdy than bellows for fieldwork, and retain the FAD capability of the camera. There is some advantage in using a longer focal length of macro lens — 105mm or 200mm, for example, with a 35mm camera — as the working distance is greater and so less likely to disturb the insect. Increasing the magnification with a longer lens, however, calls for a proportionately greater extension, and in this case a bellows may be more useful.

■ **CAMERA TECHNIQUE** For most photographs of insects in the field, the camera is, of necessity, hand-held. At typical magnifications — $\frac{1}{2}$x and greater — it is nearly always easier to focus by moving the entire camera bodily backwards and forwards rather than to try and adjust the focusing ring on the lens. With flash, pre-setting the focus also makes it possible to pre-set the aperture confidently.

Depth of field is always shallow at magnification, but the depth needed varies according to the circumstances and the style of the picture. The usual ideal is just enough depth to show most of the insect sharply, but to leave the background smoothly blurred. In practice, there is normally less depth available than the photographer would like. Stopping down improves depth of field but the reduction in light means a higher flash output, or a slower shutter speed in daylight. Depth of field can also be used more efficiently by photographing the shallowest part of an insect (side-on to a dragonfly or other long insect, for example).

■ **CLOSE-UP FLASH** Because of the problems with depth of field and subject movement, portable flash is the usual lighting in insect photograph. A dedicated flash system (see page 79) automatically compensates for the closer flash distance and extra lens extension, but otherwise a small manual flash unit is convenient — the sensors in ordinary automatic flash units are not designed for work at close range. To simplify the calculations for flash exposure, the surest system is to devise a standard arrangement, as shown (opposite). Once tested and calibrated for a few likely magnifications, it can then be used without adjustment in the field.

It is important to mount flash units close to the subject, to give some modelling and to avoid throwing the shadow of the lens onto the insect. Various propietary brackets and mounts allow this. Specialized alternatives are a ringflash and purpose-built macro-flash.

WILDLIFE

Perhaps because it is so difficult even getting near the subject, let alone taking good pictures, wildlife photography tends to lean heavily towards the documentary rather than the interpretative or lyrical. This is not to say that wildlife photography is limited to a kind of record-keeping; there are as fine examples of individual, interpretative treatments as in other fields of photography. But the foundation of consistently good wildlife photography is experience and long fieldwork.

In a field dominated by technique, there are two basic working methods: stalking and photography from a concealed position (generally known as a blind in the United States and as a hide in Britain). In one, the photographer actively seeks out the subject and must use a high level of fieldcraft to approach closely; in the other, the photographer hides near a regular haunt of the creature, such as a nesting site or a water hole, within clear camera view. A third method, highly specialized and much less often used, is remote control, in which the camera alone is positioned close to the site and triggered from a distance or by an animal's arrival. Remote control techniques are described in detail on pages 61-62, but an automatic trigger for birds is shown on the following page.

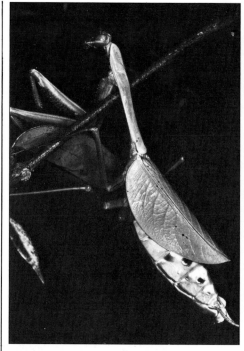

Flash is virtually essential for insect photography. A standard arrangement is one or two small units arranged in the way shown on the right, as for the mantis above.

A more specialized system is a ringflash, useful in enclosed spaces, such as a hunting spider's burrow (below).

A standard set-up for field photography of insects is two small flash units mounted close to the end of a macro lens, calibrated beforehand:
1 Choose a number of fixed magnifications.
2 For each, focus the lens and aim the flash units at the point of focus.
3 Set up a flashmeter (right) and move the camera until the dome is sharp in the viewfinder.
4 Trigger the flash and take the reading.
5 There will be aperture setting for each magnification. In the field, just move the pre-focused camera until the insect appears sharp in the viewfinder.

Birds

Just as wildlife is distinct from other nature subjects because of the special photographic techniques involved, so different groups of animals tend to be categorized by the way they are most easily photographed. In the number of photographers they attract, birds are by far the most popular subject. This is probably due in part to a loose aesthetic appeal — birds appear naturally elegant and are usually highly active — and in part, to their visibility, which contrasts with the stealth and secretiveness of most mammals. Such facilities as exist for wildlife photography — organized sanctuaries and permanent hides, for example — are more common around bird colonies and other regularly visited sites.

■ RANGE OF TECHNIQUES Stalking is less commonly used than a hide; virtually all birds can fly, and so are not bound by the terrain as is the photographer. The small size of most birds also makes a visible approach unlikely. Nevertheless, in certain situations it may not be necessary to stay concealed: dense vegetation in forests sometimes offers opportunities during a nature walk, while large colonies have so many individuals and are so noisy that a human presence is often tolerated. Species vary in how wary they are of humans.

Most serious bird photography, however, requires a hide, and the techniques for using one are fairly specific. Permanent hides exist at certain bird sanctuaries; otherwise a hide must be built and introduced to a site, which requires care and judgement. For very close camera positions and nervous subjects, remote control may be necessary (see page 62).

■ **PHOTOGRAPHING BIRDS FROM A HIDE** By far the majority of successful bird photographs are taken from a hide or with a remote-controlled camera. Hides are camouflaged covers that allow the photographer to work very close to the birds without being seen. Some bird sanctuaries have permanent hides, equipped with double-glazing and central-heating, but elsewhere hides must be carried carefully to the site and erected without disturbing the birds. Typically, hides are set up near a nest or feeding site where the birds regularly appear. Occasionally, though, birds may have to be lured to the hide with food (see box on 'Baits and lures').

Success with a hide depends very much on the birds accepting it as part of their surroundings. If their normal routine and behaviour is upset, it may not only prevent the photographer getting any photographs; it may also drive the birds away from their feeding and nesting sites. So hides must not only be camouflaged and positioned carefully so as to avoid disturbing the birds; they must also be moved into place gradually so that the birds accept the new feature in their environment. If ever the birds' behaviour seems disrupted, the hide must be withdrawn some distance or not used for a while. Once the hide is set up, the photographer must time arrival and departure carefully so as to cause the minimum disturbance. Permanent hides administered by a park ranger will already be accepted by the birds.

Hides are generally tailored to meet the circumstances, but a basic design, which is adaptable to most normal situations,

Hides are the standard technique for almost any comprehensive coverage of a particular species — especially nesting birds, such as the young Openbill storks above right and the egret with chicks at right. A portable, tent-like hide, as described right, can be used in different locations, or a sanctuary may already have a permanent structure (below).

Precautions in use
1. Enter and leave the blind out of sight and hearing of the subjects. This usually means when the birds are absent. A concealed approach to the back of the blind is an advantage.
2. If birds are present, enter with a companion, who then leaves. Few birds appear to be able to count.
3. Avoid touching the walls, once inside; and stay quiet.
4. Movement of the front of the lens may alert the birds. When the lens is removed at the end of the day, replace it with something that looks similar, such as a bottle.

Basic design for a hide
This multiple-use hide is constructed from sectioned aluminium poles of the type used for tents, covered with a camouflage material. The material, which can be bought from a camping supplier, should be waterproof and strong enough not to flap in a wind. The camouflage pattern is optional and can be dyed into plain, drab material. A box-frame construction is the simplest design; if the uprights are sectioned as shown, with a *short* lower pole, it will be easier to erect on a slope.

5. Extra comfort makes it easier to stay quiet and still. A folding chair, food and drink may be worth taking.

Specialized hides
For certain different kinds of habitat, such as forest and wetlands, a specific design may be necessary.

Baits and lures
Food, water recordings of appropriate calls, and even decoys can be used as an inducement to encourage birds to land at a certain site, and can be used in conjunction with a hide (there may be legal restrictions in some countries). For efficiency, food is best when offered when it is scarce in nature (winter, for example, rather than spring). Any bait or lure, however, should only be put down with full awareness of likely disruptive effects: regular food offerings may cause a bird to delay migration too long, or alarm calls may cause stress. Place baits in a location that is open enough to be visible, but which offers some close cover (few animals like to eat in an unprotected place).
Seed-eaters: Use cereal grains (make sure that they are untreated and non-toxic), sunflower seeds.
Fruit-eaters: Fresh fruit, raisins.
A small artificial pool can be made from a weighted plastic sheet in a scooped-out hollow. A water-drip overhead will make this especially attractive to small birds.

is shown below. Although similar hides can be bought from specialist dealers, this one is designed to be made by the photographer, using tent materials.

The location of the hide must be selected with care. Not only must it offer a clear view that is close enough for a reasonably large image — this depends on the focal length of the lens, which normally needs to be at least 400mm — but you also need to have an eye on the background to the shot and the direction of the light falling on the subject at the important times of the day. From the birds' point of view, the hide should blend with the background, such as the edge of a thicket, and should never appear silhouetted against the sky. Upwind locations should also be avoided, since the birds will be just as alarmed at a strange smell, as at unfamiliar sights or sudden movements.

There are two principal ways of introducing the hide to the site. In one, the hide, fully assembled, is moved closer each day from a distance. In the other, the hide is gradually erected, day by day, on its chosen site. In both cases, it is important to move when the birds are absent, and to pay special attention to any changes in behaviour.

■ **BIRDS IN FLIGHT** Some of the best opportunities for photographing birds are, naturally enough, when they are flying. Technically, the problems of shooting any travelling action (see page 208) are compounded here by the lack of reference points — focusing on a predetermined spot is not possible.

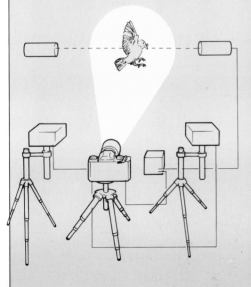

Automatic trigger One way to get high-quality pictures of birds in flight, like the picture of the starling on the right, is to arrange for the bird to trigger the camera itself. Camera and flash are set up to photograph the bird on a known flight path — typically the entrance to a nest. Flash is essential both to freeze all movement and to allow the photographer to stop down the lens for maximum depth of field. Then a photo-electric trip beam (visible or infrared) is set across the bird's flight-path to trigger the camera in the way described on page 63.

Focusing techniques for flying birds are variations of either follow-focus or fixed-focus. In the former, the focusing ring is turned (bottom) at a rate to match the bird's flight, as in the shot far left. In the second, easier method (left), the focus is fixed just ahead of the bird; after each shot, the lens is re-focused.

Camouflaged lens Very long focal length lenses of the type used in most serious wildlife photography are conspicuous because of their size. In certain situations, including hide photography, there may be some value in using camouflage tape or cloth to help conceal the barrel (below).

Following the focus by turning the lens focusing ring to keep pace with the bird's approach is one method, but demands considerable practice to avoid falling behind or advancing too quickly. Continuous refocusing, another method, involves focusing sharply, shooting, and then deliberately *de*focusing to begin again; the advantage of this is positive focusing at each attempt. A third method is to focus approximately on the approaching bird and then quickly pull the focus forward, waiting until the bird flies into sharpness; this technique is the surest, but may only allow one shot.

TTL exposure readings will be over-influenced by the sky background, which is likely to be much lighter than the bird, possibly by two or three stops. A substitute reading off an average-toned subject on the ground, or an incident reading, are more reliable.

Mammals

The great variety of behaviour among different species of mammals make different techniques applicable. Some mammals — generally larger mammals such as certain deer — are very easy to photograph; others such as weasels and stoats are very difficult indeed.

Stalking depends on fast, quiet movement, so equipment must be kept to a minimum. Even a shoulder bag may restrict movement too much. The choice of lens depends on the size of animal and type of cover, but many situations can be covered by a medium telephoto and the accessories above.

For fair-skinned people, the face and hands may be clearly visible parts. Military face paint is one answer, but messy. An alternative is camouflage netting and gloves. The netting, which doubles as a scarf, is draped over head and camera when necessary.

Camouflage for stalking: concealing appearance
Cover or darken anything bright — face, hands and chrome camera parts. Use dark face paint for the skin (military paint is ideal) and black tape for the chrome. Remove unnecessary bright objects, such as watch and sunglasses. A shapeless cap, camouflaged netting and a few sprigs of leaves will help to break up the body's recognizable outline.

Concealing scent Wear long sleeves and full-length trousers. The less exposed skin, the less scent. Use no commercial scents such as deodorant or after-shave. Movement propels scent molecules. Stay as still as possible.

Concealing noise Remove anything that rattles, such as coins or keys. Wear cotton rather than synthetic fabric.

■ **STALKING** Larger mammals, particularly grazers and browsers, tend to be the most suitable subjects for stalking. They are more visible than, say, the majority of rodents, and do not have to be approached so closely for a frame-filling image. Deer are probably the archetypal stalking subject, and common species such as the White-tailed in the United States are ideal for practising fieldcraft. Dangerous animals, such as large predators and certain large herbivores, should never be stalked on foot.

Successful stalking calls for an unobtrusive, and perhaps camouflaged appearance, and the ability to move silently and smoothly over rough terrain. Skill in fieldcraft is essential if the photographer is to get close enough to the subject animals for a satisfactory shot. However, a telephoto lens removes some of the need for a really close approach.

Most animals define for themselves a perimeter of safety and, provided that this is not crossed by a potential threat, they may not bother to take evasive action. The size of this perimeter varies, naturally, according to the species, its activity at the time, the terrain, and so on. Nevertheless, a noise made by a photographer at, say, 100m may not count as a threat, whereas the same disturbance at 50m may be reason enough to take flight. Practical experience gives a feeling for the limits to a close approach.

Stalking can have certain stages: the first is likely to be patrolling to find some sign of the animal's presence; the next, following the trail until the animal is in sight; and the last, making the approach to a shooting position. Finding animals depends on knowing their habits, being familiar with the marks they leave, such as tracks and droppings, and, often, on specific information about the location. For all these reasons, an experienced guide is extremely valuable.

Camouflage works best when it takes into account the principal senses of the animal. While sight is the most important for a human being, many mammals rely heavily on smell so scent concealment, silence and stillness may well be the most important aims of camouflage when stalking mammals. A smooth walking action also helps.

Sunlight must be avoided where possible. So must making a silhouette on skylines. The photographer may sometimes have to make use of natural cover, or even crawl. If the animal is alerted at close range, the photographer must freeze and stay motionless, avoiding eye contact, until it resumes its normal behaviour.

■ PHOTOGRAPHY FROM VEHICLES For many animals that live in the open, a vehicle is likely to be the best camera platform. Not only does it speed up the search, but it acts as a kind of moving hide — few mammals seem to identify a vehicle as a container for human beings. It is also the only safe method of approaching large, dangerous animals such as buffalo, lions and rhinoceros.

The vehicle should be suited to the terrain — a Land-Rover, Jeep or other 4WD vehicle is ideal. The best shooting positions are usually from a roof hatch or through the interior windows, although some professional wildlife photographers prefer a custom-mounted bracket on the door. Without a bracket, a soft support, such as a folded cloth or a bean bag, protects the lens from scratching and gives some steadiness.

As with other kinds of wildlife photography, a long focal length and wide maximum aperture are the ideals for a lens, although certain large animals may allow such a close approach in a vehicle (lions particularly) that a medium telephoto is also valuable. Early in the morning, after a kill, lions will lie lazily in the sun interested in little more than their breakfast. Often the amateur photographer's main problem is avoiding framing the dozens of other spectators.

■ PHOTOGRAPHING ANIMALS FROM HIDES Essentially, the same precautions apply as described for bird photography (see pages 226-7). The most common site for a hide is a watering place; in the dry season, if pronounced, visits by animals may be predictably regular. Freshness and quantity of trails at the water's edge give an indication of use. Early morning and late afternoon and evening are often the busiest times at a water hole.

■ REMOTE CONTROL Many mammals are so wary that only a remotely triggered camera is practical. In addition, for small mammals a camera position of only a few feet away is necessary — too close to allow a photographer as well. At a site where the animal is expected to cross (a trail close to the entrance of a burrow, for instance), the camera is fixed in position, focused and camouflaged. The shutter can then be triggered either by the photographer (watching from a distance), or by the arrival of the animal.

■ BAITS FOR SMALL MAMMALS A good, general-purpose bait mixture for small mammals is: roughly equal parts of suet, peanut butter, raisins and oatmeal. Never handle any bait without gloves: most mammals are very sensitive to human scent and will avoid such food. Proprietary scents are available for some game animals, particularly deer. Anise oil attracts bears and some deer. Catnip attracts some cat species. If the bait is to appear in the photograph, it is usually worth making it look as 'natural' as possible. Animals rarely respond instantly to baits and continued baiting over a few days is usually essential. For more on baits, see the box on the right.

Photography from vehicles In open country, such as the Savannah grasslands of Tanzania shown here, a 4WD vehicle is by far the most practical means of finding and photographing animals. It is also, with such large mammals as a rhinoceros, the only safe way. A roof hatch gives the clearest all-round visibility.

Baits and lures Baiting may be the only practical method of photographing many small species. Food and scent are the usual enticements, although some mammals, notably deer, will respond to calls. Items from the known diet of a mammal are generally reliable, and in addition there are certain favourite flavours:
Wild cats: Fish, meat, catnip oil, canned catfood

Chipmunks, gophers: Peanuts, peanut butter
Fieldmice, voles: Cheese, bread, small nuts, sunflower seeds, peanut butter
Weasels, stoats: Fish, fresh offal
Squirrels: Cereal grains, peanuts, sunflower seeds
Rabbits: Carrots, lettuce, onions, apples
Snakes: Mice, whole eggs
Raccoons: Fish, cooked bacon, honey
Foxes: Chicken, rabbit

Night equipment Many mammals are active only by night, and photographing them demands special equipment and materials. At stalking distances and with the moderate maximum apertures available on most telephotos, for instance, the majority of portable flash units can only be used with fast film.
1 Flashlight A flashlight on a head-strap or taped onto the lens frees the hands to operate the camera, and is useful not only for focusing but for finding animals at a distance — eye-shine (reflections from the retina) is strong from many animals and can reveal their presence even at a distance. A flashlight can also mesmerize some animals, making them easier to approach.
2 Tele-flash A parabolic mirror attachment or a condensing Fresnel lens concentrates the beam of a flash unit. This can increase the illumination over a small angle by up to three stops. The mirror unit must be calibrated for greatest effect.
3 Infrared Black-and-white Kodak High Speed Infra Red film, although grainy, can be used in situations where an animal may react to visible light. A regular flash unit is masked with a visually opaque filter, such as a Wratten 87. The infrared emission is unaffected.

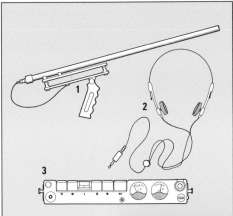

Electronic lures Animal calls can be used to attract subjects by recording them on tape and then playing back later. The basic equipment for this is a highly directional microphone such as the shotgun design shown here (**1**), a good quality portable tape recorder (**3**) and headphones for monitoring the recording (**2**). Using this method, however, calls for experience and thought for the animals — alarm calls recorded on one field trip, for instance, may create stress in the subject.

Catching the moment
While more difficult to shoot and rarely predictable, moments of action and interest nearly always make better photographs than static portraits. For bursts of activity, such as the picture above of two hyenas fighting over part of a carcass, rapid reactions are needed. Occasional activity in one location, such as the yawn of a hippopotamus (left), calls for patience and prolonged observation.

UNDERWATER PHOTOGRAPHY

Underwater photography was formerly a highly specialized field of photography, undertaken only by a few professionals and dedicated amateurs, but in recent years it has become very popular. This has been due partly to the growth of diving as a hobby, and partly to the production of relatively low-cost equipment and reliable electronics. In shallow water, underwater photography is possible without any knowledge of diving technique at all.

Camera equipment

There are two alternative underwater cameras: a purpose-built amphibious camera or an ordinary camera in an underwater housing. The advantages of an amphibious camera, sealed against water at pressure, are compactness, ease of operation, and lenses specially designed for water use (where the refraction is greater than it is in air). The drawbacks are the extra expense and the travelling weight of a completely separate camera system. An underwater housing minimizes extra expense but is bulky underwater, may be difficult to operate, and does not have lenses corrected for the higher refractive index of water.

Unfortunately, there is only one high-quality amphibious camera widely available, the Nikonos (see opposite), and its non-reflex design is for many divers a serious drawback. By contrast, a wide variety of housings are manufactured, for virtually all makes of regular camera, in moulded plastic or cast aluminium. Further details of equipment and lenses are given in the box opposite.

Diving technique

In what is an unfamiliar and potentially dangerous environment, any kind of diving must be taken seriously and it is important never to dive alone. Underwater photographic equipment adds weight and takes concentration, so it is essential first to be proficient at diving *without* cameras.

Snorkelling is relatively easy to master and needs no diving equipment other than a face mask, snorkel, fins and knife. A weight belt is also useful because photography takes up both hands, and the body's natural buoyancy makes it difficult to stay in one place when shooting. Shooting time is severely restricted — to between about 30 seconds and one minute — and it is usually easiest to make repeated short dives to take photographs rather than to attempt to make camera adjustments and several exposures all at once. Snorkelling is adequate for back reef areas at depths of about two or three meters, and is easiest at low-water. At these snorkelling depths, the level of natural light during the middle of the day can be quite light and this may affect exposure when flash is being used, unless the camera can be synchronized at a high shutter speed.

Snorkelling has one important advantage apart from simplicity over scuba diving: there is no stream of air bubbles and many fish will tolerate the closer approach of a snorkeller than that of a scuba diver. Nevertheless, to allow time for finding subjects, composing, and making a number of exposures, as well as opening up more interesting deeper locations, scuba technique is ideal. It needs thorough training, not only because there is equipment to master, but also because deeper diving is potentially more risky.

The Nikonos system
The Nikonos is the only amphibious camera system designed for serious use. The specifications have been regularly improved over the years: the Nikonos V, introduced in 1984, features both TTL metering with daylight and the facility for dedicated flash operation (with its companion SB 102 and SB 103 flashguns). The parts of the camera that open — the back and the lens — are protected by O-rings made of synthetic rubber tubing. The sealing ability of these rings increases with depth because of the extra pressure, with a normal safe limit of 50m (165ft). The Nikonos system for close-up photography features a supplementary lens rather than extension tubes (although the latter are available from independent manufacturers and can be fitted). The lens attaches to the 28mm, 35mm or 80mm camera lens and is used in conjunction with a corresponding metal field-frame, as shown below.

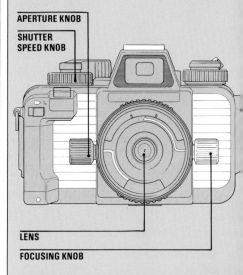

APERTURE KNOB

SHUTTER SPEED KNOB

LENS

FOCUSING KNOB

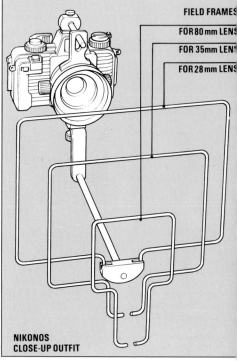

FIELD FRAMES

FOR 80 mm LENS

FOR 35 mm LENS

FOR 28 mm LENS

NIKONOS CLOSE-UP OUTFIT

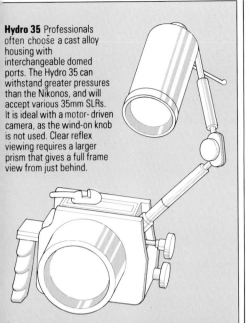

Hydro 35 Professionals often choose a cast alloy housing with interchangeable domed ports. The Hydro 35 can withstand greater pressures than the Nikonos, and will accept various 35mm SLRs. It is ideal with a motor-driven camera, as the wind-on knob is not used. Clear reflex viewing requires a larger prism that gives a full frame view from just behind.

Light-duty housings For shallow-water use, there is a choice of transparent housings. Shown below is a soft vinyl bag with built-in glove insert and a flat port. Below that is a moulded Ikelite case made of GE Lexan — a range of models is available for different makes of camera.

Natural light photography

Underwater landscapes, can only be taken by natural light. But light is often poor. Water absorbs light very strongly, and, only a few feet under the surface, exposure may have to be increased by two or three f-stops. Bright sunlight midday sunshine is really essential, and the exposure must be measured carefully. Through-the-lens automatic exposure is ideal, but close attention must be paid to the shutter speed: with a slow film or poor lighting, the exposure will be adequate, but even at maximum aperture the shutter speed may be slow enough to cause camera-shake and blurring of moving fish. $\frac{1}{60}$ second is usually the slowest speed that is satisfactory for a static view, and $\frac{1}{125}$ second is much safer.

A second problem with natural light underwater is colour balance. Water not only absorbs light, but does so selectively, beginning with the red end of the spectrum. Even at a depth of a few feet, photographs have a distinctly blue cast. At depths of several meters, the light is blue, and no practical amount of filter correction will make any significant difference. In shallow water, however, a red filter should improve colour. Ideally, the strength of the filter should correspond to the depth, but carrying a selection of filters is usually

Cleaning equipment To avoid a damaging build-up of salt deposits, it is absolutely essential to clean housings and amphibious cameras after each day's diving. First soak in fresh water for at least 30 minutes (**1**). Then hose down (**2**), dry thoroughly and dismantle (**3**). Remove the O-rings (**4**) and clean with fresh water. Then apply a light coating of O-ring grease (**5**). Finally, re-assemble, protecting the port with a cap or wash-leather (**6**). However, always dry your hands and hair before starting to clean the equipment.

BASIC SURFACE DIVE
A smooth, efficient dive is particularly useful when snorkelling, as the time submerged is limited and it is important not to frighten away the fish that has been spotted. From the normal swimming and watching position on the surface (**1**) the technique is first to bend sharply at the waist (**2**), then to lift the legs straight up vertically (**3**). This action alone propels the diver smoothly under the water, with the minimum of water disturbance.

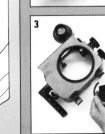

UNDERWATER LIGHT

Water modifies sunlight in three ways: it reflects some light back to the sky, especially if the water is rough; it absorbs light underwater progressively; and it absorbs the light selectively, so the light becomes increasingly blue at depth. The problems of overall light loss make a calm sea and a high, bright sun ideal, but even so, colour filtration is necessary.

DIRECT SUNLIGHT

LIGHT REFLECTED BY SURFACE OF WATER

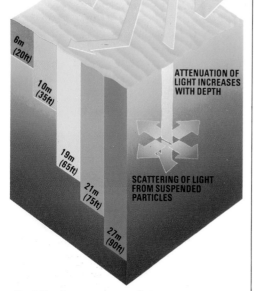

6m (20ft)
10m (35ft)
19m (65ft)
21m (75ft)
27m (90ft)

ATTENUATION OF LIGHT INCREASES WITH DEPTH

SCATTERING OF LIGHT FROM SUSPENDED PARTICLES

Pearl diver At two metres, even in relatively poor visibility, as below, sunlight alone is sufficient illumination. Here, a 20mm lens was used inside a housing, as f3.5 and $\frac{1}{60}$ second on ISO 64 film, with a red filter.

Red sea coral A red correction filter, the underwater equivalent to CC 30 red gives a reasonable rendering of the colours of red sea corals (above right).

impractical, and for most conditions, a single filter of strength CC30 red or CC40 red is satisfactory. The shallower water at low tide gives more light and less blueness. A low sun also gives warmer colours, but the water must be clear to allow shutter speeds fast enough to stop camera-shake.

Flash Photography

Over short distances, sufficient for shooting corals and fish, for example, the only practical means of restoring colours fully and freezing movement is to use flash. Since handling equipment is usually less easy underwater than on land, a single camera-mounted flash unit is the normal arrangement. A special underwater problem for flash is that suspended particles reflect back light from the camera position, so that if the flash head is close to the lens, the effect in the photograph will look something like a snow storm. This is known as 'back scatter'. To avoid back scatter, most flash units are fixed to brackets that position them a little away from the camera. In addition, flexible or jointed extension arms can be fitted or, failing that, the photographer or a companion can hold the flash separately from the camera and bracket. There is something to be said for moving the flash to achieve a variety of effects, even if back scatter is not a problem. Lighting from directly overhead, for instance, looks very natural.

A growing number of underwater flash systems are automatic, and some even feature through-the-lens automatic exposure with certain cameras (the Nikonos V and SB102

flash, for example). These can be a great help in unfamiliar and difficult conditions. Nevertheless, it is worth testing the equipment in normal diving conditions and check a variety of settings. Many professional underwater photographers now use Polachrome instant slide film for testing.

■ **CLOSE-UPS UNDERWATER** Close-ups underwater are nearly always taken by flash, which provides, as well as natural colours, enough light to give good depth of field. For the maximum depth of field in close-up photography, it may be better to set the flash to manual operation; if the output is then too high, a diffusion cap may lower it sufficiently.

As with land-based, close-up nature photography, by far the most convenient way to focus is to pre-set the equipment to particular distances and magnifications, and then move towards and away from the subject, rather than to attempt to focus the lens underwater.

To increase the magnification, either a supplementary close-up lens or an extension ring is needed. With amphibious cameras, a supplementary lens can be fitted and removed underwater, whereas an extension ring cannot and will allow only close-up photography during one dive.

For fairly static subjects, such as corals, a close-up frame is very useful. This is set for a particular magnification, and is simply placed against the subject; the rectangular metal frame marks the boundaries of the picture area, with a centimetre or so to spare. Once set, the camera can be used without even having to look through the viewfinder — an important advantage when snorkelling, for there is little time for composing and framing. Active underwater life, however, generally reacts badly to the approach of one of these frames.

Close-ups Probably the greatest range of subject material is at close-up scales — small fish, anemones, and so on. Flash is essential, for depth of field, colour accuracy, and to freeze both subjects and camera movement. Static or slow-moving subjects, such as the anemone and tiger cowrie below left, can be photographed easily with a close-up frame assembly, but fish such as the clown fish below, will rarely tolerate the close approach of a frame.

CLOSE-UP TECHNIQUES are determined very much by the type of equipment. With an SLR in a housing, extension tubes give good results and the best way to focus is to leave the lens focusing ring in a set position and move the whole housing backwards or forwards. With a Nikonos, parallax and accurate distance measurement are the problems: a frame finder, as illustrated on page 232, is the most convenient system, used with either extension tubes or a supplementary lens. Flash is essential.

ARCHITECTURE

As a photographic subject, architecture has both sociological and artistic interest. In its simplest, functional forms it can reveal a considerable amount about a culture; on a grander level, frequently in public buildings, architecture can be an expression of the aesthetic. The scope for interpretation, however, is rather more limited than in most areas of photography. The subject matter is not only usually well defined in advance — a particular building — but there are practical restrictions, not the least being that there are normally only a few good viewpoints. As with any large-scale subject, such as landscapes, the photographer has very few possibilities for making alterations — even providing artificial lighting is a major, and costly, effort when shooting a large building.

THE SINGLE BUILDING

Most architectural photography tends to be of one distinct structure and there is a basic repertoire of skills that all architectural photographers have at their command.

Finding a satisfactory viewpoint is the first step, and if the object is to make a straightforward, frame-filling image, the alternatives should be reasonably obvious. The more enclosed the building, by others or by trees and the landscape, the fewer possibilities there are likely to be. The viewpoint is also determined by the choice of lens, and there may be a number of permutations, ranging from close camera positions with wide-angle lenses to distant views with telephotos. The wide-angle possibilities are the easiest to check, by walking around the building, but telephoto shots may not be so obvious and can take much longer to investigate. One method of speeding up the operation is to look for visible positions from the building itself — a hillside, for example, or the roof or balcony of another building. These will be the likeliest to give clear views.

One complicating factor is that viewpoint cannot be considered completely separately from lighting, and checking the camera positions at any one time of the day will not necessarily give a good idea of the building's appearance at others. In built-up surroundings, other buildings, if nearby or tall, will cast shadows that shift with the hour and are not necessarily easy to predict. Anticipating the lighting according to time and the weather comes with experience, and is vital.

Certain types of lighting have advantages, but this depends very much on the construction of the building and on its aspects. A low sun can be useful in lighting the side of a tall building evenly, and for a facade with strong relief (such as columns) one of the most effective lighting conditions is when the sunlight rakes it at a very sharp angle, throwing the relief into contrast. Buildings that have large frontages of glass, particularly tinted mirror finishes, may look interesting by reflected light — when they are in shadow but when the buildings opposite are brightly lit. The more diffuse light on a hazy or partly cloudy day may be better for other architecture by reducing contrast and giving a clearer image of the details. Probably the two lighting conditions that are the least useful in most situations are very light overcast weather, which will give a high building-to-sky contrast, and a high midday sun.

Filters can be useful in architectural photography. With black-and-white film, yellow, orange and red filters darken the appearance of clear skies, which will help to make a light-

Correcting convergence with an enlarger For an enlarged print, converting verticals can be corrected by tilting enlarger and print for the exposure. The technique is similar to the shape-changing camera movements so useful in view camera work (see page 19). Tilting the easel up at the base of the pictures enlarges the top of the picture more than the base, spreading out the converging verticals. When the angle of the easel is just right, the sides of this building appear vertical (as in the photograph below). Unfortunately, tilting the easel also causes keystoning of the whole picture, and it puts most of the image out of focus. This keystone shape can be cropped — providing there is sufficient room — and the picture can be re-focused by tilting the lens in the opposite direction to the tilt of the easel. The diagrams (right and below right) show how.

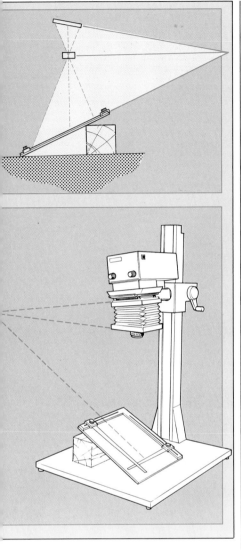

Correcting convergence without a shift lens Tilting the camera up to include the top of a building inevitably causes the verticals to converge (left). One way to reduce this effect is to move further away and use a telephoto lens — in the middle of the three pictures at left, a 400mm lens was used. Alternatively, a wide-angle lens can be aimed level to include the entire building, as in the bottom left picture, taken with a 20mm lens. This wide-angle shot can then be cropped in the printing to give the unconverging view below.

Distant view For many buildings, particularly those in a dense, built-up setting, a distant view with a telephoto lens may be clearer than a wide-angle shot from nearby (left).

A shift lens (below) contains a geared mechanism that shifts the lens elements laterally to project different areas of the lens image onto the film. So the top of even a tall building can be framed without tilting the camera upwards.

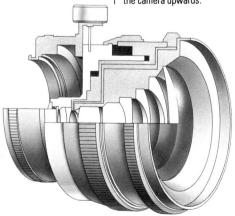

toned building stand out prominently. With colour film, a polarizing filter will have a similar effect at approximately right angles to the sun, although if used with a wide-angle lens will darken only a part of the sky, which can look odd. The reflections in the glass of modern city architecture can be controlled, also with a polarizing filter.

Converging verticals

An important technique in architectural photography is correcting 'converging verticals'. Any upward tilt of the camera will cause vertical lines to converge in the picture, and although this does not look unusual to the eye at the time (through familiarity), it normally does in a two-dimensional image. While there is no such thing as an aesthetic rule that the sides of a building must always appear to be parallel, a formal, no-frills photograph of a building is generally the better for lack of perspective distortion. In fact, while extreme convergence from a very wide-angle lens pointed strongly upwards may be acceptable through being obviously deliberate, mild convergence tends to look like an error.

With a telephoto lens from a distance, the camera is not

likely to have to be tilted very much, if at all, and convergence is mainly a problem with close, wide-angle shots. There are a few standard methods of overcoming it, all concerned with keeping the film vertical.

The simplest method, if the surroundings make it possible, is to elevate the camera to about half the height of the building; then it can be aimed horizontally and still include the top of the building in the image (given the right focal length). A window or balcony of another building nearby may give this opportunity. Another way of shooting horizontally with a regular fixed-body camera is to switch to a wider-angle of lens that will include the roof, and then to shoot from a position that has something of interest in the foreground to balance the composition.

The traditional method of correcting converging verticals, however, is to shift back either the lens or the film. This can be done with a view camera or with a specially designed, perspective-control lens on a small-format camera. In either case, the camera is aimed horizontally and the lens shifted upwards to slide the image of the building lower in the picture frame (with a view camera, shifting the film back downwards has virtually the same effect). This technique relies on having a lens that projects an image that is considerably larger than needed to cover the film format; sliding it up makes use of the edge of its projected image.

The same principle can be used with a regular wide-angle lens if a print is to be made. The photograph is taken horizontally, disregarding the 'empty' foreground which is cropped during printing.

If mild convergence has occurred already, it can be overcome to a degree in an enlargement by tilting both the printing frame that holds the paper *and* the negative carrier holding the film. The procedure is to tilt the print frame up at the base of the picture until the verticals are parallel, and then to tilt the negative carrier in the opposite direction until the entire picture is back in focus. The result will be a corrected image but converging frame edges, which must then be cropped by adjusting the easel mask.

The setting
While the full-frame portrait of a building is the most common approach, there are situations in which changing the scale of the view can be more interesting or relevant. Pulling back or using a shorter focal length of lens has the effect of putting a building in its context. This may be of architectural interest — if, for example, the building has been clearly designed to fit in with much older styles that surround it — or it may simply be attractive visually to include, for instance, a large area of sky.

Details
Decorative and structural details of architecture are often important enough to merit special treatment, and a close view of one of the capitals in a colonnade or a gargoyle on a stone church may be as relevant as an overall view. For high details, a long-focus lens is usually a satisfactory answer, although a higher camera position, such as from an upper window from a building opposite, is likely to be better than a view from ground level.

Mixed lighting
Photographing an interior by the light available often helps capture character but presents all kinds of problems with colour balance. In the picture above, the available light was a mixture of daylight, fluorescent lighting in the fireplace and the hall, and a tungsten spot. The film was therefore balanced for daylight; the fluorescent

Details Close views add variety to architectural shots, although getting in close to details can be difficult. A telephoto lens is useful, but high details do not always look their best from an upward-looking perspective, as used at left. For the interior sculpture below, only a level view was satisfactory and a raised platform was needed to carry the large-format camera and mains-powered flash.

INTERIORS

Technically, architectural interiors tend to be more difficult than outside views, principally because of the lighting, but also because viewpoints tend to be restrictive. There are certain differences between the way in which interiors are perceived and how they appear in a photograph — the most important being that they are seen by means of looking around rather than at a single glance. To come close to this effect, the photograph needs to be taken with a very wide-angle lens, and then reproduced large enough for the viewer's eye to travel around the image, taking in all the details. The latter is not always practical, and while a wide-angle lens of some kind is nearly always necessary in order to give some sense of a room, when reproduced small, the details that it shows tend to be lost.

Lighting often needs special attention because, without extra lamps or flash, the levels are low for most film, and because the contrast is usually high. Most interiors have windows, and this gives a choice of lighting conditions, not only depending on natural light at different times of the day and in different weather, but also between day-time and night-time shooting. At one end of the scale of alternatives, daylight alone can be used, at the other, room lighting only, or any combination. In either case, contrast is likely to be high: the light from one window or doorway falls off very

lights were covered with weak magenta gels, and the tungsten spot left uncorrected to add warmth.

Balancing photographic and available lights To light the foreground adequately in this library, additional photographic lights were essential. Yet the photographer wished to include the window. The set-up chosen was daylight-balanced tungsten lighting (with blue gels) close to the camera and behind the nearer stand of shelves, and magenta gels taped over the concealed fluorescent lights. Even with an 800 W lamp bounced off the wall next to the camera (see below) and tilt movement on the 5 × 5in view camera, a six minute exposure at f45 on ISO 64 film was needed to give enough depth of field to show the details of the old ledger and the room beyond. Polaroid tests in black-and-white and colour were made to check the balance of lighting for both intensity and colour.

rapidly across the room, while most existing room lamps tend to create pools of light with dark shadow areas in between.

The camera angle can solve some of these difficulties, and a neutral gradated filter can compensate for any steady fall off in light across the room. More commonly, however, photographic lighting is introduced. This can be used as an unobtrusive addition to the existing lighting — basically filling in shadows — or it can be used to create a new lighting design from scratch. The danger is that extra lighting might destroy the character of the interior.

If either daylight or the existing artificial lamps are to be the basis for the lighting of the photograph, the colour temperature will affect the film and filtration used. Daylight is 5500K or higher, domestic tungsten between about 2700K and 3000K, and fluorescent can be unpredictable (but most likely to need a 30 magenta filter with daylight film). As with the lighting considered for reportage shots indoors (see pages 202-3), these conditions will suggest flash or tungsten, possibly with colour-balancing gels. Placing magenta gels over fluorescent strip-lighting balances them with daylight and flash.

Even with additional lighting, exposures are likely to be long and a tripod is almost always needed. This is especially true if good depth of field is required since the aperture must be small. To avoid severe reciprocity failure in colour photography, tungsten film (which is designed for long exposures) is often a better choice than daylight film, even if an 85 B filter has to be used to balance it to daylight.

In large interiors, where the addition of full-scale lighting is not practical, an alternative is to work in darkness, with the camera's shutter open, and a flash unit fired repeatedly in different parts of the view (keeping the flash unit itself out of sight of the camera).

STYLES

Architectural photography provides less scope for individual interpretation than most other fields and this, naturally, makes for fewer detectable individual styles. Apart from certain practical restrictions in viewpoint and lighting, the creative input of the architect is often so strong that it dominates any picture. Architectural photography certainly calls for a high level of craftsmanship, but it tends to be descriptive rather than imaginative.

This descriptive bias has had an influence on the working methods, quite apart from such practical needs as shift lenses to avoid perspective distortion. It has noticeably encouraged the traditional values of image quality: good resolution of detail and a clear range of tones. Not surprisingly, large-formats are still used extensively by professionals for the greater amount of information they can carry and the reduction in apparent graininess (because of more moderate enlargements than would be needed from a small-format film).

Nevertheless, within these more limited parameters, some differences in style can be seen, although some of the distinctive ones verge on other fields of photography, such as urban landscapes.

Documentary

The documentary style is the most common style of architectural photography, and is shown well in the work of

Ceilings Angle of view becomes something of a problem when the ceiling of an interior is important enough to be included in the shot. Even an extreme wide angle lens, if used horizontally to prevent converging verticals, will not show most of the ceiling. One approach is to aim the camera at a fairly steep angle to take in most of the ceiling and some of the rest of the interior (below). If the shot is formally composed, as here, convergence is not likely to be objectionable.

Church and cathedral interiors need long exposures; the exposure for the shot at right of Chartres cathedral (with a 20mm lens) was four minutes at f3.5 on ISO 64 film. Detailed

selections of stained glass windows can be made easily from the floor with a telephoto lens. Colour balance depends on the weather; a clear blue sky is the most difficult to judge without a colour temperature meter.

Eugène Atget, who deliberately worked at the times of day when no people were around, producing quiet, unspectacular, but carefully observed images, mainly of his native Paris.

Graphic/Abstract
In contrast to the formal approach of the documentary architectural photographers, a number of modern photographers have abandoned traditional portrayal of buildings in favour of more extreme, dramatic design. This has been encouraged — and even made possible — by the deliberate originality of some modern architecture, using strong and unusual shapes combined with surface finishes such as all-glass. Strong camera angles, unusual viewpoints, eccentric composition and, sometimes, high contrast, are the principal techniques.

Functional
While the majority of architectural photography excludes people from its images (even to the extent of using long exposures to blur their passage in unavoidably populated shots), one style deliberately shows the buildings as they are used. Most architecture is, after all, designed functionally rather than for decoration alone. Differences in scale between buildings and the people who work and live in them, however, make successful juxtapositions difficult.

URBAN LANDSCAPES

Although the focus of architectural photography is the design of buildings, the edges of this field merge with the wider issue — the artificial landscape of which buildings are a part. Photographic interests reflect cultural changes, and as cityscapes and other urban environments become more and more a part of most people's lives, they are developing into a distinct field of photography, with its own pattern of techniques, approaches, and styles. Sociologically, this is a field that provides ample scope for comment and interpretation, from a celebration of new and dramatic development to criticism of population and poor conditions for living. Graphically, too, there is plenty of interesting material, from traditional settlements that fit harmoniously into their surroundings to unrestricted industrial growth — more variety, perhaps, than in natural landscapes.

One of the consequences of this variety is that it is possible to select very different impressions of the same place according to the photographer's choice. A typical situation might be the coverage of one city lasting several days, and in this time the usual approach will be to get some personal feeling for the place and to convey this through a series of pictures. Most photographers aim for a *distinctive* set of images, a combination of views that typify that city — at least in the photographer's eye — and set it apart visually from others. It is, of course, possible to show similar views in *different* cities, if the object were, for example, to stress the sameness of urban environments, but searching for the distinctions tends to be more common, if only because it is usually more interesting.

If each place does have a definable character and this can be translated in visual terms, it may take time and research to uncover. To avoid wasting time, it may be necessary to begin shooting before the full impression of a city begins to take shape, and this means working to a predetermined plan — the kind of approach that will work almost anywhere. Indeed, the standard plan of action for investigating a city is often the best way of developing an idea of its character; some of its special nature will only gradually become apparent.

Research into subjects and viewpoints is generally easier for cities than many other subjects, as they tend to be well-documented. There are, to begin with, other photographs

Overall view A high building is a prime site for an overall view of a city. But there can be considerable variety. The pictures here were all taken within an hour from the top of one building in the centre of Caracas. With a good viewpoint such as this, it is standard technique to explore the opportunities with the full range of lenses available. A panoramic wide-angle view (above), is supplemented by more concentrated telephoto shots. The photograph upper right was taken with a 400mm lens; that far right with a teleconverter added (effectively 800mm); while a 180mm lens was used for the pair to the right, taken an hour later.

Clear views Clear establishing shots of downtown city areas are rarely tidy. Foreground obstructions, such as telegraph wires, can be avoided by finding a different viewpoint, but there may be a variety of other obstructions. One of the most common is temporary activity, such as construction or renovation work. The problem with the shot of Singapore (right), is not that cranes and scaffolding are visually untidy, but that they are evidence that the view will soon be different. To include the construction work would shorten the picture's useful life.

Downtown activity Another basic city photograph shows the maximum activity of people and traffic at the busiest time of day. The busiest time varies from place to place — in some cities, early morning, for example, is the busiest time. In others it is the lunch hour. But the busiest time may not necessarily coincide with the best lighting — an early sunset in winter restricts shooting in the afternoon rush-hour. So the shooting time must be something of a compromise. A slightly elevated viewpoint looking along the busiest main street generally gives a good impression. This late afternoon view of Srinagar was taken from the rise of a bridge.

already taken and published in guide books, postcards, travel magazines and other places. These are invaluable, not for plagiarism, but to show some of the problems and opportunities, especially of viewpoint, faced by other photographers. With experience, it is possible to gather a great deal of useful information from other pictures of a city, such as good times of day for lighting, and the degree of freedom or restriction in framing and composing from a viewpoint (see caption on page 245). Guide books of all kinds, even unillustrated, are useful, as is a map (particularly if used from viewpoint such as the top of a building or a tower).

Many historically famous cities, particularly those well visited by tourists, can be interpreted in many different ways. Kyoto, for example, is the former capital of Japan and renowned for its temples and carefully preserved culture. However, the Kyoto postcards and typical travel documentaries would be unrecognizable to a visitor arriving by train, for a first overall view of the city shows it to be little different from most other modern Japanese cities. The special character that Kyoto is supposed to have needs to be looked for — in an undiscriminating glance it appears to be overwhelmed by the less special office blocks and apartments, cars and factories. Both ways of looking at the city, the selective and the apparent, are equally valid but call for some decisions on the part of the photographer on approach and intention. The matter of style in urban landscape photography, discussed below, is important.

Clear views

In a general coverage of a town or city, one of the top priorities is to find one or more overall views, to include some of the principal features. These are often surprisingly difficult to find, because the height and density of construction at the centre tend to get in the way. Surrounding buildings, pylons, overhead cables and so on are common obstructions.

In many cities there are publicized high viewpoints — the top of the Eiffel tower in Paris, the Empire State Building in New York, and their equivalents in other cities. These are obviously worth checking out, although if glassed-in may not be so useful. But any high-rise building is a potential viewpoint though special permission may be needed to gain access. If access to the roof is restricted, an upper floor window or balcony may be adequate.

Hills, in or around the city, are another place to find overall views though they are usually far enough away to make a long-focus lens essential.

A third method of gaining height is from an aircraft, helicopter or blimp, but the practicality of aerial photography varies greatly from city to city. At its easiest, some resort cities, particularly in America, have inexpensive facilities for tourists, such as short over-flights in a blimp or helicopter. In other countries, rates for hiring aircraft are exorbitant and overflying is forbidden anyway for reasons of security and safety. Nevertheless, if possible and affordable, an aerial viewpoint is always worth trying.

An alternative to a high viewpoint is one that gives a clear view across an open space. In cities, the best places for this are likely to be large parks, and across water (a river, lake or the sea).

With all these viewpoints, time of day and weather are a prime consideration, and more than one visit is often needed: to check out the view, and for shooting when the lighting is appropriate. For as attractive an image as possible, a low sun is often the best choice of natural light, but a useful alternative, not so dependent on the weather, is evening, at the point when the city lights are switched on but when there is still some twilight to give an outline to the buildings.

From high viewpoints, particularly high-rise buildings in the centre of a city, there may be a number of different shots that can be taken with several focal lengths of lens. Because of the narrower angle of view, there is always more choice with a telephoto, but a wider-angle lens can give a broader, less selective view. If it is possible to look down without obstruction, the horizon line can be placed high in the frame (or even left out of the composition altogether). If there is a foreground in the way, an alternative is to place the horizon low — this is likely to be more successful with an interesting sky. Horizontal views across open spaces usually need a telephoto lens to cut out irrelevant detail in the foreground and middle distance.

Faces of the city

In searching for variety both visually and in content, it is usually possible to find examples of most of the following types of picture in a large city. In towns, the variety is likely to be less. In many of these, some kind of juxtaposition can be used to emphasize certain features: for instance, between people and buildings, or between slums and better housing.

■ **DOWNTOWN ACTIVITY** The downtown area of any city is likely to be the most consistently busy. For individual close-ups of people, basic candid photography at street level is likely to be the best approach, but for more general views, some elevation is needed: overhead pedestrian walkways, overpasses, upper storey shopping malls and cafés are among the many places. To enhance the impression of crowds on sidewalks, choose the busiest times of day, such as when offices are about to open and at lunch-time, and use a telephoto lens from slightly above and head-on for compressed perspective.

■ **COMMUTING RUSH-HOUR** Most cities have a massive influx of commuters every working day. The effect is most concentrated at bottlenecks in the commuter flow, early in the morning and late in the afternoon. For crowds of people, the exits of railway and subway stations are usually good locations, as are the walkways and bridges that lead from them. For traffic, freeway ramps and converging lanes are typically congested. For massed views of traffic actually on an urban freeway, a view of an underpass from ground level is usually effective, with a telephoto lens.

■ **NIGHT LIGHTS** Entertainment districts offer the brightest concentration of illuminated signs and street lights; otherwise late shopping nights offer similar conditions. Tripod-mounted shots allow depth of field to be improved even with telephoto shots, and slow film for better resolution, but movement of crowds and people is inevitably blurred (most

Rush-hour One or two locations in a city have a concentration of commuters, especially the 'rush-hour'. In London thousands of commuters stream across London Bridge each day to reach the City from railway stations to the south of the river. From one location — an office block on the City side — a long-focus (600mm) lens emphasizes the crowding.

suitable for long-shots and details of neon signs, etc.). Fast film (ISO 400-1600) and wide apperture lenses (f1.2-f2) allow hand-held shooting. Flash has a limited range, but can be used to help general street views if combined with a slow shutter speed (this can give some blurring and overlapping of images).

■ **DAWN STREETS** For a contrasting atmosphere, downtown and business district streets are usually quite empty in the very early morning, particularly on non-working days. In east-west aligned streets, or areas where the buildings are low, a raking sun can give a very different impression of a city.

■ **FAMOUS SIGHTS** These are the obligatory tourist views, well-publicized and easy to find. They can usually be treated architecturally (see page 241) but also in relation to the constant stream of visitors to the cityscape around.

Night lights One way to produce an attractive image from ordinary downtown city areas is to photograph at night. The picture then depends very much on how late in the evening buildings are used and on how early darkness falls. Working hours in Tokyo offices are late by Western standards, as this view of Shinjuku (right) from a hotel room shows. The exposure is rarely critical but a 30 magenta filter may help colour balance where there is a great deal of fluorescent lighting.

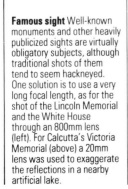

Famous sight Well-known monuments and other heavily publicized sights are virtually obligatory subjects, although traditional shots of them tend to seem hackneyed. One solution is to use a very long focal length, as for the shot of the Lincoln Memorial and the White House through an 800mm lens (left). For Calcutta's Victoria Memorial (above) a 20mm lens was used to exaggerate the reflections in a nearby artificial lake.

Dawn streets The central square of this well-visited South American colonial town (above) is normally crowded with vehicles during the day, but at first light it regains something of its original atmosphere.

Quiet corners Among the predictable downtown architecture there may be interesting remnants from earlier days. This balcony in the French Quarter of New Orleans (below) contrasts strongly with the modern.

■ **QUIET CORNERS** Most cities contain pockets that have escaped the normal pace of development. Unless intentionally preserved and used for tourism, such as in the case of the French quarter in New Orleans, the reasons for the existance of these small 'villages' may be accidental and their future not assured.

■ **INDUSTRIAL SECTORS** These are normally on the outskirts of cities, or in poorer districts. Large developments, such as oil refineries, port areas, martialling yards and power stations make the most impressive subjects, although access to most is severely restricted. Nearby freeways may sometimes give the clearest views, if elevated, but then there are likely to be difficulties in stopping.

■ **DORMITORY SUBURBS** Socio-economic differences are likely to be reflected in strong visual differences. Terraced housing and apartment block complexes appear distinctive, especially from a distance with a telephoto or from the air.

■ **RECREATION** Parks, fairgrounds, nearby beaches, lakes and river banks can provide opportunities for photographing large-scale recreation, mainly at weekends.

■ **FREEWAY CULTURE** Where automobiles are heavily used, as in California and in most of North America, a particular type of urban landscape has evolved, featuring large areas of concrete and roadway, a noticeable lack of people on foot, and prominent advertising hoardings and displays. This is usually at its most typical between urban centres.

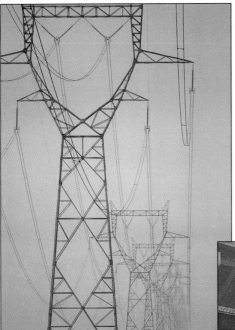

STYLES

While individual photographs of towns and cities are nothing new, the field of urban landscape photography has been recognized as distinct relatively recently. Although it could be argued that a simple mixture of architectural and street photography would deliver similar results, the fact that there are recognizable styles of approach is evidence enough that the urban landscape is a major subject that provokes different reactions in photographers. As already touched on above, the immense variety of subject material, from overall views to details of street furniture, encourages synthesis — the idea of analyzing an urban environment, one's own impressions of it, and producing an individual summation. As the complexity of cities is such that they cannot adequately be summarized in one or two pictures, most photographers that work in this field tend to see the end product of a single subject as a set of

Industrial sectors can make strong images. A long-focus lens (to compress the perspective), small aperture (to keep all the visible pylons sharply focused), and a nearly-end-on camera position (to show as much of the row as possible) made the most of the army of pylons above. The people provide a sense of scale (right).

Freeway culture Arguably at its most extreme in Southern California, the scenery of the freeway has a strong, distinct atmosphere of its own. One of its features is a strong element of the bizarre, as in the backlot of a filling station east of Los Angeles (below).

Pictorial Just as with natural landscapes, cities and other urban scenery offer plenty of opportunities for the visually attractive. The techniques are in principle the same, and include, as in this view of the Transam building in San Francisco, strong compositional design, exploration of viewpoint, and the use of the traditionally attractive natural light early or late in the day.

Social commentary An emphasis on the social aspects of urban landscapes frequently shows the less satisfactory conditions of cities. The views below and right are both of Barrios in Caracas, Venezuela, and are actually located within the view shown by the main wide-angle photograph at the top of pages 242 and 243. The direct comparison is a salutary one. In this style, the choice of subject is clearly the main element, but the visual treatment may also be distinctive. Prettification tends to work against the strength of social comment shots, and is usually avoided — in principle, it *is* possible to use pictorial techniques with a depressing subject for irony, but the effect may not be obvious to the viewer and so fail. While this does not necessarily suggest waiting for unattractive lighting or poor weather in the same way that a pictorialist photographer might wait for sunset, such conditions obviously help the picture's case. Similarly, viewpoints that concentrate on the worst aspects of a scene will heighten the negative responses.

People in the landscape One of the principal distinctions between urban landscape and architecture as a motif is that in the former, people are frequently an important element, as in the photograph (left) of a Tokyo intersection.

Formalist In city landscapes, the abundance of geometric shapes in the architecture — shadows, reflections and so on — makes it relatively easy to experiment with design. In the photograph at right, in downtown Los Angeles, a 20mm lens helps to make graphic use of the reflections in an angled window.

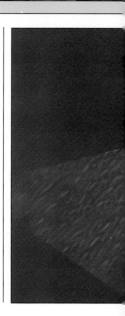

images — in other words a photo-essay. In art photography, the result is likely to be a glossy book; in professional editorial photography, magazines, such as *National Geographic* and *Geo*, or book publishers like *Time Life*, present picture stories on specific locations.

The following styles are identifiable, although a reportage photographer working on an assignment may well cover more than one in an effort to fulfil what is often seen editorially as a main criterion: variety of image. The subject naturally encourages variety, and this can, therefore, make an individual style less distinctive. As with other subjects that are complex or cover different areas, it is not uncommon for book and magazine publishers to draw on more than one source of photograph.

Anthropocentric
In a way that is often difficult for the straight architectural photographer, charged with shooting specific structures, the environment of towns, cities and industry can be shown in relation to the people who inhabit them. Indeed, avoiding people in an image often takes some effort, such as working very early or late in the day or waiting a very long time for the view to clear.

The techniques for showing the urban environment as a populated one may often be those of candid street photography, but the aims are generally restricted to showing how the surroundings affect people. Various kinds of juxtaposition of people are usual.

Pictorial
Cities can be experienced, and therefore photographed, in a variety of moods from criticism to enjoyment. The pictorial style of urban landscape photography seeks to show the most attractive versions, enhancing the appearance with judicious points of view and glamorous lighting, such as at dawn and dusk. A regular, non-critical report by a magazine, for example, would normally include one or two pictorial, evocative images of a location, probably to open or close the article.

Social commentary
Probing deeper and more critically into the subject material, some photographers concentrate on showing the social consequences of urban life. Although two of the most common, or most stock, responses in this style are 'urban blight' and 'concrete jungle', social commentary can be positive.

Formalist
The resurgence of formalism in the late 1970s among American photographers such as Joel Meyerowitz and Stephen Shore embraced the urban landscape as its special subject of interest. This is not the first time that this happened — Edward Weston did similar things several decades earlier — but the modern movement has done much to show how those urban surroundings that have *not* been designed to be architecturally significant can be interesting photographic subjects. This includes, for example, gas stations, diners, and freeways, but treated in a manner previously reserved for cathedrals and other famous buildings. Large-format photography is common in this style.

AERIAL PHOTOGRAPHY

Aerial photography for surveys and reconnaissance is a highly specialized technique, using special large-format, stereo-image cameras attached to the air frame. But a wide range of unusual, and often spectacular, pictures of the world from the air can be taken with an ordinary camera. From the air, familiar scenes take on a new and fascinating perspective and the landscape can reveal eyecatching patterns difficult to appreciate at ground level. The meanders of a slow-flowing river, for example, or the lines of paths in a city park, can only be seen properly from the air. From a height of 600m (2 000ft) or more, many individual objects cease to be easily recognizable, but take on a fresh appearance as part of a larger grouping: yachts in a marina, for example, might look more like outgrowths of crystals, while terraced housing can look like a frieze for the pattern of streets.

Pictures of the ground from above can be taken from any kind of aircraft, but some are much more suitable than others. The least satisfactory of all are commercial passenger aircraft, for several reasons. Most of the flying time is at high altitude, from which very little can be distinguished, even with a moderate telephoto lens, and ultraviolet haze and clouds generally obscure the view. A further obstacle is the thick, curved, often scratched window of the plane which restricts the view and reduces image quality severely.

Probably the best kind of aircraft for photography is a high-winged, single-engined light aircraft with room for between about three and five people, such as the Cessna Skywagon. These planes combine the advantages of good visibility, manoeuvrability at slow speeds, and low fuel costs. Manoeuvrability is important in order to be able to position the aircraft precisely for a particular shot, and this is easier if the aircraft can be flown slowly without the risk of stalling. Although the slow speed of such a single-engined model increases the time it takes to reach a shooting location, the low flying costs more than compensate.

The high wing is also important, for it allows a reasonably unrestricted view through the window of one of the doors, and if the wheels are retractable, so much the better. It is important, incidentally, to be able to open or remove a window, as any glass or plastic will make the image poorer. On most Cessnas, the pilot's window can be opened in flight. An even better view can be obtained by removing the door of some planes — though, of course, photographer and equipment must be safely strapped in.

The most expensive to hire of all forms of aerial camera platform are helicopters, but if the budget is not an important issue (on certain professional assignments, for instance), they provide unrivalled manoeuvrability. Removing a door or window is usually easy and as the lift comes from overhead rotors, downward visibility is excellent. An important precaution, however, when using a wide-angle lens, is not to include the rotor blades in shot; they may not be apparent to the eye but at a shutter speed of $\frac{1}{250}$ second or faster, they will register clearly in a photograph.

Planning and preparation

To make the most efficient use of expensive flying time, a flight must be planned as thoroughly as possible on the ground. This is particularly important if the photographer

Equipment and film
While virtually any camera that can be held by hand is suitable for aerial photography, a smaller camera is easier to use. A 35mm SLR is ideal, particularly when loaded with a slow or medium film for high resolution — though high-speed film may be needed if weather conditions change or if the flight continues through sunset. Because results are so unpredictable and because flying time is expensive, most photographers will take 10 or more rolls of 36-exposure film and shoot hundreds of frames to ensure that they have at least some usable pictures.

The wide-angle limit for lenses is set by the maximum clear view from the aircraft — normally the vertical angle from the wings above to the wheels underneath. Focal length is limited very much by camera-shake: and only the most experienced, steady-handed photographer will use a lens much longer than 200mm.

and pilot have not worked together: each may be unaware of the specific needs and problems of the other, and the noise level inside a light aircraft with the window open is sufficiently high to make in-flight communication difficult.

The first step is to define the objectives. With specific locations, the route and time can be plotted on an aeronautical map, and the photographer can brief the pilot on the height, the altitude of the plane and the time needed to take the photographs. It is rare that one single pass over the subject will be sufficient. Usually the most efficient approach is to circulate at a distance. The size of the circle depends on the angle of view of the lens and how close to vertical the shot will be. Pilots unused to this kind of photography often tend to circle too tightly, so that the subject is almost out of sight beneath the aircraft. The pilot should bank quite steeply towards the subject for the clearest view. Throttling back reduces vibration, so reducing the risk of camera-shake.

Even when there is no specific subject, some kind of preplanning and flying brief helps. For instance, the pilot should be aware that the wider the angle of the lens, the less manoeuvrability the photographer has. The pilot should also be aware that film-changing and lens-changing take time.

Weather and lighting conditions are crucial in aerial photography. Even a slight haze barely noticeable at ground level is likely to reduce contrast and colour significantly from 300-600m (1000-2000ft), the normal flying height for most photographic subjects. Photographing down through atmosphere is much the same as long distance telephoto photography on the ground, and clear air is essential. Usually, strong sidelighting from a low morning or afternoon sun is also needed, to bring out the texture and relief of the landscape. Unfortunately, in most parts of the world, these times of day are the least predictable in terms of weather, as even a distant cloud bank can obscure the sun. As well as checking broadcast weather reports, it usually pays to recruit local knowledge — local pilots and airport staff are among the most reliable sources of information.

Shooting techniques

Vibration and airflow are major problems, making a fast shutter speed essential: $\frac{1}{500}$ second is ideal, $\frac{1}{250}$ second usually satisfactory, but anything less needs care and luck. With standard and wide-angle lenses, the focus setting can be left at infinity; a telephoto lens may need focusing. In all cases, depth of field is virtually irrelevant, and the maximum aperture will allow a faster shutter speed. The best image quality is through an open window, but the airflow will tug at the camera if it is held too far out. Under no circumstances should the camera, hands or arms be rested against any part of the aircraft — it will simply transmit vibration. With an upwards-hinged window, as in a Cessna, it may be best to leave it closed for take-off and landing, opening it during flight for shooting; the pressure of the airflow will hold it steady against the underside of the wing without the need to prop it open.

As well as using an ultraviolet or polarizing filter, the most effective way of reducing the effects of haze is to fly low, using a wide-angle lens, rather than high with a telephoto — the lower the aircraft, the less haze there is to shoot through.

STUDIO PHOTOGRAPHY

On location and in the field, the photographer is completely at the mercy of the prevailing conditions. The subject must, on the whole, be accepted as it stands, and if the lighting and weather are unsuitable, there is no choice but to wait, or give up the shot altogether. A studio, in contrast, offers the photographer almost total control over every aspect of the photograph. In particular, it allows photographers to arrange the setting and the lighting in just the way they want.

Studio photography inevitably loses some of the sense of reality that is important in much location work; studio photographs are indeed more artificial. But for many photographers the degree of control possible in the studio more than compensates for this loss. In commercial fields such as advertising and fashion photography, where the photographer must be able to guarantee results, the predictability of the studio environment is invaluable. Yet in fine art photography as well, the studio is clearly attractive.

Studio layout

Photographic studios can vary enormously, from giant purpose-built rooms to makeshift tents, but in all, space is at a premium. There must be space to build sets and space to store set material; space to set up the subject; space to move lights around; space for the camera; and space for the photographer. Yet because of the range of equipment and material used in the studio, it is very easy for it to become untidy and cluttered. So meticulous organization of the studio space and arrangement of equipment and fixtures are vital.

While the floor area is a natural place to stand and store equipment, it is better to keep the floor clear for photography. There are many ways of keeping things off the floor. Both walls and ceiling are often underused, yet can carry a great deal of the equipment needed in a studio. In a reasonably high studio, equipment can be stored above head-height and lights can be swung from the ceiling. Ceiling fittings include plates attached firmly to a beam and carrying a hook, lug or screw attachment, and ceiling tracks that allow lighting attachments to be moved along them on a runner. From either of these, lamps can be suspended at a fixed height or, better still, raised and lowered.

Cupboards and shelves can be kept out of the way by placing high on walls, and extra space can be saved by fitting sliding rather than hinged entrance doors — and attaching cupboards to these. Trianguar corner shelving and cupboards can also occupy otherwise unused space. Tools, tape and cables may be more conveniently kept on a peg board attached to a wall, or on a castored trolley.

Among the largest objects needed in a studio are flats (normally used as lighting reflectors) and background materials, and they must usually be stored on the floor so that they can be moved quickly into place. Background paper rolls can be stacked on end. Rigid flat surfaces, such as perspex sheets and wooden boards, are usually best stacked against a wall — though as they tend to slide out, it helps to fit either a stop on the floor, or a simple frame rack to hold them upright.

Working surfaces are often needed in studios for construction and assembly of props and settings. These take up less space if collapsible — for instance, a hinged work surface fixed to a wall or folding trestles and a plain flat board.

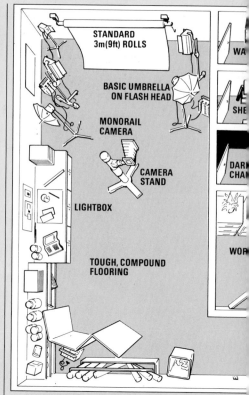

STANDARD 3m(9ft) ROLLS

BASIC UMBRELLA ON FLASH HEAD

MONORAIL CAMERA

CAMERA STAND

LIGHTBOX

TOUGH, COMPOUND FLOORING

WA

SHE

DAR CHA

WOR

Although more time-consuming than a simple, drawn plan, a scale model of the space available is by no means an extravagant preparation. it makes it easier to visualize exactly how the studio will function and, at the same time, gives a good impression of the height. After calculating the shooting angle from the most commonly used lenses (**1**), the shooting area can be transferred to the floor of the model (**2**). The height of studio equipment can be calculated (**3**), and the model gradually fitted fully (**4**).

PREPARING A STUDIO DESIGN The usual starting point for the design of a studio layout is the space that is available. At the least, the minimum shooting area should be calculated, then this fitted into the plan in the most convenient place. Other equipment and fittings needs, all of which depend on the kind of work the studio will be used for, should then be worked into this plan.

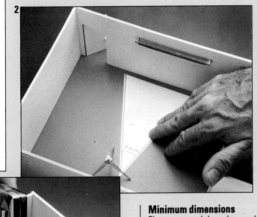

Minimum dimensions
Plans or a model can be used to calculate what type of shot will be possible in a given space. Room sets, for instance, normally need a great deal of room, but by planning a view that takes in just a corner, and by bouncing light off wall-mounted reflectors, some shots can be undertaken in average studio spaces (below).

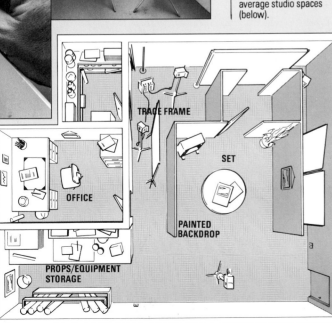

TRACE FRAME

SET

OFFICE

PAINTED BACKDROP

PROPS/EQUIPMENT STORAGE

STUDIO DESIGN
The design of a studio has a lasting effect on future work and demands careful consideration of all the variables, balancing cost with the ideal environment for the type of photography it is to be used for:

Size and configuration
The larger the subject, the greater the working distance, and so, the larger the set area must be. The largest subjects in most studio photography are room sets and vehicles, followed by group full-length portraits, after which in scale are single full-length portraits, head-and-shoulders portraits and the majority of still-life shots. In addition to the camera-to-subject distance (itself depending very much on the lens focal length) extra space must be allowed in the calculations for light fittings, reflectors, shades and ancillary items such as supports for props, wind machines, and others.

REMOVE AMBIENT LIGHTING
Except in a daylight studio, all extraneous lighting must be excluded. Windows can be boarded over, painted opaquely, fitted with special blinds that run in grooves, or shuttered. If flash is being used, complete light-proofing is not necessary for shooting, but will nevertheless help in setting up shots and judging the illumination from the flash unit's modelling lamps.

Neutral setting
Any colour in the studio walls, floor and ceiling may create a colour cast in the photograph. So the studio must usually be painted in a neutral colour — either black, white or a shade of grey. Black kills all reflections, so the lighting can be built up very precisely, but a black studio can be oppressive to work in day after day. White gives a lighter and more airy atmosphere, but may need masking off with black cards for some shots. Grey is a compromise.

Lighting equipment
The choice of lighting equipment (see pages 74-89) depends not only on the type of photography, but also on the space available. If space

Backgrounds and settings
Again, the size of these depends on the type of subject, and storage requirements vary. Larger backgrounds, such as for group portraits, generally need some hanging system, whereas horizontal surfaces for small-scale still lifes can be placed on an ordinary table, trestles or trolley. In virtually all cases, however, a variety of stock backgrounds is necessary.

Flooring and walls
Because of heavy wear, and the use of wheeled equipment, the best flooring is both smooth and durable, such as compound tiles. Walls and ceiling are usually painted a neutral colour. For continuous-light photography — that is, tungsten rather than flash — the floor must be solid, for camera-shake is a potential problem at slow shutter speeds — passing traffic or just the movement of people around the studio may vibrate the camera.

is limited, off-floor integral flash may be more convenient than cable-connected, free-standing power units and separate heads. Also, lighting modifiers that attach directly to the lamp are usually more manageable than separate trace frames and the like.

Storage and access
The largest items regularly used must be borne in mind when deciding the size of both the entrance(s) and the non-working storage space. The doorway may need to be enlarged.

Power and utilities
Standard domestic electricity supply may not be adequate for heavy power requirements, such as from high-wattage tungsten lamps and heavy-duty flash capacitors. Separate circuits may need to be installed with power outlets and fuses to match. Flash capacitor units draw power in surges. Plumbing may also be needed, in food photography, for example.

Ventilation and air conditioning
Light-proofing usually seals off the studio from outside air, so that an extractor or air conditioning unit may have to be installed.

Daylight studios

While the majority of studios use artificial lighting — either tungsten or flash — natural daylight has certain special advantages for certain kinds of work, notably portraits. While it is harder to control, daylight from skylights and windows can give a large area of diffuse illumination which it is not always easy to achieve when working with small, point-source lamps. The preconditions for a daylight studio are a relatively large window area and a north-facing aspect (in the northern hemisphere) — this will give diffuse lighting even on the sunniest day. A top-storey traditional artist's studio with sloping skylights is probably ideal, but it is quite important that the room does not receive direct sunlight, which needs diffusing and, depending on the weather, can create change-able conditions. Clouds passing regularly in front of the sun both lower the light levels significantly and raise the colour temperature, which can interfere with shooting.

For some measure of control, dark blinds can be fitted; the more the better, as then the size of the light source and its direction can be adjusted. A second set of transluscent blinds can be useful if direct sunlight is likely to strike the room for at least part of the day. To control contrast, large white and black flats can be used to fill in shadows and hold back reflec-tions respectively. One of the great advantages of a daylight studio is that there is little additional expense involved — except if colour film is used, when a colour temperature meter is absolutely necessary, as the eye accommodates colour casts too easily to judge them accurately. Colour-balancing filters of different strengths, both straw-coloured (81 and 85 series) and bluish (80 and 82 series) are also needed.

Temporary studio space

A temporary studio converted for only a few hours from a living room is as valid as any full-time professional layout. But even for a temporary studio, it pays to plan a system that involves the least disturbance to the existing room layout and furniture and which can be applied quickly.

Just as with the design of a permanent studio, it is import-ant to work out exactly how much space will be needed: the size of a typical subject area, the angle of view of the lenses that will be used, and the working distance from camera to subject. The height of most modern domestic rooms tends to be low, and this can restrict the angle of view. Carpet is generally unsatisfactory as studio flooring: not only does it give under pressure and so is less steady for a tripod and other supports, but the legs of equipment may damage it. If it can be rolled back, so much the better, but otherwise a firm sur-face, such as plastic matting or a solid board, can be overlaid, at least for the camera tripod.

Total black-out is often difficult to achieve in a temporary studio, but if flash is used rather than tungsten, this may not matter, particularly if the shooting area is located away from the windows. For occasions when all lighting must be excluded, large black cloth drapes can be hung over windows and, as a last resort, the photographs can be taken at night. Regular mains-powered studio lamps can be used as well under these temporary circumstances as in a permanent studio although the power-loading of the circuit *must* be checked. But because a small room may heat up relatively

TEMPORARY STUDIO To show what can be done, the steps needed to convert this fairly typical modern living room (above) to both a still-life studio and a small portrait space are outlined. The room has the advantage of tiled rather than carpeted flooring, but the common problems of large window area and a low ceiling.

quickly under high-wattage tungsten lamps, flash is usually easier to use.

In a low-ceilinged room, lamp installations may be a problem. For standing portraits in particular, the normal lamp position is quite high, and if a diffusing attachment is fitted — an area light for example, or an umbrella — even more space is needed. This may restrict the kind of shooting that can be undertaken, but one advantage of a low ceiling is that, if painted white, it makes a good reflector to diffuse light.

A small basic studio (far left) Even within this modest 5 × 6m (16 × 20ft) basement, careful and economic use of the space makes it possible to work on two small sets at one time — and still have room to walk about. Note the use of expanding poles and ceiling fittings for the lights.

A daylight studio Existing skylights (near left) allow the photographer to work with natural light as well as flash or tungsten, though blinds and diffusing materials may sometimes be needed to alter the lighting quality.

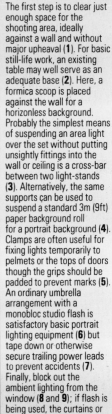

The first step is to clear just enough space for the shooting area, ideally against a wall and without major upheaval (**1**). For basic still-life work, an existing table may well serve as an adequate base (**2**). Here, a formica scoop is placed against the wall for a horizonless background. Probably the simplest means of suspending an area light over the set without putting unsightly fittings into the wall or ceiling is a cross-bar between two light-stands (**3**). Alternatively, the same supports can be used to suspend a standard 3m (9ft) paper background roll for a portrait background (**4**). Clamps are often useful for fixing lights temporarily to pelmets or the tops of doors though the grips should be padded to prevent marks (**5**). An ordinary umbrella arrangement with a monobloc studio flash is satisfactory basic portrait lighting equipment (**6**) but tape down or otherwise secure trailing power leads to prevent accidents (**7**). Finally, block out the ambient lighting from the window (**8** and **9**); if flash is being used, the curtains or blinds may be sufficient. ●

STUDIO PORTRAITS

The portrait is the classic and traditional subject of the photographic studio. Skill in studio portraiture is partly a technical matter, with a strong emphasis on lighting, and partly a matter of relationships — being able to encourage a particular kind of response from the sitter. Indeed, the dealings between the photographer and the subject often contribute more to the success of a portrait than any other factor. While the techniques of lighting and set arrangement take more time and space to describe, these alone cannot guarantee a powerful or revealing photograph.

Choosing backgrounds

One of the most persistent features of studio photography is that everything, including the setting for the subject, must be selected by the photographer. On location, backgrounds are chosen from the existing scenery; in the studio, there *is* no background until one has been deliberately hung.

Most portraits concentrate so determinedly on the face of the sitter — its form and expression — that the setting usually plays a very subsidiary role. The most common type of portrait background is, therefore, plain and unobtrusive. Its function is mainly to complement the tones and colours of the subject — in other words, to help the design of the picture. And because demand is greatest for simple backgrounds, the standard material is heavy, seamless paper in a variety of colours. Typically in nine-foot rolls, background paper is designed to be supported horizontally from wall or ceiling fittings; if the frame of view takes in the floor, the free

Front projection

Using axial lighting and a special highly reflective screen, front projection equipment is basically a sophisticated version of ordinary slide projection. But it allows a bright image of any slide to be projected onto the background screen, without any visible effect on people or objects in front. It works in the following manner. A flash-powered slide projector is positioned exactly at right angles to the axis of the camera and lens. A half-silvered mirror in front of the lens diverts the projected image along the lens axis towards the screen. The screen itself contains many very small transparent beads which reflect the light back in one direction only — towards the lens. From even a few inches to one side of the camera, the projected image is invisible, and the skin and clothes of the subject reflect nothing.

The screen material is 3M Scotchlite, and this can be bought separately to make larger screens. If different sheets are attached together, they should overlap away from the centre, so that no shadow lines show.

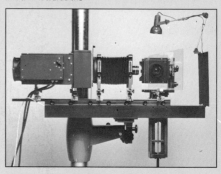

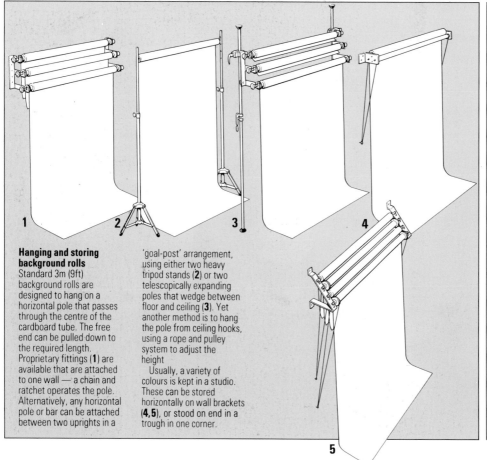

Hanging and storing background rolls

Standard 3m (9ft) background rolls are designed to hang on a horizontal pole that passes through the centre of the cardboard tube. The free end can be pulled down to the required length. Proprietary fittings (**1**) are available that are attached to one wall — a chain and ratchet operates the pole. Alternatively, any horizontal pole or bar can be attached between two uprights in a 'goal-post' arrangement, using either two heavy tripod stands (**2**) or two telescopically expanding poles that wedge between floor and ceiling (**3**). Yet another method is to hang the pole from ceiling hooks, using a rope and pulley system to adjust the height

Usually, a variety of colours is kept in a studio. These can be stored horizontally on wall brackets (**4,5**), or stood on end in a trough in one corner.

end of the paper can be draped to give a smooth, continuous sweep that extends through to the foreground.

If handled carelessly or hung crookedly, paper will crease and, even though it may be out of focus, this may be visible and distracting. After a session, it is often necessary to trim off the used portion.

In addition to standard paper rolls, there are very many other possibilities for creating differences in texture as well as tone and colour. Fabrics of various kinds can be used, including velvet, old tapestries, drapes and canvas. Heavy paper and canvas can be painted or sprayed. All backgrounds must be considered in relation to the lighting (described on pages 259-61): the colour and shaping of background lights can transform their appearance.

While plain backgrounds are the most common in portraiture, shots that show more of the sitter than just the head and shoulders may need various props. These can range from as simple an object as a chair or table to a full-blown room set. For 'environmental' portraits (see pages 182-3), it is usual to select props that are specifically relevant to the sitter's work or interests.

A special type of background sometimes used in portraiture is a projected image. Using a *front projection* system (see box), any slide can be enlarged to fill the background, either for realistic or dramatic effect. This calls for special projection equipment and screen, and places some restrictions on the normal studio lighting, but once installed offers a limitless choice of background images.

Backgrounds for black-and-white portraits In portraiture, choose simple background materials. Shooting in black-and-white makes fewer demands on backgrounds, in two ways: the colour of the material is irrelevant; and considerable adjustments to the tone can be made during printing (by choice of paper grade or by using printing controls). The three most basic backdrops are shown in three photographs below: plain white (bottom left), black (bottom), and textured canvas (immediately below). It is useful, however, to be able to light the background separately from the person.

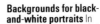

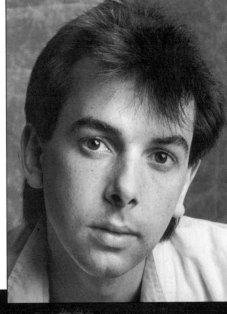

Background materials
This small selection of
background materials for
head-and-shoulders
portraits gives an idea of the
possible range.
  1 Coloured netting
  2 Black velvet
  3 Painted flatboard
  4 Tenting canvas
  5 Plastic wrapping
  6 Patterned fabric
  7 Plastic ciré
  8 Calico
  9 Mirror foil
 10 Painted brick

Portrait formats and poses

Portraits tend to be taken in a few distinct scales: frame-filling views of the face; head-and-shoulder shots; three-quarter torso shots, truncated around the waist or thighs; and full-length portraits. In addition, there are group portraits, which need even larger settings and more working distance. The larger the scale, the more attention is placed on the setting, so that backgrounds and props usually need more care in selection. If the figure of the subject is prominent in the picture, some thought will also have to be given to the choice of pose.

The pose is important because of its graphic effect — on the general design of the photograph — and because of its influence on the attitude of the subject. In front of the camera, most people have some tendency to feel apprehensive and tense, and this often shows itself in excessive concern over where to place hands and feet.

Both relaxed and alert poses can be flattering to the subject, and these can be encouraged by the photographer in one of two ways. The photographer can direct the subject into a pose, giving instructions on how to sit, where to place hands, and so on. Alternatively, specific props can be provided that encourage a certain posture. Whether the direct or the indirect method is used depends on the photographer's own preferred way of working and on the character of the subject.

A low armchair encourages slouching, and places the knees and legs well in front of the torso. A high stool encourages a more compact pose, with the subject leaning forward. Armrests on a hard chair give the sitter something natural to do with hands and elbows. A selection of chairs and stools of different kinds gives a useful choice for different sitters and different types of portrait.

Portrait lighting

There is a strong tendency for photographers to use set patterns of lighting for portraits, particularly if these have a proven record of success. Clearly, there is a danger of becoming stuck in a rut but in portraiture more than most other kinds of photography, there is some justification for using standardized lighting methods. The reasons are twofold.

First, the human face has a relatively complex set of planes, projections and recesses, which in hard lighting can obscure expression. Second, the interest of most portraits lies more in the personality conveyed than in the graphic design

Poses The more of a subject that appears in a portrait, the more important it usually is to consider this pose and stance. Generally the aim is to produce a relaxed and comfortable effect. There is a limitless variety of pose, but the small selection above may be a useful starting point.

Facial expressions are susceptible to the influence of the photographer. The relationship between photographer and sitter is clearly important in encouraging a particular manner (below). Close crop portraits (top) can be very strong.

Common portrait problems and solutions

Problem	Cause	Solution
Nose and mouth out of proportion — too large.	Distortion caused by shooting too close with too short a focal length of lens	Use a medium telephoto (between 100mm and 200mm on 35mm format)
Reflections in spectacles	Light or reflector card too far forward	Have subject lower head slightly, or place black card just out of shot in position to reflect in spectacles. Extreme solution: remove lenses from spectacles.
Chin folds prominent	Head held down on neck	Have subject lean forward, to stretch neck slightly. Shoot from higher.
Fixed stare	Tension; photographer too slow in making technical adjustments	Have subject close eyes tightly, or look away; then look back to camera on suggestion
Rigid smile	Tension; over-concern to please photographer	Distract with conversation; have subject puff out cheeks to relax muscles around mouth.
Subject looks slightly arrogant	Probably because head tilted back, forcing subject to look down at camera	Raise camera position; have subject lean forward.
Eyes appear small and ungenerous	Ambient lights too bright, causing irises to contract, giving small pupils	Use flash, dim room lights, wait some seconds between shots
Crows feet around eyes and other skin wrinkles obvious	Harsh lighting angles	Diffuse lights more, and position more frontally. Use soft focus filter
Spots and blemishes prominent in black-and-white portrait	Undersensitivity to red of most black-and-white films (most skin blemishes reddish)	Shoot with red or orange filter
Skin shine	Perspiration and natural skin oil	Wipe skin. Diffuse lights more. If necessary, apply light dusting of make-up powder

BASIC UMBRELLA LIGHTING The diffuse light reflected from standard photographic umbrellas, round or square, is very popular for head-and-shoulders portraits, whether toplit (below) or sidelit (bottom).

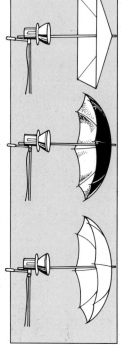

of the photograph. As a result, diffuse lighting from a conventional position — above and fairly frontal — is standard for the majority of portrait photographs.

The technical problems in lighting a face include: recessed eyes, which can give a disturbingly expressionless look if strongly shadowed; cross-shadows cast by a prominent nose; over-bright highlights on the upward-tilted planes such as the forehead, cheekbones and bridge of the nose, particularly if the skin is shiny; and a tendency towards high contrast. For clear, uncomplicated lighting that gives more prominence to the expression than to the sculpting of the face, all of this suggests moderate diffusion — sufficient, at least, to take the edge and intensity off shadows. At the same time, totally shadowless lighting would give a flat, formless treatment, and the usual compromise is to rely on one principal light source.

To avoid blurred facial movements, flash is much more commonly used than tungsten, and the most convenient diffusing attachment, at least for head-and-shoulders shots, is an umbrella used from about two or three metres. Alternatives for a diffused main light are an area light (see page 86), bounced lighting from a flat, or, in a daylight studio, a north-facing window.

Refinements to this basic, conservative lighting include shadow fill and effects lights. The function of shadow fill is to lower the contrast range, and so depends first on whether the photographer wants to show all the facial details (the aim may be a graphically strong image with dramatic lighting), and then on the degree of diffusion in the main lighting and on its position. The softer it is, and the more frontal, the less need there is for shadow fill. Side-lighting, however, will give quite high contrast between the two sides of the face, hence one name for it — 'hatchet lighting'. Reflectors include white card, crumpled foil, smooth shiny foil, mirrors, and secondary lights, in increasing order of efficiency. For the most natural effect, shadow fill should be approximately one quarter of the level of the main illumination. Secondary shadows from a strong shadow fill are usually distracting.

The two most common effects lights added to this basic set-up are back spots and catch-lights. Back spots give an intense beam, and are usually located directly behind the subject or else behind and just out of frame; their effect is to light the edges of the hair (or the face in profile). With fair hair, the effect is that of a glowing halo.

Catch-lights are small spots, or even a mirror used as a reflector, that give small bright reflections in the eyes. These can help to enliven the expression and compensate for any tendency for the eyes to fall back into shadow.

Pulling back for large-scale portraits — full figure and groups of people — usually calls for more lights and more diffusion. For an even illumination, a standing figure needs a strong element of side-lighting, and the most common lighting techniques are two or more umbrellas mounted vertically, a tall trace frame, a white-painted cupboard used to bounce the light from two or three lamps, or a very large area light. Under most circumstances, the size of the light should be approximately that of the figure — about two metres by one metre (seven by three feet). Shadow fill is generally necessary, unless the studio is small and painted white.

USING LIGHTING FOR SPECIFIC EFFECTS

Single spot In the photograph at top right, a single, undiffused spot was placed at a low angle and directed up towards the man's face to give the impression of someone working in an office by the light of a desk lamp.

Lighting for mood The pair of studio shots at right show how the contrast and angle of the lighting can help the mood of the shot. Sidelighting without shadow fill is moodier than the less contrasty, higher-key effect above.

High-key light In the photograph at left of an artist painting on glass, a high-key lighting effect emphasizes the lines of the sketch against a completely white background.

Louis Daguerre's portrait of his wife (right), made in 1837, has a simple, unaffected appearance that is evidence of familiarity between photographer and model. The more traditional picture of photographer Edouard-Denis Baldus (below) has the formal air that characterized most early studio portraiture.

André Kertesz's photograph of a young man in a café in Budapest is typical of his work. Taken in 1912, when the photographer was barely 18, | it seems at first to be a casual, throwaway shot. Yet close examination reveals the characteristic geometric composition with strong crossed diagonals.

STYLES OF PORTRAITURE

Photographic style is more of a contentious issue in portraiture than in most other fields, because there is doubt about how much control and personality the photographer should impose on the sitter. As in all the arts, an identifiable style is achieved only if the photographer places a distinct and consistent stamp on the images. Yet this means that the photographer may over-ride individual nuances of the sitter's character, and can even result in pictures that are distortions of the sitter's personality. For this reason, a number of photographers deliberately avoid attempts at imposing a style; Snowdon, for example, says, 'I want my sitters to be recognized, not my work.'

Nevertheless, there is an enormous variety of styles in portraiture, even if they cannot always be tied down to individual photographers. Indeed, because 'personality' must be added to elements such as lighting and composition that normally help to identify a style, there may be even more variations of style in portraiture than in any other type of photograph. Some of the most common and most distinctive are as follows:

■ **FORMAL** The traditional, formal style of portraiture dates back to 19th-century studios. There, the long exposures needed — several seconds or even minutes — and fairly rigid

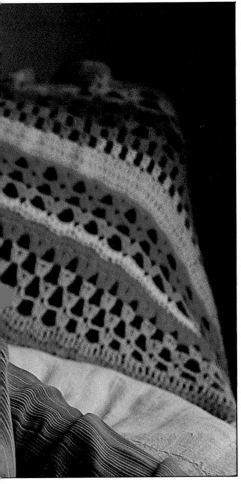

Informal but sombre, Fay Godwin's portrait of the author Doris Lessing (above) employs two techniques to create a serious mood: the downcast eyes of the subject and the low-key lighting from one window. The contrasting and very stylized treatment below, by Rose Jones, gives an air of graphic theatricality to a portrait of three young actors.

social ideas about 'proper' appearance, combined to produce a pose and demeanour that was direct and unsophisticated, if also stiff and often physically uncomfortable. Although little used now, it can have certain advantages, adding an air of occasion and seriousness to the session.

■ **INFORMAL** In direct contrast to the old-fashioned formal style, relaxed and casual portraiture is possible with fast film and fast lenses, and by shooting a sufficiently large number of frames to allow the subject to become accustomed and comfortable. For most people, a relaxed pose and attitude is evidence of being 'natural'.

■ **ENVIRONMENTAL** Even within the artificial confines of the studio, it is possible to photograph a person with visual references to their work or way of life — in other words, in the context of an environment. Among modern photographers, Arnold Newman is probably best known for his development of this technique, both in the studio and on location. A sculptor framed by a piece of work, or a musician with instrument are examples of what are essentially environmental portraits.

■ **INTRUSIVE** In contrast to the fairly cool manner of working involved in the detached style, with its unspoken respect for the subject's privacy, intrusive portraiture probes its sitters' character, not always in a kindly way. The aim is usually a 'revealing' view of the subject's personality in the photographer's eye, and the techniques may include a lengthy session in which the relationship between photographer and sitter is not always comfortable. Richard Avedon's portrait work has this quality and he sometimes creates pictures that the sitters themselves would rather not have displayed. Harsh lighting and shorter focal length lenses used close to give some distortion contribute to the effect.

■ **FLATTERING** Commissioned portraits for the personal use of the sitter are usually intended to flatter. The flattering style of portraiture is the stock-in-trade of commercial portrait studios. Techniques such as the use of soft-focus lenses, textured and framed colour prints, and what many photographers choose to call 'Rembrandt' lighting are common.

■ **GLAMOROUS** In a sense, glamour portraits are an extension of visual flattery and, because of a basic 'softness' of approach, they are usually of women. The aim is beauty, and a formal, mannered beauty at that. As a result, in addition to the usual techniques of the above style, make-up, hair styling, dress and jewellery accessories are important.

■ **HEROIC** Like glamour portraits, 'heroic' pictures aim to flatter but in a way that suits just certain types of sitter, principally men. Through a small range of poses, strong tonal contrasts in the picture, formal dress and props, and heavy effects lighting (usually a number of spotlights from positions behind the sitter), a subject can be given stature and made to appear statesmanlike. Karsh of Ottawa is easily the most recognizable of the photographers regularly using these techniques, and is rightly identified with this style.

FASHION

Fashion has a special place in photography, for although its ostensible subject matter is clothes, jewellery, dress accessories and make-up, it has considerably more significance for its audience — as entertainment and even as an indicator of social behaviour.

Fashion photography is principally a professional concern, because the market for this kind of image is commercial (advertisements and fashion magazines), and because there is a strong element of elitism. Fashion imagery, which calls on the talents of art directors, fashion designers, models and stylists as well as the photographer, has the considerable task of setting trends and influencing public taste. This requires in the photographer a strong sense of design (and one that is sufficiently flexible to move with changing fashion), a fine attunement to the current social ideals of fashion, and an ability to stage-direct models.

An essential feature of fashion is its fashionability — regular change with each season is necessary in the industry — and this frequently means that the *presentation* of new fashions must exaggerate their stylistic differences (which may not always be so great). This in turn places some onus on the photographer and art director to improvize. The editorial pages of fashion magazines are filled with essentially similar subjects — usually dresses on women — and achieving a different look in each set of pictures is something of a problem. Usually, each set, which may be shot in a session of as little as an hour or two, or over a period of several days, is given a definite theme. If this theme is suggested by the dress collection itself — for instance, a particular combination of colours or a new type of material — so much the better. If not, one must be invented. It may be purely graphic, such as a compositional style, an overall colour arrangement, or a technique such as motion blur. Alternatively, it may be built around a setting or a collection of props. Currently, a significant proportion of fashion shooting takes place on location, using unusual and exotic settings to give a stylistic identity.

Lighting

When the subject is clothing, as it normally is, the scale of sets calls for reasonably powerful lighting. However, while most portraiture tends towards the conservative in lighting, the demand in fashion photography for stylistic difference tends to produce a greater variety of technique, favouring experiment and originality. The exception to this is lighting for beauty shots, which must usually conform to certain standards of what is considered attractive.

Styles

Fashion photography is dominated by style, and identifiable differences are often exaggerated. However, within any one market, there is usually a consensus of style at any one time, with certain photographers leading the way. The history of fashion photography, therefore, shows pronounced differences, while a survey of the photography published at any one time usually shows consistency. Because of the elitism in the fashion industry, there is much more critical judgement of style than in most other fields, and this tends to suppress any that are not in line with the ideas of the major opinion makers (that is, the principal couturiers and magazines.)

As fashion photography is chiefly a commercial activity, usually advertising specific items, the style, atmosphere and setting of the pictures must generally reflect the needs of the market. The unusual and the exotic may seem to be the most prominent type of images, but the majority of fashion photography is workmanlike. The picture above, high-key, soft and with quite strong back-lighting, advertises wool — customers tend to be conservative, the sensual appeal of the material is important, so that in practice a romantic treatment is more appropriate than a dramatic one. The male fashion shot on the right, part of a series advertising leather clothing, was carefully lit and arranged to appear as if taken outdoors, for a casual, in-the-street look. It is often easier to achieve a consistent light by imitating natural light in the studio than by shooting outdoors.

Poses in fashion photography are, by convention, more stylized than the naturalistic manner that is common in portrait shots (compare these with the selection of poses on page 259). Being stylized, the poses are as subject to changing fashion as the clothes themselves.

BEAUTY

This is a specific aspect of fashion photography, and exists chiefly for the presentation of make-up and hair-styles. Standards of beauty in the face change more slowly than they do in dress, and while the sculpted precision of the early 1950s stands in clear contrast to the more natural and casual looks of the late 1970s and early 1980s, very little is attempted in the way of outrageous experiment.

Beauty photography is almost exclusively of women. As the principal work is that of the make-up artist and hair-stylist, the photographic emphasis is on a set of techniques that will enhance the attractiveness of the face. As a result, those lighting techniques which in portraiture are designed for flattery are here developed to a high degree of sophistication. As the make-up itself can take some of the load of shaping the face, it is usual for the lighting to be heavily diffused. This, in effect, gives the make-up artist more choice. A typical lighting arrangement is shown (opposite): broad frontal light with strong shadow fill gives an evenly lit area for the application of make-up, at the same time conveying some structural form through very soft shadows.

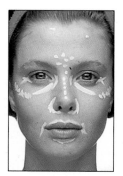
1 Apply concealer.

2 Cover blemishes.

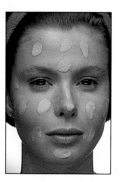
3 Apply liquid foundation.

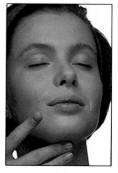
4 Blend in foundation.

MAKE-UP STEP BY STEP
Although there is no single standard approach to make-up, the sequence illustrated here is a good basic routine.

Concealer and foundation is essential preparatory work; the main stages are illustrated at left. Concealer is available in light and tan tones (for fair-to-medium and dark skin respectively), in the form of cover sticks, creams and cakes.
1 Use concealer sparingly to cover flaws, placing dots under the eyes, on the forehead, and around the nose and mouth.
2 Blend into the skin with short wipes to cover spots and soften wrinkles.
3 The easiest type of foundation to apply is liquid. Using a tone that closely matches the skin colour, place dabs as shown. Blend into the skin with fingers, lightly to avoid pressing it into the pores.
4 Finish blending the foundation with long strokes down the neck to the collar bone. Absorb excess with a tissue.

Lips First define the shape by outlining dry lips with a lip pencil as shown (far left). With the mouth closed, extend the outline outwards at the corners in small, quick strokes. Next, brush in the colour, working outwards (near left). Either smudge the brushed colour into the pencil outline or leave the outline distinct.

1

Eyes For basic eye make-up, pencil along the lower lid just above the lash line (**1**). Then shade the upper lid with a pale tone (**2**). Apply highlight just below the brow (**3**), and strengthen the appearance of the eyelashes with mascara, using a zigzag movement for the lower lashes (**4**).

2

3

4

5
Define the shape of the eyebrow with an eyeline pencil (**5**), and finally brush the eyebrows upwards (**6**).

6

Make-up styles clearly differ — the bold blacks, whites and reds in the picture above right match the scarves; the softer colours at right are more 'natural'. But in general, the aims are masking defects, making the skin look smooth, modelling the shape of the face, and making eyes larger and lips fuller and softer.

Professional beauty shots often demonstrate a new style of make-up, and so a model is chosen for the suitability of her face for the style. In non-professional beauty photography, the make-up usually has to make the subject look as attractive as possible — enhancing best features and hiding or suppressing worst ones. Large, well-spaced eyes are usually considered the most attractive, and make-up can do much to convey this impression even when they are not; applied to the outer edges of the eyes, for instance, it will help to make them appear more widely spaced. Similarly, eyebrows can be re-shaped, and the lips made to appear fuller, while the combined application of highlight and shadow make-up can re-model the structure of the face — for example, making the cheekbones seem more prominent by lightening the upper ridges and darkening the area underneath to give a very slight hollow to the cheeks. The skin texture can be smoothed and coloured easily. Some make-up artists have recently even been using cosmetics to make living artworks for a photograph.

THE NUDE

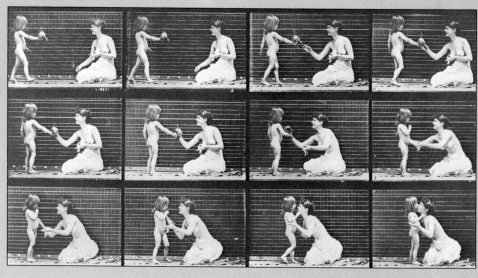

Motion pictures This sequence of semi-nude photographs, taken in 1885 with a special camera equipped with 12 lenses, was part of a vast documentary project by Eadweard Muybridge. These pictures served basically as anatomical references.

There is a certain amount of ambivalence in the photography of the human body. There are two elements — the sculptural and the erotic — and while these might seem at first glance to be distinct from each other, there is some overlap. On the one hand, the lens-distorted nudes of Kertesz and Brandt were purely concerned with form; in Brandt's case, the work explored the visual relationship between the body and the natural landscape. On the other hand, the photographs on the centrefold of *Playboy* magazine are strictly pin-ups, designed to be sexually stimulating. Between these extremes, however, is a whole, varied field of photography in which the sculptural and the erotic are intertwined.

In both cases, the lighting is of fundamental importance, and it is principally for this reason that studios, with their opportunities for precise lighting control, are used more often than location settings (other reasons are privacy and comfort). The role of the lighting can differ, however. If the aim is more for a sculptural effect, the lighting is used to display the physical qualities of the body, such as form, skin texture and musculature. A strong erotic bias calls for lighting that evokes atmosphere and, incidentally, helps to conceal some parts of the body and reveal others in a pattern that is stimulating to the viewer without being too obvious.

Sculpturally, the human body is both complex and familiar, a combination which gives the photographer, or artist, substantial freedom for visual experiment. Much of the formalist appeal of still-life photography applies here, and lighting is the principal means of exploration.

While portrait photography, even of full-length figures, features facial expression very strongly, in nude photography the face is often a distraction. It may, of course, play a part in generating eroticism in a pin-up, but in most other forms of nude photography the face tends to be suppressed, by positioning it in shadow, or having it turned away from the camera, or cropping it out of the picture.

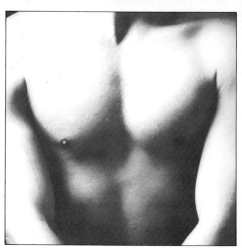

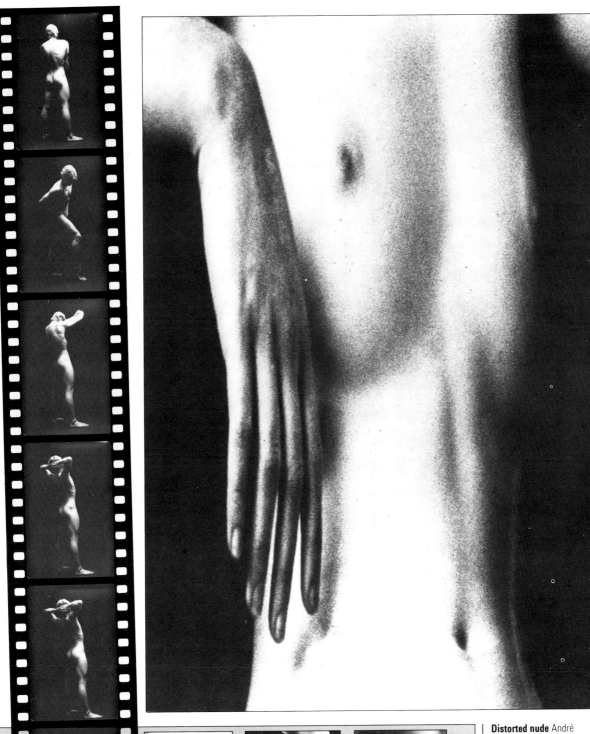

Physique With strongly directional, but diffused, lighting, this series of studies demonstrates variety of muscalature (left, right and above). A black paper background and absence of shadow-fill opposite the light gives the maximum relief effect to the skin texture.

Distorted nude André Kertesz's 1933 nude torso (above) entitled 'Distortion No 6' was an attempt to play with form using an optical trick (a fairground distorting mirror).

LARGE-SCALE SETS

Certain types of studio subject need special consideration simply because of their size — calling not only for scaling-up of operations, but also for different working methods. Cost becomes an important factor. Suitable large studio spaces are not easy to come by and rents or hire charges are high while the amount of lighting, props and background increases *geometrically* with the size — at twice the shooting distance the same lens takes in four times the area of set. As a result, the variety of large-scale studio photography is limited principally by commercial considerations, notably those of the advertising industry.

Room sets and automobiles are by far the most common large-scale sets. Both require such specific techniques that they are mainly undertaken by specialist photographers. Certainly, the actual studio space must be large and fitted with certain equipment and materials, and, in some cities, room sets and automobile studios are leased by the day as a commercial proposition.

ROOM SETS

Room set photography is often used to display large household equipment, such as furniture, wallpaper, and so on. But a set may also be built to recreate a particular type of interior not otherwise available, such as a period setting. Location photography in existing rooms is a natural alternative, but for various reasons is not always practical. To begin with, location research is time-consuming and therefore costly, while it is unlikely that a room can be found that exactly meets the demands of an agreed layout. Moreover, there may be physical difficulties in installing photographic lighting, and this is often needed in order to be able to maintain control over the colour balance and exposure settings — installing lamps outside windows, for instance, can sometimes be as much work as building a set indoors.

Therefore, while large set construction is a major effort and can easily take a few days even with experienced carpenters and decorators, the results can be guaranteed. In advertising photography this and not cost is nearly always the main consideration. The normal sequence of events is to begin with a sketch of the finished picture and work backwards from this to assign camera and lighting positions, perspective and angles of view. Then a precise plan and section of the set can be drawn, and construction can begin. One reason for working in this logical order is that any changes to the camera position and angle of view that are made *after* the set is completed will be costly. In fact, even building the set so that its area extends beyond what will be shot, in order to allow some freedom in composition, is more costly than providing the exact minimum.

There are certain inherent advantages in building a room set for still photography within a larger studio area. One is that only the surface appearance is important, and structural considerations are minimal. Walls, for example, can be erected very rapidly, using thin boarding and struts; only if they have to carry weight will they need to be strengthened. Some main fittings, such as windows and doors, can be bought already assembled. In addition, the field of view is unlikely to take in even half of the room, so that normally only two walls and a small corner of ceiling have to be built.

Room sets Both these re-creations of period settings were built indoors and lit artificially, even though the effect is of natural daylight through windows. In both cases the windows were covered on the outside with translucent plastic sheeting to diffuse the light from several 1000 watt tungsten lamps placed outside.

A specialist in complex, highly orchestrated studio photographs, principally for advertising, Michael Joseph has here arranged a simple light set-up to make it easier to move and pose this huge crowd of people to best effect. Diffused overhead banks of lights give a blanket illumination of the crowd of 60 models, who have been assembled in such a way that the important activity takes place in one nearly flat plane. Since directing the cast was the most critical part of the photography, it would have been an unnecessary complication to include side-lighting that might have restricted the positions and movements of the models.

The outstanding benefit of the studio, however, is that it gives complete choice of lighting. Typically, room sets occupy about half of the studio floor space, leaving room on the other side of windows and doors and above for arranging lamps. For a natural day-lit effect, one method is to light a painted or photographically enlarged backdrop beyond a window.

While either tungsten or flash can be used, the quantity of light usually needed — small apertures for great depth of field on a large-format camera are normal — tends to favour tungsten. With tungsten lamps, exposure is simply a matter of time, whereas flash units need to be tripped a number of times in order to increase the exposure.

AUTOMOBILES

The commercial market for automobile photography is sufficient to support a number of specialist studios and photographers. While on the face of it, location photography may seem the obvious choice — showing automobiles on the road

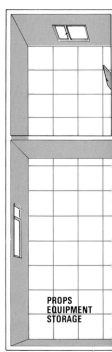

and in use — there are often good reasons for going to the considerable trouble of constructing sets large enough and lighting sophisticated enough to work inside. Considered as a large-scale, still-life subject, an automobile poses significant problems because of its reflective finish on curved and multi-angled surfaces, and the difficulty of manipulating outside surroundings severely restricts control of these reflections. Linked to this drawback is that the most suitable conditions for natural lighting (often twilight or close to sunrise and sunset) are relatively unpredictable in most parts of the world because of weather changes.

A different kind of problem in taking a car out on location is the logistics. Most commercial car photography is for purposes of advertising, and the usually tight production schedules, which allow little leeway, mean that the conditions of the shoot must be guaranteed. Additionally, for the launch of a new model, automobile manufacturers are usually concerned with security, needing to keep the design secret until its launch.

Even the tightest shot of an automobile, showing minimum background, will normally call for a working distance in the order of 20m (65ft) or so when a standard lens is fitted to the camera and proportionately greater with a long focus lens (often used to improve perspective). Behind the vehicle, extra distance is needed for the backdrop, and there must also be sufficient room to drive the automobile into position.

Car photography In the set-up above, arranged by photographer Ric Hawkes for an Alfa Romeo advertisement, the final product was to be a cut-out of the three vehicles set on a background of painted perspective lines, as shown. This simplified some of the studio details, in that the lighting and reflectors could be installed without regard for the setting, concentrating only on the effect they would have on the cars themselves. Nevertheless, the dimensions of the shot and the curved reflective surfaces in the bodywork demanded a large-scale treatment in all respects. Even though only one car needed to be photographed at a time, the studio had to be fairly large to give the photographers a reasonable choice of shooting angles. The cyclorama alone was over 7m (21ft) long. An important, though often difficult to find facility, was suitable access for the car into the studio.

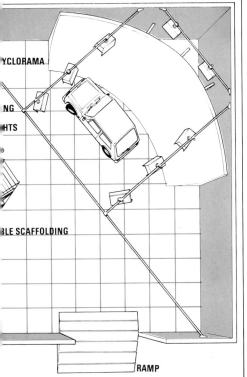

For good access, most automobile studios are at ground level (the alternative is a heavy-duty goods lift) and all need large, warehouse-style doors.

It is, however, the lighting that makes the greatest demand on studio design and fittings. As a highly reflective object, an automobile needs much the same lighting as any shiny object (see page 279): broadly diffused lighting that will reflect smoothly in the paintwork, and great attention to the detail of the surroundings to avoid distracting reflections. However, the sheer scale complicates matters. The most important reflective panels are usually one side, the bonnet and roof. The shaping of the radiator grill and other parts of the front is normally sufficiently complex *not* to give a broad reflection, and the visible side can usually be treated with free-standing flats or trace frames. The bonnet and roof, however, are more difficult, as they will reflect a large area of the upper background. When curved, as they often are, they can reflect a very large angle which, at a normal distance that allows room for aiming lights, can be well over 100 sq m (330 sq ft) of backdrop. In most automobile studios, backgrounds and lighting are indistinguishable one from the other, the surrounds functioning as large reflectors to give even or smoothly shaded lighting.

To ensure that this reflective lighting is completely smooth, the normal procedure is to construct a specially curved surround, from floor to ceiling, and sometimes even taking in a corner. Known as a *cyclorama*, this has the additional function of removing the floor/wall join to give a horizonless picture (although such a limbo setting is not always wanted, it is easier to build a 'horizon' in a cyclorama than to remove it from an unaltered studio).

Once constructed, a cyclorama must be carefully maintained, for while small marks and blemishes will not be prominent at a distance, large areas of unevenness will. Careful plastering and constant repainting are usually needed. The foreground area of the floor needs special attention, taking up a significant part of most photographs. Unless it is intended to be rough or textured, it may not be easy to provide a really clean, smooth surface. Unit flooring, such as tiles, is relatively easy to lay down (and does not need to be fixed), but for a mirror-like finish, one standard technique is to flood the floor area with water. For this, even if the area is bordered by low, waterproof barriers and if the depth is only 5cm (2in) 1000-2000 l (220-440gal) of water may be needed. With this and other floor coverings that must be spotless, it may be easier to drive the car into position first.

For all this reflective background area, larger numbers of lamps are usually needed, often with shaped dishes to give an even array. Bouncing the light from a backdrop reduces its quantity, so that a shot may call for upwards of 50,000W to illuminate the subject properly.

The reflected light can be even or gradated, and it is possible to simulate the appearance of a clear twilit sky quite closely, by concentrating the lighting on the lower part of the cyclorama, and by fitting coloured gels over the lamps. Gradated spraying with coloured paint can help. An alternative lighting technique is direct diffusion, with overhead lamps aimed down through a false ceiling of diffusing material.

STILL LIFE

Despite the extensive use of still lifes in editorial and advertising photography, still life remains the form in which photography seems to be most capable of approaching fine art. It demands an input of time and effort from the photographer that few other fields of photography do. The photographer must carefully select the elements that are to be included and then, slowly and deliberately, create a design — gradually altering a composition, lighting, colour and so on until the desired effect is achieved. In contrast to candid, and most other forms of photography, a still-life image is not seized as an opportunity, but built up.

To David Hockney, a painter who has also experimented with photography, this is crucial, for he believes that the time and effort the artist puts in are essential qualities of an image. He argues that most photographs, unlike paintings, take very little time to make and so cannot hold the viewer's attention for long. 'Look at a Rembrandt for hours and you're not going to spend as much time looking as he spent painting — observing, layering his observations, layering the time.' By contrast, 'The reason you can't look at a photograph for a long time is because there's virtually no time *in it*.' If there is a valid argument here — that the effort and consideration show through in the finished image — the photographic still life should reward closer observation than most other forms. Certainly, the details and arrangements in a still-life image are deliberate rather than accidental. A photographer has full control over a still life, from the choice of objects to the method of treating them.

Backgrounds and settings

In still-life photography, the background is a vital element of the picture design and demands as much consideration as the choice of subject — even if the background is to be subdued or neutral. The variety of possible background materials is immense, as the chart opposite shows, and the choice must inevitably depend on whether the background is to act merely as a backdrop for the main subject or whether it is used to create an elaborate setting.

One of the most popular simple backdrops is a featureless 'limbo' setting, which allows the subject to 'float' visually against it. The best materials for this kind of background are colourless — white, black or grey — and textureless. For light-toned backdrops, plastics and laminates such as formica are ideal because they are so smooth — many papers have a texture that is noticeable in close-up, and paper is also prone to wrinkling and creasing. For a completely 'dead' black, that kills all shadows and has no recognizable tone or texture, good-quality black velvet is excellent.

The appearance of these floating backdrops can be altered dramatically by the lighting. Back-lit translucent plastic will give a completely white setting that carries no shadows. A curved white background — sometimes known as a *scoop* — partially lit from overhead gives a horizonless gradated zone (see Basic lighting style below). A gradated scoop can actually do more visually than just provide a limbo setting. Used with a particular camera angle to suit the subject, as in the example (see page 276), the upward change in tone from light to dark can be made to coincide with the downward gradation from light to dark in a typical object that is lit from

SILK

CLOTH

BOOK

BALLBEARINGS

MARBLE (FRONT LIT)

GLASS OVER COLOURED PAPER

MIRROR

WOOD

COLOURED PAPER (FINE)

WHITE FORMICA

LEATHER

COLOURED PAPER (COARSE)

MYLAR

TEXTURED BLACK PLASTIC CARD

BLACK VELVET

MARBLE

LATTICE

MARBLE (LIT BY REFLECTION)

A library of backgrounds
The variety of useful background surfaces for still lifes is immense. The glass filter is included for size reference and to show the degree of reflection from an overhead area light. The light over the subject, tilted very slightly towards the camera, is common for still lifes. In fact, colour saturation and tone depend very much on the lighting direction; in the pair of photographs at left, the same marble looks quite different when lit by the reflection of an area light (near left) in the same way as the pictures above, to when the light is placed more frontally (far left).

overhead. In this way, the tones of an object stand out much more clearly.

Other simple backdrops are those that contrast with the appearance of the subject, and those that are complementary to it. This applies not only to tone — an ivory carving, for example, has quite a different appearance when seen against a light or a dark background — but to colour, pattern and texture. As a general rule, the *less* neutral the background, the more important it is to be sure why it is being used. Attention-getting backgrounds chosen indiscriminately can overwhelm a subject and appear tasteless. Whether a background is selected for contrast or similarity is a matter of personal taste: either can work well, the one through enhancement, the other through restraint.

Atmospheric settings are often chosen for their association rather than simply their appearance but can complement or contrast with the subject. Certain smooth, shiny surfaces, such as stainless steel and plastic, for example, tend to be associated with precision, science and technology, and may even appear a little 'cold' — an obvious complementary background for a piece of equipment. An example of the use of a contrasting background might be a delicate piece of jewellery photographed against a roughly hewn block of stone. Contrasting associations probably have more scope for an interesting and imaginative interpretation of the subject.

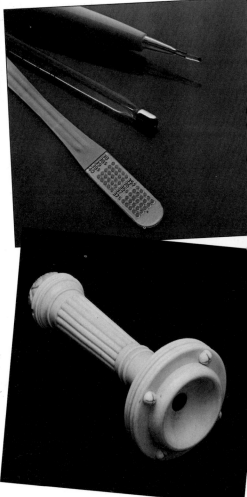

Choice of background
These examples show how texture, association and tonal contrast can be used. The delicacy of the emerald and gold necklace (above) is exaggerated by contrast with the rough surface of fossil-embedded rock. The clinical thermometers (above right) are given a suitably clean, sterile setting on smooth reflective perspex. An antique ivory telephone receiver (right) stands out sharply against a perfectly black background of velvet.

Scoop backgrounds Firm but flexible surfaces such as formica, certain other laminates and plastic sheets can be arranged to form an upward-curving background, as shown below. If secured at its front edge, the sheet will fall naturally into this shape if placed up against a wall or some other vertical support. Depending on the camera angle and the height of the scoop, the background of the photograph can be filled completely without any 'horizon' line in a relatively small space (see also box at right). If an overhead area light is then suspended fairly low, its soft shadow will give the impression of receding distance, as in the photograph at left. Moreover, the darker background behind usually contrasts well with the more brightly lit upper part of the subject.

Camera angle The area of the picture occupied by the background surface often depends simply on the camera angle. As the diagrams below show, the more horizontal the lens axis, the larger the area of background. It often makes little difference to the look of the shot to tilt the camera down slightly, but can save a great deal of background preparation.

Backgrounds need not be plain and consistent, or even a single surface. Many still-life photographs use what is basically a set, constructed to create a certain atmosphere or to simulate a location, either contemporary or period. If the shot is tightly framed and the camera angle kept sufficiently high not to take in a large area of background, convincing reconstruction can be made with quite modest props, carefully selected.

Basic lighting style

Even more than in studio portraiture, lighting is critical to the success of a still life. When a person is the subject, the fairly consistent shape of the head and body, and the need to show recognizable facial expression, set limits to lighting style. But with still life there are many different styles of lighting, and fashions are forever changing. Whatever the style, though, lighting for still life needs to be efficient. It must clearly reveal all the relevant aspects of the subject, form, shape, texture, colour. With a simple subject, for which the aim is to do little more than make an accurate record, lighting efficiency may indeed be the only consideration. But where there are more interesting aspects to take into account, such as the atmosphere and impression of the shot, efficiency may be compromised.

With most still-life subjects, lighting usually benefits from some diffusion — enough, at least, to kill the hard-edge, dense shadows thrown by a naked lamp that tend to confuse the appearance of most objects. Extreme diffusion, however, shows the *form* of an object poorly, as some light/shade contrast is necessary to show the contouring. In practice, this is not usually a problem, as it is hard to create the kind of enveloping light that gives this effect outdoors within a studio. The usual compromise for 'straight' still-life lighting is

Diffusion, contrast and tone Even a limited degree of diffusion in front of a single lamp can make a significant difference to the distribution of tones. In the upper picture, one light in a 23cm (9in) reflector bowl gives hard shadows and a noticeable fall-off in illumination from left to right. The second photograph was lit by the same lamp, bounced off a 1m (3ft) square white card, for a softer, more even effect.

one main lamp diffused through a sheet of material rather larger in area than the subject. A single main light is simple and practical and its clear, uncomplicated effect resembles natural light, whether from the sun outdoors or from a window.

As the illustrations (opposite) show, it is the *relative* size of the light compared with the object that controls the amount of diffusion: it can be increased, therefore, by making the light area larger, by moving it closer, or by photographing a smaller subject from closer. Overhead lighting positions tend to be considered as normal and traditional, and so are relatively common. Overhead diffused lighting on a scooped background, if positioned relatively low and forward, as shown in the diagram (opposite), has a useful gradated effect, creating and increasing shadow backwards and upwards. If the camera is low, this combines well tonally with the appearance of objects placed on the surface. But the best direction and position for the light depends on the shape and characteristics of the subject. To light an upright bottle, evenly, for example, it is usually easier to aim the light more horizontally than vertically.

As lights in still-life photography are often used quite close to the subject, lens flare is a common problem. While flare can sometimes be used intentionally to soften an image, it is usually better avoided. The position of the lights is crucial, but there are many other ways of cutting down flare. The camera lens can be provided with a lens hood, for instance, and the lamps shaded with French flags (see pages 88-9) and barn doors. It is important to remember that flare may come not only from light spilled directly from the lamps, however, but also from bright reflections from in and around the subject. This is why many photographers cover the bright metalwork on their cameras and lighting equipment with

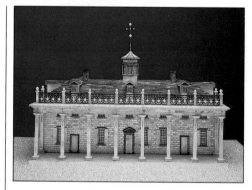

Shiny surfaces The over-riding principle for lighting very shiny surfaces is to plan the reflection over every square inch of surface area very carefully. Essentially, the reflected surroundings are being photographed as much as the subjects themselves. The classic technique is to use a light source that is large enough to cover most of the reflective surfaces, as in the photographs at right and below. The proportions of subject area to light area are extreme — in the close-up of the gold bar below they are in the order of 1:20 — and the light source is as close as possible. In addition, the angles of the surface of the subject and the camera are arranged to catch as much reflection as possible. For the picture of the gold bar, the illumination was the tent light illustrated below. For the pearls and mother-of-pearl shells, illumination was a natural light from a north-facing window on a cloudy day.

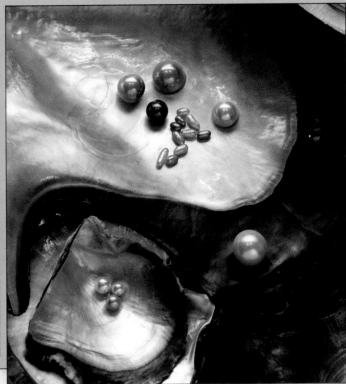

Light tent Although normally practical only for small objects, the subject can be completely enveloped in diffuse light with what is usually called a light tent. The aim is to surround the cone-shaped area that is visible through the camera lens, but just out of frame.

Any neutrally coloured diffusing material will do, provided that it can be supported firmly; here, ordinary tracing paper is used. The cone is first rolled to the dimensions of the lens (at smaller end) and the picture area (at larger end).

black gaffer tape, and sometimes hide the camera behind black card, leaving only a small hole for the lens. Coping with reflections can be particularly difficult to spot when working with flash without modelling lights — even with modelling lights, bright spots that are obtrusive with the flash may not be obvious while the shot is being set up. So many photographers shroud every possible source of unwanted reflection in black.

The final element in efficient lighting is shadow fill, to control contrast. The normal shadow fills are reflectors of white card or paper, cooking foil, mirrors, or a second lamp, also diffused. The degree of shadow fill is largely a matter of taste, although if very obvious it can appear distracting. This is more likely to be a danger with a fill light than with reflectors. It is difficult to assess the level of fill needed by eye and the most accurate method is to measure the different levels with a meter. Shadow fill is most likely to be needed with a degree of back-lighting, when the light is aimed towards the camera, and least likely when the lighting is frontal, from the camera position to the subject.

Even with basic still-life lighting, using one main diffused light, there is scope for different effects, and relatively small changes in position and direction can make a significant change to the appearance of a photograph. When the lighting possibilities are extended to include the many other styles, with spotlights, multiple lights, degrees of lens diffusion and the many types of light modifier illustrated on pages 88-9, it is easy to create a distinctive and unusual lighting design.

Lighting for reflective surfaces

Although the surface qualities of any still-life subject influence the choice of lighting, shiny surfaces call for a very specific technique. The problem with shiny surfaces, such as glass, polished metal, many plastics, and glazed ceramics, is that they tend to reflect both the lamps being used to light them and the unwanted studio surroundings, including the camera and photographer. In fact, the problem can be both aesthetic and technical, for not only are the studio surroundings likely to be distracting if noticeable in the picture, but the reflection of a light source will usually make the contrast range of the image much too high for the film to record adequately. Although proprietary dulling sprays are available (these give a matt or semi-matt coating to the surface, taking away its natural shininess) these are not usually a satisfactory solution as they change the nature of the subject completely — and the greasy deposit they leave may be difficult to remove.

The skill in making a straight photograph of a reflective subject is in simplifying the reflections while still retaining the impression that the surface is shiny. The technique is to control the surroundings. A shiny surface will always reflect something, but by arranging for broad, even surfaces to surround the subject, the reflections can be made to blend smoothly with its form and shape.

The light source can be softened by diffusing through a textureless translucent screen, such as tracing paper or perspex, or bouncing off a large white surface, such as a wall or a sheet of card. If the subject has one principal flat surface,

Controlling flare Obvious sources of lens flare are directly visible lights close to the picture's frame edge. Less easily noticed is the subdued flare from white areas outside the picture area common with white studio backgrounds such as those shown here. The result is a lowering of maximum density, contrast and colour saturation. The standard solution is to lay black surfaces (cloth, card, paper) right up to the edges of the picture area, as shown below.

Glazed pottery The shape of a reflective object determines the lighting position and viewpoint very closely. These upright vases offer limited choice of camera angle — they cannot reasonably be laid flat, and to keep the vases correctly positioned the camera must be at approximately their level. Side-lighting with a close, fairly large area light is therefore almost the only acceptable arrangement for a conventional shot.

it is usually easy to position the light at such an angle and at such a distance that its reflection covers the subject. The reflections in other flat surfaces that lie at different angles can be treated by placing reflector cards in appropriate positions. By using reflectors of different strengths — white card, grey card and silver, for instance — the form of the subject can be presented in several ways.

Curved surfaces, however, tend to reflect much more of the surroundings, and can even give an effect similar to that of a fish-eye lens. One way of simplifying these reflections is to surround the object almost completely with diffusing material, to make what is sometimes known as a *light tent*. The simplest light tent is a cone of tracing paper spreading out from the lens. The hole at the apex is just large enough for the lens, while the base is broad enough for the background. Lamps can then be positioned outside the light tent so that it becomes an enveloping light source. The number and distance of these lamps determines whether the light appears even or gradated — gradated lighting helps to give modelling to the object. With very shiny, strongly curved objects, the lens can appear in the shot as a dark central spot. If absolutely necessary this can be taken out with a small local application of dulling spray to the appropriate place on the subject.

A variation of the light tent is to bend a flexible piece of diffusing material over the object so that its shape matches the curve of the reflective surface. Another is to accept that the shape of the light source will appear distinctly within the

Exposure for transparent objects
Where the subject is either transparent or light toned, the key for exposure calculation is the background. If the subject is back-lit, it is the light source that must be measured by taking a direct reading. To get the exposure for the subject, add 2 or 2½ stops to the reading. An alternative is to take an incident reading.

reflection, and to make it as clean and simple as possible — a rectangle, for example. Some photographers add dark strips of tape to the front of an area light to simulate a window-frame.

Lighting for transparent objects
Just as shiny surfaces reflect their surroundings, transparent ones show their backgrounds, so the lighting technique must always take into account what appears *through* the subject. Glass and clear liquids are the two most common transparent subjects, and there is a considerable variety of each. Both are reflective as well as transparent, and this can make clean lighting very difficult indeed.

The most common technique for lighting glass and liquids is back-lighting with a broad, diffuse light source that fills the picture frame. With this method, it is refraction of light through the glass or liquid that defines its shape and details — thicker areas and edges tend to look darker, so that a wine glass, for example, appears thinly outlined against the light. This technique does not suit all subjects, however, as some edges and important features may be too thin to register clearly. Edge-darkening can be enhanced by placing black card or paper as close as possible to either side of the glass without actually appearing in shot.

Full back-lighting for transparent objects can be created either directly, by aiming a light (or lights) towards the camera through a clean, textureless diffusing sheet, or indirectly, by bouncing a light off a white opaque background. In either case, the surface on which the object stands tends to appear darker and so will affect the refraction of the glass. Also, the line where the surface and the light meet may produce an unwanted 'horizon'. One solution is to rest the glass on a translucent surface that transmits some of the light. Another is to use a reflective surface and shoot from a low angle, so that the base picks up the back-lighting and, incidentally, appears to merge with the back-light. Some photographers even make a transparent porthole directly beneath the glass and shine diffuse light up into the glass to give the liquid a rich glow.

With most transparent subjects, less exposure gives stronger definition to the darker edges and richer colours. The limit to underexposure is the appearance of the brightest areas and of the background itself; a reliable exposure method is to measure the brightest part and then give about two or two and a half stops more than indicated. According to the exposure principles on page 56, the back-lighting is the key tone.

If the edge-darkened outline is not quite sufficient to show the form of the object adequately, an extra conventional light can be added. The roundness of a drinking glass, for example, can be enhanced by using a rectangular *area light* (see page 278) from one side to give a faint curved highlight in addition to the back-lighting.

An alternative to full back-lighting, which depends on the refraction of the subject, is *rim-lighting*, typically created with two spotlights facing the camera but out of frame, behind the glass. This technique tends to suit thick, solid transparent objects rather than thin-walled containers — old bottles are particularly suited to this treatment.

Eliminating the horizon Unless a scoop is used, as above, the edge between the level surfaces and the vertical back-light will tend to appear like a kind of horizon. A relatively easy way to eliminate it is to use a shiny surface and a low camera angle, as in the photograph of the antique perfume bottle below. The camera angle increases the visible reflection, which becomes bright enough to merge with the light source.

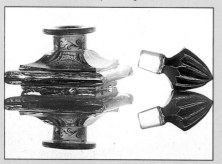

In this close-up of a cherry in a wine glass, what mattered were the composition, the precise positioning of objects to control the refraction effects, and elimination of flare (achieved with a professional bellows lens shade).

Combining transparent and opaque subjects The four-part exercise below illustrates the effect of different basic lighting positions when, as often happens, transparent subjects must be photographed in proper settings with other objects. Clockwise from the upper left, the arrangements are side-lighting, base lighting, back-lighting, and the conventional three-quarter frontal lighting. The colour saturation and sense of transparency of the olive-oil bottle is different in each case, and this affects its prominence in the pictures. With side and frontal lighting, the liquid is best treated simply, placing it in front of a light-toned part of the setting.

Special equipment

The key to success with still-life photography is often meticulous preparation. Cleaning and polishing is vital, for instance, because the close, clear views tend to reveal dust and dirt that the eye might miss at the time of shooting. Many backgrounds, as well as the subjects themselves, need to have a pristine appearance, particularly for product shots and other commercial applications. A studio used regularly for still-life photography usually has a range of special cleaners to suit most possible surfaces: metal polish, detergent, perspex polish, clear spirit, among others. Also valuable are various tools for removing dust and other small particles, including dusters, brushes of different sizes, a compressed-air spray, a miniature vacuum cleaner, and an anti-static gun.

In still-life work, objects must often be held in awkward positions by unseen supports and it is worth having a variety of support materials to hand. Particularly useful are adhesives, including permanent and removable bonding agents, double-sided and ordinary tape, and putty-like sticky compounds. Pins, clips and staples are also valuable, while some objects that do not appear completely in shot can be clamped from the side, using retort stands, screw and spring clamps, and other devices.

Ragged edges and loose fibres can be trimmed and perfected with a sharp scalpel or a nail-file. Indeed, a sharp scalpel is useful for making all kinds of clean cuts — all cuts must usually be very neat for they will be under close scrutiny.

Adding the final touches to an arrangement might call for very delicate movement. A range of manipulation tools, including prodders, tweezers, fine brushes and jeweller's claws makes this much easier, particularly if there are clean, polished surfaces in shot that must not be touched by hand.

Liquids need special handling, particularly if they are to be applied precisely, without spilling. An atomizer, such as a simple garden plant spray, can be used to spray tiny drops of water to simulate condensation on surfaces that are supposed to look cold or fresh. Pipettes and syringes can be used to place drops and other small quantities of liquids exactly in place. Stirrers can be used to give movement and removed just before shooting. Flexible or glass tubes can be used to introduce bubbles, either by blowing or by attaching to a compressed-air source. Clear glass tanks are needed for photographing submerged objects.

Preparing still subjects
1 Tape
2 Compressed air
3 Magnifying loupe
4 Needle file
5 Jeweller's claw
6 Needle-nosed pliers
7 Jeweller's screwdrivers
8 Epoxy glue

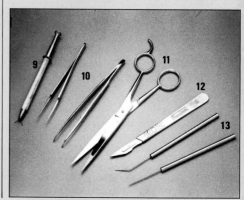

TYPES AND STYLES

Because of the high degree of imaginative control possible in studio still-life photography, it probably has the greatest stylistic variety, or at least the potential for it, of any field. Neither the subjects nor their treatment are under the same external influences as people or outdoor locations, so the image can be much more a product of the photographer's intentions and working methods. The following are the most identifiable of a very large range of types and styles of still-life images and approaches.

■ **STRAIGHT** The least distinctive of styles, but the most common of professional treatments, is the straight record shot — an efficient, informative portrait of an object sets out to give a clear, recognizable view, with maximum detail and the least overlay of obvious technique. Commercially, the demand for this kind of image is high, and it is often found in advertising and in catalogues in a subsidiary role; known as a 'product shot' or 'pack shot', its function is information rather than persuasion. The basic skills of still-life photography, particularly in lighting and camera technique, are demonstrated in an uncomplicated manner in such images, and craftmanship is usually much more in evidence than imagination but it should not be assumed that individual photographers will stick rigidly to any one style.

■ **FORMALIST** Because of the ease of selecting, arranging and lighting still-life objects, there is, not surprisingly, great scope for exploring form. There is great flexibility in the construction of a still-life image, allowing a long sequence of

These Victorian dolls were arranged simply in an appropriate setting — a Victorian chest-of-drawers. Within this framework, the dolls were displayed for maximum visibility. The lighting from a large window was strongly diffused to avoid shadows that might confuse the 'readability' of the picture.

Moving delicate objects
9 Jeweller's claw
10 Tweezers with different grips
11 Scissors
12 Surgical scalpel or fine craft knife
13 Prodders for moving microscope specimens

14 Ball and socket head on miniature tripod
15 Double-sided tape
Holding subjects in place
16 Screw clamp on ball and socket head
17 Small magnets
18 Malleable adhesive compound (eg Blu-Tack)

19 Alligator clip on heavy, bendable copper wire
20 Black cotton thread for suspending objects invisibly against dark backgrounds
21 Miniature C-clamps
22 Adjustable clamping arm on heavy base

Photographing scale models is in many ways a form of close-up photography and borrows a number of techniques. But the need to make small models look realistically large poses the photographer with a number of unique difficulties. Models are used easily in movies because the eye is not allowed to dwell for long on each image, but still photographs of models often have to be much more carefully made.

The usual techniques for giving a sense of scale are to use a very wide-angle lens from very close, and minimum aperture to give a depth of field similar to that at full scale. A low viewpoint also looks more realistic. These techniques are used in the photograph at left, of a $\frac{1}{3}$nd scale architectural model of a synagogue in Amsterdam.

change and assessment in the position of the subjects, camera, lighting and so on. This type of procedure suits a formalist approach, although there may at times seem to be rather too much choice.

■ CONSTRUCTIVIST Echoing the constructivist movement in pre-war Europe, this is a relatively recent style in studio photography, and principally concerns the design of the image. Angular composition, and a precise geometry are strongly in evidence, and understandably the general impression of constructivist photographs tends to be of assembled planes rather than of great depth. There is often an element of the abstract in these images, and even some illusory qualities. More specifically, constructivist design often makes more use of the edges and covers of a picture than does the more conventional 'centred-subject' type of composition. In its original form, constructivism made deliberate use of different materials; now it frequently involves the assembly of a subject from plastics, mirrors and specially prepared shapes.

■ ABSTRACT A more general exploration of the graphic possibilities in still-life subjects, composition and lighting can be described as abstract. Whereas the visual element — line, shape, tone, colour and so on — are in the formalist approach treated as expression of the subject's basic nature, here they are extracted and isolated. Often the subject itself is physically unrecognizable, and is used only as a source of interesting visual arrangements; at other times, the identity of the subject *is* revealed, but slowly, and the degree of abstraction is treated as a demonstration of graphic skill.

■ **MULTIPLE IMAGES** Although the still life is normally thought of as a single image (and the planning and care that is usually taken encourages the production of one final, considered image), interesting use can be made of sets of related pictures. These can be related graphically, designed to appear in a block or strip, or sequentially, showing progressive stages of action, rearrangement, or other changes.

■ **RECONSTRUCTIVE** In this style, a miniature set is produced to evoke a realistic impression of a location, historical period or other situation. It is heavily used in advertising, where evocation of atmosphere is often an important sales ingredient. Authenticity is a central concern, involving research and a selection of props, both of which can be time-consuming. As normally a fairly restricted area of view and number of elements is being used to convey a wider impression, reconstructed sets are often at least slightly idealized and match viewer's preconceptions. Many period reconstructions of 19th-century still-life sets, for example, are lit and arranged to have a Dickensian flavour.

■ **ILLUSTRATIVE** A style that often draws on and incorporates other styles as well, the illustrative still life visualizes specific ideas, and is frequently used in magazine features (and especially the covers) and in advertising. The ideas treated in this way are often abstract, or at least difficult to

Reconstructed sets As the photographs below illustrate, creating a suitable ambience for a still-life subject need not involve the kind of large-scale set construction described on pages 270-1. In both cases, the key is a selection of appropriate props. In the photograph immediately below, the props were collected mainly from antique dealers.

illustrate with a straight photograph, hence the common use of studio photography, which can be ordered and planned. For example, a magazine article on banking would be inadequately illustrated by a photograph of a bank building, but might be successfully treated with some unusual presentation of various elements of banking practice, such as cheques or bank notes. Juxtaposition, in which two or more normally unassociated objects are brought together, is the most widely used technique in this style.

■ ILLUSIONARY The extreme control that is possible in still-life photography, and the development of various specialized equipment and techniques to manipulate objects (see page 284 above), facilitates deliberate illusion — tricks with perception that involve, for example, suspending objects with supports and other kinds of impossible looking images.

■ SURREALIST Closely related to the illusionary still life, and often using the same techniques, surrealism involves both unexpected (and often illogical) juxtaposition and a join-free authenticity in the image. Post-production techniques, including retouching and photo recomposition, are often used to polish the effect. The elements of fantasy and realistic technique apparent in much of the original Surrealist movement, including the work of Dali and Magritte, has been a natural inspiration for photographic surrealism.

Surrealism and illusion
With the help of special effects techniques, photographs can be used to alter the appearance of reality. For maximum control, this is usually easiest to do in the studio. In the photograph above, using an idea from a Magritte painting, an original transparency was placed behind a miniature broken window and back-lit. A copy transparency was cut and re-touched to resemble shards of glass below. The curtains were added later with another exposure. In the photograph at left, everything except the moon was assembled and photographed in the studio. The brick was laid flat on a large sheet of translucent plastic, giving a graded effect to simulate a dawn sky. The horizon was produced by cutting a strip of back card to shape and placing it directly underneath the brick. To exaggerate the perspective, a wide-angle lens was used close to the brick, at a small aperture, and a miniature flash used to simulate a spotlight, as if the brick were a large building. The moon was added by double exposure.

CLOSE-UP PHOTOGRAPHY

Close-up photography, simply defined, is the photography of things at less than the normal close distance of a normal lens. The relative size of the image on film and the real subject is important, and different degrees of close-up photography are often described in terms of magnification. In terms of magnification, close-up photography extends from images about $\frac{1}{7}\times$ (one-seventh times life size) up to about $20\times$, at which point the optical system of a microscope (see page 308) is usually more efficient and resolves more detail. There are, nevertheless, no hard and fast limits: the definition is essentially a practical one. According to another method of definition, close-up photography extends up to life-size magnification ($1\times$) only. Enlargements that are greater than those of photomicrography are considered to be the province of 'photomacrography'. The reason for this is that greater-than-life-size photography involves certain additional techniques, including reversing the lens — partly because beyond $1\times$ magnification, the lens is closer to the subject than it is to the film. Here, the entire range is considered.

Types of subject
Close-up photography is, strictly speaking, a technique, but the subject matter is usually very distinctive. There are 'close-up' views of people or, indeed, whole mountains, but close-up photography is generally concerned with tiny subjects.

Magnification and reproduction ratio
Because the basis of many calculations and settings is the degree of enlargement of a close-up image, this is the fundamental measurement. In practice, there are two related and interchangeable ways of expressing it. One is magnification, in which a lifesize image is unity ($1\times$) and all other magnifications are proportionately less or more ($\frac{1}{2}\times$ is half lifesize, $2\times$ is twice lifesize). The other is reproduction ratio, in which the degree of enlargement is given as a ratio to the size of the subject; lifesize is 1:1, twice lifesize is 2:1, and so on. The two forms of measurement are shown in the table opposite.

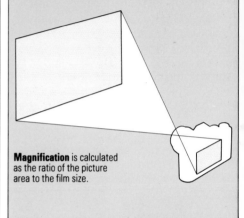

Magnification is calculated as the ratio of the picture area to the film size.

Close-up Equipment: Practical Comparisons

Equipment	Advantages	Disadvantages	Best uses
Extension tubes	Simple, rugged, allow FAD use, known lengths make calculations easy	Non-variable, bulky for long extensions	Field use and moderate close-ups
Bellows extension	Variable magnification, large extension, some models have swings and tilts	Relatively fragile for field use, may prevent FAD use or need double cable release	Indoor close-ups, especially at high magnification
Ordinary lens & reversing ring	Improves optical quality at magnifications greater than lifesize	Cannot use FAD	Occasional high-magnification use
Close-focusing lens (usually macro zoom)	Uncomplicated	Close-up image quality poorer than at larger scales	Non-critical use
Macro lens	Designed for best optical performance in close-up, focuses unaided to $\frac{1}{2}\times$, good for general purpose photography also	More costly than ordinary lenses, relatively small maximum aperture	All close-up photography: alone up to $\frac{1}{2}\times$, more with extensions
Supplementary lenses	Quick to fit, light, need no exposure adjustment	Limited magnification, image quality not high	Fast field use up to about $\frac{1}{6}\times$, and for fixed-lens cameras
Medical lens	Easy to use, fast changes of magnification, built-in light	Expensive, bulky, ringflash may not suit all subjects	Medical, insects
Supplementary telephoto lens	If both lenses already available, needs only a coupling ring	Bulky, limited magnification	Emergency field use

Extension and focal length
The magnification of the image depends not only on the length of the extension, but also on the focal length of the lens. To achieve a given magnification, lenses of different focal lengths must be extended proportionately: for $1\times$ magnification (lifesize) a 50mm lens must be extended by 50mm — its own focal length — and a 100mm lens by 100mm. So, a simple means of achieving high magnification is to switch to a shorter focal length.

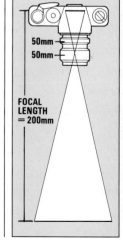

50mm
50mm

FOCAL LENGTH = 200mm

REPRODUCTION RATIO TABLE

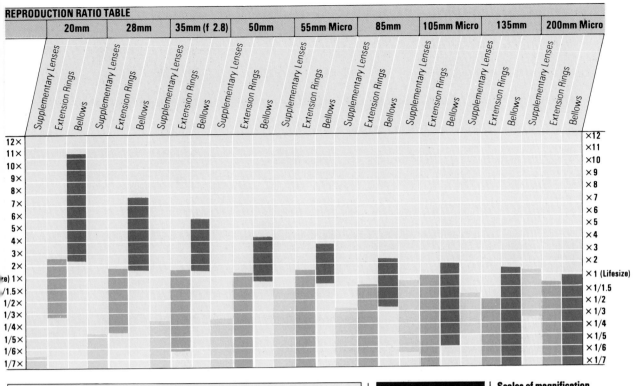

	20mm			28mm			35mm (f 2.8)			50mm			55mm Micro			85mm			105mm Micro			135mm			200mm Micro		
	Supplementary Lenses	Extension Rings	Bellows	Supplementary Lenses	Extension Rings	Bellows	Supplementary Lenses	Extension Rings	Bellows	Supplementary Lenses	Extension Rings	Bellows	Supplementary Lenses	Extension Rings	Bellows	Supplementary Lenses	Extension Rings	Bellows	Supplementary Lenses	Extension Rings	Bellows	Supplementary Lenses	Extension Rings	Bellows	Supplementary Lenses	Extension Rings	Bellows

Scale (vertical axis, left): 12×, 11×, 10×, 9×, 8×, 7×, 6×, 5×, 4×, 3×, 2×, 1×, /1.5×, 1/2×, 1/3×, 1/4×, 1/5×, 1/6×, 1/7×

Scale (vertical axis, right): ×12, ×11, ×10, ×9, ×8, ×7, ×6, ×5, ×4, ×3, ×2, ×1 (Lifesize), ×1/1.5, ×1/2, ×1/3, ×1/4, ×1/5, ×1/6, ×1/7

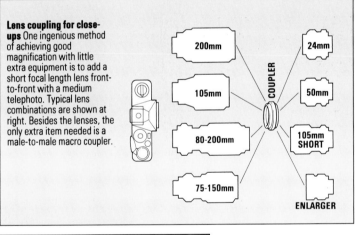

Lens coupling for close-ups One ingenious method of achieving good magnification with little extra equipment is to add a short focal length lens front-to-front with a medium telephoto. Typical lens combinations are shown at right. Besides the lenses, the only extra item needed is a male-to-male macro coupler.

COUPLER

200mm — 24mm
105mm — 50mm
80-200mm — 105mm SHORT
75-150mm — ENLARGER

Scales of magnification
Different close-up equipment is needed, depending on the degree of magnification. For the photograph at left of a butterfly measuring 50mm (2in) wingtip-to-wingtip, an unaided 55mm macro lens could handle the magnification. The series of pictures below show different degrees of magnification.

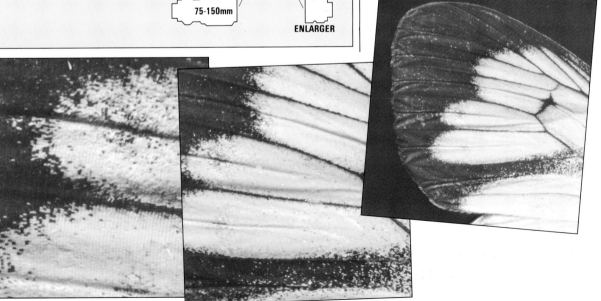

Abstract patterns Close-up photography is very good for creating abstract images. While at most scales photographs have a strong tendency towards realistic representation, at magnifications greater than the eye is accustomed to, pictures may seem a little difficult to place. The photograph at right, apparently an aerial view of drainage channels, is in fact a large magnification of pigments trapped in a damaged Polaroid print. More recognizable are the arrangement of feathers below, and the pattern of bubbles in a liquid below right.

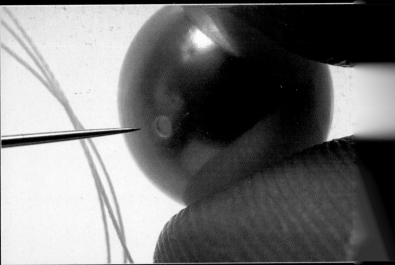

Technical close-ups Unlike the pictures opposite, the photographs on this page are meant to inform. In each case, there is a technical need to show a magnified view of something small. Illustrating an article on malaria research, the photograph at top left combines two disparate scales — mosquito and human researcher. At top right, the subject is the method of threading pearls onto strands. The large photograph at left combines scales in another way — by focusing on the small quartz sphere and using its refraction to show part of the laboratory. The photograph above, of teeth, uses a medical lens equipped with ringflash to make a clear, shadowless record of hard-to-reach locations.

MINIATURE NATURAL OBJECTS Small plants, insects and individual details of larger things — the scales of a fish, for example, or the texture of tree bark — offer an almost limitless choice of close-up subject. Not surprisingly, therefore, the most widespread use of close-up photographic techniques is in nature photography, and some of the specific methods for treating insects and flowers are dealt with on page 224. These are often interesting precisely because they are not normally noticed by the eye, so the most common treatment is realistic, using lighting, viewpoint and depth of field to show the maximum amount of information as accurately as possible.

MINIATURE MAN-MADE OBJECTS Miniaturization in various fields, including electronics and engineering, provides a rich modern source of close-up images. Circuitry, components, and, as in close-up nature photography, the surface details of larger, more familiar things, are important subjects.

UNUSUAL TREATMENTS Precisely because small-scale views are unfamiliar to the unaided eye, many close-up subjects offer opportunities to experiment with unusual and sometimes dramatic treatments. These often involve a careful selection of viewpoint and lighting techniques.

ABSTRACT IMAGES Visual experiment can also produce images that are so unfamiliar that they become abstract. For purely graphic pictures, with no hint of the content, close-up photography excels.

Exposure
Any close-up system that involves lens extension reduces the amount of light reaching the film. In practice, this means that the greater the magnification the more exposure is needed. Exposure is increased either by extending time, or by widening the aperture, or by increasing the amount of light (moving the light source nearer or boosting the light output).

  TTL metering removes the problem of tedious calculation, when working by available light. And many SLRs now have off-the-film flash metering to solve the problem when working with flash. Where it is not available, the precise settings must be located in tables or calculated. Additional compensation may have to be made for reciprocity failure with long exposures.

  As with telephoto photography, a magnified image also magnifies camera-shake, and all the usual precautions must be taken with continuous light photography: a rigid support, cable release, shelter from wind and locking up the mirror.

Depth of field
Depth of field decreases with magnification, and is always shallow in close-up photography. At high magnifications, even the smallest aperture may not give enough depth of field to keep all of the subject in sharp focus. This is not necessarily a problem. Out-of-focus blur in the background or foreground may actually help to make the main subject appear to stand out sharply. Normally, though, the lack of depth of field means that precise focusing is critical. A point to bear in mind is that at normal distances there is more depth of field beyond the sharpest focus than there is closer to the camera. At close distances, the difference is almost irrelevant.

Basic macro set-up
For controlled conditions indoors, a basic arrangement for macro photography centres on a copystand or equivalent. Shown below is a monorail that clamps to a horizontal surface such as a desk-top. The camera mount can move freely up and down, and a separate, movable frame below acts as a macro stage. This be fitted with an opaque plate or a translucent sheet as needed. Adjustable arms and small mirrors (dental mirrors are ideal) can be used either to introduce main lighting or shadow fill.

Exposure calculations For non-TTL metering cameras, the two most usual ways of calculating the exposure increase needed are:

$$\left(\frac{\text{lens focal length} + \text{extension}}{\text{lens focal length}}\right)^2$$

or

$$(1 + \text{magnification})^2$$

For example, if a 100mm lens is extended half its own focal length — 50mm — to give a magnification of ½X

$$\left(\frac{100 + 50}{100}\right)^2 = (1.5)^2 = 2.25$$

and

$$(1 + 0.5)^2 = 2.25$$

This means that the film needs to receive 2¼ times more light, which can be achieved by increasing the exposure time by a little more than twice — in practice, halving the shutter speed from, say, 1/125 sec to 1/60 sec — opening up the lens aperture by 1 or 1½ stops, or by moving the light closer by about 1/3 of its distance.

Magnification	Depth of field at f/11	
	A	B
0.2X	30mm	15mm
0.5X	6mm	3mm
0.8X	3mm	1.5mm
1X	2mm	1mm
1.2X	1.5mm	0.7mm
0.3mm	15mm	7mm
1.5X	1mm	0.5mm
2X	0.8mm	0.4mm
3X	0.4mm	0.2mm

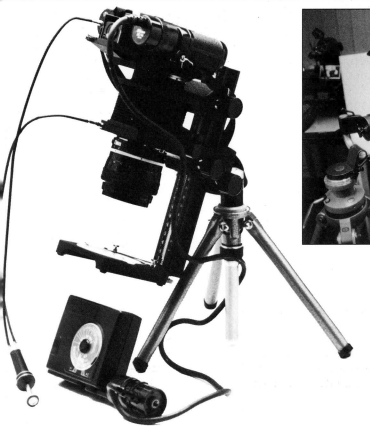

High-magnification set-ups When working with extension bellows (generally at magnifications greater than 2×), a specimen stage at the end of the bellows rail is a useful accessory for mounting specimens securely (left). This can usually be fitted with glass or translucent plastic if backlighting is needed. Large-format macro shooting is simply an extension of the normal working procedure with a view camera — flexible bellows are already a part of the monorail, and greater magnification needs only extra sets of bellows (above).

Depth of field This is a critical matter in all close-up photography. The greater the magnification, the less depth of field there is, and the only way to increase it is to stop down the aperture. This itself creates some new problems: one is the difficulty of seeing the effect at the smallest apertures because of the dim image on the focusing screen. Another is the deterioration of image quality at the smallest apertures due to diffraction. The table at left offers a quick guide to the most commonly used magnifications. For a lens setting of f11, the first column gives the depth for a circle of confusion of 0.06mm (satisfactory but not critical). The second column is for the more exacting 0.03mm (use this if the picture will be printed or reproduced large).

Trans-illumination (the more usual macro term for backlighting) is so commonly used in close-up photography that an efficient, controllable light source may be a worthwhile investment. In the example used for the photograph above of a fluorite crystal, a slide duplicating machine doubler as macro set-up (left). The monorail copystand, itself adapted from a view camera, is the same as that illustrated on the opposite page.

The smallest apertures may not give quite such sharp results as optimum apertures (see page 51), but the extra depth of field means that the picture may be sharper overall. Re-positioning either the camera or the subject can help to align the important parts with the plane of sharpest focus. The swings and tilts on some bellows extensions can be very useful to redistribute the sharpness.

Another, highly specialized, means of increasing the apparent depth of field is slit-scan lighting, described below.

Lighting

In close-up photography extra lighting is needed for a variety of reasons: to compensate for the light loss in the extension; to allow small apertures; and to introduce illumination into the small confined spaces of a tiny subject. In addition, the small size and structure of close-up subjects means that many are translucent or transparent, so that back-lighting, (or 'trans-illumination', as it is sometimes called in photomacrography) is useful.

Light sources used in normal-scale photography appear larger and so more diffused when used closer with small-scale subjects. Consequently, it is usually easy to achieve soft lighting, though of relatively low intensity. Close-up lighting equipment, therefore, tends to be miniaturized in keeping with the reduced scale, and small flash heads and miniature spots are commonly used. Fibre optics are also useful for directing light into exactly the right place — and to light subjects which may be sensitive to heat sufficiently brightly.

Controlling reflections
Most of the techniques in lighting shiny surfaces described on pages 278-83 apply in close-up photography, yet it is important to be flexible. In the photographs of a cowrie shell below, the difference between naked, undiffused lamps and the same lights diffused through a cone of tracing paper is obvious, yet the diffused version is *so* flattened as to give an inaccurate impression.

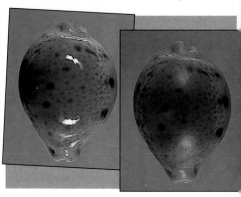

In the photograph of an art nouveau brooch (below), diffused frontal lighting was combined with trans-illumination to give depth to the image and to display the texture of the leaf selected as a background. The slide duplicating machine shown on page 293 was used, and the levels of brightness were matched by Polaroid testing. The close-up of the gold bar (below right) was an exercise in controlling reflections — diffuse lighting was needed for an even effect, but the direction was angled to throw the stamping into relief.

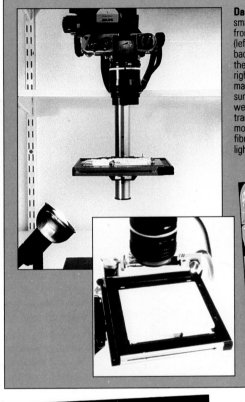

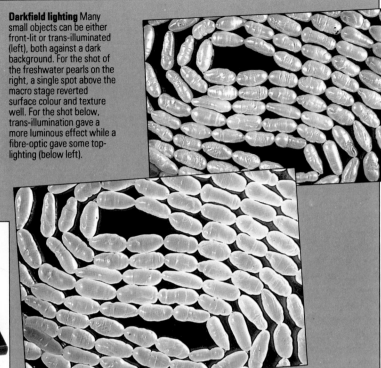

Darkfield lighting Many small objects can be either front-lit or trans-illuminated (left), both against a dark background. For the shot of the freshwater pearls on the right, a single spot above the macro stage reverted surface colour and texture well. For the shot below, trans-illumination gave a more luminous effect while a fibre-optic gave some top-lighting (below left).

When the working distance is very small, the best lighting position may actually be just where the camera is. One answer is to use a 'ringflash', a circular tube that surrounds the lens to give virtually shadowless illumination. Medical lenses contain their own built-in ringflash. Macro lights have a number of small tubes surrounding the lens. The tubes can be switched off and on independently for different degrees of modelling effect. Another answer is 'axial lighting', in which a semi-reflecting mirror is placed at 45° to the lens axis in front of the lens. Light is aimed at right angles from one side, and half of the beam travels along the lens axis. This technique can be useful with coins as it permits some diffusion.

For most of these miniature lighting systems, close-up brackets are needed. Some brackets attach to the base of the camera, others to the hot-shoe, and others screw onto the front of the lens. Most are jointed to allow manouevrability.

The two most common methods of trans-illumination, useful with thin subjects that are at least partly translucent, are 'brightfield' and 'darkfield' lighting. Brightfield lighting is usually created by placing the subject on an opal plastic base and aiming light up through this. In darkfield lighting, the subject is usually placed on a clear glass base, over a black background. One or more spotlights are then aimed diagonally upward from the sides.

A highly sophisticated lighting system is the slit-scan technique, in which the subject is moved towards the camera at a fixed rate, illuminated only by a narrow band of light from the sides. As the band of light is fixed relative to the camera and is narrow enough to fall within the depth of field of the lens, an apparently spectacular depth of field is possible — matched only by other scanning systems.

FOOD AND DRINK

The demands of the commercial world have transformed the photography of food and drink into a highly specialized art that demands a combination of very particular still-life techniques and a knowledge of cuisine. Food and drink could be approached in the same way as any still life, but the overriding need for food and drink to look attractive when a photograph accompanies a recipe or advertises a food product has educated us to expect food to look almost unnaturally appetizing in photographs.

The greatest obstacle to making food and drink appealing in a photograph is the loss of its prime ingredients, taste and smell. The skill of the food photographer lies in using a combination of setting, careful preparation, lighting and colour to suggest these missing ingredients to the viewer.

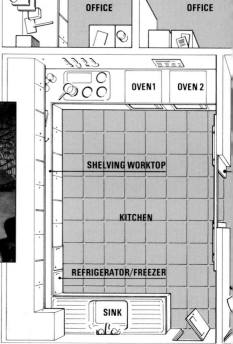

Set pieces A classic food photograph is a fully arranged still-life setting including suitable utensils, associated objects, and some of the raw ingredients. For the food to appear fresh, the normal procedure is to prepare the set and compose the picture in advance, using an empty dish of the same size. As soon as the set is ready the food is prepared and put in place.

Setting

In many ways, the setting is crucial in establishing the mood and appeal of the shot. Very few food shots do not have some kind of suggestive setting, even if it is only a knife laid ready to cut the food. Commercial food photographers go to a great deal of trouble to make sure the setting is just right. Most employ a stylist (also known as a 'home economist') to do precisely this.

Details, such as wooden pepper grinders, proper chef's knives, sprigs of herbs and so on are all arranged within an appropriate country kitchen set complete with well-worn wooden table and chopping board. Or candles, silver cutlery and sparkling wine glasses are combined on a perfect lawn tablecloth for an elegant dining table. A common ploy is to surround the food with the raw ingredients and utensils needed to prepare it. High value is put on authenticity. Tradition is very much to the fore, because tradition plays such an important role in people's expectations of food.

Preparing the food

Preparing the food is perhaps the most difficult part of food photography and demands considerable care and attention. Food should always look perfect, so photographers buy only top-quality fruit, meat and vegetables. Then they may spend hours sorting through to find blemish-free and perfectly coloured examples. Chopping and slicing must be equally meticulous and should only be done with the proper, sharp knife.

If the food is to be cooked, adequate kitchen facilities are essential. However, cooking and photography mix poorly, as liquids, heat and fumes and oil droplets in the air can damage equipment. Professionals usually have a separate kitchen

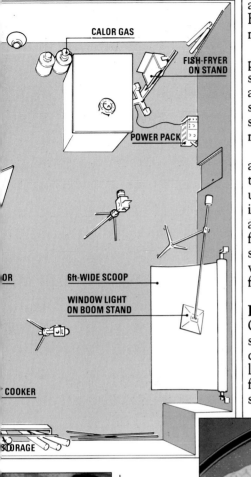

CALOR GAS

FISH-FRYER
ON STAND

POWER PACK

OR

6ft-WIDE SCOOP

WINDOW LIGHT
ON BOOM STAND

COOKER

STORAGE

attached to the studio with rapid access to the working area. But working at the far end of a large, well-ventilated kitchen may be just as effective.

Food generally looks better slightly under-cooked and photographers will often add almost raw vegetables to dishes such as casseroles at the last minute, so that both their shape and colour is perfect. But it is important that hot dishes should look hot and cold dishes cold. The working area should be cool, so that hot food steams and cold food does not shrivel or melt. A dark backdrop shows off steam well.

There are various tricks to make food look appetizing, although editorial and advertising ethics limit what substitutes can be used for commercial work. Common tricks are: using smoke from a cigarette as a substitute for steam; painting sausages and other foods with glycerine to give them an attractive sheen and to prevent them drying out; soaking fruit in lemon juice to stop it going brown; substituting shaving foam for whipped cream; spraying salads and green vegetables with droplets of water (or water and glycerine) from a garden plant spray to make them look fresh.

Lighting for mood and texture

Careful lighting is especially important because the taste and smell can be suggested by the skilful handling of texture, colour and atmosphere by the photographer. This is why light is often shone at a low angle across the surface of the food, to reveal the detailed texture. A light positioned to face slightly towards the camera, from overhead and a little

Simple table setting The simplest of all food shots is a single dish in a plain table setting. When both food and tableware are strongly designed, as with many traditional Japanese dishes, such a treatment is ideal. To make the most of the textures in this photograph, an area light was placed over and beyond the picture area, aimed slightly towards the camera to provide a visible reflection.

Close-up Closing in on graphic details of shape and texture can be an effective way of photographing certain foods. This kiwi fruit was sliced thinly and arranged carefully on a sheet of glass. This was then backlit by a diffused light source, and the surfaces of the fruit kept moist by brushing them with glycerine.

out the surface texture, though at the expense of colour saturation and some foreground shadow fill is often necessary. A third method, which removes some detail and increases the sensual, atmospheric impression, is to use quite hard directional lamps at a raking angle, and achieve diffusion by using filters over the lens rather than translucent materials over the light housings.

In commercial food photography, lighting tends to be rather conservative — largely because people have very fixed expectations of what food should look like; a photographer can only make food appetizing by conforming to these expectations. Gentle, diffuse lighting, more or less overhead, is probably the most traditional and natural-looking, and it features strongly in food photography.

Drinks

Drinks photography can be as difficult to light as any reflective subjects (see pages 278-9) and calls for similar solutions. Dark and opaque liquids (such as some red wines and milk) need to be treated only for reflections in the glass and surface. But some form of back-lighting is commonly used for light-toned translucent drinks, such as whisky or lemonade.

Back-lighting is simple to arrange and will intensify the colours if you expose accurately. But it may distract from other elements in the subject. If drinks are combined with other food, a local back-light can be arranged by concealing a shaped bright reflector, such as a small mirror or crumpled tin foil, behind the glass.

Movement, by stirring, pouring, or introducing bubbles, gives not only a sense of action to the shot, but also helps to give form to the liquid and even conveys some impression of its viscosity. For this, flash is essential, and you usually have to take a number of shots to guarantee one attractive arrangement.

In a deep container, such as a full-bodied glass, it may be necessary to dilute the liquid slightly to ensure an intensity of colour that *looks* authentic. Common substitutes used in photographing drinks are acrylic ice-cubes (which are well-shaped and do not melt while the drink is being arranged) and glass bubbles for both eye-level views of clear liquids and downwards shots of opaque liquids (such as bowls of soup).

Substitute props Two of the more common substitutes in drinks photography are for ice and for bubbles. Real ice melts and changes its shape in much less than the time needed to arrange it for shooting. Moreover, in active shots that involve pouring or stirring, real ice means the glass and set must usually be cleaned for each shot. Acrylic ice cubes solve these problems, although unlike real ice they do not float (right). Small, hand-blown glass 'bubbles' (below) last indefinitely and can be positioned carefully.

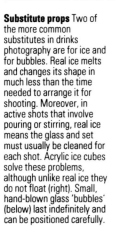

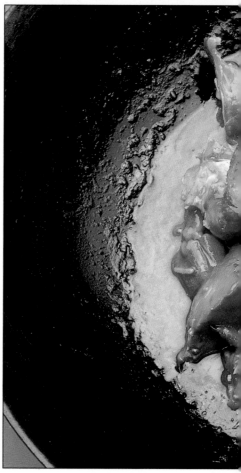

Cooking One way of introducing a little activity into a food shot is to photograph the food being cooked. The approach naturally depends on the method of cooking, but frying in an open pan works well, as the photograph of crab claws at left illustrates. The fire-pot (above) was photographed in the same way. Rather than photographing the food on the cooker, though, it is better to cook the food on a portable gas stove in the studio.

Graphic arrangements
Where the form of the food or natural style of presentation is appropriate, another style of photography is to adopt a formal design. This could be symmetrical and geometric, as in the Korean food at the top of the opposite page.

Eating Most food is photographed in a pristine condition as if just ready to be eaten. Many dishes, indeed, cease to look attractive once they are broken into. Some, however, can be photographed as they are eaten, like the prawn-fried rice at the top of this page.

Simple treatment The simplest and most informative approach of all is a plain, frame-filling view of one entire dish, laid out for serving (main picture above).

SCIENTIFIC PHOTOGRAPHY

Photography's inherent capacity for recording information makes it of tremendous value to the scientist. In many fields, visual documentation is a straightforward, rather unexciting business, yet it can make a vital contribution. Scientific photography is the most innovative variety of such record-keeping, constantly demanding new techniques to match the progress of research. Quite incidentally, many of its images are aesthetically powerful in their own right.

Astrophotography

Photography of the stars has assumed tremendous importance in the science of astronomy. Long exposure can record pinpricks of light from distant stars so dim that they cannot be seen by the eye even through the most powerful telescope. But the photographer wanting to photograph the night sky faces a number of problems.

The first problem is achieving sufficient magnification to record tiny stars on film. Telescopes can be either refracting (like telephoto lenses) or reflecting (like mirror lenses). For most photographers, a reflecting telescope is better because it gives a wider aperture (typically f5), is less prone to chromatic aberration, and is generally cheaper and lighter. Some telescopes based on the Schmidt-Cassegrain principle, such as the 2000mm Celestron 8, can be attached to a 35mm SLR with a T2 adapter and an inverter. Others must be adapted so that the telescope's area of *prime focus* falls on the film (see panel).

A second problem is supporting the camera and lens. Because of the earth's movement during a long exposure, stars are recorded only as bright streaks — unless the camera is moved continuously during the exposure in a direction exactly counter to the earth's rotation, so that the star stays in the same place on the film. There are a number of ways of doing this, but the most common is to provide the camera with an 'equatorial' telescope mount which rotates about an axis pointed at the celestial pole — that is, parallel to the earth's axis of rotation. With lenses much greater than 1200mm, the mount must be driven by an accurate synchronous electric motor; acceptable results can be achieved with shorter lenses on a home-made, hand-driven mount (see panel).

Surprisingly, perhaps, resolution is not a significant problem and most photographers find a medium-fine grain film records all the detail they need. Exposure is difficult, for with long exposures reciprocity failure is inevitable. Indeed, exposures longer than 30 minutes are a waste of time unless the film is *hypersensitized*. There is no point using fast film, for fast film is even more prone to reciprocity failure than slower films. For shots of the stars, Kodachrome or a high contrast black-and-white film such as Kodak 2415 recording film is ideal. Typical exposures are given in the table.

A fourth problem with astrophotography is simply getting a clear view of the stars. Even on a clear night, the stars still twinkle, showing that their light is being distorted by the earth's atmosphere. And near cities there will be considerable interference from city lights reflected in the sky. There is no real solution, but the distortion can be minimized by moving as far away from cities and as high up as possible, and waiting for the right weather conditions.

SUBJECT	LENS SYSTEM	f NUMBER
Star trails	Regular camera	Maximum Aperture
Meteor trails	Regular camera	f6.3+
Satellite trails	Regular camera	f4.5+
Comets	1in + telescope	f6.3+
Planets	6in + telescope for detail	Varies according to f. number of system
Stars	1in + telescope	f6.3+
Nebulae & galaxies	1in + telescope	f6.3+
Moon	1in + telescope	f4.5—

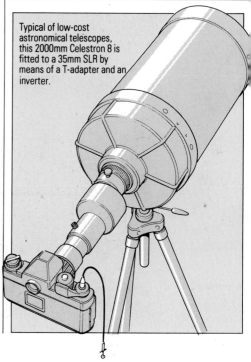

Typical of low-cost astronomical telescopes, this 2000mm Celestron 8 is fitted to a 35mm SLR by means of a T-adapter and an inverter.

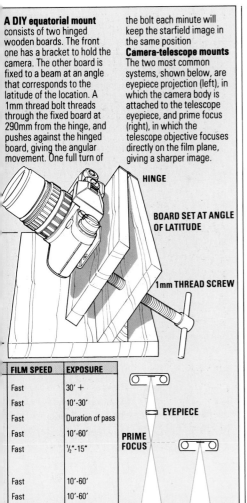

A DIY equatorial mount consists of two hinged wooden boards. The front one has a bracket to hold the camera. The other board is fixed to a beam at an angle that corresponds to the latitude of the location. A 1mm thread bolt threads through the fixed board at 290mm from the hinge, and pushes against the hinged board, giving the angular movement. One full turn of the bolt each minute will keep the starfield image in the same position

Camera-telescope mounts The two most common systems, shown below, are eyepiece projection (left), in which the camera body is attached to the telescope eyepiece, and prime focus (right), in which the telescope objective focuses directly on the film plane, giving a sharper image.

HINGE

BOARD SET AT ANGLE OF LATITUDE

1mm THREAD SCREW

FILM SPEED	EXPOSURE
Fast	30′ +
Fast	10′-30′
Fast	Duration of pass
Fast	10′-60′
Fast	½″-15″
Fast	10′-60′
Fast	10′-60′
Medium	¹/₁₂₅″ -10″

EYEPIECE

PRIME FOCUS

Holography

Holograms are three-dimensional images that look so remarkably lifelike that viewers often reach out to touch the subject that appears to protrude from the surface of the holographic plate.

Superficially, photography and holography seem closely related: both use light-sensitive film to record a visible image. But apart from these two common characteristics the two media are quite different.

The camera makes a two-dimensional record of the subject using light rays that obey simple-to-understand laws of geometry, and forms a picture that can be seen in all types of light. A hologram on the other hand records three-dimensional space in a complex interference pattern, and replays this only when suitably illuminated. Viewers of a hologram see the subject just as if it was in front of their eyes, behind or in front of the surface of the holographic plate — or as sometimes nowadays, 35mm film.

Holograms are made using the pure light of a laser. The laser is split into two or more beams, which are then spread out into broad shafts. One of these, the reference beam, strikes the plate directly. The others, the object beams, hit the object before striking the plate. The object encodes its own shape on the object beams by diffraction, and when these 'scrambled' beams strike the plate, they form the diffraction pattern that makes a permanent record of the subject's contours. Illuminating the hologram appropriately 'unscrambles' the diffraction pattern, and we see the object — in full depth.

Holography is widely used in industry for non-destructive testing; in certain specialized areas of optics; for security purposes (certain types of hologram cannot be copied); and as an art-form in its own right. As the cost of creating holograms continues to fall, it seems likely that these remarkable three-dimensional images will become commonplace in security, printing, packaging and display applications.

Holograms By recording the interference between crossing beams of laser light on photographic plates, the photographic process can create remarkable three-dimensional images. The picture above shows a hologram made by James Cobb of a sculpture of Punch. Because the process is so sensitive to vibration, holograms are often made on massive concrete tables — the holographic table in the picture on the left weighs 42 tons.

Schlieren photography of a soap bubble In schlieren photography a schlieren interferometer is used to record relative densities, an electronic flash freezes the

patterns. The results are colour coded to allow measurement. Even the minutest differences in surface thickness of the bubble show up clearly.

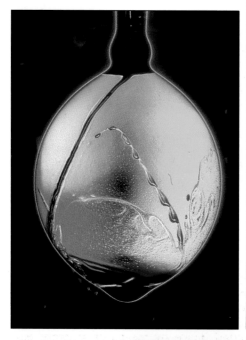

Schlieren photography

Schlieren photography is a method for making the mixing within gases and liquids visible. It is used, for example, to record airflow in a wind tunnel and shock waves in ballistics tests. Turbulence in a gas or liquid creates slight local differences in the refraction of light. If lit by a concentrated beam and photographed next to a knife edge, the turbulence appears in high contrast — and in different colours if a filter is used. Great precision is needed, and for fast movement, flash illumination. In practice, the image is projected by means of concave mirrors, which do not suffer from the chromatic aberration that affects lenses.

Electron photomicrography

The resolution, and so the useful magnification, of an optical microscope is limited by the wavelength and 'spread' of white light. The rays defract against sharp edges, and details smaller than about one micron (0.001mm) across cannot be distinguished. However, this lower limit to the visibility of things can be overcome by using radiation that has a shorter wavelength. An electron microscope uses electrons, directed and focused by means of electromagnets (rather than lenses as for light).

As the information is stored electronically, a scanning system can be used, giving high resolution and an extraordinary depth of field. A tight beam of electrons plays in a programmed pattern across the surface of the subject, and the

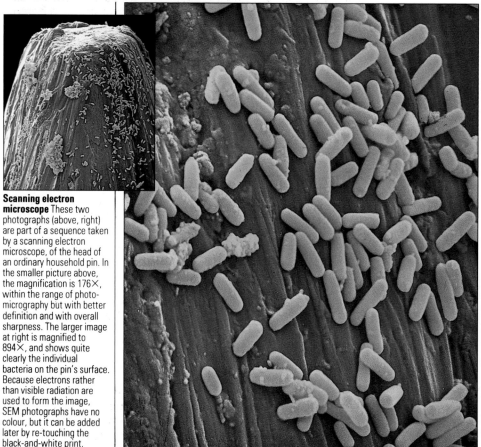

Scanning electron microscope These two photographs (above, right) are part of a sequence taken by a scanning electron microscope, of the head of an ordinary household pin. In the smaller picture above, the magnification is 176×, within the range of photomicrography but with better definition and with overall sharpness. The larger image at right is magnified to 894×, and shows quite clearly the individual bacteria on the pin's surface. Because electrons rather than visible radiation are used to form the image, SEM photographs have no colour, but it can be added later by re-touching the black-and-white print.

Interference and stress polarization Interference between beams of light can be used to make visible phenomena and distortions that would otherwise be too small to

Thermography As this portrait shows, recognizable images can be produced by heat alone. Light is irrelevant: the different colours show only variation in temperature. The hair is cooler than the skin, and the glass of the spectacles, being a poor conductor of heat, is coolest.

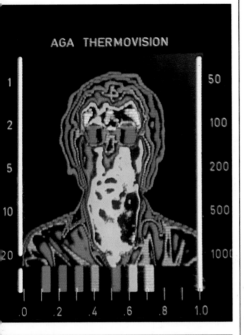

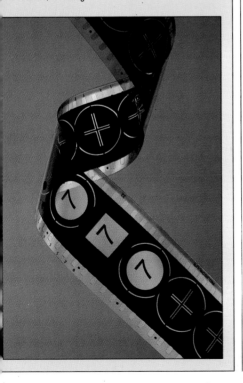

see — of less than the wavelength of light itself. In the negative images below, acoustic deformation is made visible by laser interference, revealing how the shape of a violin alters slightly as it is played. Below, a strip of movie film reveals colourful patterns when back-lit through crossed polarizers.

resulting image is built up in overlapping raster lines on a monitor. This is then recorded on film. The image is of course, monochromatic, although it can be coloured, either arbitrarily or, with larger specimens, from an optical reference.

Scanning electron microscopes (SEMs) can work at magnifications of up to a few millions of times. A major limitation is the need for a vacuum around the subject (to prevent electrons colliding with gas particles and scattering) and special preparatory treatment for the subject, such as freeze-drying or gold-coating — both can traumatize organisms severely.

Thermography

Although infrared film, as described on page 108, can record infrared emissions that are close to the visible spectrum, for the deep infrared wavelengths associated with differences in temperature, a different electronic system is needed. Thermal imaging cameras use a heat detector kept at low temperatures (usually with liquid nitrogen). The signals generated in the detector are amplified and imaged on a video display unit. This electronic image is then photographed on regular film, either with a built-in camera-and-filter system, or directly off the screen by the user. The most sophisticated thermographic equipment produces coloured pictures directly — the colours are arbitrary, but coded to a scale of temperature. More basic systems produce black-and-white images, but these can be used to make a coloured image by means of separate exposures of each temperature, each through a different coloured filter. When photographing the screen with a regular camera, follow the recommendations for video recording.

Thermography is used widely in medicine, as temperature differences in the human body can be diagnostic of some diseases, including cancer. They also have industrial uses, to show heat loss through insulating materials, for example, or rates of flow of heated fluids and gases through pipes.

Stress polarization

Certain crystals and plastics transmit light in two rays that are polarized at right angles to each other. If photographed through polarizing filters, these crystals show interference patterns in vivid colours. Under stress, such as bending, the play of colours is quite striking. This has scientific uses in analyzing the stresses in certain shapes, by making models of the appropriate plastic.

Stress polarization photography is straightforward: the light is covered with a polarizing sheet or filter, and directed through the material. A polarizing filter is placed over the camera lens. Rotating either polarizing lens or the subject changes the patterns and play of colours.

Radiography

Radiography uses invisible light waves of extremely short wavelengths, called X-rays, to form shadow images of the internal structure of objects. These rays are so energetic that they can penetrate many apparently opaque structures. The shadows are formed by bombarding the target with X-rays. Special film beyond the target records where these X-rays pass through the target and where they are held back, notably by bone. In this way certain internal structures are clearly revealed. This is why they are so useful for medical diagnosis.

In practice, X-ray film is placed next to the subject, which is then bathed in a timed dose of X-rays. The developed result is a shadow negative of the denser parts of the subject. The structural details that are revealed depend of the dose of the X-rays or on the use of even more penetrating particles, such as gamma rays from a radioactive isotope or neutrons from a nuclear reactor.

Radiography Although the most common use of X-rays is medical, they have other applications, too. In an impressive demonstration of large-scale, high-intensity radiography, this Mercedes sports car was radiographed onto five large strips of special Agfa-Gevaert film. The intensity of the exposure in an X-ray determines which internal details become visible, as a radiograph such as this is essentially a shadow picture of parts having a certain density or greater. In this example, to penetrate most of the bodywork, a lethal 50-hour exposure to radioactive combalt was necessary. Interestingly, this exposure reveals just the cross-sections of the tyres. The solid rectangle near the radiator grille is the battery — lead-lined, it is the densest barrier to X-rays.

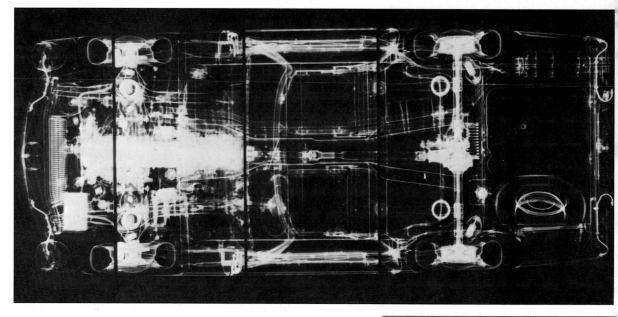

Tomography is a special medical application of radiography, in which the apparatus is rotated about the patient so as to scan a particular area. This scanning technique, in which a very large number of readings are made and then processed in a computer, makes it possible to form images of sections of soft tissue, such as the brain.

X-rays can also be used to *project* an image in certain conditions, although the result is a diffraction pattern rather than a recognizable picture of the subject. The subject is placed next to the source of X-rays, and the film at a distance. This is used, for example, in the analysis of certain gems.

Certain materials fluoresce under radiation, and X-ray fluorescence can be a useful way of detecting them.

Endoscopy

Miniature and flexible optical systems allow photographs to be made in small spaces that would otherwise be too restrictive for a regular camera. Endoscopy has obvious uses in medicine, making it possible to see, and photograph, internal organs; industrial uses include machinery inspection, on piping, for example, and internal combustion engines.

Endoscopes can be either flexible or rigid. Flexible endoscopes channel the light through bundles of optical fibres that are precisely assembled so that each individual fibre is in exactly the same place at either end (otherwise, the image

Endoscopy A relay of miniature lenses in a stainless steel tube transmits the image from the tiny taking lens to either a viewing eyepiece or, as here, a regular 35mm SLR. This endoscope is used here to photograph inside an oyster (see right).

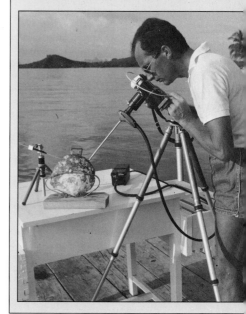

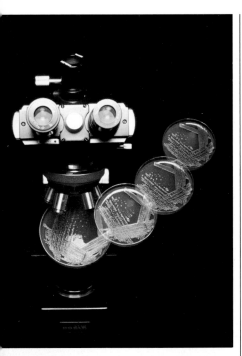

Step photography This is a form of regular controlled multiple exposure shot. For the picture below, a Petri dish with its bacterial culture was photographed in three steps. To do this, the camera was racked back and left by a predetermined amount. Step photography needs gradated scales for accuracy — in this case, a monorail. Any kind of gradated scale will do, even if it is drawn just for the rising centre column of a tripod, or marked on the floor for moving the entire tripod. If a large number of closely spaced steps is used, the result in the picture is almost a continuous line.

The endoscope gives a circular image, reaching within a few millimetres of this soft-bodied parasitic crab that lives permanently among the internal organs of the oyster. The small lens has good depth of field with aperture wide open.

would be scrambled). Rigid endoscopes, also known as bore-scopes, use a relay of lenses, which is less expensive and can give better image quality — (the resolution of fibre optic bundles is limited to the diameter of each fibre relative to the diameter of the whole bundle).

The three essential components of any endoscope are a miniature lens, a light channel for the image, and a light channel to introduce lighting into the subject. The taking lens, being small, has considerable depth of field and very close focusing (down to a few millimetres); there is often a choice of angle of view and of angle of orientation. For introducing lighting, a light guide is attached to a high intensity, focused lamp and run alongside the image transmitting channel. For this, either fibre optics or a liquid light channel are used — in both cases, high refraction keeps light loss to a minimum.

For photography, the eyepiece is attached directly to the camera body via an adapter, which has a simple lens. The image is usually circular, but can be made to fill the film simply by fitting a close-up lens extension.

Electro-photography

With limited but visually interesting applications, an electrical charge can be passed directly through or across a film emulsion. The result, more or less controllable, has some of the appearance of a photograph of lightning.

There are a number of ways of doing this, but the most vivid effects occur with low-current, high-voltage electricity. In one system, known as Kirlian photography after its inventor, any small object, typically a hand, can be pressed against a sheet of photographic film or paper and the charge is passed between two electrodes. Some unusual diagnostic claims have been made for Kirlian photography, including the detection of emotion.

Another method is to attach a sheet of film to one ball of a Van de Graaf Generator in darkness, and then to bring the second ball close until an electrostatic charge passes between the two. Daylight-balanced colour film produces a range of colours from red to blue.

Step Photography

Closely related to streak photography, but performed with a number of separate still exposures, is step photography. If the bright light or subject is moved in steps instead of continuously, and photographed each time, the result is a sequence of images on the same frame of film. Essentially, this is a form of multiple exposure with some kind of motion control; the same thing performed in cinematography would be stop-motion animation.

The actual technique can be simple or complex. At its most straightforward, the subject may be moved just two or three times in a single direction. Using a precise, graduated scale, a large number of steps can be overlapped to produce an effect which has almost the appearance of controlled streak photography. A simple animation guide makes it possible to make tiny adjustments for complex, irregular steps, such as with an articulated model — this is, in fact, exactly the method used in film animations. A variation is a mixture of step and streak photography — 'go-motion' as it is called in the special effects industry. In this, each step is performed with a little continuous movement, to leave the image of a slight trail.

Streak Photography

In any time exposure, movement appears as a blur, and although most photographers in most situations take precautions to avoid blur (sharpness being one of the conventions of photography), it can be used to advantage, especially if controlled. Basically, a bright moving object against a dark background will produce the image of a line or band; a bright background, however, will wipe out the image of a passing dark object (a small streaked tail may remain). Under controlled studio conditions, the simplest way of producing useful streaked images is to fix a light on a moving track or arm. The type of movement determines the shape of the image: a light at the end of a rotating arm, for example, will photograph as a circle, if the camera is directly above, or as an ellipse if the camera is at an angle.

For a smooth streak, motorized movement is usually best — an electronic wheeled motor on a track, for example, or an adapted record turntable. Hand-cranked movement tends to produce a banded effect.

An alternative to a moving light (or a light-toned object that is lit) is to move the camera itself. Or, the camera can be moved or rotated as the subject moves, to build up a complex pattern. In all cases, if only the streak is wanted, the rest of the set will have to be blacked out with black velvet.

Slit-scan photography

By moving film and subject in exact relation to each other, and recording just a small area of the image at a time, a type of linear distortion can be produced. In its simplest form, this can stretch or compress the image, depending on the direction and speed of movement, in a way that is loosely related to the focal plane shutter distortion mentioned on page 47. In a more serious application, the full circumference of a rotated object can be recorded in one single strip of film.

The principle is that part of the scene in front of the camera is projected not onto the entire film, but through a narrow slit. If this slit passes across the film as different parts of the image are projected through it, the result is as if the surface of the three-dimensional subject has been peeled off and laid down flat.

In its scientific application — 'periphery' photography — the film holder is motorized, and so is the turntable carrying the subject. The two motors are linked so that their rates of movement match. Because the parts of the subject which are further from the camera appear to move more slowly across the film, there is some depth distortion. A subject that contains real differences in movement as well produces very unusual distortion — a runner or cyclist, for example. A much less precise method of slit-scan photography can be done very simply. A vertical slit is fitted in front of the lens, and the camera is panned to follow a moving subject as the film is wound. With some dexterity, the film can be moved by turning the rewind crank, or the motor drive can be operated (weak batteries can be used to reduce the speed of winding). At least one proprietary make of slit-scan filter is available.

Streak photography involves moving either the subject or the camera during a long exposure to record the streak of movement. In this example (below), a light attached to a motor-driven rotating arm was photographed in darkness (and against a black background), to give a representation of an electron in orbit around a nucleus. The camera was also rotated between revolutions.

Video recording

Apart from simply photographing transmitted pictures on a television receiver, the computer boom has created a new need for hardcopy photographs of video displays. Although some professional computer graphics systems have built-in means of transferring the images onto film, direct photography of the monitor screen remains a standard option for most people. The two basic precautions are to match the colour balance and to match the exposure time to the scanning period of the video.

While phosphors on the screen that display the image (as they are struck by the electron beam) appear realistically coloured to the eye, they are actually bluish. The amount varies according to the equipment, but the normal filtration with daylight-balanced film is 30 red plus 20 yellow. Testing is essential for good results.

As a video image is created by scanning, line by line, it takes a finite amount of time to build up each image. If the shutter speed of the camera is faster than this, some of the picture will be missed, and a diagonal band will appear on the photograph. A slow shutter speed avoids this — slower than one thirtieth of a second is usually safe. The brightness of the screen can be adjusted, but the high settings tend to reduce sharpness. Typical exposures on ISO 64 film are about $\frac{1}{15}$ second at f4. With a moving image, it may be necessary to time the exposure for moments of least movement, or to record the transmission and freeze-frame the picture. Screen reflections can be reduced by darkening the room and by shielding the bright parts of the camera with black cloth.

A higher resolution technique is to isolate the individual pixels along each raster line; this calls for special equipment, such as the Polaroid Model Four Videoprinter.

Video subjects Any video image can make a satisfactory subject for a still shot, providing the movement is not great. In particular, graphically processed images such as this, of an American football player, make clear, simple still photographs.

'Banding' The importance of a slow shutter speed is demonstrated by the shots below, taken from a standard television monitor. At 1/30 second, the image is clean, but at 1/125 second (bottom) the electron beam has had insufficient time to scan the entire screen, giving a dark diagonal stripe.

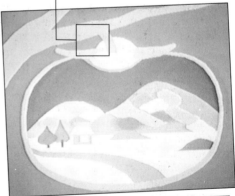

Hardcopy videoprinters The increasing use of computer graphics has created a need for making photographic hardcopies, and to date it is the instant film manufacturers who have made the strongest entry. The Polaroid Video-Printer Model 48 colour film recorder connects by cable to a variety of host video sources, accommodating different standards from medium to high resolution computer graphic systems. The base unit shown at left below contains the CRT and electronics, with simple operator controls. The incoming signals are digitalized by the microprocessor into 256 grey scale levels, and red, blue and green signals are then displayed in sequence through appropriate filters so that a full-colour image can be built up on one print. There are two optical attachments, which between them allow 10×8 inch and 5×4 inch instant film prints to be made, in addition to slides.

PHOTOMICROGRAPHY

The range of magnifications in small-scale photography — close-up, photomacrography and photomicrography — is subdivided because each uses different optical techniques. Close-up photography covers subjects needing a lens extension large enough to effect the exposure — that is, with an image $\frac{1}{7}x$ life size — up to about life size (1x). This needs only regular camera equipment. In photomacrography, with magnifications from 1x to about 20x, the lens is closer to the subject than the film, and special, or at least reversed, lenses are desirable. At greater magnifications — indeed even at more modest ones around 10x — the best image quality comes from an entirely different optical system — that of the microscope.

In a microscope, the image is magnified in two stages: by the *objective* lens, which is the primary lens, close to the subject, and by the *eyepiece* lens. The magnification is inscribed on each, and the total is calculated by multiplying the two. The power of objective lenses is mainly between 5x and 100x, and that of eyepieces between 5x and 25x. In photomicrography, only the microscope's optical system is used; the camera body is attached directly to the microscope lens. The camera is usually attached with a special collar, but it can even simply be mounted above the microscope, provided that the room is darkened. Depth of field at these magnifications is negligible, and virtually all photomicrography is of completely flat specimens. Apertures in photomicrography are used to maximize resolving power rather than to increase depth of field. The numerical aperture (NA) of an objective lens is a measure of how well it can resolve detail, and limits

Most modern microscopes have lights built into their bases, requiring less operator skill in adjusting the illumination. Nevertheless, it is important to make sure that, where the position of the light can be moved, there is no vignetting. In the upper of the two photographs below, taken with brightfield illumination, the light was off-centre.

The pair of photographs at right, of a pearl section, illustrate the difference between brightfield (above) and darkfield (below) illumination. Often, either lighting system is acceptable, but here brightfield lighting may be prone to flare.

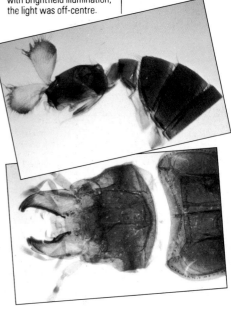

Microscope optics The most common photographic set-up, as shown at left, is a 35mm camera body attached to the eyepiece — the adaptor collar may also have a simple optical system. The sub-stage condenser focuses an image of the field diaphragm in the specimen plane. This focused light picks up an image of the specimen and projects it into the objective. A sharp aerial image is formed at the entrance pupil of the eyepiece, which then projects it up to either the observer's eye or, as here, the film plane of the camera. When using a large-format camera, as shown at right, the eyepiece is adjusted to focus the image further back. In this case, the camera is too large and heavy to be mounted on the microscope, and must be separately supported.

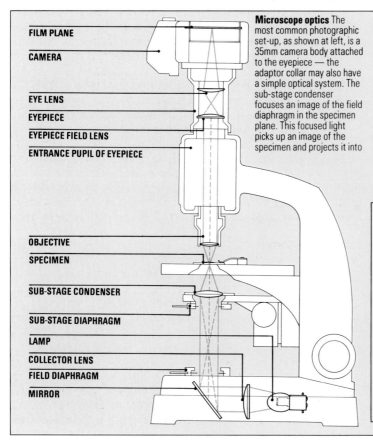

FILM PLANE
CAMERA
EYE LENS
EYEPIECE
EYEPIECE FIELD LENS
ENTRANCE PUPIL OF EYEPIECE
OBJECTIVE
SPECIMEN
SUB-STAGE CONDENSER
SUB-STAGE DIAPHRAGM
LAMP
COLLECTOR LENS
FIELD DIAPHRAGM
MIRROR

Preparing specimens
As there is virtually no depth of field in photomicrography, the surface of a specimen must be flat. Most can be sliced into translucent sections, and this preparation is performed with a microtome. To enhance contrast in thin tissue sections, stains of various types and colours are regularly used. Liquids can be smeared between two cover glasses, and crystals can be formed from solutions by allowing a drop to evaporate on a cover glass.

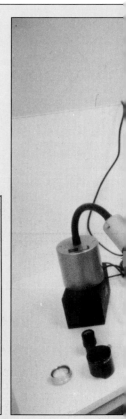

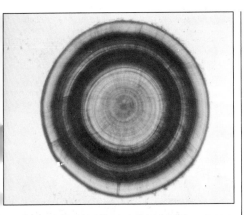

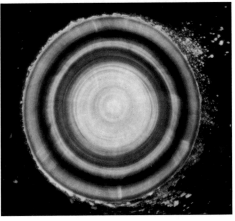

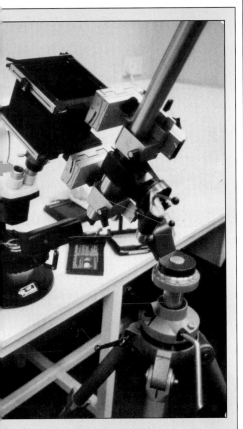

the use for magnification. 1000x the NA gives an approximation of the maximum useful magnification.

Lighting

In microscopy, the lighting can virtually be considered as part of the optical system. For the best results, the light must be focused. In modern, sophisticated microscopes, the lamp is built into the base; in simpler models a separate lamp is focused up onto the 'stage' (where the specimen is placed) with the aid of a swivelling mirror.

Standard lighting is tungsten, colour balanced for type B films. Any 3200 K balanced film is suitable, although fine grain is usually needed because resolution is essential. Kodak Photomicrography Colour Film 2483 is specially designed for this work, and has both fine grain and high contrast. For active specimens, flash must be used.

The most common lighting methods are brightfield and darkfield. Both are transmitted through the specimen from below the stage. Brightfield lighting is basically backlighting. In darkfield lighting an opaque stop is placed in the beam of light below the stage, so that the specimen is lit from the edges. Brightfield lighting is about four times brighter than darkfield and so needs less exposure. For opaque specimens that cannot be sliced sufficiently thin to be transluscent, 'axial' lighting must be used, in which light is introduced into the microscope's optical system above the objective with a semi-reflecting mirror.

Camera technique

Small cameras (35mm) can be mounted directly onto the eyepiece (or one eyepiece in the case of binocular microscopes) with a special adapter available from the camera manufacturer. Large-format cameras are better supported on a tripod or copy stand separately. The important first step is to centre the light in the field of view and focus it so that the entire picture area is evenly illuminated. The easiest way to judge the exposure is with a TTL meter, or an instant film test. Exposure is regulated by either the shutter speed and/or neutral density filters. With a large-format camera, the exposure may be up to several seconds, so vibration is a potential problem: use a cable release and lock up the mirror. Even with fairly brief exposures, the small size of the subject means that any movement is significant, so all the equipment should be mounted on a solid bench to minimize vibration.

Special systems

With some specimens — especially certain metals and crystals — polarization has vividly colourful effects. Two filters are used: one, known as the polarizer, between the specimen and the objective; and another, the analyzer, between the objective and the eyepiece. The analyzer can be rotated, in the same way as an ordinary polarizing filter on a regular camera lens.

Two special lighting systems, phase-contrast and interference-contrast, split the light passing through the specimen into two beams, delaying one to create a contrast-enhancing effect. By these means, specimens that would otherwise be virtually invisible through being transparent reveal fine detail.

COPYING

Photographing flat artwork — paintings, art prints, documents, type-setting and photographic prints — can be very demanding technically. Usually the aim is to reproduce the original as accurately as possible, and the approach needed depends on the nature of the artwork.

There are three main kinds of flat original: continuous tone, halftone and line. In continuous tone artworks, tones and colours merge gradually into each other, even at magnification. Halftones (see page 161) are produced by photomechanical reproduction and are composed of a pattern of dots of solid ink, fine enough to appear continuous — the photographs in this book are of this type. Line originals such as type are solid ink on a toneless background.

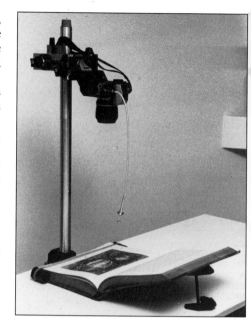

Fidelity

Copying always involves some loss of image quality, however small. These losses occur in three areas — detail, tonal range and colour. A fine-grained film, particularly in a large format, helps to preserve detail and avoids adding a texture of grain. Careful processing, with most films except Kodachrome, provides some control over the tonal range (see page 113). Contrast can be increased by pushing, or reduced by pulling, the development.

Colour is more of a problem. This is because the dyes in the film do not react to the dyes or pigments in the original in the same way as our eyes react. Imperfect colour response does not usually matter in normal photography, as the differences are usually quite small, but a side-by-side comparison of an original and its photographic copy will show up any inaccuracies clearly. The best that can usually be done is to filter for the most important colours. For photomechanical reproduction, it helps to include in the copy shot a standard colour reference, such as a Kodak separation guide; the printer can then adjust to this.

In black-and-white copying, filtration offers some control over staining. The yellowing of paper, for example, can be dealt with by using a yellow filter.

Alignment

The easiest way of making sure that the lens axis is exactly at right angles to the original is to copy vertically, as shown opposite, and use a spirit-level. An even more precise check is to place a hand mirror flat against the centre of the original, and focus the lens on its own reflected image: the alignment is exact if the image of the lens is precisely in the middle of the viewfinder.

With a large painting, however, this may not be possible. To copy *in situ*, the angle at which the painting hangs must be measured (with a clinometer), and the camera adjusted to the same angle. Alternatively, and more laboriously, a cross-grid viewfinder screen shows if the opposite edges of the painting's frame are parallel.

Lighting

To illuminate the artwork evenly, two lights can be positioned at either side, each aimed towards the *opposite* edge of the original. In this way, their beams cross. The evenness of illumination can be checked with several incident light readings from different parts of the original, or with spot

Copying artwork from books The basic requirement for copying artwork is a flat base for the original and a firm camera support — a vertical bar and sliding mount is easier to work with than a tripod. The copy stand must be aligned so that the lens axis is perpendicular to the base. Books, unfortunately, rarely lie completely flat, and the following alignment technique is useful: raise one side of the book to help flatten the page being copied (left top); focus on the reflection of the lens in the mirror (left bottom) and adjust either book or camera until the image appears centred (left centre). Line artwork, such as engravings (right), is best copied on line film, which has sufficiently high contrast to reproduce the lines black and background clear white.

Copying paintings in situ
While it is always easiest to bring a painting to the camera, it is not always possible. With oil paintings in particular, their size and the way they are hung may make it necessary to photograph them in place — in this example (above right), the height of the painting made it hard to remove. The lighting problem can be solved by using lighting stands that extend to ceiling height: at least two are positioned so that their beams strike the painting at an angle of about 45°, and they themselves are shaded from the camera lens to reduce flare. The verticals can only be maintained parallel by using a shift lens (on a small camera) or rising front standard on a view camera, as shown here (see also pages 18-19). Allowing for the small angle at which the painting is tilted is more difficult, especially if it is too inaccessible to be measured. Generally, a certain amount of trial and error is necessary, using etched grid lines on the camera's viewing screen as a guide.

readings from a plain white or grey card placed in different positions over the original. A pencil held perpendicular to the original in the centre will provide a rough guide — if light is even, the two shadows of the pencil should be identical in length and intensity.

To avoid reflections from the surface of the original, the lights should be at a fairly acute angle. However, if the angle is too extreme, they may cast shadows from the frame. An angle of 45° to the original is usually the best. Still, the lens should be shaded from the lamps to reduce flare.

If the original is covered by glass, there are two ways of cutting reflections of the camera itself. One is to black out the camera, by hanging in front of it a large sheet of black cloth or paper with a hole cut just large enough for the lens. The other is to polarize the light, with polarizing sheets across the lamps and a polarizing filter over the lens.

GLOSSARY

A

Aberration. Lens fault in which light rays are not focused properly, thereby degrading the image. It includes chromatic and spherical aberration, coma, astigmatism and field curvature.

Achromatic lens. A lens constructed of different types of glass, to reduce chromatic aberration. The simplest combination is of two elements, one of flint glass, the other of crown glass.

Acutance. The objective measurement of how well an edge is recorded in a photographic image.

Additive process. The process of combining lights of different colours. A set of three primary colours combined equally produces white.

Aerial perspective. The impression of depth in a scene that is conveyed by haze.

Amphibious camera. Camera which is constructed to be waterproof without the addition of a separate housing, by means of O-ring seals.

Anastigmat. A compound lens, using different elements to reduce optical aberrations.

Angle of view. Angle of the scene included across the picture frame by a particular lens. This varies with the focal length of the lens and the film format.

Angstrom. Unit used to measure light wavelengths.

Aperture. In most lenses, the aperture is an adjustable circular opening centred on the lens axis. It is the part of the lens that admits light.

Aperture-priority. Automatic camera mode in which the photographer selects the aperture manually; the appropriate shutter speed is then set automatically according to the information from the camera's metering system.

Area light. Photographic lamp/s enclosed in a box-like structure, the front of which is covered with a diffusing material such as opalescent plastic. Light is diffused by increasing the area of the light source. Also known as soft light, window light or 'fish-fryer' depending on size.

Archival techniques. Methods of handling, treating and storing photographic emulsions so as to lessen the deteriorating effects of ageing.

Astigmatism. A lens aberration in which light rays that pass obliquely through a lens are focused, not as a point but as a line. Astigmatism is normally found only in simple lenses.

ASA. Arithmetically progressive rating of the sensitivity of a film to light (American Standards Association). ASA 200 film, for example, is twice as fast as ASA 100 film. This is currently being replaced by the ISO rating.

Audio-visual (AV). Method of slide presentation to an audience in which the sound-track of music, voice and effects is synchronized to the projected images.

Auto-focus. System in which the focus is adjusted automatically, either passively by measuring the contrast of edges, or actively by measuring the reflection of an ultrasonic pulse.

Automatic exposure control. Camera system where the photo-electric cell that measures the light reaching the film plane is linked to the shutter or lens aperture, adjusting exposure automatically.

Axial lighting. A method of illuminating a subject in which the light travels along the lens axis, thereby casting no visible shadows. The normal means is by an angled, half-silvered mirror, which is a part of front-projection systems.

B

Back projection. Slide projection systems in which the image is projected onto a translucent screen from behind. It is both a method of presenting slides to an audience and a method of creating an apparently realistic background for a studio photograph. In the latter use it is less efficient than front projection.

Back scatter. The visual result of using a flash underwater from the camera position when the water contains particles or air bubbles. It appears as a 'snowstorm'.

Background roll. A standard type of studio background, in the form of heavy-gauge coloured paper, in 3m (9ft) wide rolls.

Barn doors. Adjustable flaps that fit at the front of a photographic studio lamp to prevent light from spilling at the sides. Normally two or four hinged flaps on a frame.

Barrel distortion. A lens aberration in which the shape of the image is distorted. The magnification decreases radially outwards, so that a square object appears barrel-shaped, with the straight edges bowed outwards.

Base. The support material for an emulsion — normally plastic or paper.

Base density. The minimum density of the film base in a transparency or negative. Determines the maximum brightness of highlights in a transparency.

Base lighting. Lighting directed upwards from beneath a subject. Also known as ground lighting.

Bas-relief. A method of producing images that appear to stand out slightly in relief. It is produced by sandwiching a positive and negative of the same image slightly out of register, and then printing the combination.

Bellows. Flexible black sleeve of concertina-like construction, connecting the camera-back or body with the lens. Used in view cameras and in close-up attachments.

Between-the-lens shutter. A leaf shutter located inside a compound lens, as close as possible to the aperture diaphragm.

Blind. American term for 'hide' — camouflaged camera positions in wildlife photography.

Boom. Counter-weighted lighting support in the form of a metal arm that pivots on a vertical stand. Useful for suspending lights high over a subject.

Borescope. A rigid endoscope, developed artificially for industrial inspection.

Bounce flash. Diffusion of the light from a flash unit, by directing it towards a reflective surface, such as a ceiling or wall. This scatters the light rays, giving a softer illumination.

Bounce light. Diffusion of any light source in the same way as described for bounce flash.

Bracketing. A method of compensating for uncertainties in exposure, by making a series of exposures of a single subject, each varying by a progressive amount from the estimated correct aperture/speed setting.

Brightfield illumination. The basic lighting technique for photomicrography, directing light through a thin section of the subject. In effect, a form of back-lighting.

Brightness range. The range of tones in a photographic subject, from darkest to lightest. Usually measured as a ratio or in f-stops.

C

Camera angle. Common term to describe the direction of view of a camera, particularly in reference to its angle from the horizontal.

Camera movements. Mechanical adjustments normal on view cameras that permit the lens panel and/or film back to be shifted laterally and pivoted. They allow adjustments to the coverage and geometry of the image and the distribution of sharpness.

Capacitor. Electrical device that allows a charge to be built up and stored. An integral part of electronic flash units.

Cartridge camera/film. Photographic system in which the film is enclosed in a plastic cartridge, simplifying loading and unloading. Designed for amateur use.

Catadioptric lens. See *Mirror lens*.

CdS cell. Cadmium sulphide cell used commonly in through-the-lens light meters. Its proportionate resistance to the quantity of light received is the basis of exposure measurement.

Centre of curvature. The centre of an imaginary sphere of which the curved surface of a lens is a part.

Central processing unit (CPU). In an automatic camera, the part of the electronic circuitry that coordinates the programming.

Centre-weighted exposure. Standard method of exposure measurement in TTL-metering cameras in which extra value is given to the tones in the centre of the picture.

Characteristic curve. Curve plotted on a graph from two axes — exposure and density — used to describe the characteristics and performance of sensitive emulsions.

Chromatic aberration. A lens aberration in which light of different wavelengths (and therefore colours) is focused at different distances behind the lens. It can be corrected by combining different types of glass.

Chromogenic film. Photographic emulsion in which dyes are formed at the sites of the silver grains. Normal for colour film.

Circle of confusion. The disc of light formed by an imaginary lens. When small enough, it appears to the eye as a point, and at this size the image appears sharp.

Click stop. The graduation of the aperture ring on a lens that allows the change between individual f-stops to be felt and heard.

Clinometer. Device for measuring angles from the vertical. Useful in copying paintings that hang at an angle.

Clip test. A short strip from an exposed film that is processed in advance to determine whether any adjustment is needed in processing. Useful when the exposure conditions are uncertain.

Coating. A thin deposited surface on a lens, to reduce flare by interference of light waves.

Colour balance. Adjustment made at any stage of photography, from film manufacturers to post-production, to ensure that neutral greys in the subject appear neutral in the photograph.

Colour cast. An overall bias in a photograph towards one particular colour.

Colour compensating filter. Filter used to alter the colour of light. Available in primary and complementary colours at different strengths, and used to correct deficiencies in the lighting and film manufacture.

Colour conversion filter. Coloured filter that alters the colour temperature of light.

Colour coupler. A chemical compound that combines with the oxidizing elements of a developer to form a coloured dye. It is an integral part of most colour film processing.

Colour temperature. The temperature to which an inert substance would have to be heated in order for it to glow at a particular colour. The scale of colour temperature significant for photography ranges from the reddish colours of approximately 2000°K through standard 'white' at 5400°K, to the bluish colours above 6000°K.

Coma. A lens aberration in which off-axis light rays focus as different distances when they pass through different areas of the lens. The result is blurring at the edges of the picture.

Combination printing. Method of combining images during enlargement by sandwiching two negatives.

Complementary colours. A pair of colours that, when combined together in equal proportions, produce white light (by means of the additive process).

Compound lens. Lens constructed of more than one element, making optical corrections possible.

Condenser. Simple lens system that concentrates light into a beam. Often used in enlargers.

Contact sheet. A print of all the frames of a roll of film arranged in strips, same-size, from which negatives can be selected for enlargement.

Contrast. Difference in brightness between adjacent areas of tone. In photographic emulsions, it is also the rate of increase in density measured against exposure.

Contrast range. The range of tones, from dark to light, of which film or paper is capable of recording. Usually measured as a ratio or in f-stops.

Convergence. In terms of perspective, the appearance of parallel lines in the subject as they are reproduced in the image when photographed from an angle.

Converging lens. Lens which concentrates light rays towards a common point. Also known as a convex lens.

Covering power. The diameter of usable image produced at the focal plane by a lens when focused at a given distance. An important consideration when choosing view camera lenses, which must cover more than just the film format if the camera movements are to be used.

Coving. A concave shape of background, usually moulded, that smooths out the normally sharp edge between a studio wall and floor. Gives a 'horizonless' background.

Cyan. Blue-green, complementary to red. Produces white in combination with magenta and yellow by the additive process.

Cyclorama. See *Coving.*

D

Darkcloth. Black cloth used by view camera photographers to eliminate the distraction of ambient light when looking at the image on the ground-glass screen.

Darkfield lighting. Lighting technique used in photomicrography and in photomacrography in which the subject is lit from all sides by a cone of light directed from beneath the subject. The background appears black.

Darkslide. A lightproof sheet used to protect film from exposure until it is mounted in the camera. Used with sheet film and certain rollfilm systems.

Daylight film. Colour film balanced for exposure by daylight or some other source with a colour temperature of 5400°K, such as electronic flash.

Dedicated flash. The integration of a flash unit with the camera's automatic exposure system.

Definition. The subjective effect of graininess and sharpness combined.

Densitometer. Device for measuring the density of specific parts of the image in the film or on paper. Allows precise measurement of tones. Necessary for making separation negatives.

Density. In photographic emulsions, the ability of a developed silver deposit to block transmitted light.

Depth of field. The distance through which the subject may extend and still form an acceptably sharp image, in front of and beyond the place of critical focus. Depth of field can be increased by stopping the lens down to a smaller aperture. It is a subjective measurement.

Depth of focus. The distance through which the film plane can be moved and still record an acceptably sharp image.

Diaphragm. An adjustable opening that controls the amount of light passing through a lens. Often referred to as the aperture diaphragm.

Diffraction. The scattering of light waves when they strike the edge of an opaque surface.

Diffuser. Material that scatters transmitted light and increases the area of the light source.

Digital. Principle of recording, storing and processing information in discrete units.

DIN. Logarithmically progressive rating of the sensitivity of a film to light (Deutsche Industrie Norm). Currently being replaced by the ISO rating.

Diopter. Measurement of the refractive ability of a lens. It is the reciprocal of the focal length, in metres; a convex lens is measured in positive diopters, a concave lens in negative diopters. Used, for example, for supplementary close-up lenses.

Direct reading. Common term for reflected light reading.

Disc camera/film. Amateur photographic system in which the film frames are arranged on a flat disc.

Diverging lens. Lens which causes light-rays to spread outwards from the optical axis.

D-Max. Abbreviation for maximum density.

Documentary photography. Type of photography in which an accurate, objective record, undistorted by interpretation, is held to be the ideal.

Dolly. A rolling trolley to support either a camera tripod or a lighting stand. The wheels can be locked when it is in place.

Dye cloud. Zone of colour in a developed colour emulsion at the site of the developed silver grain, which itself has been bleached out during development.

Dye-image film. See *Chromogenic film.*

Dye-sensitization. The standard manufacturing process of adding dyes to emulsion in order to control its spectral sensitivity. Used in the manufacture of normal black-and-white films to make them panchromatic.

Dye transfer process. Colour printing process that uses colour separation negatives which in turn produce matrices that can absorb and transfer coloured dyes to paper.

E

Effects light. A photographic light used to produce a distinct visual effect rather than to provide basic illumination. A spotlight to give a halo effect to hair in a portrait is one example.

Electromagnetic spectrum. The range of frequencies of electromagnetic radiation, from radio waves to gamma rays, including visible radiation (light).

Electronic flash. Artificial light source produced by passing a charge across two electrodes in a gas. The colour balance is about 5400°K.

Electrophotography. The formation of images on emulsion by means of passing an electrical charge. Kirlian photography is one form.

Emulsion. Light-sensitive substance composed of halides suspended in gelatin, used for photographic film and paper.

Endoscope. Device built around a miniature lens for photography in small, normally inaccessible places, such as internal organs of the body.

Exposure. In photography, the amount of light reaching an emulsion, being the product of intensity and time.

Exposure latitude. For film, the increase in exposure that can be made from the minimum necessary to record shadow detail, while still presenting highlight detail.

Exposure value (EV). Notation of exposure settings for cameras that links aperture and shutter speed. A single EV number can, for example, represent 1/125 at f5.6 and 1/1500 at f2.8.

Extension. A fixed or adjustable tube placed between the lens and camera body, used to increase the magnification of the image.

F

F-number. The notation for relative aperture, which is the ratio of the focal length to the diameter of the aperture. The light-gathering power of lenses is usually described by the widest f-stop of which they are capable, and lens aperture rings are normally calibrated in a standard series: f1, f1.4, f2, f2.8, f4, f5.6, f8, f11, f16, f22, f32 and so on, each of these stops differing from its adjacent stop by a factor of 2.

Fibre optic. Optical transmission systems in which light is passed along flexible bundles of light-conducting strands. Within each fibre, the light is reflected with high efficiency to prevent any significant loss over a distance.

Field camera. Traditional folding design of view camera, often of mahogany construction with a flat-bed base, that is sufficiently portable for carrying on location.

Field curvature. In this lens aberration, the plane of sharpest focus is a curved surface rather than the flat surface needed at the film plane.

Fill. The illumination of shadow areas in a scene.

Fill-flash. As fill (above) but performed with an electronic flash, usually camera-mounted.

Film holder. Specifically, a container for sheet film for loading in the back of a view camera. The standard design has room for two sheets, one in each side of the flat holder, each protected by a dark slide. Film is loaded by the user in darkness.

Film plane. In a camera, the plane at the back in which the film lies and on which the focus is set.

Film speed rating. The sensitivity of film to light, measured on a standard scale, now normally ISO, formerly either ASA or DIN.

Filter factor. The number by which the exposure must be multiplied in order to compensate for the loss of light due to absorption by a filter.

Fish-eye lens. A very wide-angle lens characterized by extreme barrel distortion.

Flag. A matt black sheet held in position between a lamp and the camera lens to reduce flare.

Flare. Non-image-forming light, caused by scattering and reflection, that degrades the quality of an image. Coating is used to reduce it.

Flash. See *Electronic flash.*

Flash guide number. Notation used to determine the aperture setting when using electronic flash. It is proportionate to the output of the flash unit.

Flash synchronization. Camera system that ensures that the peak light output from a flash unit coincides with the time that the shutter is fully open.

Focal length. The distance between the centre of a lens (the principal point) and its focal point.

Focal plane. The plane at which a lens forms a sharp image.

Focal plane shutter. Shutter located close to the focal plane, using two blinds that form an adjustable gap which moves across the film area. The size of the gap determines the exposure.

Focal point. The point on either side of a lens where light rays entering parallel to the axis converge.

Focus. The point at which light rays are converged by a lens.

Follow focus. Lens focusing technique with a moving subject, in which the focusing ring is turned at exactly the rate necessary to maintain constant focus.

Fresnel screen. A viewing screen that incorporates a Fresnel lens. This has a stepped convex surface that performs the same function as a condenser lens, distributing image brightness over the entire area of the screen, but is much thinner.

Front projection. System of projecting a transparency's image onto a background screen from the camera position, thus ensuring minimum loss of image intensity and quality (the chief problem with back projection). The system relies upon axial lighting via a half-silvered mirror, and on a super-reflecting screen.

Full-tone. An image containing a continuous gradation of tones, as in an original photographic print (see *Half-tone*).

Fully automatic diaphragm (FAD). System in an SLR camera which allows full-aperture viewing up to the moment of exposure; linkages between the mirror box and the lens stop down the aperture to its selected setting an instant before the shutter opens.

G

Gamma. Measure of the steepness of an emulsion's characteristic curve being the tangent of the acute angle made by extending the straight line position of the curve downwards until it meets the horizontal axis. Average emulsions averagely developed have a gamma of about 0.8, while high contrast films have a gamma greater than 1.0.

Gel. Common term for coloured filter sheeting, normally used over photographic lamps.

Gelatin. Substance used to hold halide particles in suspension, in order to construct an emulsion. This is deposited on a backing.

Gelatin filter. Thin, coloured filters made from dyed gelatin that have no significant effect on the optical quality of the image passed. Normally used over the camera lens.

Grade. Classification of photographic printing paper by contrast. Grades 0 to 4 are the most common, although they are not precisely comparable across makes.

Grain. An individual light-sensitive cyrstal, normally of silver bromide.

Graininess. The subjective impression when viewing a photograph of granularity under normal viewing conditions. The eye cannot resolve individual grains, only overlapping clusters..

Granularity. The measurement of the size and distribution of grains in an emulsion.

Ground-glass screen. Sheet of glass finely ground to a translucent finish on one side, used to make image focusing easier when viewing.

Ground light. A design of studio light that sits on the floor and is aimed upwards, normally to illuminate a background.

Gyro stabilizer. Electrically powered camera support that incorporates a heavy gyroscope to cushion the camera from vibrations. particularly useful when shooting from helicopters, cars and other vehicles.

H

Half-tone. An image that appears at normal viewing distance to have continuous gradation of tones, but which is made up of a fine pattern of dots of solid ink or colours.

Hardener. Chemical agent — commonly chrome or potassium alum — that combines with the gelatin of a film to make it more resistant to scratching.

Heat filter. Transparent screen used in front of a photographic lamp to absorb heat without reducing the light transmission.

Hide. Term for camouflaged camera position in wildlife photography.

High key. Type of image made up of light tones only.

Hyperfocal distance. The closest distance at which a lens records a subject sharply when focused at infinity. It varies with the aperture.

Hypo. Alternative name for fixer, sodium thiosulphate.

Hypo eliminator. Chemical used to clear fixer from an emulsion to shorten washing time.

I

Incident light reading. Exposure measurement of the light source that illuminates the subject. It is therefore independent of the subject's own characteristics.

Infrared radiation. Electromagnetic radiation from 730 nanometers to 1mm ($\frac{1}{32}$in), longer in wavelength than light. It is emitted by hot bodies.

Instant film. Photographic system pioneered by the Polaroid corporation, in which processing is initiated as soon as the exposed film is withdrawn from the camera and is normally completed within a minute or so.

Instant-return mirror. The angled viewing mirror in a SLR camera, which flips up to allow the film to be exposed and then immediately returns to the viewing points.

Integral film. Type of instant film in which the entire development process, chemicals, and materials take place and remain within a sealed packet.

Integral masking. The addition of dyes to colour negative film in its manufacture to compensate for deficiencies in the image forming dyes.

Intensifier. Chemical used to increase the density or contrast of an image or an emulsion. Particularly useful with too-thin negatives.

Internegative. A negative copy of a transparency. Internegative film is formulated to prevent any build-up of contrast.

Inverse square law. As applied to light, the principle that the illumination of a surface by a point source of light is proportional to the square of the distance from the source to the surface.

 ISO (International Standard Organization). Film speed notation to replace the ASA and DIN systems, made up of a combination of these two.

J

Joule. Unit of electronic flash output, equal to one watt-second. The power of different units can be compared with this measurement.

K

Kelvin (K). The standard unit of thermodynamic temperature, calculated by adding 273 to degrees centigrade/Celsius. In photography it is a measure of colour temperature.

Key light. The main light source.

Key reading. Exposure reading of the key tone only. A form of spot metering.

Key tone. The most important tone in a scene being photographed that must be rendered accurately.

Kilowatt. Unit of electrical power, equivalent to 1000 watts.

Kirlian photography. Form of electrophotography in which the subject is placed against film and its image appears as an outline of electrical discharge.

L

Latent image. The invisible image formed by exposing an emulsion to light. Development renders it visible.

Latitude. The variation in exposure that an emulsion can tolerate and still give an acceptable image. Usually measured in f-stops.

LCD (Liquid crystal diode). A solid-state display system used in viewfinder information displays particularly. Consumes less power than LEDs (light emitting diodes).

Lens. A transparent device for converging or diverging rays of light by refraction. Convex lenses are thicker at the centre than at the edges; concave lenses are thicker at the edges than at the centre.

Lens axis. A line through the centre of curvature of a lens.

Lens flare. Non-image-forming light reflected from lens surfaces that degrades the quality of the image.

Lens shade. Lens attachment that shades the front element from non-image forming light that can cause flare.

Lens speed. Common lens designation in terms of maximum light-gathering power. The figure used is the maximum aperture.

Light tent. Enclosing device of translucent material placed so as to surround a subject, the lighting is directed through the material to give an extremely diffused effect, useful with rounded shiny objects to simplify reflections.

Line film. Very high contrast film, which can be developed so that the image contains only full-density black, with no intermediate tones.

Long-focus lens. Lens with a focal length longer than the diagonal of the film format. For 35mm film, anything longer than about 50mm is therefore long-focus, although in practice the term is usually applied to lenses with at least twice the standard focal length.

Low key. Type of image made up of dark tones only.

Luminaire. Large photographic tungsten lamp which focuses by means of a Fresnel lens.

Luminance. The quantity of light emitted by or reflected from a surface.

M

Macro. Abbreviation for photomacrographic, applied to close-up photography of at least life-size reproduction. In particular, used to designate lenses and other equipment used for this purpose.

Macrophotography. The photography of large-scale objects. Hardly ever used to mean this, but often misused to mean 'photomacrography'.

Magnification. Size relationship between image and its subject, expressed as a multiple of the dimension of the subject.

Manual operation. The operation of camera, flash or other equipment in non-automatic modes.

Maximum density. The greatest density of silver or dye image that is possible in a given developed emulsion. In transparency film, the dark rebate is at maximum density.

Masking. Blocking specific areas of an emulsion from light. For example, a weak positive image, when combined with the negative, can be used to mask the highlights so as to produce a less contrasty print.

Matrix. Sheet of film used in the dye transfer process that carries a relief image in gelatin. This is temporarily dyed when printing.

Mean noon sunlight. An arbitrary but generally accepted colour temperature to which most daylight colour films are balanced — 5400° Kelvin being the average colour temperature of direct sunlight at midday in Washington DC.

Medical lens. Type of lens designed specifically for medical use, having close-focusing capability and a built-in ringflash.

Mercury vapour lamp. Form of lighting sometimes encountered in available light photography. It has a discontinuous spectrum and reproduces as blue-green on colour film.

Mid-tone. An average level of brightness, halfway between the brightest and darkest areas of scene or image (that is, between highlight and shadow areas).

Mired value. A measurement of colour temperature that facilitates the comparison of different light sources. It is calculated by dividing 1,000,000 by the colour temperature of the light source in Kelvins.

Mirror lens. Compound lens that forms an image by reflection from curved mirrors rather than by refraction through lenses. By folding the light paths, its length is much shorter than that of traditional lenses of the same focal length.

Mode. In camera technology, the form in which the basic functions (including exposure measurement, aperture and shutter speed settings) are operated, many automatic cameras have a choice of modes, from a high degree of automation to manual operation.

Modelling lamp. A continuous-light lamp fitted next to the flashtube in studio flash units that it used to show what the lighting effect will be when the discharge is triggered. Modelling lamps are usually low-wattage and either tungsten or fluorescent, and do not interfere with the actual exposure.

Modular construction. Method of camera construction in which several elements can be assembled by the user in a variety of combinations to suit particular uses. Monorail view cameras, for example, are designed in this way.

Monopod. Single leg of a tripod, as a lightweight camera support for hand-held shooting.

Monorail. The base support for the standard modern design of view cameras, in the form of an optical bench. Also, abbreviation for such a camera.

Motor-drive. Device that either attaches to a camera or is built into it, that motorizes the film transport, enabling a rapid sequence of photographs to be taken.

Multiple exposure. Method of combining more than one image on a single frame of film by making successive exposures of different subjects.

Multiple flash. The repeated triggering of a flash unit to increase exposure (with a static subject).

Multi-pattern metering. The metering system in which areas of the image frame are measured separately, and weighted according to a predetermined programme.

N

Nanometer. 10^{9} metre.

Negative. Photographic image with reversed tones (and reversed colours if colour film) used to make a positive image, normally a print by projection.

Neutral density. Density that is equal across all visible wavelengths, resulting in absence of colour.

Night lens. Camera lens designed for optimum use at a wide maximum aperture, usually about f1.2. Often incorporates an aspherical front element.

Non-substantive film. Colour film in which the colour-forming dyes are not present in the film as manufactured, but added during the processing. Kodachrome is the best known example.

Northlight. The light, usually large in area, from a north-facing window. Also, sometimes used to refer to artificial lighting which delivers the same effect. Noted for its diffuse but directional qualities.

O

Opalescent. Milky or cloudy white, translucent quality of certain materials, valuable in the even diffusion of a light source.

Open flash. Method of illuminating a subject with a flash unit, by leaving the camera shutter open, and triggering the flash discharge manually.

Optical axis. Line passing through the centre of a lens system. A light ray following this line would not be bent.

Optimum aperture. The aperture setting at which the highest quality images are formed by a lens. Often two or three f-stops less than maximum.

Orthochromatic film. Film that is sensitive to green and blue light, but reacts weakly to red light.

OTF metering. Off-the-film metering — a TTL system in which the exposure is measured from the image that is projected inside the camera at the film plane.

Outrig frame. Open metal frame that fits in front of a lamp and can be used to carry filters, gels or diffusing material.

P

Panchromatic film. Film that is sensitive to all the colours of the visible spectrum.

Panning. Smooth rotation of the camera so as to keep a moving subject continuously in frame.

Pantograph. In photography, a device constructed of interlocking, pivoted metal arms that allows the extension and retraction of lamps.

Parallax. The apparent movement of two objects relative to each other when viewed from different positions.

Peel-apart film. Type of instant film comprising two sheets, one carrying the negative image, the other receiving the positive image. After the short development time, the two sheets are peeled apart and the negative discarded.

Pentaprism. Five-sided prism, which rectifies the image left-to-right and top-to-bottom.

Peripheral photography. Photographic system in which the image of a revolving subject is projected through a moving slit onto the film. By correlating the two rates of movement, the circumferences of the subject can be recorded in a continuous strip.

Perspective correction (PC) lens. A lens with covering power greater than the film area, part of which can be shifted to bring different parts of the image into view. Mainly used to correct converging verticals in architectural photography.

Photo composite. A photograph assembled from two or more photographs. Normally a transparency, the assembly being accomplished by line film masks and duplication.

Photo-electric cell. Light sensitive cell used to measure exposure. Some cells produce electricity when exposed to light; others react to light by offering an electrical resistance.

Photoflood. Over-rated tungsten lamp used in photography, with a colour temperature of 3400°K.

Photogram. Photographic image made without a camera, by placing an object on a sheet of emulsion and briefly exposing it to light. The result is a kind of shadow picture.

Photojournalism. Relating a newsworthy story primarily with photographs.

Photomacrography. Close-up photography with magnifications in the range of about $1\times$ to $10\times$.

Photomicrography. Photography at great magnifications using the imaging systems of a microscope.

Picture area. The area in front of the camera that is recorded as an image.

Pincushion distortion. A lens aberration in which the shape of the image is distorted. The magnification increases radially outwards, and a square object appears in the shape of a pincushion, with the corners 'stretched'.

Pixel. Smallest unit of digital picture information in a digitalized picture, it is usually an extremely small square, of a certain tone and hue.

Plane of sharp focus. The plane at which an image is sharply focused by a lens. In a fixed-body camera it is normally vertical and perpendicular to the lens axis, but it can be tilted by means of camera movements.

Polarization. Restriction of the direction of vibration of light. Normal light vibrates at right angles to its direction of travel in every plane; a plane-polarizing filter (the most common in photography) restricts this vibration to one plane only. There are several applications, the most usual being to eliminate reflections from water and non-metal surfaces.

Port. In underwater photography, the window in the front of a housing. To avoid image distortion, it should ideally have a curve similar to that of the front element of the lens.

Posterization. Photographic image produced in blocks of solid tone, by means of tonal separation.

Post-production. The photographic processes that take place after the image has been developed, including retouching, special effects and treatment.

Printing controls. Shading and printing-in techniques used during enlargement to lighten or darken certain parts of a photographic print.

Printing-in. Printing technique of selectively increasing exposure over certain areas of the image.

Prism. Transparent substances shaped so as to refract light in a controlled manner.

Process lens. Flat-field lens designed to give high resolution of the image on a flat plane. This is achieved at the expense of depth of field, which is always shallow.

Programmed shutter. Electroncially operated shutter with variable speeds that is linked to the camera's TTL meter. When a particular aperture setting is selected, the shutter speed is automatically adjusted to give a standard exposure.

Pull-processing. Giving film less development than normal, in order to compensate for overexposure or to reduce contrast.

Push-processing. Giving film more development than normal, in order to compensate for underexposure or to increase contrast.

R

Rangefinder. Arrangement of mirror, lens and prism that measures distance by means of a binocular system. Used on direct viewfinder cameras for accurate focusing.

Rebate. The margin surrounding the image area on film; dark on a developed transparency, clear on a developed negative.

Reciprocity failure (reciprocity effect). At very short and very long exposures, the reciprocity law ceases to hold true, and an extra exposure is needed. With colour film, the three dye layers suffer differently, causing a colour cast. Reciprocity failure differs from emulsion to emulsion.

Reciprocity law. EXPOSURE = INTENSITY $\times$ TIME. In other words, the amount of exposure that the film receives in a camera is a product of the size of the lens aperture (intensity) and the shutter speed (time).

Reducer. Chemical used to remove silver from a developed image, so reducing density. Useful for overexposed or overdeveloped negatives.

Reflected light reading. Exposure measurement of the light reflected from the subject (cf *Incident light reading*). Through-the-lens meters use this method, and it is well-suited to subjects of average reflectance.

Reflector. Surface used to reflect light.

Refraction. The bending of light rays as they pass from one transparent medium to another when the two media have different light-transmitting properties.

Register system. System used in darkroom and assembly work in which separate pieces of film can be aligned exactly in position. The usual method is a matching punch and pin bar.

Relative aperture. The focal length of a lens divided by the diameter of the entrance pupil, normally recorded as f-stops, eg a 50mm lens with a maximum aperture opening 25mm in diameter has a relative aperture of f4 $\left(\dfrac{100mm}{25mm}\right)$.

Reportage photography. Capturing images on film that manage to sum up a typical news story.

Reproduction ratio. The relative proportions of the size of the subject and its image.

Resolution. The ability of a lens to distinguish between closely spaced objects, also known as resolving power.

Reticulation. Crazed effect on a film emulsion caused by subjecting the softened gelatin to extremes of temperature change.

Reversal film. Photographic emulsion which, when developed, gives a positive image (commonly called a transparency). So called because of one stage in the development when the film is briefly re-exposed, either chemically or to light, thus reversing the image which would otherwise be negative.

Rifle stock. Camera support that enables a camera normally with a long lens, to be hand-held more securely, in the same manner as a rifle.

Ringflash. Electronic flash in the shape of a ring, used in front of and surrounding the camera lens. The effect is of virtually shadowless lighting.

Rollfilm. Film rolled on a spool with a dark paper backing. The most common current rollfilm format is 120.

S

Sabattier effect. Partial reversal of tone (and colour when applied to a colour emulsion) due to brief exposure to light during development.

Safelight. Light source used in a darkroom with a colour and intensity that does not affect the light-sensitive materials for which it is designed.

Sandwich. Simple, physical combination of two sheets of film: transparencies for projection, negatives for printing.

Scheimpflug principle. Principle by which the orientation of the plane of sharp focus varies with the orientation of both the front and rear standards of a view camera: the plane and lines extended from the two standards meet at a common point.

Scoop. Smoothly curving studio background, used principally to eliminate the horizon line.

Scrim. Mesh material placed in front of a lamp to reduce its density, and to some extent to diffuse it. One thickness of standard scrim reduces output by the equivalent of about one f-stop.

Selenium cell. Photo-electric cell which generates its own electricity in proportion to incident light.

SEM. Scanning electron microscope.

Sensitometry. The scientific study of light-sensitive materials and the way they behave.

Separation guide. Printed guide containing a set of standard colours, when photographed alongside a subject that must be reproduced with great colour accuracy by printer (a painting for example), the separation maker can match the image against another, identical guide.

Separation negative. Black-and-white negative exposed through a strong coloured filter to record an image of a selected part of the spectrum, normally one-third. Used in dye transfer printing, and also in non-photographic printing.

Serial flash. See *Multiple flash.*

Shading. Photographic printing technique where light is held back from selected parts of the image.

Shadow detail. The darkest visible detail in a subject or in the positive image, often sets the lower limit for exposure.

Shadow fill. See *Fill.*

Sharpness. The subjective impression of acutance when viewing a photograph.

Sheet film. Film used in the form of flat sheets rather than rolls or strips. The most common formats are 4 × 5 inch and 8 × 10 inch.

Shift. Lateral camera movement (qv) — of either the front standard or rear standard.

Shift lens. See *Perspective control lens.*

Short-focus lens. Lens with a focal length shorter than the diagonal of the film format. For the 35mm format, short-focus lenses generally range shorter than 35mm.

Shutter. Camera mechanism that controls the period of time that image-focusing light is allowed to fall on the film.

Shutter priority. Automatic camera mode in which the photographer selects the shutter speed manually; the appropriate aperture is then set automatically according to the information from the camera's metering system.

Single lens reflex (SLR). Camera design that allows the image focused on the film plane to be previewed. A hinged mirror that diverts the light path is the basis of the system.

Skylight. Light from the blue sky (as opposed to direct sunlight).

SLR. See *Single lens reflex.*

Slave unit. Device that responds to the light emission from one flash unit, to activate additional flash units simultaneously.

Slit-scan. Method of photography in which the image is projected onto the film through a moving slit (or else the film moves and the slit remains still). Periphery photography is one form of this.

Snoot. Generally, cylindrical fitting for a light source, used to throw a circle of light.

Soft-focus filter. A glass filter with an irregular or etched surface that reduces image sharpness and increases flare in a controlled fashion. Normally used for a flattering effect in portraiture.

Solarization. Reversal of tones in an image produced by greatly overexposing the emulsion. A similar appearance can be created by making use of the Sabattier effect.

Spectral response/sensitivity. The pattern of response of an emulsion to the different wavelength of light.

Spherical aberration. In this aberration, light rays from a subject on the lens axis passing through off-centre areas of the lens focus at different distances from the light rays that pass directly through the centre of the lens. The result is blurring in the centre of the picture.

Split-field filter. Bi-focal filter, the top half of which consists of plain glass, the lower half being a plus-diopter lens that allows a close foreground to be focused at the same time as the background.

Spotlight. A lamp containing a focusing system that concentrates a narrow beam of light in a controllable way.

Spotmeter. Hand-held exposure meter of great accuracy, measuring reflected light over a small, precise angle of view.

Standard. The upright unit of a monorail view camera. The front standard carries the lens panel; the rear carries the film back and viewing screen.

Standard lens. See *Normal lens.*

Step photography. Type of multiple-exposure photography in which either the camera or subject (or both) are moved in measured steps between exposures.

Step wedge. Strip of developed film containing a measured graduated scale of density. Used for exposing alongside separation negatives to check accuracy of exposure.

Stereography. Type of photograph in which two simultaneous exposures are made, the receiving frames of film being separated by at least a few inches, and the developed pair presented to the view in such a way as to reproduce the impression of three-dimensional depth.

Stop bath. Chemical that neutralizes the action of the developer on an emulsion, effectively stopping development.

Streak photography. Type of photography in which the camera or subject (or both) are moved during a continuously lit exposure (usually long). The image shows the trace of the movement.

Stress polarization. Stress patterns in materials that polarize light made visible by viewing them through crossed polarizing filters.

Strobe. Abbreviation for 'stroboscopic light'. A rapidly repeating flash unit, used for multiple-exposure photographs of moving subjects.

Substantive film. Colour film in which the colour-forming dyes are included at manufacture. Most colour films are of this type.

Substitute reading. Exposure measurement of a surface of subject that is similar in tone or appearance to the subject about to be photographed.

Subtractive process. The process of combining coloured pigments, dyes or filter, all of which absorb light. Combining all three primary colours in this way produces black (an absence of light).

Swing. Rotating camera movement of the front or rear standard around a vertical axis. See *Camera movements.*

T

Technical camera. Flat-bed view camera, similar in basic construction to a field camera but of metal and to greater precision.

Tele-converter. Supplementary lens that attaches between a telephoto lens and the camera body to increase the focal length.

Telephoto lens. Design of long-focus lens in which the length of the lens is less than the focal length.

Test strip. Test of various exposures made with an enlarger.

Thermography. Method of imaging heat emission from a subject.

Through-the-lens (TTL) meter. Exposure meter built into the camera, normally located close to the instant-return mirror of a single lens reflex or to the pentaprism.

Tilt. Rotating camera movement of the front or rear standard around a horizontal axis. See *Camera movements.*

Time exposure. Exposure of several seconds or more that must be timed by the photographer.

Tone separation. The isolation of areas of tone in an image, normally by the combination of varying densities of line positives and negatives.

Toner. Chemicals that add an overall colour to a processed black-and-white image, by means of bleaching and dyeing.

Trans-illumination. See *Back-lighting.*

Transposed processing. The processing of reversal film as if negative, or negative film as if reversal, for special effect.

Tri-chromatic. Method of reusing or reproducing specific colours by the variable combination of only three equally distributed wavelengths, such as blue, green, red or yellow, magenta, cyan.

Tri-pack film. Colour film constructed with three layers of emulsion, each sensitive to a different colour. When exposed equally, the three colours give white.

Tungsten-balanced film. Film manufactured for use with tungsten lighting without the need for balancing filters. Type A film is balanced for 3400°K; the more common type B film is balanced for 3200°K.

Tungsten-halogen lamp. Tungsten lamp of improved efficiency, in which the filament is enclosed in halogen gas, which causes the vaporized parts of the filament to be re-deposited on the filament rather than on the envelope.

Tungsten lighting. Artificial lighting caused by heating a filament of tungsten to a temperature where it emits light.

U

Ultraviolet radiation. Although it is invisible, most films are sensitive to this electromagnetic radiation.

V

Variable contrast paper. Printing paper with a single emulsion which can be used at different degrees of contrast by means of selected filters.

View camera. Large-format camera in which the image is projected onto a ground-glass screen. After viewing, the film is inserted into a holder in the same position as the viewing screen.

W

Wavelength of light. The distance between peaks in a wave of light. This distance, among other things, determines the colour.

Wetting agent. Chemical that weakens the surface tension of water, and so reduces the risk of drying marks on film.

Wide-angle lens. Lens with an angle of view wider than that of the human eye and having a short focal length.

Z

Zoom lens. Lens with a continuously variable focal length over a certain range at any given focus and aperture. It is generated by differential movement of the lens elements.

INDEX

Page numbers in *italic*
refer to illustrations

ACKNOWLEDGEMENTS

The pictures on these pages were reproduced by courtesy of the following:

11 (t) Nikon UK Ltd; **12** Keith Bernstein; **16** Sotheby's; **21** (b) Rose Jones; **23** (b) Kodak Ltd; **26** (tl) Polaroid UK Ltd, (t) Clive Boden; **30** Keith Bernstein; **31** Nikon UK Ltd; **34** Keith Bernstein; **44** Rose Jones; **47** (tl, tr) George Selwyn, (b) Neyla Freeman; **48** Rose Jones; **58** (tr) Keith Bernstein; **59** (tr) Keith Bernstein; **60** A. Arthur; **61** Hasselblad Ltd; **65** (b) Keith Bernstein; **76** (t) Rose Jones; **78-9** (t) Keith Bernstein; **85** (b) Keith Bernstein; **87** (b) Rose Jones; **90** (c) Robert Golden, (b) Kobal Collection; **91** (b) Kobal Collection; **92** (b) Keith Bernstein; **94** (t) Gustave le Gray (Victoria and Albert Museum), (b) William Henry Fox Talbot (Fox Talbot Museum); **96** (l) Ilford Ltd; **104** Rose Jones; **108** (c) Polaroid UK Ltd; **118** (tr, cr) Keith Bernstein; **119** Keith Bernstein; **125** Keith Bernstein; **137** Polaroid UK Ltd; **143** Sue Wilks; **146-7** Neyla Freeman; **156-7** (b) Keith Bernstein; **158-9** John Claridge; **167** (t) Neyla Freeman; **172** (t) Henri Cartier Bresson/Magnum/John Hilleson Agency, (b) Eric Salomon/Magnum/John Hilleson Agency; **173** (t) Victoria and Albert Museum, (b) E.T. Archive; **177** (b) Romano Cagnoni; **180** (m) Victoria and Albert Museum; **184-5** (b) Keith Bernstein; **186** Felix H. Mann/Creative Camera; **191** (t) Keith Bernstein; **205** (t) Rose Jones; **206** (b) Keith Bernstein; **209** (b) George Selwyn; **211** (t) Keith Bernstein, (c) Fotobank International, (b) Clive Boden; **212** (t) Royal Photographic Society; **213** (t) Eston Gallery, Carmel, California, (b) Royal Photographic Society; **214** (b) John Pfahl (Robert Freidus Gallery); **227** (b) Steve Dalton/NHPA; **234** (t) Seaphot; **235** (br) Spectrum Colour Library; **248** (b) Keith Bernstein; **254-5** (t) Rose Jones; **256** (t) Bob Elsdale; **256-7** Rose Jones; **258** Rose Jones; **259** (t) Keith Bernstein, (b) Rose Jones; **261** (bl) Keith Bernstein, (tr, br) Rose Jones; **262** (b) André Kertesz; **262-3** (t) Fay Godwin; **263** Rose Jones; **264** (t) Sanders, (b) Rose Jones; **265** (t) Rose Jones; **267** (t) Sanders; **268** (t) Victoria and Albert Museum; **269** (tr) André Kertesz; **270-71** (t) Michael Joseph; **272-3** (t) Ric Hawkes/Marshall Advertising; **277** (b) Rose Jones; **279** (tl) Rose Jones; **282** (c) Rose Jones; **294** (t) A. Arthur; **301** (bl) Applied Holographics PLC, (br) Richard Platt; **302** (tl, br) Science Photo Library; **304** (t) Science Photo Library; **306-7** Polaroid UK Ltd.

All other photographs are the property of the author or Quarto Publishing Limited.

Key: (t) top; (b) bottom; (l) left; (r) right; (c) centre; (m) middle.

While every effort has been made to acknowledge all copyright holders, we apologize if any omissions have been made.